T0323289

The Leap of Faith

The Leap of Faith

The Fiscal Foundations of Successful Government in Europe and America

Edited by
Sven H. Steinmo

OXFORD
UNIVERSITY PRESS

OXFORD
UNIVERSITY PRESS

Great Clarendon Street, Oxford, OX2 6DP,
United Kingdom

Oxford University Press is a department of the University of Oxford.
It furthers the University's objective of excellence in research, scholarship,
and education by publishing worldwide. Oxford is a registered trade mark of
Oxford University Press in the UK and in certain other countries

Published in the United States of America by Oxford University Press
198 Madison Avenue, New York, NY 10016, United States of America

British Library Cataloguing in Publication Data

Data available

Library of Congress Control Number: 2017963306

ISBN 978-0-19-879681-7

Printed and bound by
CPI Group (UK) Ltd, Croydon, CR0 4YY

Links to third party websites are provided by Oxford in good faith and
for information only. Oxford disclaims any responsibility for the materials
contained in any third party website referenced in this work.

Preface and Acknowledgments

It was late October 2011. I was teaching at the European University Institute in Florence, Italy, where I had been working for over three years. By now I had become fairly well adjusted to many of the idiosyncrasies one confronts living in this wonderful and frustrating country. Though I can't say I was perfectly comfortable driving in this country yet, I had learned many of the informal driving rules here. I had also gotten used to waiting in long lines to fill out bureaucratic forms—only to have the bureaucrat who was supposed to deal with them tell me that I was at the wrong window. I had gotten used to the fact that my Internet connection was sporadic at best and that buses follow a schedule—but only most of the time. I also truly enjoyed the slower pace of life, the longer conversations, and fabulous food that this country has to offer.

I was walking home from my office in the early evening and saw a car with a young couple and two small children pull up next to the large garbage bins parked on the side of the street near my apartment. I watched as a hand reached out through the open window and the male driver dropped a plastic bag full of garbage on the street. I couldn't believe it. Not only was this man throwing garbage on the street next to the garbage bin, he was also teaching his small children that it was okay to behave this way.

While staring aghast as the car drove off, I began to think about whether such behavior was imaginable in Scandinavia. As a Norwegian American who has lived for a number of years in Sweden and Norway, I could scarcely imagine a Scandinavian throwing a bag of garbage out of his car window even in the middle of the night in a dark forest. Why, I kept wondering, do people behave so differently in different countries?

As far as I know, no one likes to see the garbage strewn around on the streets. So why do some people do it? In my experience Italians are genuinely lovely, warm, and deeply friendly people. Their homes are incredibly clean and orderly and despite the stories one hears about pickpockets in Rome and house robberies in the hills above Florence, it has been my experience that Italians are honest and remarkably trustworthy. When I ask my Italian friends about the kind of socially inappropriate behavior I witnessed that evening, they typically just shake their heads and say, "It's Italian culture." For the most part, they are just embarrassed. "It's like tax evasion," one colleague suggested.

"We all know it's wrong, but lots of people do it just because they can get away with it."

My first reaction to my colleague's comment was, "that makes sense." Italy has a serious tax evasion problem and it is a commonplace narrative that Italians cheat on their taxes. In fact the former prime minister, Silvio Berlusconi, was being tried for tax fraud at the time and no one doubted that he was guilty. As the *New York Times* reported, "Italians have been accused by some of making tax evasion a national sport."[1]

Tax evasion seemed like just another example of the many socially dysfunctional behaviors you witness living in Italy. Even a tourist will notice the apparent absence of driving rules in this country . . . to say nothing of their creative parking techniques. Living here you confront literally hundreds of examples where people do not seem to have the same sense of civic responsibility apparent in other countries. Tax evasion seemed to be just one more example of how perfectly good people sometimes behave in socially dysfunctional ways.

I wondered why.

After my experience at the garbage bin, I became increasingly fascinated with the *why* question. As I thought about it, I was especially puzzled by my untested assertion: that a Scandinavian would be much less likely to throw a bag of garbage out of their car—even if they knew no one would see them—than his Italian counterpart. I thought it was so, but the truth is I did not know.

Having lived in Italy, Sweden, Norway, the UK, and Japan, I have often noticed that not only do social behaviors differ across countries, but so do each country's public institutions and systems of enforcement. Perhaps the real differences between Italian and Scandinavian behavior, I began to wonder, is more a product of what people can get away with, rather than some deeply internalized pro- or anti-social values. I also realized that seeing a guy drop garbage out his window in public tells me very little about how most people would behave. In short, I came to realize that I, like most people who notice differences in different societies, extrapolate from specific personal experiences and draw conclusions about whole societies.

Maybe, I began to suspect, the differences between Italian and Scandinavian behavior is not a product of some deep-seated cultural variation. Maybe it is simply because in Scandinavia rules (driving, littering, etc.) are enforced, whereas in Italy they rarely are.

This puzzle stuck with me. This book is the product of a five-year-long research project which examines this puzzle.[2]

I decided to study tax evasion. Tax evasion is illegal everywhere. For the most part people believe that it is wrong to avoid taxes. But the actual practice of tax evasion differs dramatically from one country to another. In Sweden, for example, the government estimates that it loses roughly 8 percent of potential tax revenue through what is called the "tax gap." The Bank of Italy estimates that nearly 27 percent of public revenue is lost in its tax gap (Santoro 2010). The tax gap in the US is estimated to be nearly 16 percent which is $450 billion a year in lost revenue (IRS 2017).

In February 2012 I submitted a grant proposal to the European Research Council (ERC) for a "Frontier Grant" in which I proposed to compare tax compliance behavior in a small set of democratic nations. A key feature of this proposal was that I would approach my puzzle through two quite different methodologies—comparative historical analysis and laboratory experiments. The idea was to examine the relationships between taxpayers and their states in different countries over time and then use experimental/laboratory methods to see whether people in these countries today would respond similarly or differently when faced with exactly the same institutions and choices. I hoped to combine these approaches and methods to gain insights into the fundamental question of whether outcomes and behavior are so different in different countries because citizens confront diverse systems (tax and otherwise), or whether the systems differ because they confront disparate people.

At that point, there had already been a significant amount of work in behavioral economics focusing on tax compliance behavior. I read the fascinating studies by James Alm, Ernst Fehr, Simon Gachter, Benedikt Hermann, Luigi Mittone, Benno Torgler, and many others.[3] I learned from these scholars that it was already well understood that taxpayers did not behave as classical economic theory would expect them to behave. Instead, there seem to be other motivations for paying taxes driven by what the scholars titled "tax morale." In addition, it appeared that tax morale varies from country to country. Several of the scholars explicitly argued that more studies should be done using laboratory experiments to test for differences in tax compliance behavior across countries.

This project attempted to do just this. But in addition to running experiments in a number of countries[4] we attempted to build the experimental protocols around questions of interest to country specialists and policymakers. In short, the experiments did not stand alone. The results from our behavioral experiments are reported in a series of articles as well as in the forthcoming book, *Willing to Pay?*[5] I cannot fully summarize the range of findings uncovered in our experiments here, but I can at least report that the behavioral work casts significant doubt on classical culturalist explanations. It simply does not seem to be the case that Italians, for example, are much more likely to cheat each other than most other Europeans—when they are given transparent and consistent rules. Italians *are* more willing to cheat their state, however. Why? Because Italians tend to believe that their state cheats them.

In contrast, most Swedes cheat less on their taxes than do people in almost any other country because they tend to believe that their government treats them fairly and gives them value for their money (D'Attoma 2017; Pampel, Andrighetto, and Steinmo forthcoming).

We also found that while some behavioral patterns do seem to vary from country to country, the differences between individuals *within countries* are often larger than the differences between countries. In every society, including Sweden, there are some people who distrust other people as well as their state and appear willing to cheat both their government and those around them. At the same time, there are some who will pay taxes and/or sacrifice their own short-term self-interest for the larger public good in every society. Interestingly, the distribution of types of individuals (e.g. whether pro-social or more self-centered, for example) does appear to differ across countries.

Finally, we find that the way people behave in the laboratory does not necessarily reflect how they behave in the real world. Perhaps most surprisingly, we found that Italians and Romanians in the laboratory were *more* likely to contribute to a public good in our experiments (or less likely to cheat their colleagues) than our British subjects (Andrighetto et al. 2016; Zhang et al. 2016).

None of these laboratory results suggests that there is no such thing as "culture" or that there are no attitudinal or behavioral differences between countries. On the contrary, there are important differences in the ways people behave in different countries. These differences, however, are rooted in the *lived experiences* that people find themselves confronted with. These lived experiences affect attitudes towards the state, expectations about others' behavior, social norms, and, perhaps ultimately, social values. Italians and Romanians cheat more on their taxes than Swedes or Americans not because they are more dishonest as a whole. Instead, compliance is lower in some countries than in others because some states are less efficacious, efficient, and trustworthy than others. In short, institutions matter.

In sum, our behavioral experiments do suggest that there are some differences in behavior and attitudes across societies. But the experiments cannot tell us why these differences exist. To understand the relationship between taxpayers and their states, we obviously needed to examine the states as well as citizens. You cannot simply study citizens' attitudes and behavior in order to understand what citizens and taxpayers believe about their state. Whether people pay their taxes, abide by the rules and laws, or vote, is defined by this relationship. To understand this relationship we need to examine both sides of the coin.

Having said this, I realize of course that I have just peeled another layer of the onion. If it is the case that differences in citizens' willingness to pay more and/or cheat their states less is mostly driven by difference in the character of the states themselves, then why are states so different? Specifically, how has the relationship between the taxpayer and the tax collector evolved over time?

This is the central focus of this book.

Each chapter in this book examines the fiscal history of one of the countries in the "Willing to Pay?" project (Sweden, Italy, the United Kingdom, the USA, and Romania). It is clear both from previous work and from the behavioral experiments conducted for this study that institutions are fundamental for explaining why people behave the ways they do in different societies. This book, then, explores how and why different countries have developed such different relationships between taxpayers and their states.

If one wants to understand how human beings generally behave when faced with specific incentives and disincentives, then behavioral experiments can and do offer significant insights. But if you want to understand why people behave differently in different countries, you need to examine the social, institutional, and historical context in which those decisions are made. That is what this book attempts to do.

While I believe that we can learn a great deal from behavioral experiments, I have learned that they also need to be interpreted and placed into context. While the ambition of some experiments might be to isolate the decision maker from the social or political context in which choices are usually made, this has *not* been my goal. Instead, a central aim of this project has been precisely to understand how broader social, political, and even cultural contexts structure and inform individual decisions.

After the introduction, the central chapters in this book each examine a particular epoch in the development of the relationship between taxpayers and their particular state. In each case we explore the evolution of that relationship focusing on when and why this relationship has been a positive one or not. The concluding chapter, written with the Argentinian scholar and student of tax evasion, Marcelo Bergman, attempts to draw specific lessons from the case studies for developing countries today. This, to be sure, is an unusual twist for a largely historical volume. But I believe that we study history and compare countries' pasts not just because the comparisons are interesting. We study them precisely because we hope and believe that these narratives have implications for today.

This book is also unusual in that it will be offered "open access." The European Research Council has pressed us to make all our publications open access on the logic that taxpayers have paid for this research, and therefore all taxpayers (and many beyond) should be able to easily reach this material and its findings. I have to admit that this first seemed like an odd suggestion for a comparative historical volume. After some consideration, though, I concluded that this was a wonderful opportunity that would allow us to present our work and findings far beyond a traditional academic readership. It seems to me that there may be a number of policymakers, public officials, and policy activists who might be interested in the lessons that can be drawn from these histories.

What is it about the Swedish case that has made it so successful? Why, in contrast, have the Italians and Romanians been so much less successful in building a positive relationship between taxpayers and their states? Our experimental work shows clearly that the main reason some countries have very low levels of tax evasion while it is very high in other countries is *not* because some people are more honest or willing to contribute to the public good than others. It is instead because some governments are more efficacious, treat taxpayers more fairly, provide better services for the taxes collected, and are generally more trustworthy than others. Having said this, it is also clear that there are even more specific lessons one can draw from the historical narratives presented in this book concerning types of tax and revenue policies that have proven to be most effective, and types of policies that appear to work or not work well from the citizen/taxpayer point of view. The last chapter of this book is specifically devoted to these policy issues.

A large number of other scholars have been integral to this project at different stages. My first and perhaps most important intellectual debt is to Giulia Andrighetto. Giulia is one of the pre-eminent young scientists in Italy today and it has been my pleasure to work with her and learn from her since she first came to work with me as a Max Weber Fellow at the EUI back in 2011. It is no exaggeration to say that this project would not have been possible without her. A second person who deserves special recognition is John D'Attoma who came to this project in 2015, first as a research assistant and then as a postdoctoral fellow. He has been an integral part of both the historical and behavioral analysis and has been essential to its success. James Alm, Benedikt Hermann, Ryan Murphy, Stefania Ottone, Ferruccio Panzano, and Nan Zhang contributed enormously to the design, development, and interpretation of the experimental portion of this project.

For the current volume, I would also like to specifically acknowledge the contributions of the scholars that have contributed directly: Marcelo Bergman, Michelle D'Arcy, John D'Attoma, Martin Daunton, Joseph Hien, Romain Huret, Jenny Jansson, Carolyn C. Jones, Marina Nistotskaya, Liam Stanley, Arpad Todor, and Clara Volintiru. Their willingness to continually revise and rethink their papers in light of the arguments and themes developed throughout the project have made this what I think of as a "constructed volume" and not just an edited book. This volume was also significantly advanced by the cogent and thoughtful comments from a number of scholars and policy experts who participated in one or several of the "Willing to Pay?" workshops and conferences we held over the past five years. Their criticisms and suggestions have significantly improved this volume in specific and the research project as a whole: Cornel Ban, Pablo Beramendi, Mark Blyth, Christiano Castelfranchi, John Cullis, Ray Duch, Jonas Edlund, Philipp Genschel, Benedikt Hermann, Edgar Kiser, Isaac Martin, Matthias Matthijs, Monica Noll,

Fred Pempel, Stefano Pisani, Alan Plumley, Bo Rothstein, Mario Scala, and Lennart Wittberg. It has been an honor and inspiration to work with these scholars, policymakers, and friends.

Finally, Julia Hiltrop, Daniel Schulz, and Martina Selmi have been fundamental to the success of this whole affair. Without their diligence, patience, and attention to detail none of this would have been possible. I cannot thank them or any of the people mentioned above enough.

Notes

1. Elisabetta Povoledo, *New York Times*, Aug. 8, 2011.
2. The research leading to these results/publication has received funding from the European Research Council under the European Union's Seventh Framework Programme (FP7/2007–2013)/ERC Grant Agreement n. 295675. This publication reflects only the authors' views and the Union is not liable for any use that may be made of the information contained therein.
3. Some of these works include: Alm, McClelland, and Schulze 1992; Alm and Torgler 2006, 2011; Bergman and Maicis forthcoming; Frey and Meier 2004; Gangl et al. 2013; Kallgren, Reno, and Cialdini 2000; Kastlunger et al. 2013; Kirchler, Maciejovsky, and Schneider 2003; Nicolaides 2014; Smith and Kinsey 1987; Torgler 2002, 2007; Torgler et al. 2008; Torgler and Schneider 2007; Traxler 2010; Wenzel 2005.
4. We conducted laboratory experiment in multiple locations in all five countries with more than 3,000 subjects.
5. Several articles reporting these research finding have recently been published, or are forthcoming. These include: Andrighetto et al. forthcoming; Andrighetto et al. 2016; Bruner, D'Attoma, and Steinmo 2017; Colombo and Steinmo forthcoming; D'Attoma 2017; D'Attoma, Volintiru, and Steinmo 2017; Pampel, Andrighetto, and Steinmo forthcoming; Steinmo and D'Attoma 2017a, 2017b; Zhang et al. 2016.

Bibliography

Alm, J., G. H. McClelland, and W. D. Schulze (1992), "Why Do People Pay Taxes?" *Journal of Public Economics* 48(1): 21–38.

Alm, J. and B. Torgler (2006), "Culture Differences and Tax Morale in the United States and in Europe." *Journal of Economic Psychology* 27(2): 224–46.

Alm, J. and B. Torgler (2011), "Do Ethics Matter? Tax Compliance and Morality." *Journal of Business Ethics* 101(4): 635–51.

Andrighetto, G., N. Zhang, S. Ottone, F. Ponzano, J. D'Attoma, and S. Steinmo (2016), "Are Some Countries More Honest than Others? Evidence from a Tax Compliance Experiment in Sweden and Italy." *Frontiers in Psychology*. doi: http://dx.doi.org/10.3389/fpsyg.2016.00472.

Andrighetto, G., A. Szekely, S. Ottone, N. Zhang, and S. Steinmo (forthcoming), *Context and Preferences Shape Cooperative Decision-Making.*

Bergman, M. and F. Maicis (forthcoming), *Tax Reform in Latin America.* Ithaca, NY: Cornell University Press.

Bruner, D. M., J. D'Attoma, and S. Steinmo (2017), *Going Dutch? The Role of Gender in the Provision of Public Goods through Tax Compliance.* Working Paper.

Colombo, C. and S. Steinmo (forthcoming), "Why People Follow Rules: A Reasonable Choice Approach."

D'Attoma, J. (2017), "Divided Nation: North–South Cleavages in Italian Tax Compliance." *Polity* 42(1). doi: 10.1086/689982.

D'Attoma, J. and S. Steinmo (2016), "Why are some nations' citizens more likely to cheat on their taxes? What we found surprised us." *The Washington Post Online, The Monkey Cage* (April 15).

D'Attoma, J., C. Volintiru, and S. Steinmo (2017), "Willing to Share? Tax Compliance and Gender in Europe and America." *Research & Politics* 4(2). doi: 10.1177/2053168017707151.

Frey, B. S. and S. Meier (2004), "Social Comparisons and Pro-Social Behavior: Testing 'Conditional Cooperation' in a Field Experiment." *The American Economic Review* 94(5): 1717–22.

Gangl, K., S. Muehlbacher, M. D. Groot, S. Goslinga, E. Hofmann, C. Kogler, . . . E. Kirchler (2013), "How Can I help You? Perceived Service Orientation of Tax Authorities and Tax Compliance." *FinanzArchiv/Public Finance Analysis* 69(4): 487–510.

IRS (2017), *The Tax Gap.* Retrieved from www.irs.gov/uac/the-tax-gap.

Kallgren, C. A., R. R. Reno, and R. B. Cialdini (2000), "A Focus Theory of Normative Conduct: When Norms Do and Do Not Affect Behavior." *Personality and Social Psychology Bulletin* 26(8): 1002–12.

Kastlunger, B., E. Lozza, E. Kirchler, and A. Schabmann (2013), "Powerful Authorities and Trusting Citizens: The Slippery Slope Framework and Tax Compliance in Italy." *Journal of Economic Psychology* 34: 36–45.

Kirchler, E., B. Maciejovsky, and F. Schneider (2003), "Everyday Representations of Tax Avoidance, Tax Evasion, and Tax Flight: Do Legal Differences Matter?" *Journal of Economic Psychology* 24(4): 535–53.

Nicolaides, P. (2014), *Tax Compliance, Social Norms and Institutional Quality: An Evolutionary Theory of Public Good Provision.* Retrieved from https://ec.europa.eu/taxation_customs/sites/taxation/files/resources/documents/taxation/gen_info/economic_analysis/tax_papers/taxation_paper_46.pdf.

Pampel, F., G. Andrighetto, and S. Steinmo (forthcoming), "How Institutions and Attitudes Shape Tax Compliance: A Cross-National Experiment and Survey."

Santoro, A. (2010), *L'evasione fiscale: quanto, come e perché.* Bologna: Il Mulino.

Smith, K. W. and K. A. Kinsey (1987), "Understanding Taxpaying Behavior: A Conceptual Framework with Implications for Research." *Law and Society Review* 21(4): 639–63.

Steinmo, S. and J. D'Attoma (2017a), "Our survey reveals even Trump supporters want a fairer tax deal." *The Conversation* (December 12). https://theconversation.com/our-survey-reveals-that-even-republicans-want-a-fairer-tax-deal-for-america-89043.

Steinmo, S. and J. D'Attoma (2017b), "Trump's tax proposals are wildly out of sync with what most Americans would do." *The Washington Post Online, The Monkey Cage* (September 20). www.washingtonpost.com/news/monkey-cage/wp/2017/09/20/trumps-tax-proposals-are-wildly-out-of-sync-with-what-most-americans-would-do-our-new-study-shows/?utm_term=.174227a876fa.

Torgler, B. (2002), "Speaking to Theorists and Searching for Facts: Tax Morale and Tax Compliance in Experiments." *Journal of Economic Surveys* 16(5): 657–83.

Torgler, B. (2007), *Tax Compliance and Tax Morale: A Theoretical and Empirical Analysis.* Cheltenham: Edward Elgar.

Torgler, B. and F. Schneider (2007), "What Shapes Attitudes Toward Paying Taxes? Evidence from Multicultural European Countries." *Social Science Quarterly* 88(2): 443–70.

Torgler, B., I. C. Demir, A. Macintyre, and M. Schaffner (2008), "Causes and Consequences of Tax Morale: An Empirical Investigation." *Economic Analysis and Policy (EAP)* 38(2): 313–39.

Traxler, C. (2010), "Social Norms and Conditional Cooperative Taxpayers." *European Journal of Political Economy* 26(1): 89–103.

Wenzel, M. (2005), "Motivation or Rationalisation? Causal Relations Between Ethics, Norms and Tax Compliance." *Journal of Economic Psychology* 26: 491–508.

Zhang, N., G. Andrighetto, S. Ottone, F. Ponzano, and S. Steinmo (2016), "Willing to Pay? Tax Compliance in Britain and Italy: An Experimental Analysis." *PLOS ONE* 11(2). http://journals.plos.org/plosone/article?id=10.1371/journal.pone.0150277.

Contents

List of Figures   xvii
List of Tables   xix
Notes on Contributors   xxi

Part I. Introduction

1. Introduction: The Leap of Faith   3
   Sven H. Steinmo

Part II. Sweden

2. Getting to Sweden: The Origins of High Compliance
   in the Swedish Tax State   33
   Marina Nistotskaya and Michelle D'Arcy

3. Creating Tax-Compliant Citizens in Sweden: The Role
   of Social Democracy   56
   Jenny Jansson

Part III. Italy

4. Tax Evasion in Italy: A God-Given Right?   81
   Josef Hien

5. Explaining Italian Tax Compliance: A Historical Analysis 106
   John D'Attoma

Part IV. United Kingdom

6. Creating Consent: Taxation, War, and Good
   Government in Britain, 1688–1914   131
   Martin Daunton

7. "When We Were Just Giving Stuff Away Willy-Nilly":
   Historicizing Contemporary British Tax Morale   155
   Liam Stanley

Contents

Part V. United States

8. The Not-So-Infernal Revenue Service? Tax Collection, Citizens,
    and Compliance in the United States from the Eighteenth
    to the Twentieth Centuries   181
    Romain Huret

9. Seeing Taxation in the Mid-Twentieth Century:
    US Tax Compliance   198
    Carolyn C. Jones

Part VI. Romania

10. Tax Collection without Consent: State-Building in Romania   225
    Clara Volintiru

11. Willing to Pay? The Politics of Engendering Faith in the
    Post-Communist Romanian Tax System   250
    Arpad Todor

Part VII. Conclusion

12. Taxation and Consent: Implications for Developing Nations   273
    Marcelo Bergman and Sven H. Steinmo

Name Index   293
Subject Index   299

List of Figures

2.1. Cadastral map (*geometrisk jordebok*) of a Royal Domain in Danmarks
Parish, Uppsala County, 1635   38

2.2. Enlarged elements of the same cadastral map   39

2.3. A page from the tithe register for a farm in Hjärnarp Parish, Skånia,
Sweden, 1766–83   42

5.1. Rates of evasion of IRAP by region 1998–2002   107

5.2. GDP per capita in the Mezzogiorno as a percentage
of Northern GDP per capita   112

7.1. Attitudes to taxation and spending 1983–2011   158

7.2. Attitudes to unemployment benefits 1983–2011   165

7.3. Percentage who "almost never" trust UK governments (of any party) to
place the needs of the nation above the interests of their own
political party   167

List of Tables

3.1. Mechanisms of compliance   58

4.1. Country, confession, and belief in God as a percentage of population (2005) and size of the shadow economy (1999–2010)   87

4.2. Budgetary allocations in millions of lire in 1811   91

5.1. Quality of government: 14 Western European countries   107

5.2. Quality of government: Italian regions   109

10.1. Number of newly established monasteries in Romanian territories   235

10.2. Duties and loans in Wallachia (1694–1703)   238

10.3. Comparative fiscal duties in the sixteenth century   243

Notes on Contributors

Marcelo Sergio Bergman is Professor at Universidad Nacional de Tres de Febrero in Buenos Aires and the founding director of the Center for the Study on Violence and Insecurity (CELIV). He holds a BA and MA degree in Political Science from the Hebrew University of Jerusalem and a PhD from the University of California at San Diego. He has worked and published on state and law enforcement in Latin America, on tax evasion and tax compliance, as well as on criminality and public security in Latin America. His books include, among others, *Tax Evasion and the Rule of Law in Latin America* (2009), *Drogas y Narcotráfico en América Latina* (2016), and *Crime and Prosperity: The Latin American Paradox* (forthcoming).

Michelle D'Arcy is an Assistant Professor at the Department of Political Science, Trinity College Dublin. Her research focuses on the relationship between democracy and state-building in historical and contemporary comparative perspective. She has published in journals including *Governance*, the *European Journal of Political Research*, and *African Affairs*, and has received funding for this work from the Swedish Research Council.

John D'Attoma is currently a Postdoctoral Research Associate at the Tax Administration Research Centre (TARC) at the University of Exeter. Previously, he was a Research Fellow at the European University Institute, working on the project "Willing to Pay?" His research lies in the field of comparative political economy and investigates the varied relationship between citizens and their states. Most recently, he has published articles in *Research and Politics* and *Polity*.

Martin Daunton was Professor of Economic History at the University of Cambridge from 1997 to 2015, as well as the Master of Trinity Hall from 2004 to 2014, and Head of the School of the Humanities and Social Sciences from 2012 to 2015. He was previously Astor Professor of British History at University College London. He is currently completing a book on the economic governance of the world since 1933, and recently published an edited collection with Marc Bugglen and Alexander Nutzenadel on *The Political Economy of Public Finance: Taxation, State Spending and Debt since the 1970s* (Cambridge University Press, 2017). Previous publications include *Trusting Leviathan: The Politics of Taxation in Britain, 1799–1914* (2001) and *Just Taxes: The Politics of Taxation in Britain 1914–1979* (2002), as well as two surveys of British economic history between 1700 and 1951.

Josef Hien is a Postdoctoral Fellow at the REScEU project. Funded through a European Research Council advanced grant and hosted at the University of Milan, REScEU aims at reconciling social and economic Europe. Hien is interested in the ideational and cultural foundations of European political economies. He received his PhD from the European University Institute and has worked as a postdoc at the Max Planck Institute for the Study of Societies (Cologne), at the Collegio Carlo Alberto (Moncalieri/Turin), and the Berlin Social Science Centre (WZB, Berlin). His key publications include "The Ordoliberalism that never was" (*Contemporary Political Theory*, 2013), "The Religious Roots of the European Crisis" (*Journal of Common Market Studies*, 2017), "From Private to Religious Patriarchy" (*Politics & Religion*, 2017), *Ordoliberalism, Law and the Rule of Economics* (together with Christian Joerges, Hart Publishers, 2017), and *Competing Ideas: The Religious Foundations of the German and Italian Welfare States* (EUI, 2012).

Romain Huret is Professor at the School for Advanced Studies in the Social Sciences in Paris (France). He works on inequalities in the United States and has published many books and articles on this topic, including *American Tax Resisters* (Harvard University Press, 2014). He is currently completing a book on the Andrew W. Mellon trial for tax evasion.

Jenny Jansson is a researcher at the Department of Government, Uppsala University. She publishes in the areas of industrial relations, labor history, and archival studies. Her work has appeared in journals such as *Labor History, International Labor and Working-Class History,* and *Slagmark*. She has also written several contributions to edited volumes on trade unionism and labor history. She is currently building an e-archive for the Swedish trade unions. Her research interests include labor studies, digitalization, and e-archives.

Carolyn C. Jones is the Orville L. and Ermina D. Dykstra Chair in Income Tax Law at the University of Iowa College of Law, where she was formerly the dean. Her research interest is in the legal history of American tax law and much of her works focuses on World War II and the postwar era when much of the current income tax system developed. Jones has written on tax arguments in the woman suffrage movement, World War II tax propaganda, and women's roles in the economy and tax law during the war and Cold War. Other works focus on tax policy analysis by women home economists in the early twentieth century, and the role of the National Council of Churches in tax policy.

Marina Nistotskaya is Associate Professor of Political Science at University of Gothenburg and a Research Fellow at the Quality of Government Institute, Sweden. Her research interests include state capacity, with special focus on comparative public bureaucracy, and socio-economic development. She has published on causes and consequences of strong states and Weberian bureaucracy in historical and comparative perspectives.

Liam Stanley is Lecturer in Politics at the University of Sheffield and Associate Fellow at the Sheffield Political Economy Research Institute (SPERI). His research interests include comparative and international political economy; the politics of austerity, tax, and welfare; everyday narratives of politics, the economy, and the state; and political analysis and political science methodology. He has published in *New Political Economy, Political Studies,* and *Economy and Society* among others, and is currently completing a British Academy/Leverhulme-funded project on public attitudes to redistribution and inequality, and a book manuscript on the politics of austerity.

Sven H. Steinmo is a professor of Political Science at the University of Colorado, Boulder. While working on this project he was "Research Professor" at the Robert Schuman Center for Advanced Studies (RSCAS) of the European University Institute (EUI) in Florence. He received his BA from the University of California Santa Cruz and his MA, MPH, and PhD from the University of California Berkeley. His major teaching and research interests are in the areas of Institutional Theory, comparative public policy, and comparative historical analysis. He is perhaps best known for his work in institutional theory, having been one of the founders of the subfield of Historical Institutionalism. His book with Kathleen Thelen, *Structuring Politics: Historical Institutionalism and Comparative Analysis* (1992), is widely considered to be one of the defining statements in this area of research. Steinmo's other works include *Taxation and Democracy: Swedish, British and American Approaches to Financing the Modern State* (1993), *Restructuring the Welfare State: Political Institutions and Policy Change* (2002, co-edited with Bo Rothstein), and *The Evolution of Modern States: Sweden, Japan and the United States* (Gunnar Myrdal Prize, 2010).

Arpad Todor holds a PhD degree from the European University Institute, a PhD from the National University of Political Studies and Public Administration (NUPSPA), and is lecturer at the National University of Political Studies and Public Administration (NUPSPA) in Bucharest, Romania. Since 2006 Todor Arpad has worked as expert and program manager at Asociatia Pro Democratia, the most important human rights NGO in terms of volunteers, number of projects, and advocacy capacity. His main efforts have focused on the APD's Electoral Code, the introduction of the Score Card system for evaluating MPs' activity, and Participatory Budgeting. Between 2013 and 2015 he was Executive Coordinator of the Constitutional Forum, a public consultation project whose aim is to propose amendments to the Romanian Constitution. Besides his NGO activity, Todor Arpad is active in the academic community. He is editor of the *CEU Political Science Journal*, has been involved in more than forty research projects and has written several papers concerning Romania's political evolution.

Clara Volintiru is Associate Professor of International Business and Economics at the Bucharest University of Economic Studies (ASE), and researcher in the Government Department of the London School of Economics and Political Science (LSE). Her research interests include clientelism, informal linkages, behavioral studies, and international political economy. Recent publications can be found in chapters of edited volumes, as well as articles in *European Political Science Review*, *East European Politics*, and *Research & Politics*.

Part I
Introduction

1

Introduction

The Leap of Faith

Sven H. Steinmo

Where would you rather live—Sweden or Sudan? To libertarians the choice is obvious. Of course they would rather live in Sudan: there are no taxes, it is a truly "free market" economy, government regulation is nonexistent, and everyone is allowed to have a gun. Sweden, in contrast, has some of the highest taxes in the world, a very large and extensive welfare system and virtually everything—including guns—is highly regulated by a very strong state.

Most of us, however, would rather live in Sweden. The standard of living and the quality of life is incomparably better in Sweden than it is in Sudan. People have more personal freedom, poverty is almost nonexistent, and violence is rare. By any measure of health, happiness, and well-being, Sweden is a far better country than Sudan. Why? The simple answer is that Sweden has strong, stable, and efficient institutions and Sudan does not. Indeed, the extensive and expensive Swedish state is at the foundation of the positive outcomes that Swedish society enjoys. Sweden is not successful simply because Swedes live there, but also because Swedish institutions regulate a well-functioning society.

Surely states can also be too strong. A government that is too powerful might be nearly as bad as having no government at all. Successful societies are those that have built political institutions that are strong enough to act effectively and at the same time responsive enough to act responsibly. Striking a balance between having a strong, effective, and efficient state on the one hand, and a responsive government on the other is both difficult and rare. Only a few handfuls of societies in the history of the human race have been able to strike this balance. They are mostly democratic capitalist regimes.[1]

In this book we look at the history of fiscal policy in five different democratic countries with an eye toward understanding how and why some have been more successful than others in striking this balance. We focus specifically on taxation. As Joseph Schumpeter once said, "Taxation is the skeleton of the state." Indeed, without taxes there can be no state. But, perhaps more importantly, precisely because individuals have strong incentives to avoid their taxes there is an inherent conflict between the first-order preferences of citizens and the first-order preferences of the state. A successful country must be able to collect revenues without oppressing its citizens. Taxation, in short, lies at the heart of the balance between a strong state and a successful society.

We will not compare Sweden with Sudan. But we do try to understand why countries such as Sweden have become so successful in generating compliance. The book focuses on how countries built or attempted to build the fiscal capacity that could make them successful nation states. We then explore how these countries further evolved in the twentieth century. Here we try to understand the connection between the emergence of state capacity and the foundations of consent. In short, this volume tries to connect two fundamentally interrelated questions of concern to students of politics and history. How do states build capacity to govern and collect revenue, and how do states develop successful systems into which citizens are "willing to pay"?

As Marc Berenson puts it: "states cannot govern effectively if they cannot collect revenue" (Barenson 2017: 3). This is not simply because you need money to finance government, but as we shall see in the chapters that follow, the act of building fiscal capacity is integral to the act of building a successful state. Of course, just because a state is able to collect lots of tax revenue does not necessarily mean that its citizens pay willingly. To be sure, some states can extract extensive resources from hostile taxpayers. But they expend huge resources in the extraction process. The problem with this method of self-financing is that it is both very expensive and does not exactly endear subjects to their state.

In recent history, however, a relatively small number of countries figured out another means for self-financing that turns out to be hugely more efficient: Get your subjects to pay taxes willingly. It is hard to overstate how rare this is. Yet it can scarcely be denied that self-monitoring is much more efficient than extortion.

Jean Baptist Colbert once famously argued: "The art of taxation consists in so plucking the goose as to obtain the maximum amount of feathers with the smallest possible amount of hissing." In the most successful societies, the geese pluck themselves.

The Leap of Faith

No one likes to pay taxes. Some dislike it more than others. Most of us pay taxes because we recognize that to get what we want from government, we need to help pay for it. There is a kind of moral or social responsibility to pay our taxes—even if it hurts. But of course not everyone feels this way. Many will do whatever they can to avoid taxes even though this means that others will have to pay more just to make up what they have avoided.

To willingly pay taxes requires a "leap of faith." We have to believe that we will get something in return for the money we shell out *and* that other people will share the burden. It might seem reasonable that Swedes or Danes are willing to pay for the high-quality public services they currently receive, just as it might seem understandable that citizens in countries with less efficient institutions are less willing to pay taxes for low-quality services. We can also understand why people are more resistant to paying taxes when they feel that the tax burden is unfair, or that many people get away without paying their fair share. In short, if we take a static view, we may be able to explain current attitudes and taxpayer behavior in different countries. But this static view cannot help us understand how or why these different societies have developed such different tax systems and, ultimately, different relationships between citizens and their governments.

This book explores the evolution of this relationship in a set of widely different democratic countries (Sweden, Italy, the United Kingdom, the United States, and Romania). We examine how these relationships evolved in each country and why they have come to differ so much. The book is organized as case studies of each country. Each case is presented in two chapters. In the first chapter for each country we examine the fiscal foundation upon which "successful" societies have been built. The central question these chapters address is: How did this country develop the capacity to tax and monitor its citizens and its society? How was it possible for some early rulers to build institutions that could effectively monitor, measure, and collect sufficient revenue to build a modern state? In the second of the two chapters we examine the relationship between citizens and their states in the twentieth century. With the exception of Romania in this study, by the mid-twentieth century most democratic and capitalist countries had surprisingly similar tax laws. As we shall see, however, how well and efficiently they have implemented these rules varies widely—as do the ways citizens perceive their states and consequentially their "willingness to pay."

As the reader will quickly see, this is not a typical edited volume. Instead, it has been conceived and written as a constructed volume. This book has grown out of a five-year-long project called "Willing to Pay?" which focuses on behavioral experiments conducted in these five countries. We began this project with the desire to better understand the sources of national policy variation. Our behavioral work uncovered a large set of fascinating and some-times surprising results (see Andrighetto et al. 2016; D'Attoma et al. 2017; Zhang et al. 2016; as well as Steinmo (forthcoming), *Willing to Pay?*). We found that while there are significant differences in behavior between people from different nations with respect to their willingness to contribute to a public good in the laboratory setting, this variation is only loosely connected to actual tax compliance behavior at the country or national level. Along with the national and individual differences we discovered, however, the most robust finding we have is that most people in all countries are far more compliant and honest than standard economic theory predicts.[2] When faced with identical institutional choices most people, most of the time, *are* willing to contribute to the public good. We were surprised to find, for example, that Italians are *more* willing than British subjects to contribute to a common fund *if they believe that the institutions and rules are fair, efficient, and reliable*.

Our experimental methodology allowed us to test how people in different societies behave when faced with identical choices. But, of course, citizens and taxpayers in different countries are *not* faced with identical institutions or choices. In the real world, tax and compliance decisions are motivated in the context of hugely different institutions and incentives. As Marcelo Bergman cogently argued,

> People maximize utilities inasmuch as they pay as little taxes as they can. But the environment in which people operate fundamentally shapes how they frame the maximization benefits.... Tax evasion, then, [should be] understood as highly sensitive to social, political, and cultural processes; any attempt to understand variation in tax evasion across cases must incorporate social, political, cultural, and economic perspectives on the problem. (2009: 10)

In other words, *Willing to Pay?* demonstrates that when Italians are presented with the same institutions as Swedes, they make similar (but not identical) choices to the Swedes. The implication is that if Italians were given the opportunity to pay taxes in a system as efficient as Sweden's, they would avoid far fewer taxes than they do today.

In sum, the "Willing to Pay?" experiments strongly support the institution-alist theory that people respond to the political and social incentives they face and that if we want to explain behavior in different countries we need to examine the ways in which the social and political institutions governing that society structure that behavior (Steinmo, Thelen, and Longstreth 1992). But as interesting as this behavioral analysis and methodology is, it cannot help us to understand how and why different societies have developed such different political and social institutions. This is the central question explored in this volume.

The Co-Evolution of Political Culture and Political Institutions

It is rather obvious that a purely institutional analysis is insufficient to explain how individual systems have evolved and changed in the ways they have over the decades. Indeed, as any observer with international experience will notice, there are real and substantive differences between countries in the ways in which citizens interact with their states—and what they expect of them. These broad attitudinal and even cultural differences must also matter for policy outcomes. Americans, for example, do seem to be more committed to the concept of individual freedom than most of their European counterparts. Similarly, Swedes are far more tolerant of high levels of taxation and are far more willing to cooperate with their government authorities than citizens in most other countries.

In short, attitudes, beliefs, and even "political culture" do seem to matter in politics. However, cultural analyses have rarely been taken seriously in modern political science.[3] The key reason for this is that political culture is (a) hard to define and therefore test; (b) not fully consistent—or perhaps not even coherent—across a polity; and (c) attitudes and beliefs (the building blocks of culture) are dynamic and not static.

Importantly, the exact same criticisms can be leveled at institutional analysis. Political institutions are hard to define (especially when we consider informal institutions), often remarkably inconsistent, and constantly evolving (Mahoney and Thelen 2009; Steinmo 2010; Thelen 2004). A plausible and perhaps reasonable response to these truths is that we cannot or should not study institutions, culture, or, for that matter, history. These subjects of inquiry do not lend themselves to precise, falsifiable, and predictable scientific inquiry. Perhaps we, as scientists, should restrict ourselves to the kind of analysis presented in our forthcoming book *Willing to Pay?* in which we conduct rigorous experiments and repeat these experiments over and over in multiple locations with thousands of subjects. I, personally, am a strong advocate of this kind of work and believe it is interesting and important. *But*, if we want to understand *why* different societies have developed such different institutions, incentives, and outcomes, I believe we need to understand how and why the institutions have evolved in such different ways in different societies.

In this volume we try to develop just such analyses by building a nuanced understanding of the iterative relationship between citizens' attitudes and beliefs about their states, the behavior and policies of those states, and the institutions through which citizens' preferences are transmitted. We believe that the focus on fiscal history and tax compliance offers a particularly useful window to view this relationship. No other policy is such a good test of the relationship between citizens and their states. Most people want more from their governments and at some level most people would prefer to pay less tax. The dilemma is that unless everyone pays, no one is willing to pay. In other words, this is a giant collective action dilemma in which the state and the citizen are engaged in a kind of "ultimatum game." Unlike the standard game played in laboratories around the world, however, it is far from evident who the first player is, in the real world. This is quite simply because this is a repeated game with a history that is far longer than anyone can remember.

Following the insights offered by Marcelo Bergman in his excellent book, *Tax Evasion and the Rule of Law in Latin America*, we argue that the different levels of tax compliance observed in different countries can be understood as different kinds of "compliance equilibria" in each of these different societies (Bergman 2009). We build on this analysis, arguing that these equilibria are dynamic. To be sure, there is a considerable amount of path dependency (Pierson 2004) and historical legacy shaping these equilibria, but they are not linear progressions. We will see multiple examples showing that what the state can do is in large measure defined by what citizens believe about their state. But what citizens believe about their state is in large measure defined by what their state has done and how it has behaved toward them in the past. Simply put, states that have low capacity to enforce their laws and rules tend to have citizens who distrust that state. When citizens distrust their state it is difficult for the state to collect the revenues that could make the citizen more satisfied with their state.

Sweden is perhaps the premier example of a country that has developed a high compliance equilibrium. We believe that we can understand this outcome as a virtuous cycle in which the state has earned the trust and support of its people and is thus able to lower monitoring costs at the same time that it works to improve delivery of its services (see Jenny Jansson, Chapter 3 in this volume). Italy and Romania, in contrast, find themselves stuck in much lower compliance equilibria, which can be seen as vicious cycles. In each of these countries the state so far has proven unable to develop the capacity to effectively and efficiently collect taxes or deliver services to a nation. Consequentially, citizens have not developed a sense of common purpose or trust in the state. Instead, to deliver services and collect revenues these states have built a sometimes quite burdensome and ultimately inefficient administrative apparatus that works to further undermine citizens' willingness to pay (see, in this volume, Josef Hien (Chapter 4), John D'Attoma (Chapter 5), Clara Volintiru (Chapter 10), and Arpad Todor (Chapter 11)).

Britain and the United States lie in between. These two cases are obviously quite different from each other even while they share something of the middle ground between Sweden and Italy. These states are relatively efficient and at least at some point possessed relatively high levels of trust on the part of their citizenry. But again, the relationship between citizens and their state is not fixed. Instead, culture, attitudes toward the state, political institutions, and public policies interact with one another over time. Moreover, the relationship between the state and its citizens has not always been positive (see, in this volume, Martin Daunton (Chapter 6), Liam Stanley (Chapter 7), Romain Huret (Chapter 8), and Carolyn C. Jones (Chapter 9)). Governments can get things right and thereby increase trust and compliance, or they can pursue policies that undermine their own legitimacy and thus undermine consent. Looking at the history and evolution of these five different countries, the chapters in this volume provide fascinating insights into how these cycles became established, how they are nurtured, as well as how and why they can be undermined.

Fiscal Capacity and the Evolution of Modern States

The current volume stands on the shoulders of some of the greatest works in the history of political science and fiscal sociology. We owe great intellectual debts to several of the foundational insights offered in the classic texts of, for example, Charles Tilly's *The Formation of National States in Western Europe* (1975); Joel Migdal's *Strong Societies and Weak States* (2009); Theda Skocpol's *States and Social Revolutions* (1979); Samuel Huntington's *Political Order and Changing Societies* (1968); Rudolf Braun's *Taxation, Sociopolitical Structure, and State-Building* (1975); and Peter Evans et al.'s *Bringing the State Back In* (1985). Though taxation and fiscal policy have not exactly been at the center of political science's interest in recent years,[4] there have been a number of more recent works that have also deeply informed our current work. Some of the most important of these include: Margaret Levi's *On Rule and Revenue* (1988), Sven Steinmo's *Taxation and Democracy* (1993), Peter Lindert's *Growing Public* (2004), and finally the insightful volume by Isaac Martin, Ajay Mehrota, and Monica Prasad, *The New Fiscal Sociology* (2009)—these have been particularly influential in our thinking and the development of this book.

We hope to add to these literatures in several ways. First, this book explicitly compares five quite different regimes in both their early state-formation processes and in the modern twentieth century. The majority of the great books noted here and elsewhere tend to focus on the formation of states and state capacity and leave it to the reader to draw conclusions about how these states would manage in the modern era. In this volume we explicitly build on the analyses of state-building and try to show how these different emergent states managed in the twentieth century. Secondly, by focusing on taxation and compliance we drill down into one of the most difficult and important points of contact between citizens and their states. Finally, we believe that these analyses of tax capacity and tax compliance have broad implications for developing societies and welfare states. In the last chapter of this volume, Marcelo Bergman and Sven Steinmo explicitly lay out the policy implication of these historical analyses for countries whose citizens are reticent to take the "Leap of Faith." No country can become Sweden. But learning how and why Sweden developed such a positive relationship between taxpayers and their government and comparing this history to countries that have been much less successful in this regard, offers both general and specific insights into what can build and what can undermine legitimacy.

Sweden

We begin our volume with the case of Sweden. This country is widely noted for having one of the heaviest tax burdens in the world and at the same time the highest level of tax compliance. It might be easy to say that today Swedes understand that they get a lot for their tax money and/or that Swedes have particularly high levels of trust in their public institutions, but this just raises the question: How and why did this come about?

In their essay, "Getting to Sweden: The Origins of High Compliance in the Swedish Tax State," Marina Nistotskaya and Michelle D'Arcy open our volume with a careful and fascinating analysis of the emergence of state capacity in Sweden. They argue that as far back as the sixteenth and seventeenth centuries, Sweden was already developing advanced methods for monitoring society's main economic assets for tax collection purposes. These early foundations were enormously influential for subsequent developments in terms of the tax net coverage, fairness of tax assessments, and also for the development of a vertical fiscal contract directly between the king and his subjects.

Their explanation for this early and remarkably efficient system hinges on the special role that the newly formed Lutheran church played in collecting information and legitimizing state actions. Reliable and stable fiscal foundations enhanced the state's ambitions both domestically and internationally and this created a virtuous cycle where citizens could enjoy direct benefits, in terms of first-order public goods provision (peace, freedom from foreign rule, law and order) in return for paying taxes. At the same time, these developments were facilitated by Sweden's relatively unique social structure: a free peasantry and weak nobility led the state into a direct fiscal contract with the broad bulk of the peasantry rather than, as happened elsewhere, the land- and capital-owning nobility. Finally, they suggest that the structure of the Swedish economy, particularly the late onset of industrialization, forced the state to find innovative administrative technologies that produced a tax structure and administration that could easily adapt to the collection of modern taxes. Nistotskaya and D'Arcy tell us:

> Between 1500 and 1750 Sweden transformed into a tax state with certain characteristics that would become the hallmarks in later periods. The result of the transformation was that the state had both the "hard" capacity needed to collect taxes—such as digital information on the resource base and ability to monitor the entire population—and "soft" capacity in the form of a meaningful fiscal contract between the state and its subjects that supported quasi-voluntary compliance.

The keystones of the successful Swedish case were, first, that the state adopted sophisticated methods for monitoring their citizens' ability to pay. Second, the Swedish Reformed Lutheran Church effectively acted as an agent of the state both by helping to collect information on citizens and by legitimizing state tax collection. Third, due to the unique features of the Swedish early military conscription system in which communities contributed soldiers to the King's Army and then supported the soldier's family while he was away, these communities were keen to monitor each other to ensure that everyone paid their fair share. The direct contribution of soldiers to the state reinforced a type of horizontal contract in which citizens developed a sense that the state owed them something in return. In short, the foundations of "quasi-voluntary compliance" were built even before Sweden became a modern democratic society (Levi 1988).

Jenny Jansson's chapter, "Creating Tax-Compliant Citizens in Sweden: The Role of Social Democracy," builds on Nistotskaya and D'Arcy's argument, but brings it forward into the twentieth century. In her chapter we learn that the Social Democrats built on the strong administrative traditions present in this country and explicitly and intentionally propagandized their voters to accept the idea that if they paid high taxes, they would get better services. Socialism, they argued, did not mean taking money or wealth from the rich or the corporations, but, instead, meant that everyone had to share the burden.

Certainly, having developed efficient monitoring institutions as described by Nistotskaya and D'Arcy, this country was able to develop more efficient and effective governance institutions. But this was far from an over-determined outcome. Looking back upon history, the path taken seems like it was obvious. Standing at the other point in history and looking forward, however, it seems highly unlikely you would take such a view. At the end of the nineteenth century Sweden was a poor country, peripheral to the main developments in Europe. It had no colonies (except, perhaps, Norway) and was late to develop an industrial sector. Early in the twentieth century it was rife with labor unrest and social conflict. Democracy had yet to be extended to the working classes. It seems unlikely that anyone would have looked at this little country at the dawn of the century and said: "Sweden will become one of the richest countries in the world in sixty years."

But it did become rich. How did this happen? First, Sweden's electoral and political institutions were captured by a Social Democratic party that then decided to compromise with its political adversaries and build a Social Democratic identity, *convincing its own members they should pay for their own welfare state*. Jansson shows us how the Social Democrats convinced these workers that they lived in "the good society" (*Folke Hemet*, "The People's Home") and that their common identity gave them solidarity with not just other members of their class but with society as a whole. The new Social Democratic leaders first had to come to an agreement with the other parties and interests outside the party, but once they did, the relatively efficient administrative apparatus they inherited made it possible to implement their main goals. The fact that they could execute their goals enabled a new kind of virtuous cycle in which the government could provide good services to both the working class and the capitalist elite. These positive outcomes in the end encouraged them toward ever broader goals. Still, the policy history that Jenny Jansson describes was not one of continual success. Instead, there were moments in their own history where the very foundations of the social democratic idea seemed to be at risk.

Jansson's chapter explains how the Social Democratic Party created the high tax morale for which Sweden is so famous. In her argument it was the intentional propagandizing of the Social Democratic Party in favor of taxes for everyone that helped build a system in which everyone felt that they must contribute and therefore had a right to benefit. Whereas the politics of taxation in the twentieth century in many countries has been a politics of trying to displace the burden onto someone else, the Social Democrats understood quite early that if they were going to have a successful welfare state they needed to have everyone in.

In her analysis it was both the perception that the state had the capacity to collect taxes and the state's emphasis on fairness across society that are key to the high levels of "quasi-voluntary compliance" we see in Sweden today. Jansson points to the fact that simply having state capacity does not necessarily imply that citizens will comply. Instead citizens need to believe that taxes are distributed fairly and that they will benefit from those taxes. Sweden benefited from high state capacity but this in itself was not enough to create the kind of tax-compliant citizen that we now see in this country.

An especially important part of Jansson's chapter shows how even in Sweden, tax compliance was hardly a foregone conclusion. In the 1970s and 1980s Swedish leaders were genuinely concerned that the tax system itself was creating "a people of cheats." The increasingly burdensome and complicated tax system was encouraging more and more people to complain about not just their taxes, but the way in which the state functioned. As we will see in several of the upcoming chapters in this volume, Jansson's case study shows how if people do not feel that the system is "fair" they will be unwilling to pay taxes. This apparently applied even to "honest" Swedes.

Fortunately for the Swedes and their welfare state, Sweden was able to reform its tax system. Ironically, these reforms were very similar to the types of tax reform pushed for by neoliberals in the United States and Britain. However, while the American neoliberals pressed for flat taxes and cutting back on tax expenditure in order to reduce the role of the state, in Sweden the Social Democratic elite came to believe these reforms would support Social Democracy because they would reaffirm citizens' belief in the fairness of the system. Social Democracy was about fairness, they argued, not about creating divisions within society (Steinmo 2003).

In the end, the dominant theme of Jansson's chapter is that the success of the modern Swedish tax system is that it is fundamentally based on the concept of fairness. Whereas Nistotskaya and D'Arcy emphasize state capacity and explain how Sweden could achieve it, this chapter explains how that capacity was used to build a fair and equitable system into which the Swedish are willing to pay.

Italy

We next look at a very different case: Italy. Whereas the Church worked with the state in Sweden, the Catholic Church did the opposite in Italy. As Josef Hien shows in "Tax Evasion in Italy: A God-Given Right?" the Catholic Church saw the modernizing Italian state as a competitor. Rather than working to build the fiscal foundations for a successful social welfare state, Catholics were threatened by the prospect that the government might provide the kinds of services that had up to that point been their domain. Instead of legitimizing state activity and tax authority, church officials in Italy actively undermined the state and even at times encouraged citizens to evade their taxes as a moral duty.

Hien's analysis of the nineteenth-century state formation argues that the high levels of tax evasion in Italy—for which this country has become so infamous—have their foundations in the conflict between the Church and the new "liberal" state during Italian unification in the nineteenth century. To the Vatican, the territorial integration of the Italian nation state posed an existential threat both on the political (loss of territory) and spiritual (diffusion of liberalism) levels. The chapter shows that after unification the

Vatican took strides to undermine the legitimacy of the Italian state and even specifically worked against Italians' willingness to pay.

The Italian case shows the contrast with the Swedish case in deep relief. Italians, it appears, were unwilling early on to take the "leap of faith" in large measure because the Catholic Church warned them not to. What this demonstrates is perhaps less about the specific institution of the Church and more about the difficulty any state has in generating the levels of trust *and competence* needed for the "leap." Swedish elites were quite simply more successful in their ability to eliminate the alternative sources of power than Italian elites.

In Italy's case, however, these factors worked against the state's ability to exercise effective control over the country. Hien's fascinating account of the Italian case aligns nicely with Joel Migdal, who argues, "in societies with weak states the continuing environment of conflict—the vast, but fragmented social control embedded in non-state organizations the society—has dictated a particular, pathological set of relationships within the state organization itself, between the top state leadership and its agencies" (1988: 207).

As Migdal later argued, "local and regional strongmen, politicians, and implementers accommodate one another in a web of political, economic, and social exchanges. [And therefore] the strongmen end up with an enhanced bargaining position or with posts in the state itself that influence important decisions about the allocation of resources in the application of policy rules" (Migdal 2001: 92). In short, "a society fragmented in social control affects the character of the state, which, in turn reinforces the fragmentation of society" (Weiner and Huntington 1987: 429).

There can be no gainsaying that Italians are far less "willing to pay" than Swedes. Indeed, in many ways Italy provides the opposite story to the Swedish case. To be sure it is a complicated story (everything about Italian history is complicated) but the overwhelming theme that comes through—especially in comparison with the Swedish case—is the fact that the Italian state was never able to take control over its citizens' hearts or pocketbooks. This case reminds us of how unique and precious the Swedish case is. Hien reminds us that the experiments in our "Willing to Pay?" project demonstrated that contrary to many people's expectations, Italians on average are not a great deal less willing to pay when the monies will be shared or distributed in a system that could be considered fair. Hien also argues that the Church's role in Italy was a double-edged sword: at the root of much Catholic teaching were the ideas of forgiveness, indulgence, and repentance, which could be used to justify evading the state's taxes. As a consequence, Italians appear more willing to "fudge," meaning that they might cheat a little.[5] But of course if everyone cheats a little, or even if a lot of people cheat a little, the perception is that there is a lot of cheating. If the perception is that there is a lot of cheating then it may become an accepted norm and more and more people will do it when they have the opportunity. That does not mean, however, that they are necessarily willing to cheat or even steal from their neighbors. Italians may pay less in taxes, but that does not mean that they are more dishonest than Swedes.

John D'Attoma's chapter picks up on this theme with his opening quote from former Prime Minister Silvio Berlusconi: "evasion of high taxes is a God-given right." Of course, Mr. Berlusconi was famous for his own tax evasion and indeed for illegal behavior more generally, but one cannot fail to notice how remarkable it is that a leader of a country would invoke God in a justification for not paying taxes. Not even Donald Trump would suggest that God gave him the right to evade his taxes.

D'Attoma's chapter begins with a focus on the differences in tax payment in the North and the South of Italy. Picking up on the theme of "The Southern Question," D'Attoma shows us that rates of tax evasion vary enormously across the country, being as high as 80 percent in the far South and as low as 2 percent in the North.

Many (including Putnam and Banfield) have argued that these differences can be explained by differences in "civic virtue" between the North and the South (Banfield 1958; Putnam, Leonardi, and Nanetti 1993). D'Attoma disagrees, arguing instead that tax evasion in the South is especially high because of the low efficiency/low trust equilibrium that has been struck in this part of the country. A better explanation for the low compliance in the South is that institutions are less efficient and equitable than in the North. Echoing the themes that we see over and over again in this book, D'Attoma's thesis is that people are willing to pay when they believe they get something in return for their payments. When citizens believe that the state does not reciprocate, then evading tax is not theft, it can be justice. In his words, "Taxation mobilizes citizens to demand accountability from their government, but . . . a lack of government accountability can actually have the opposite effect, motivating individuals to evade their responsibilities."

Picking up on one of the main themes in Hien's chapter, the Catholic Church plays a large role in modern Italy as well. But for D'Attoma it is the difference in relationship between the Church and state in the North and South that is critical. It is not just the Church and its teachings that matter, but the Catholic Church as a political party has been especially significant. The particular structure of Italian electoral institutions and the presence of the powerful Christian Democratic Party enabled the two other largest parties (the Liberals and Socialists) to essentially divide the country into their own domains. The result was that high taxes were extracted from the South to finance the economic development of the North, facilitating the development of a more or less successful modern state. In the South, on the other hand, politics continued to be ruled by a traditional elite that did not offer services and thereby further alienated the Southern Italian citizen.

D'Attoma elaborates the ways in which Italy's incomplete unification has worked to further undermine the legitimacy of the Italian state. Early in the Republican period, there was a massive redistribution of wealth from South to North. Today, however, the politics of redistribution work in the opposite direction. Citizens on both sides of the regional divide tend to view the national government as *ladri* (thieves) who take too much from us and give too much to the other. These regional conflicts also contributed to vote buying and neo-corporatist administrative arrangements that further undermine the efficiency and legitimacy of the national state.

D'Attoma's analysis of twentieth-century Italian tax administration provides powerful examples of how government policies affect citizens' attitudes toward government and eventually even political culture. Certainly, Italy did not begin the twentieth century advantaged. As Joseph Hien's analysis demonstrates, the construction of the modern Italian state was problematic from the beginning. Surely, other caveats are in order as well—not the least of which was the fascist interlude and war. But despite the disadvantages, Italy did build a large and extensive state apparatus and does tax its subjects quite heavily. What the Italian state does not seem to be able to do, however, is tax its subjects or deliver its services efficiently and effectively.

D'Attoma's examination of the "sector analysis" method of tax collection from small- and medium-sized businesses provides remarkable insights into how the system was constructed and how it works today. The story here is of how and why a political regime that was as fragmented as Italy's could not make coherent tax law in the first place. Consequentially, they legislated a tax administrative/collection system that in some fundamental ways seems designed to fail. Today, small businesses and their employees are enormously frustrated by the very system that was supposedly more effective and efficient than the one it replaced. Not only does this system collect very low revenues, it also deeply angers the very people who are supposed to find it easier to use. And because everyone knows that small businesses pay so little in taxes it encourages others to avoid as much as they can *and* distrust their government.

Finally, the repeated amnesties for tax evaders introduced by several Italian governments have worked to further exacerbate the problems of Italian tax collection precisely because they convince citizens that the system will never be fair. When asked about their opinions on tax amnesties, over 50 percent of respondents thought that they were unfair. Once again we see that tax compliance is deeply affected by people's perceptions of equity and justice.

Remember, "Getting to Sweden" is hard. Even Sweden barely got to Sweden. Our analysis of the Italian case is one of an ineffective state implementing inefficient policies. Certainly Italy did not start with a strong sense of identity and common purpose. The structure of the state institutions and the fragmentation of the polity have worked to further exacerbate these problems. When we look more carefully and closely at the actual implementation of tax policies, it becomes more and more obvious why Italians disparage and try to ignore their state. It simply does not work very well.

Britain

Martin Daunton's analysis of the history of British fiscal capacity provides a fascinating case that lies between the Swedish and the Italian. Daunton focuses precisely on the question of how the emerging British nation built the kind of institutions that subsequent generations of British citizens could trust. In "Creating Consent: Taxation, War, and Good Government in Britain, 1688–1914," he begins with the observation that Britain was one of the first countries to become a tax state in the eighteenth century, and was marked by its ability to extract a higher proportion of national income at a very low level of resistance. This outcome is explained, he argues, by the transparent negotiation of taxation by Parliament, the creation of a bureaucratic excise service with low levels of corruption, and the incorporation of taxpayers themselves into the administration and collection of taxes. Whereas many other emerging states relied more heavily on tax framing and indirect levies, British rulers felt it important to build consent. Interestingly, Daunton also shows that these early successes did not determine the final outcomes. Instead, he shows that both state legitimacy and tax compliance were threatened after 1815 by the perception of the inequity of taxation that fell on productive capital and labor rather than rentiers and land. Further, the franchise and representation lost legitimacy. The task from the second quarter of the nineteenth century was to *re*create legitimacy and consent. This was done with remarkable success so that Britain avoided tax revolts and resistance from 1848 until after World War I.

The key, he demonstrates, was the articulation of a rhetoric of neutrality; the creation of strict rules for parliamentary scrutiny of spending; and the continued reliance on incorporating taxpayers into administration. The resulting high levels of legitimacy and consent survived the challenges of the two world wars and rising levels of extraction, but then faced new challenges after about 1970. The rhetoric changed to one of choice, stressing the need to return decisions on spending from the state to individuals. The relation between paying income tax and voting changed; as more voters came to pay tax and at higher levels, the relationship between taxpayers and tax administration shifted.

Daunton's chapter suggests quite clearly that strong fiscal foundations must be based on consent, but that consent is contingent upon taxpayers believing the system is "fair." Daunton's story is one of how British fiscal officials fundamentally understood the need to negotiate taxes with the taxpayers. Contingent consent, in the British case at least, depended on (a) the taxes being "negotiated rather than imposed" and (b) the ability of taxpayers' representatives to monitor spending, which in turn rested on the fact that the state could and did provide reasonably accurate accounts. This enabled taxpayers to challenge waste and thereby constrain the autocratic power of the state.

Though the specifics of the British case in the seventeenth and eighteenth centuries were different from the Swedish case, a common feature was that the method of collecting taxes was considered equitable and legitimate. In Britain, taxation and tax assessment was done by taxpayers themselves. Whereas in Sweden the local church authorities played a critical role, in Britain the local parish performed this function. The small size of the local parish facilitated the monitoring capacity of the authorities, much as in Sweden. Moreover, since the parish was the local source of what we might call "welfare" (especially the care of the elderly), there was a sense that taxpayers received something in return for the taxes that they had paid in.

But Daunton's chapter also shows that, even once established, contingent consent is not guaranteed. Daunton's narrative demonstrates how under the pressures of demographic change, the need to repay debt after the Napoleonic Wars and the growing perception that the distribution of the tax burden was no longer fair, the legitimacy of the British tax state was undermined. Indeed, it would have been quite possible to imagine that mid-nineteenth-century Britain could have turned itself into a battleground of some taxpayers versus others. Consent was restored, however, in part due to the leadership of Robert Peel and then William Gladstone, who both understood that consent depended upon fairness and transparency. "By constraining state expenditure and as far as possible excluding the state from involvement with economic interests, it was hoped to protect the political elite from challenge and to define the state as a neutral arbitrator," Daunton reports. "Politicians must rise above personal greed and self-interest; they must also rise above any temptation to use the state to favor one interest against another, whether a trade group in search of protection or a social group seeking tax breaks. This rhetoric of disinterestedness, of being even-handed between all types of property and the propertied and non-propertied, was central to Gladstone's budget ... "

In sum, as we saw in the Swedish case, public legitimacy was based on the idea of a level playing field between those of property and those with incomes. Fairness and even-handedness went together. Thus, by the mid-twentieth century "the income tax, despite its problems, was embedded within civil society, which helped to create a high level of compliance, trust in the fairness of the tax and the widespread acceptance of the legitimacy of the state." It was not until the last third of the century that the evenhandedness of the state came under serious threat once again. But this is the story that we learn in the next chapter by Liam Stanley.

One of the most surprising experimental results uncovered in our "Willing to Pay?" study, however, was the fact that our British subjects were *more likely* to cheat each other than our subjects in the other countries we studied in Europe or America (Zhang et al. 2016). Though tax collection rates are relatively high in Britain, it does not appear that this is because Brits (or at least young Brits) are necessarily cooperative or willing to share with each other. It seems instead that British citizens today trust their public institutions more than they trust their neighbors. Daunton's overview of the early foundations of British tax administration demonstrates precisely that even back in the eighteenth century, "good government" was paramount for British tax authorities. Even governments who aimed to cut back on their role in society and the economy focused explicitly on making their administrations something that citizens could trust.

Clearly the United Kingdom at the beginning of the twentieth century was one of the most successful states in the world. Not only was the country rich, but it had also clearly developed the political and administrative institutions that would make it a strong and successful state. After all, by the beginning of the twentieth century the sun never set on the Union Jack. A little more than a hundred years later, however, Great Britain looks quite different. Indeed, as the recent Brexit vote demonstrates, British citizens are far from confident in their political institutions and the choices made by their leaders. Rather than leading the world and exporting its version of democracy and capitalism, Britain appears to be retreating into a self-centered and increasingly frustrated society. The results from our experiments in Britain surprised us precisely because the British subjects were significantly more selfish and willing to free-ride than any of the other groups that we examined in the study. How did this happen?

Daunton demonstrates that British fiscal history was one of competence and relatively high compliance, but he suggests toward the end of his chapter that this may no longer be true. The chapter by Liam Stanley goes further into this and also helps us to make sense of the really quite remarkable finding that the British subjects in our experiments were so unwilling to contribute to the public good and/or share with their colleagues. Certainly, part of this unusual finding could have been a product of the fact that our subjects were mostly young people. And indeed, our evidence suggests that British young people are different from their elders.[6] But it also makes sense to argue that had we done these experiments twenty years ago we would have obtained quite different results. Unfortunately, we cannot go back in history and run these experiments all over again.

We suggest that, in Britain's case at least, there may have been the willingness to pay in decades past, but today that willingness is in decline. Just as in the United States where we see that reaction to the state in the election of Donald Trump, in Britain we see it in our results and in Brexit.

British citizens have long been noted for their "stiff upper lip" and their enormous sacrifice during the wars. But certainly things have changed. Many believe that Margaret Thatcher was a significant instrument in this change. "There is no such thing as society" was only one expression she employed while starting to tear down the social foundations of the British welfare state. But Thatcher clearly did not do this alone—New Labour and the Blair government made significant contributions. At the core of New Labour's idea was the attempt to individualize the welfare state and move away from class politics. Blair's welfare state would free the individual to pursue their own success. The result was hardly the new dawn they had promised. Instead, inequality grew, the rich got ever richer, and perhaps even more people started to take advantage of the welfare state because it was in their self-interest.

Liam Stanley's analysis focusing on the attitudes of British citizens gives us significant insights into this puzzle. Stanley's story is one of how a once great nation (one that could honestly tell itself that its people had beaten back the Germans twice through collective sacrifice for the common good) could become so self-centered. Stanley's analysis points to the legacy of Margaret Thatcher as well as the structure of the British welfare state and tax system itself. Combined with the decline in industrial production and jobs Britain's policies specifically worked to undermine their citizens' trust in one another and in their political institutions precisely because it felt "unfair." British tax and means-tested welfare policies worked together to create huge disincentives for the unemployed to look for and find work. Going on the "dole" was not admired or desired, but the strange mix of tax and spending policies ofttimes worked to present low income families with 100+ percent tax rates. In other words, for someone on benefits, every pound earned could mean more than a pound lost in benefits and/or increased taxes (Kay and King 1983; Steinmo 1993). Stanley's focus groups demonstrate the long-term effects of these policies on citizens' attitudes toward each other. The dysfunctional result has been that many people in full-time work believe that they have *lower* disposable income than those who live on the dole. Even welfare recipients themselves believe that everyone else is taking advantage of the system.

Our studies were conducted before the now historic "Brexit" decision, but in many ways we could say that the writing was already on the wall. Sadly, it is the young that were most damaged by this historic vote. But, as our data show, the young are hardly the most willing to contribute or cooperate. Clearly the Brits built a great country and were once "willing to pay." Both our experiments and recent events suggest that this may no longer be true. Stanley shows that British citizens increasingly believe that the state may be efficient but they are also increasingly skeptical of the very aims of the social welfare state (at least in its British form).

The USA

The United States of America provides us with a case that many might have expected to be quite like that of the British. But, when compared to Swedish or British state institutions, the fragmentation of authority in America's federal system in combination with Madisonian divided government would lead one to expect that the USA could scarcely develop the kind of tax state we find in these other successful societies. Add to this, of course, that there does seem to be a consistent anti-taxation ideology that runs through much of American history. Romain Huret argues in his chapter, "The Not-So-Infernal Revenue Service? Tax Collection, Citizens and Compliance in the United States in the Eighteenth to the Twentieth Centuries," however, that Americans may not deserve this reputation as being so "anti-state." He suggests that US history is instead marked by relatively high levels of tax compliance.

His essay examines the tax compliance process in the United States from the Early Republic to the start of the twenty-first century and proposes what he calls a "common ground model" based upon three elements that explain why Americans accepted in the past and, generally speaking, still accept the expansion of fiscal power: social legitimacy of the state, a consensus on the measurement of income and wealth, and room for negotiation.

Given the anti-tax politics that have become the hallmark of American politics in recent years, one might expect that this country would have an enormous amount of tax evasion and non-compliance. While the nearly half-trillion dollars lost each year to tax evasion does indeed seem like an enormous sum, the fact is that tax morale is actually quite high in this country and 85 percent of taxes are actually paid correctly and honestly. The puzzle for us is not why tax evasion is so high in the USA, but instead, why is it so low? Many would suggest that the answer here is clearly in the draconian powers of the Internal Revenue Service (IRS), but, as Romain Huret demonstrates, coercion is not the key. Instead, the USA has developed a relatively efficient model (despite the rhetoric often heard lately).

Americans in many ways are an enigma. This author (Steinmo) has spent much of his personal and academic life trying to better understand this strange country and its people. As almost any outside observer readily notices, Americans are generous, open, and profoundly egalitarian. The average American is not the selfish, narrow-minded *Homo economicus* that American policies seem to suggest. At the same time, the USA is the richest country in the world, has the smallest welfare state, the highest levels of inequality, and lowest taxes of any modern democracy. While Americans could afford to share their wealth more than any other country, they apparently have chosen not to. But when we look at their tax compliance behavior we find that both in our experiments and in the real world Americans do appear willing to pay. Or at least, they are willing to follow the rules. Their rules. The enigma is that Americans apparently do not want a state, but still do what the state tells them to do.

There can be no gainsaying that the politics of distrust and the fragmentation of the American polity have increased enormously in recent years. But the foundation upon which this politics has emerged was remarkably strong. Carolyn C. Jones's analysis of the relationship between Americans and their tax collector authorities is one of both patriotism and fear. Americans do not love their state but they love their country. Americans may not want taxes, but when they are asked to pay, they pay. The contrast to the Italians is remarkable. Italians want the state to do things for them, but then cheat the state. Americans say they do not want the state to do things for them, but pay for it anyway. Why?

Here we turn to the relationship between identity and compliance. As we shall see, societies that have a stronger sense of self, a stronger identity, are easier for the state to manage effectively. To put this in reverse, in more fragmented societies it is more difficult for the state to impose its will, in part because it has to compete with other sources of legitimacy. The Swedish state, probably the most effective in this regard, essentially co-opted the Church, the capitalist elite, and the labor unions. The Italian state, perhaps the least effective in this regard, continuously suffered from the fact that the Catholic Church opposed the implementation of state authority. The result, as we shall see, was that the Italian state never developed a sense of coherence, just as the Italian society never developed a common sense of identity.

But what of the United States? Certainly, the Church could not be used as a source of legitimacy by the state. Thomas Jefferson's dictates against a state Church and indeed the constitutional prohibition against Church–state cooperation made this impossible. One could look at this huge continent-sized country and the way in which many peoples who arrived here expanded across the country as evidence of a lack of common identity. But as all students of American politics and history from Alex de Tocqueville to Gunnar Myrdal have long noted, Americans are unique precisely because of their common identity. That identity is that of "Americanism." America is an "ism." It is impossible to imagine "Britishism" or "Swedishism."

At the time of the Civil War, America was obviously a very fragmented country. But Carolyn C. Jones argues that World War I and World War II helped build a more common sense of identity, much as Charles Tilly would have argued. Remarkably, it was at least in part the act of collecting taxes to finance these wars that proved critical for advancing a common sense of "us" (Americans) versus "them." Indeed, the IRS very effectively used publicity and marketing strategies to help build a sense of common identity, arguing that the USA needed "Taxes to Beat the Axis." Her story is thus not just one of publicity campaigns; it is also about building a common sense of Americanism and the role taxes played in this social construction.

Jones shows how the IRS and its propaganda instruments successfully convinced citizens—especially during World War II—that it was their civic responsibility to pay their taxes. But the tax authorities were also very successful at publicizing high-visibility tax fraud cases and thereby making average people believe that they, the authorities, were far more efficient than they in fact were. The irony may be, however, that in doing so, revenue collectors generate more fear than trust. In doing so, they play into the anti-state beliefs that have become so apparent in this country. Today even the president is proud to have avoided the taxman.

Romania

Our final case, Romania, provides a very different story. Romania has the lowest tax burden, a "flat" income tax, and the highest level of tax evasion in Europe. Here we see the difficulty of building confidence on the heels of an illegitimate regime. Both Clara Volintiru's and Arpad Todor's chapters show how difficult it is to get citizens to take the "leap of faith" when their rulers are corrupt and their institutions are inefficient. These chapters build a bridge to an understanding of the dilemmas developing countries are facing more generally. Importantly, our experimental studies offer some hope, as Romanians do appear to be willing to pay—if they can believe that their money is collected and redistributed fairly.

Volintiru's essay, "Tax Collection without Consent: State-Building in Romania," specifically explores the fiscal history of what is most certainly the least successful state in our set of countries. She shows how the evolution of Romanian fiscal institutions was fundamentally shaped by the fact that the state itself was foreign. Whereas we saw in the Swedish, British, and American cases that a common sense of identity and belonging was critical for the building of fiscal capacity, in Romania's case there could be almost no normative connection between the citizens and the state precisely because "the state" belonged to someone else. Consent, at least of the kind that Daunton emphasizes, was clearly impossible in this context. But, as both Volintiru and Todor argue, compliance does not necessarily mean consent.

Romania is perhaps the most different case in this analysis. Volintiru's chapter reveals how the Romanian state was for centuries the possession of foreign powers. In a very real sense, the Romanian state was even further disadvantaged than the Italian state at the beginning of the twentieth century. We do not examine the Communist interlude here but as Todor shows, the years of Communist dictatorship and especially Ceausescu's leadership did nothing to tie the citizens to their state. Moreover, the longstanding linguistic and cultural divisions between the Transylvanians and Romanians continue to hinder any sense of common identity.

Volintiru focuses her chapter on the evolution of the relationship between the state and the Orthodox Church, as well as the traditionally loose coupling between formal and informal institutions in Romania. One of the main propositions of this chapter is that the absence of a consolidated social contract between citizens and authority has led to remarkably divergent fiscal capacities of local and central structures of power.

Italy and Romania thus both provide examples of the consequences of a state *not* being able to fully dominate its own country. As Hien reminds us, "modern" Italy as a unified nation is scarcely 150 years old. But of course, just being a new nation does not itself prohibit unity. One need only look to Germany to find a country that is roughly the same age, but that managed to become a far more efficient and indeed coherent nation state. Romania shows how difficult it can be to develop both a sense of identity as well as administrative capacities for governance when your country has scarcely had any experience in collecting its own taxes or for that matter measuring its own resources.

At the time of the communist collapse, income taxes did not exist in Romania. This could have advantaged the national leadership for it could have built a tax system on a relatively blank slate. However, as Arpad Todor shows, both the enormous levels of corruption and public sector inefficiency undermined the nation's ambitious goals. Todor argues that the structure of incentives created in the new tax system failed to convince citizens that the system was fair and failed to motivate state actors to treat taxpayers fairly. The structure of incentives created for both those paying the personal income tax and those paying corporate taxes made it very rational to simply avoid the burden. Remember, nobody likes to be a sucker. Thus the instability and low quality of the Romanian legal framework in combination with the absence of serious political attention paid to fiscal issues helped to facilitate, if not downright encourage, tax evasion. Certainly, the fact that Romania still remains a poor and largely agricultural nation is a large part of the explanation for the nearly 40 percent tax gap. But even those individuals who pay taxes, pay less than they might in other countries precisely because the system itself is so poorly organized and poorly administered. Sadly, corruption is rampant in Romania. State spending is often used to benefit the most corrupt and most influential, public infrastructure in much of the country is in disrepair, and public services are minimal and largely financed by European instead of Romanian institutions. Finally, public expenditure on social welfare and pensions is among the lowest in the modern world. There is what Todor calls "a broken connection between contribution and benefits," which, as he says, "gives the impression that average citizens do not receive much from the state in exchange for paying their taxes."

Another of the most surprising results drawn from our experimental work is that Romanians—or at least young Romanians—appear at least as likely to contribute to a public good as those in Sweden or the United States. In other words, when Romanians are given the same institutional choices as citizens in other countries they appear to be just as willing to pay. But of course, they are not given the same choices or institutions in the real world. Thus, as Arpad concludes, "given the constant failure to create an adequate legitimacy for the tax system, the capacity to directly tax citizens and companies has slowly decreased." The result is that the state relies ever more on indirect taxes precisely because they are less felt by the citizens. The result is that the "fiscal exchange" simply does not take place. Romanians do not expect much from their state, nor are they willing to pay for it.

At the time of writing, Romania is going through a massive political crisis over exactly these issues. Perhaps the best demonstration of the argument we keep returning to in this book was captured by the *Financial Times* in their coverage of this story on February 3, 2017, when they quoted a young man who was demonstrating against the government in Bucharest: "Why should we act like honest citizens, paying taxes and being good people if they can get away with this?"

Conclusion: The State as Predator?

Early models of tax evasion were built on the neoclassical economic assumption that human beings are essentially selfish (Allingham and Sandmo 1972). In this view, the only reason someone would pay taxes is that they fear being caught and punished for tax evasion. Today, however, there is a huge body of evidence demonstrating that tax compliance behavior cannot be explained by a simple model (Alm and Torgler 2006; Cummings et al. 2009; Frey and Torgler 2007; Sandmo 2005; Torgler et al. 2008). While most of us can be strongly influenced by incentives and punishments, it is also clear that human beings are not simply the rationally selfish decision makers once imagined in classical economics. The behavioral revolution that has swept much of the social sciences in recent years shows quite clearly that human beings are social creatures who are as interested in their place in society and following social norms as they are in maximizing individual self-interest. Of course this is not to suggest that human beings are not self-interested. They are. But to understand how they define their self-interest we must understand them as "reasoning" social creatures. As Douglas North writes, "human behavior appears to be more complex than that embodied in the individual utility functions of economists' models... People decipher the environment by processing information through pre-existing mental constructs through which they understand the environment and solve the problems they confront" (North 1990: 20).

The perspective we offer here builds on this line of research and echoes Margaret Levi's notion of "quasi-voluntary compliance" (1988: 52). Each of the chapters in this book demonstrates the point that tax compliance is a type of "fiscal exchange" in which citizens are more willing to put money into the pot when they feel they have a good chance to win something back from that pot. But also, as implied by Levi, taxpayers are especially resistant to paying taxes if they feel that they are being asked to bear an unfair share of the burden. "Taxpayers are strategic actors who will cooperate only when they can expect others to cooperate as well. Compliance of each depends on the compliance of others. No one prefers to be a *sucker*" (1988: 53).

States that developed the administrative capacities to enforce laws, protect property rights, and even accurately measure their lands early in their histories were clearly advantaged. At the same time, we know that collecting taxes is not as simple as building technical capacity to enforce tax laws. When the state has the ability to enforce its laws, a positive social equilibrium is possible... but it is far from guaranteed in any particular country. As Bergman (2009: 16) says,

> Enforcement is at the heart of the tax compliance game because it elicits—or inhibits—the conditions for cooperation. It is the subjectively perceived credibility of effective enforcement that compels citizens to abide by the rules. The threat of credible sanctions creates a virtuous circle because it both develops social and human capital and economizes on individual cost-driven decisions. The perception that rules are being enforced effectively reduces free riding and optimizes resource allocation, and more widespread tax compliance raises revenues and improves the quality of public goods.

How does this rare event come about? First, the state, or rulers, must establish a fairly high degree of state capacity. State capacity is defined simply as "the ability to perform appropriate tasks, effectively, efficiently and sustainably" (Grindle and Hilderbrand 1997: 34). States with high levels of capacity are not simply strong authoritarian states, though. Having a big military or police force does not mean you have developed strong capacity. In our view, effective state capacity depends on three variables: under these conditions, a state *may* develop capacity that can lead to social and political legitimacy that is foundational to becoming a successful state. However, having gotten this far is no guarantee. On the contrary, successful states require a further set of conditions:

- Successful states deliver value for the tax money they collect.
- Successful states have relatively efficient administrative and monitoring systems.
- Successful states practice procedural fairness.

Under these conditions citizens will willingly pay taxes and even monitor themselves. Under these conditions revenue collection becomes radically more efficient than it is for a predator state.

In sum the successful state is not simply a predator who must concede some things in order to get what it wants. Instead, we believe that it is more useful to think of a successful state as one that treats people fairly and gives them things that they want. Being *legitimate* is not just about extraction or resources.

We will return to these themes in our last chapter where we explore the implications of this study for tax policy in both the developed and the developing world. As we better understand how and why some countries have been more successful building higher tax compliance, perhaps we can better understand what other countries can do (or avoid) to encourage their citizens to take the "leap of faith."

Notes

1. Interestingly, however, simply having democratic institutions—the right to vote, free elections, even a free press—is clearly not enough. Sadly, there are many countries that have those institutional features and yet are quite dysfunctional societies. Consider Jamaica compared to Singapore. Indeed, as Bo Rothstein has argued in many publications, the quality of government is not the same thing as democratic institutions (Rothstein 2011; Rothstein and Teorell 2012).
2. There are also a host of other fascinating findings discussed in *Willing to Pay?*, both national differences in behavior as well as at the individual level. We show, for example, that women in all countries and all situations are more honest than men, that people are more responsive to what they get from the public pot rather than how much they put into it, and that economists are more selfish than any other group we studied.
3. Political culture arguments were much more common in classical political science. Political science literature generally argued that political outcomes differ in different countries quite simply because their citizens want different things. See Almond and Verba (1963); King (1974); Lipset (1996); and Shafer (1991). See also Alesina and Glaeser (2004).

4. In *The Formation of National States in Western Europe*, Tilly (1975: 50) bemoans, "taxation, for example, ordinarily shows up in European histories (not to mention theories of political development) as an epiphenomenon—and a rather uninteresting one at that."

5. See Andrighetto et al. (2016) for an elaboration of this argument and evidence for the Swedish and Italian cases.

6. We subsequently tested an adult group of British subjects and found them to be substantially more compliant than their younger counterparts. See the forthcoming volume: Steinmo, *Willing to Pay?* (Oxford University Press).

References

Alesina, A. and E. Glaeser (2004), *Fighting Poverty in the US and Europe*. Oxford: Oxford University Press.

Allingham, M. and A. Sandmo (1972), "Income Tax Evasion: A Theoretical Analysis." *Journal of Public Economics* 1: 323–38.

Alm, J. and B. Torgler (2006), "Culture Difference and Tax Morale in United States and Europe." *Journal of Economic Psychology* 27(2): 224–46.

Almond, G. A. and S. Verba (1963), *The Civic Culture: Political Attitudes and Democracy in Five Nations*. Princeton, NJ: Princeton University Press.

Andrighetto, G., N. Zhang, S. Ottone, F. Ponzano, J. D'Attoma, and S. Steinmo (2016), "Are Some Countries More Honest than Others? Evidence from a Tax Compliance Experiment in Sweden and Italy." *Frontiers in Psychology*. doi: 10.3389/fpsyg.2016.00472.

Banfield, E. (1958), *The Moral Basis of Backward Society*. Banfield, IL: The Free Press.

Barenson, M. (2017), *Trust and Taxes: From Coercion to Compliance in Poland, Russia and Ukraine*. Cambridge: Cambridge University Press.

Bergman, M. (2009), *Tax Evasion and the Rule of Law in Latin America*. University Park, PA: University of Pennsylvania Press.

Braun, R. (1975), "Taxation, Sociopolitical Structure, and State-Building: Great Britain and Brandenburg, Prussia." In C. Tilly (ed.), *The Formation of Nation States in Western Europe*. Princeton, NJ: Princeton University Press, 243–327.

Cummings, R. G., J. Martinez-Vazquez, M. McKee, and B. Torgler (2009), "Tax Morale Affects Tax Compliance: Evidence from Surveys and an Artefactual Field Experiment." *Journal of Economic Behavior & Organization* 70(3): 447–57.

D'Attoma, J., C. Volintiru, and S. Steinmo (2017), "Willing to Share? Tax Compliance and Gender in Europe and America." *Research & Politics* 4(2). doi: 10.1177/2053168017707151.

Evans, P., D. Rueschemeyer, and T. Skocpol (1985), *Bringing the State Back In*. New York: Cambridge University Press.

Frey, B. S. and B. Torgler (2007), "Tax Morale and Conditional Cooperation." *Journal of Comparative Economics* 35(1): 136–59.

Grindle, M. S. and M. E. Hilderbrand (1997), "Building Sustainable Capacity in the Public Sector: What Can Be Done?" *Public Administration and Development* 15(5): 441–63.

Huntington, S. (1968), *Political Order in Changing Societies*. New Haven, CT: Yale University Press.

Kay, J. and M. King (1983), *The British Tax System* (3rd edn.). London: Oxford University Press.

King, A. (1974), "Ideas, Institutions and Policies of Governments: A Comparative Analysis, Part I." *British Journal of Political Science* 3(4): 291–313.

Levi, M. (1988), *Of Rule and Revenue*. Berkeley, CA: University of California Press.

Lindert, P. H. (2004), *Growing Public: Social Spending and Economic Growth since the Eighteenth Century*. Cambridge and New York: Cambridge University Press.

Lipset, S. M. (1996), *American Exceptionalism*. New York: W. W. Norton.

Mahoney, J. and K. Thelen (eds.) (2009), *Explaining Institutional Change: Ambiguity, Agency, and Power*. Cambridge: Cambridge University Press.

Martin, I., A. Mehrotra, and M. Prasad (eds.) (2009), *The New Fiscal Sociology: Taxation in Comparative and Historical Perspective*. New York: Cambridge University Press.

Migdal, J. (1988), *Strong Societies and Weak States: State–Society Relations and State Capabilities in the Third World*. Princeton, NJ: Princeton University Press.

Migdal, J. (2001), *State in Society: Studying how States and Societies Transform and Constitute One Another*. New York: Cambridge University Press.

North, D. (1990), *Institutions, Institutional Change and Economic Performance*. Cambridge: Cambridge University Press.

Pierson, P. (2004), *Politics in Time: History, Institutions, and Social Analysis*. Princeton, NJ: Princeton University Press.

Putnam, R. D., R. Leonardi, and R. Nanetti (1993), *Making Democracy Work: Civic Traditions in Modern Italy*. Princeton, NJ: Princeton University Press.

Rothstein, B. (2011), *The Quality of Government: Corruption, Social Trust, and Inequality in International Perspective*. Chicago, IL: University of Chicago Press.

Rothstein, B. and J. Teorell (2012), "Defining and Measuring Quality of Government." In S. Holmberg and B. Rothstein (eds.), *Good Government: The Relevance of Political Science*. Cheltenham: Edward Elgar, 13–39.

Sandmo, A. (2005), "The Theory of Tax Evasion: A Retrospective View." *National Tax Journal* 58: 643–63.

Shafer, B. (1991), "The American Way." In B. Shafer (ed.), *Is America Different? A New Look at American Exceptionalism*. Oxford: Clarendon Press.

Skocpol, T. (1979), *States and Social Revolutions: A Comparative Analysis of France, Russia and China*. Cambridge: Cambridge University Press.

Steinmo, S. (1993), *Taxation and Democracy: Swedish, British and American Approaches to Financing the Modern State*. New Haven, CT: Yale University Press.

Steinmo, S. (2003), "Bucking the Trend: Swedish Social Democracy in a Global Economy." *New Political Economy* 8(1): 31–48.

Steinmo, S. (2010), *The Evolution of Modern States: Sweden, Japan and the United States*. New York: Cambridge University Press.

Steinmo, S. (forthcoming), *Willing to Pay? Explaining Tax Evasion in Europe and America*. Oxford: Oxford University Press.

Steinmo, S., K. A. Thelen, and F. Longstreth (1992), *Structuring Politics: Historical Institutionalism in Comparative Analysis*. Cambridge and New York: Cambridge University Press.

Thelen, K. (2004), *How Institutions Evolve: The Political Economy of Skills in Germany, Britain, the United States and Japan.* New York: Cambridge University Press.

Tilly, C. (1975), *The Formation of National States in Western Europe.* Princeton, NJ: Princeton University Press.

Torgler, B., I. C. Demir, A. Macintyre, and M. Schaffner (2008), "Causes and Consequences of Tax Morale: An Empirical Investigation." *Economic Analysis and Policy* 38(2): 313–39.

Weiner, M. and S. P. Huntington (1987), *Understanding Political Development.* Boston, MA: Little, Brown.

Zhang, N., G. Andrighetto, S. Ottone, F. Ponzano, and S. Steinmo (2016), "Willing to Pay? Tax Compliance in Britain and Italy: An Experimental Analysis." *PLOS ONE* 11(2). http://journals.plos.org/plosone/article?id=10.1371/journal.pone.0150277.

Part II
Sweden

2

Getting to Sweden

The Origins of High Compliance in the Swedish Tax State

Marina Nistotskaya and Michelle D'Arcy

Introduction

Sweden is one of the strongest, most stable and high-compliance tax states in the world. As Steinmo (1993: 41) notes, "the hallmarks of the Swedish tax system have been its broad base, its stability, and its high revenue yield." Tax revenue as a percentage of GDP was at least 25 percent above the OECD average from 1965 to 2013, putting Sweden in the top five tax-yield countries for nearly the entire period (OECD 2014). Since the 1980s, collection losses (taxes levied but not paid) have been less than 1 percent of total tax receipts, standing at the level of between 0.3 and 0.5 percent for most of the period (STA 2013: 20). By comparison, in the UK a similar measure, known as the tax gap, was between 6 and 8 percent of total tax receipts in the period 2005–13 (HM Revenue & Customs 2014: 4; authors' calculations). Experimental data from the "Willing to Pay?" project show that the Swedes are the most compliant taxpayers in the sample of five countries reference to Steinmo et al "Willing to Pay?" is here. It should also feature in the reference list.

Why is this the case? How did Sweden become one of the most successful states in terms of tax yield and compliance levels? While most of the classic works on the Swedish tax state have emphasized the constitutional structure of the state that emerged in the twentieth century (Steinmo 1993) and social democratic politics in the twentieth century (Jansson, Chapter 3 in this volume), we look at earlier periods, tracing the roots of Swedish exceptionalism as far back as the sixteenth century.

Although regular taxation in Sweden dates back to the thirteenth century, for most of the medieval period Sweden was essentially a domain state, dependent on income from crown lands, rather than a tax state, supporting itself through taxes collected from subjects (Dovring 1951; Poulsen 1995; Retsö and Söderberg 2015). Between 1500 and 1750, Sweden transformed into a tax state with certain characteristics that would become hallmarks in later periods. The result of the transformation was that the state had both the "hard" capacity needed to collect taxes—such as detailed information on the resource base and ability to monitor the entire population—and "soft" capacity in the form of a meaningful fiscal contract between the state and its subjects that supported quasi-voluntary compliance.

We draw on the rich existing literature and add to it in a number of ways to make five key arguments as to how Sweden became Sweden and why it is such an exceptional case. First, we argue that the Swedish state adopted advanced methods for monitoring the availability, quality, and use of the main economic assets for tax collection purposes at a very early stage, leading to both the creation of institutional capacity and the development much earlier than in most other European states of a direct vertical fiscal contract between the king, the embodiment of the state in the early modern period, and his subjects. Second, we show how the development of both the capacity to raise taxes and the fiscal contract were assisted by the use of the newly reformed Church of Sweden, which both collected population information for the state and legitimized its actions. Third, we argue that the fiscal contract was particularly strong because the extensive, accurate data available to the state allowed for fairness in the distribution of the tax and conscription burdens, and the military successes of the Swedish state in the early period of state-building delivered benefits to the population: peace within its borders, freedom from foreign rule, and law and order. Furthermore, the military allotment system—an organizational innovation, stimulated by war, for extracting tax in kind from a peasant economy—created conditions that could foster a horizontal contract between subjects. Fourth, we emphasize that these developments were aided by Sweden's relatively unique social structure. Having a large free peasantry and a small weak nobility led the state into a direct fiscal contract with the broad bulk of the peasantry rather than, as happened elsewhere, through the land- and capital-owning nobility. Fifth, we show how the structure of the Swedish economy, particularly the late onset of industrialization, forced the state to find innovative administrative technologies, producing a tax structure and administration that could easily adapt to the collection of modern taxes. Taken together, these factors explain how Sweden, over the course of 400 years, cultivated its fiscal capacity and strengthened the fiscal contract between ordinary taxpayers and the state. Its contemporary exceptionalism was set in motion centuries ago.

Three overarching themes emerge from our analysis. The first is the importance of the early modern period as a critical juncture in the history of European states in general and Sweden in particular. Although a rich general literature has addressed this (Ertman 1997; Glete 2002; Tilly 1992), not all recognize this period as the starting point of Sweden's transition to modernity, instead arguing that the nineteenth century was the critical period of transformation (Rothstein and Teorell 2015; Teorell and Rothstein 2015). The second is the contrast between Sweden and other European countries during this period. Sweden was markedly superior in international comparison in terms of the organization of the state in relation to taxation, particularly the degree to which the information-gathering activities of the state penetrated society. Finally, the continuity between the aspects of the contemporary tax state that make it effective and the tax state that emerged in the early modern period suggests that the virtuous circle persisted over time. For example, there is remarkable continuity in key areas such as the amount of information the state collects on the population. These insights together suggest that to understand divergent performances in tax compliance today we need to take a considerably longer-term historical perspective.

Monitoring Capacity

Monitoring capacity is a critical but often overlooked aspect of fiscal capacity. Taxation has been increasingly understood as a collective action problem (CAP) whereby rational individuals have strong incentives to free-ride because they cannot be excluded from the benefits of the collective goods that taxes provide (Levi 1988). In a small group it is more straightforward to solve CAPs, as it is easier to monitor and enforce compliance (Ostrom 1990). Because of the high degree of visibility in a small group, everyone can directly observe individual contributions by other members and sanction those not cooperating. In large groups, such as states, CAPs can only be solved by an external agent with the capacity to monitor individual contributions, find the free-riders, and punish them (Olson 1965). A state with these capacities reduces the likelihood that individuals will choose a free-riding strategy both because they believe there is a high likelihood they themselves will be caught if they evade, and because they believe this power will ensure others also comply. Monitoring capacity, in particular the gathering of information needed to assess individual behavior in collective endeavors, is thus critical to curb fiscal free-riding (D'Arcy and Nistotskaya 2017).

Swedish kings were among the first European rulers to systematically gather information on the main productive assets for taxation purposes. Sweden's early modern experience of gathering data on land and its users was a critical component in making it one of the most effective tax states from a historical perspective. It has also left a legacy of exhaustive information-gathering that persists into the contemporary period.

Although attempts to draw a comprehensive list of taxpayers were made by the Crown as early as 1413 (Dovring 1951: 417), the crucial steps in developing monitoring capacity in Sweden were undertaken by Gustav Vasa (1523–1560). The newly elected monarch, faced with competition for power from the Catholic Church and the nobility, had no choice, but "to start building a new organization for mobilizing economic resources and political support" (Hallenberg, Holm, and Johansson 2008: 251; see also Ertman 1997: 311–14; Glete 2002; Hallenberg 2012; Roberts 1958: 77; Tilly 1992: 25, 135). First, Gustav Vasa appointed trusted local representatives, who held office in return for direct payment rather than as a personal fief. Research suggests that during the reign of Gustav Vasa the number of these salaried royal officials increased fourfold, reaching a total of about 200 by 1560 (Glete 2002: 189; Hallenberg 2012: 563). Second, with a view to extracting resources, these royal bailiffs started collecting and recording information about the local peasant economy. Specifically, around the 1530s, information about individual land parcels began to be gathered and methodically recorded in special registers— *jordeböcker* (Dovring 1951; Hallenberg 2012: 563–5; Lindkvist 1987: 61–2; Österberg 1977). Royal bailiffs also maintained lists of taxpayers and men eligible for conscription, and account books where the principles of tax assessments, arrears, and other issues related to the tax collection were recorded. Third, the Crown changed the basic principle of tax assessment: from collective appropriations from groups of people with the tax amounts or quantities in kind being determined somewhat arbitrarily to individual assessments, based on surveys of individual land parcels and valuations of land (Dovring 1951: 13–139; Lindkvist 1987).

These developments had several important consequences that arguably set the virtuous circle of the Swedish political economy in motion. First of all, the Swedish state developed a competence to monitor the peasant economy down to the level of "every single farm" (Lindkvist 1987: 62), which, as we argued earlier, is a key condition for curbing fiscal free-riding. Secondly, the principle of individual assessments made an individual peasant a "direct subject of the king, personally responsible for sustaining the crown by his yearly contributions" (Hallenberg 2012: 564). Furthermore, the introduction of the institution of royal bailiffs, who dealt with tax assessment and collection on a day-to-day basis, "opened up direct communication lines between the King and his subjects" (Hallenberg, Holm, and Johansson 2008: 254). Thus, the foundations of both effective monitoring and a vertical fiscal contract between the king and his subjects were laid down during the reign of Gustav Vasa. This is in stark contrast to England, for example, where even in the implementation of personal income tax in the nineteenth century, the state explicitly aimed to "minimize the direct contact between the central bureaucracy and the individual citizens" to secure consent (see Daunton, Chapter 6 in this volume; Kiser and Kane 2001). Third, reliable information about key economic assets and other local conditions made it possible for the state to tax "according to the economic capacities of the individual households" (Lindkvist 1987: 62) and to distribute the tax and conscriptions burdens between communities in a manner "that could be regarded as fair" (Glete 2002: 189), which is an important constituent of a robust fiscal contract (see "Fiscal Contract" below).

The monitoring capacity of the state was further strengthened in the seventeenth century. In 1628, Sweden launched a comprehensive program of surveying and mapping of individual land parcels of all settlements of the realm. The resultant cadastral maps (*geometriska jordeböcker*) were state-administered, methodically arranged records that identified individual land holdings in terms of their location, dimensions, and features, and were presented as drawings or sketches. One of the essential features of cadastral maps is that they securely link properties on a map to a register, containing information about the landowner or occupier (Kain and Baigent 1992: xviii). Cartographic cadasters are based on systematic observations, such as instrumental land measurement, providing accurate information on land resources. Furthermore, through cartographic representation of land *geometriska jordeböcker* standardized diverse local economic practices, making "the resource base visible and accessible to the central state" (Glete 2006: 7). For these reasons the cadastral map is considered an effective instrument of control of the governed (Buisseret 1992; Scott 1998).

Geometriska jordeböcker, which were produced by royal surveyors from a newly established government office (*Landmäteriet*), are "without contemporary European equals" because of their comprehensiveness in terms of both territorial coverage and the recorded information (Baigent 1990: 62). By the end of the seventeenth century most of the parishes in Sweden proper (except Skåne and Gotland), Finland (then part of the Swedish realm), and also in Sweden's Baltic (modern Estonia and Latvia) and German provinces had been mapped (Baigent 1990: 67; Kain and Baigent 1992: 57, 70–5). There are about 12,000 large-scaled (1: 5,000 to 1: 4,000) cadastral maps relating to the period, which include a great degree of detail, such as ownership/tenure, quality of land, field systems, types of crop, yields, and valuation (Figures 2.1 and 2.2). Taxes were assessed "almost annually" (Sköld 2004: 6), implying that the underlying observational data was also regularly updated (Baigent 1990, 63). The Swedish cartographic cadaster was an innovation that greatly enhanced the state's capacity to monitor the availability, quality, and use of the main economic asset of the time—land—and to calculate taxes based on the land's

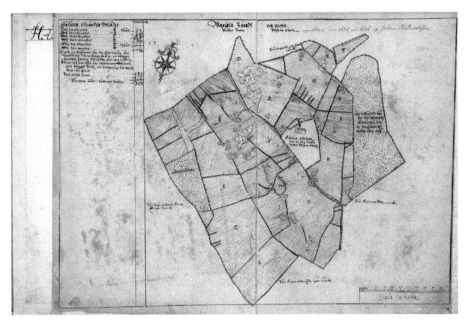

Figure 2.1. Cadastral map (*geometrisk jordebok*) of a Royal Domain in Danmarks Parish, Uppsala County, 1635
Source: The Swedish National Land Survey (Lantmäteriet), Gävle, Sweden.

size and productivity and to extract taxes from the de facto users (not *de jure* owners). In comparison, in other countries under consideration in this volume, analogous measures were initiated considerably later: in the USA the Federal Land Survey began in 1785 and its primary purpose was not fiscal; the Ordnance Survey Act of 1841 laid the foundation for cadastral surveying in England with its application to land valuation and inland revenue purposes beginning in the early twentieth century; and national cadasters in Italy and Romania commenced in 1897 and 1997 respectively.

The cadastral records were augmented by extensive population statistics collected by the state directly or with the help of the Church (see the following section, "The Role of the Reformed Church"). From around the second half of the sixteenth century the Church of Sweden kept parish catechetical registers (*husförshörslängder*), containing a wealth of information related to the Church's efforts to enforce adherence to Lutheran doctrine (for instance levels of the parishioners' catechetical knowledge and attendance), but also names of residents, relationships within the household, information on births, migration in and out of the parish, and marriages and deaths (Gille 1949;

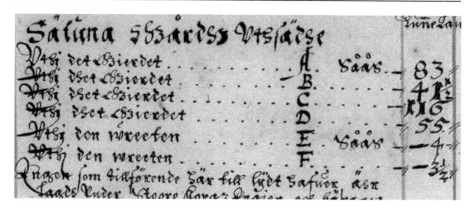

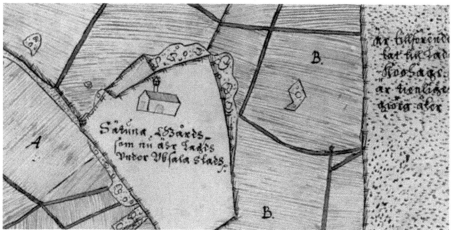

Figure 2.2. Enlarged elements of the same cadastral map
Source: The Swedish National Land Survey (Lantmäteriet), Gävle, Sweden.

Sköld 2004; Willigan and Lynch 1982; Wisselgren et al. 2014). In the middle of the eighteenth century, the Swedish state established *Tabellverket*—the world's oldest continuous national population statistics. The information for *Tabellverket* was drawn from parish registers. At the government's request, clergy had to collect information on a set of predefined items, including, for example, occupation and social status, and compile the data as summary statistics every three to five years (Gille 1949; Oden 1972; Sköld 2004; Willigan and Lynch 1982). These summary statistics served as the basis for drawing up the censuses, a method that distinguished Sweden from most

Western countries that practiced field survey-based censuses (Axelsson and Wisselgren 2016: 63). Another distinctive feature of the Swedish population statistics is that since information was collected in a number of different lists and registers that were ultimately centralized, it allowed the state to cross-check the information (Oden 1972: 269).

Cumulatively these innovations meant that in the early modern period the Swedish state acquired formidable monitoring capacity. Cadastral records and population registers made both the economic resources and economic activities of the population "visible and accessible to the central state" (Glete 2006: 7) so that it could collect taxes, both in cash and in kind, to the extent needed to support one of the largest standing armies in Europe. As Tilly (1992: 79) notes, between 1600 and 1700 the number of troops under arms in Sweden increased from 1.5 percent to 7.1 percent of the population, more than in England, France, Spain, or Russia.

Sweden's experience contrasts with that of other European states, most of which did not develop strong monitoring capacity. Most European states "had neither the administrative tools nor the information" to penetrate to the level of individual households (Scott 1998: 38). For example, although it had one of the earliest narrative cadasters in the Domesday Book, the British state never utilized it to the same extent as Sweden did. Neither did it produce a genuine cartographic cadaster, instead appropriating Ordnance Survey maps for the purpose (Kain and Baigent 1992: 260). In England the first national census was not conducted until 1801 and civil registration of vital events began in 1837. Between 1801 and 1840 censuses were "merely head-counts," and although names and addresses were included after 1841, there is little evidence that the state used this information for monitoring purposes (Higgs 2001: 179).[1]

Just as the early modern Swedish tax state was remarkable in terms of the amount of information it collected compared to its European counterparts, so too the contemporary Swedish state can be seen to hold more detailed information, in a more integrated way than many other governments. Indeed, some scholars see this early Swedish history of information-gathering as a critical predecessor to the *personnummer*—a unique identifier, introduced in 1946, used in all interactions between the state and citizens (Riches 2005: 357). *Personnummer* is central to the effective functioning of the Swedish tax state from tax collection to welfare provision as it is a crucial piece of information, present in all data on individuals officially collected, that connects these numerous datasets together, allowing for cross-referencing.

Thus, in the early modern period Sweden had established itself as exceptional in terms of its monitoring capacity. This capacity both set it apart from other European states and has remained a key element of the fiscal strength of the Swedish state.

Role of the Reformed Church

A second rather unique characteristic of the Swedish fiscal state in the early modern period was the extent to which and success with which the state used the clergy to provide copious and detailed information on the state's subjects and to legitimize state activities.

The seizure of ecclesiastic lands in 1527 and subsequent displacement of the Roman Catholic Church, which with its own laws and taxes was offering "an alternative framework of political and military power" (Glete 2002: 183), eliminated a serious rival and a source of continuous resistance to the Vasas' attempts to consolidate and expand state power. Furthermore, the newly established Church of Sweden, whose creed and organization were officially supported by the state until the year 2000, in effect became a part of the state's administrative apparatus.

By the mid-sixteenth century when Gustav Vasa's bailiffs undertook the task of assessing resources and levying and collecting taxes, local clergymen were assisting in their enumeration efforts by cross-checking the accuracy of the information provided by peasants and the bailiffs' own observations (Oden 1972: 267; Roberts 1953: 414). At about the same time, although the precise date has been difficult to establish (Gille 1949: 4; Sköld 2004: 8), the Church began collecting extensive information on the members of their parishes in parish catechetical registers (*husförhörslängder*). Although scholars noted the connection between the tax and church registers due to the timing of their commencement, but also with regard to their monitoring intentions (Nilsson 1982), it is not entirely evident that the Swedish state stood behind either the initiation of the parish registers or making them compulsory in 1686 in all 2,500 parishes (Gille 1949: 5; Oden 1972: 269; Sköld 2004: 8). What is clear, however, is that when *Tabellverket* were put into practice in 1749, it made controlling the population through list-taking as one of the legal duties of Swedish clergymen. Until very late in the twentieth century, the vicar of each parish served as the chief of the local civic registration office and the census officer (Nilsson 1979: 1). It was only in 1991 that the population registration task was fully transferred from the Church to the state bureaucracy.

Since nearly all inhabitants belonged to the Church of Sweden, the use of the clergy to collect population data meant that these records were comprehensive. They also contained a wealth of continuous and high-quality data (Gille 1949; Wisselgren et al. 2014) on demography and social welfare that became part and parcel of Sweden's formidable fiscal monitoring capacity. Parish records were often kept earlier in other European states (Sköld 2004: 8), yet they were not incorporated into state administration to the same degree as in Sweden.

Although it has frequently been noted in the literature that over the course of the early modern period the Swedish clergy were often caught in "an awkward position between their parishioners, who hoped to escape the worst of taxation, and the government and its representatives, whom they were expected to serve loyally" (Sköld 2004: 7; see also Lext 1968; Roberts 1953: 415), the clergy's direct involvement in tax and military registration lasted at least until the second half of the seventeenth century, when the Church was "eventually relieved" of this duty (Sköld 2004: 16). The clergymen remained involved in keeping records of harvests and livestock (*boskapslängder*), from which a tithe (*tiondelängder*) was levied (Figure 2.3²), and they also attended tax collection meetings at least until the beginning of the eighteenth century (Sköld 2004: 7). The Scandinavian Lutheran clergy is seen to be "more committed to state administration than was the case in most European countries" (Bregnsbo and Ihalainen 2011: 108).

The Swedish kings successfully employed the ecclesiastical organization and the social power of the Church to legitimize their authority (Forssberg 2014; Hallenberg, Holm, and Johansson 2008; Nordin 2011; Roberts 1953: 413–14).

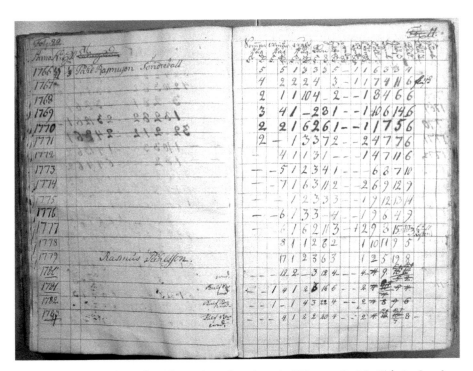

Figure 2.3. A page from the tithe register for a farm in Hjärnarp Parish, Skånia, Sweden, 1766–83

Source: SEDD: the Scanian Economic Demographic Database (Lund University).

The clergy disseminated, often under direct instruction from state officials, information and propaganda about wars and royal policy. Attendance at Sunday service was mandatory and royal proclamations were made from the pulpit. This meant that the king's edicts and letters were read out on the same day, in a uniform message by clergymen who had moral standing in their communities (Nordin 2011). The clergy were pressed to add the weight of their moral authority to these decrees, and there are records of speeches by priests to their congregations exhorting their parishioners to "faithfulness to our all-gracious king" (Forssberg 2014: 178–9). In an era of illiteracy before mass communications, this was a very effective tool for the state to legitimize its actions (Roberts 1953: 413–14). Although the clergy at times resisted the state's attempts to harness them for its own purposes, in general the message they relayed from their pulpits was "a political ideology of deference and unconditional loyalty to the ruler" (Munck 2011: xx).

Fiscal Contract

The Swedish case illustrates the well-established link between war and taxation (Downing 1992; Ertman 1997; Tilly 1992). The development of information-gathering and other administrative capacities in Sweden in the early modern period was driven by the needs of war (Glete 2002). However, in addition to stimulating the expansion of the state's fiscal capacities, described earlier, war was important to the development of the fiscal state in another way: out of the interaction between the state and society over taxation, the conditions were created for a vertical fiscal contract—between subjects and state—and also for a horizontal contract between subjects. The fiscal contract, understood as an exchange of goods in return for taxes, has been seen as the foundation for quasi-voluntary tax compliance (D'Arcy 2011; Levi 1988; Moore 1978; Spicer and Lundstedt 1976). When people get the promised goods they are more likely to honor their tax obligations without the ruler having to resort to coercion.[3] This literature has also shown that fair exchange—the perception that the tax burden is shared between the individual and other taxpayers in a fair manner—matters for compliance (Bordignon 1993; Spicer and Becker 1980). From this viewpoint, unfair distribution of the tax burden and insufficient levels of public goods' provision are seen to be the main factors that might undermine consent to pay.

When conceived of in these terms it is clear that at an early stage a virtuous circle emerged in the fiscal contract between the Swedish crown and its subjects. In exchange for taxes, the state provided a bundle of public goods that were of the highest priority in the early modern context (Forssberg 2014; Glete 2002: 194–5; Neveux and Österberg 1997): security, freedom from foreign rule, and internal law and order. Indeed, there is evidence that the rise of the Swedish tax state was accompanied by the rhetoric of fiscal contract (Forssberg 2014; Glete 2002; Hallenberg, Holm, and Johansson 2008). Thus, in the very first year of his reign, Gustav Vasa told the Estates gathered in Strängäs that he hired mercenaries "so that the native peasantry may sit at home, tend their fields and meadows, feed their wives and children, and no longer go out to get themselves killed" (Hallenberg, Holm, and Johansson 2003: 27). As "warfare marked everyday life both mentally—with widespread fears . . .—and economically" (Forssberg 2014: 171), it is plausible to argue that the subjects were rather receptive to the idea of paying taxes in exchange for the military protection of their homes and families (Glete 2002: 194–5). Sweden's multiple military successes in the second half of the sixteenth and seventeenth centuries presented the Crown with a powerful argument that it had fulfilled its promise to provide security. That this translated into compliance is suggested by a remarkably low number of tax revolts in Sweden after the Great Dacke Rising of 1542–3 (Burg 2004; Glete 2002: 194; Österberg 1990).

Second, the information the state had gathered made it possible to distribute the tax burden in a non-arbitrary way. On the one hand, information about local conditions enabled the state to tax according to the capacities of individual households (Lindkvist 1987: 62). In international comparison, "this was distinctively 'modern'. Similar systems in other countries have usually been created only in the nineteenth century" (Glete 2002: 189). For example, in England before the 1800s "taxes never adequately tapped subject wealth" (Kiser and Kane 2001: 200). On the other hand, tax registers and cadastral records gave subjects the means to question tax assessments and demand more equitable distribution of the burden (Forssberg 2014; Glete 2002; Hallenberg, Holm, and Johansson 2008; Lindkvist 1987; Österberg 1990). As empirical evidence suggests, peasants routinely bargained with central and local agents of the state over taxes and "quite often had their way" (Hallenberg, Holm, and Johansson 2008: 256), which arguably encouraged compliance.

A key institution in terms of the organizational infrastructure through which this direct vertical fiscal contract could evolve was the innovative system of *indelningsverket*—an allotment system that enabled the Crown to effectively extract resources in kind from an economy with comparatively low levels of monetization (Carruthers 1996: 94–5). One of the central challenges for all early modern rulers was to extract resources to support an army. In earlier periods the Swedish army had been supported through a rotating conscription system (*utskrivning*) based on lists compiled by the local clergy and officials and supported by contributions from non-selected enlisted men (Riches 2005: 356). This system evolved in the seventeenth century with soldiers in certain parts of the country being billeted on farms whose owners or tenants supported them directly. In the 1680s under Karl XI the system was implemented countrywide. Every province concluded agreements with the Crown as to how many regiments it would support. Within each province several farms were grouped into "files" responsible for one person, who volunteered to become a soldier (Åberg 1973: 269; Riches 2005). The extent to which this system was successful is evidenced by the fact that over the early modern period Sweden had one of the largest standing armies in Europe (Glete 2002; Tilly 1992: 79).

In addition to being a constitutive part of a vertical fiscal contract, *indelningsverket* arguably created the conditions for the emergence of a robust *horizontal* fiscal contract. The literature has emphasized that when people believe that others are paying their taxes they are more likely to do so themselves (Bordignon 1993; D'Arcy 2011; Spicer and Lundstedt 1976). For almost 300 years (until *indelningsverket* was phased out at the beginning of the twentieth century) most of the Swedish population was involved in extensive horizontal monitoring of fellow taxpayers. Through *indelningsverket* the collective action problem associated with taxation was transformed into multiple collective action problems, operating at a scale where this problem could be solved more efficiently by means of peer-to-peer monitoring. Each "file" had incentives and opportunities to ensure each individual household was contributing.

Sweden was not exceptional in terms of what stimulated the development of fiscal capacity, but was in terms of the forms, extent, and consequences of these processes. Cadasters, population registers, *indelningsverket*, and the tax bureaucracy were part of the new complex organization of the Swedish state, geared to effective resource extraction. The ability to curb individual incentives to free-ride was one of the direct consequences of Swedish monitoring institutions. Another was what in modern parlance can be called a system of evidence-based tax assessment and redress procedure, which laid the foundations for a robust fiscal contract between the state and taxpayers. Tax compliance was furthered by the state's ability to fulfill its "contractual obligations": the state delivered security both in practice and in the form of official rhetoric, promulgated by subordinated clergy. Furthermore, the introduction of yet another organization innovation—*indelningsverket*—was arguably conducive to the emergence of a strong horizontal fiscal contract between subjects themselves.

It is important to emphasize that Sweden's development as a fiscal state in response to the constant threat of war was not inevitable, linear, or immune from reversals and missteps. In common with other European states at the time, Sweden learned by doing, and by making mistakes, sometimes in the same moment as they were making advances in other areas (Hoffman 2015). The infamous *Vasa* ship, built with the wrong proportions, sank just 1,000 meters into her maiden voyage in 1628, the same year that cadastral mapping was initiated. The development of the fiscal state was subject to experimentation and evolution. For example, the state switched the mode of taxation entirely in 1621 to tax farming, only to abandon this due to resistance, as discussed further in the next section, several decades later (Hallenberg 2012: 565–8). The institution of *indelningsverket* took a century to evolve, and was the outcome of bargaining between the state and society rather than a state-engineered project imposed from the top down. Sweden's exceptional fiscal state arose in very particular social conditions, as outlined in the next section.

Unique Social Structure

The fiscal contract that emerged between the Crown and taxpayers in Sweden in conjunction with the emergence of a new complex organization of the state was direct and deep in part because Sweden had a unique social structure. In contrast to most European states in the early modern period, Sweden had a free peasantry and a small, weak nobility (Glete 2002: 174–5, 182; Lindkvist 1987; Myrdal 2011; Neveux and Österberg 1997). In the sixteenth and seventeenth centuries the Swedish hereditary aristocracy numbered about 500 adults (Liliequist 2015: 229; Retsö and Söderberg 2015: 11), and in the 1520s, before Gustav Vasa's initiatives, the nobility owned 25 percent of the land, compared to the 45 percent that belonged to freehold peasants (Myrdal 2011: 91). The Swedish nobility's low level of economic strength is mainly explained by the fact that compared to other European states there was no inheritable possession of the land (Lindkvist 1987: 61). The Crown could withdraw the right to land relatively easily, as demonstrated by the massive alienation of noble lands to the state at the end of the seventeenth century (*reduktion*). Economic weakness translated into low political power for the aristocracy, as evidenced by, for example, the absence of manorial courts in Sweden, in contrast with profound seigneurialism elsewhere in Europe (Glete 2002; Neveux and Österberg 1997; Ogborn 1998). Their political power was further weakened by the fact that, unlike in England, for example, the parliament was not a vehicle for the exclusive defense of aristocratic interests, as the freehold peasantry was also represented in the national Diet as the fourth estate (Glete 2002). Without security of tenure and a monopoly in parliament, the strength of noble resistance was weaker than in the rest of Europe.

This is not to say that the nobility did not try to resist state-building activities, nor that its relative weakness was uniform across the early modern period. In 1529, only a year after Gustav Vasa was crowned King of Sweden, the lords and the clergymen in Västergötland rose against him (under Ture Jönsson). In 1567 Gustav Vasa's son Erik XIV had to resort to murder as a preventive move against the influential aristocratic Sture family (Roberts 1968). His successor John III faced a "well organized aristocratic opposition... who demanded a larger say in the ruling of the dynastic state" (Hallenberg, Holm, and Johansson 2008: 254). Although the early Vasa kings did manage to consolidate the state's power, the end of the sixteenth to the first half of the seventeenth century was a period when the nobility controlled about two-thirds of income from the land (Myrdal 2011: 115) and had a major say in political affairs (Glete 2002; Hallenberg, Holm, and Johansson 2008). However, the return to the Crown of the land that had been granted to the nobility (*reduktion*) in 1655 and 1680 illustrates that aristocratic power was not enduring, in part because it lacked a strong institutional basis. When after *reduktion* members of the nobility became a central part of the state's apparatus, they joined the state's organization and benefited from it from within, rather than resisting it from outside. By that point they did not have an independent source of power outside the state in the way that the nobility in other countries did.

This social structure had a number of direct implications for how the Swedish tax state evolved. In other parts of Europe the strength of the nobility was a major constraint on the state's expansion in areas such as monitoring capacity. For example, due to the high strength of the resistance of the nobility, the English state never managed to introduce a genuine cartographic cadaster (Kain and Baigent 1992: 343). In France, it was only in the Napoleonic period that state-administered cadastral mapping was expanded to cover the entire country. In Sweden's Baltic territories the strength of the local nobility led to less effective mapping than in the metropole (Kain and Baigent 1992: 72).

Without a strong nobility able to effectively resist, the Swedish state was able to make numerous detailed registers of economic resources and their users (discussed in the first section, "Monitoring Capacity") and also to enter into a direct fiscal contract with the peasantry. Peasants were in contact with state officials and negotiated this relationship at both local level and in the national Diet (Hallenberg 2012). Sweden's remarkable record of a very low number of tax revolts suggests that regular interaction between crown officials, rather than leading to animosity and resistance, developed tolerable administration and a situation where the state was seen as a suitable medium for problem solving. Indeed, "the last major rebellion, in Småland 1542–3, was... directed at the new and ever stronger state. After this, peasant protest in Sweden increasingly went through more peaceful channels" (Myrdal 2011: 99). This is further demonstrated by the fact that the failure of the tax farming experiment from 1621 to 1635 was partly due to resistance from peasants, who preferred taxes to be collected by royal bailiffs rather than by private tax farmers

(Hallenberg 2012: 556–7). Thus the Crown was exceptionally successful in integrating the peasantry as the organization of the state evolved.

The strength of the relationship between the state and the peasantry also derived from the fact that they constituted an important ally for the Crown against the nobility at certain moments. Thus, the support of the peasants was key in Charles XI's successful creation of absolute rule after 1680. In return he committed not to conscript peasants as soldiers. Instead, they contributed through *indelningsverket*. Although this could constitute a heavy economic burden, "the fact that future soldiers would be volunteers was regarded as an important gain for peasant society" (Glete 2002: 195). At this and at other moments, the peasantry could exercise more agency and extract some degree of political demands in a way that their contemporaries in other European states often could not. This was enabled by both the new organization of the Swedish state and the unique structure of its society.

A direct relationship between the peasantry and the state that developed in early modern Sweden contrasted with most other parts of Europe where resources were extracted from the peasantry by the local nobility and clergy, but not directly by state officials, meaning that the nobility mediated the relationship between ordinary people and the state. As Tilly observed, Sweden's exceptional social structure "left its impact on the very organization of the state" (1992: 27) and meant that it was perhaps the only European country that had instituted "direct rule from top to bottom" before the nineteenth century (1992: 25). The fiscal contract in Sweden was arguably deeper and stronger than in other states because the social structure facilitated the state's direct engagement with the majority of the population. In what became a self-reinforcing cycle, the weakness of the nobility enabled the Swedish monarchs to effectively organize resource extraction in the ways discussed, leading to less reliance on the nobility's local organization and further weakening their position vis-à-vis the Crown.

Late Industrial Development and the Structure of Taxation

In the 1870s, 72 percent of the population was still employed in agriculture in Sweden: "Industrialization in Sweden began in earnest during the last third of the nineteenth century, a hundred years later than in England and roughly a generation later than in Germany" (Berman 1998: 42). The late onset of industrialization is one of the explanations for the relatively late adoption of local income tax in 1862 and state income (and wealth) tax in 1903 (Du Rietz, Johansson, and Stenkula 2015: 41–4), and the fact that the Swedish tax to GDP ratio was one of the lowest in the world at the beginning of the twentieth century (Rodriguez 1981). However, while the late onset of industrialization delayed the introduction of modern forms of taxation it also stimulated the state to perfect the art of extracting tax in kind from an agriculturally based economy. The set of administrative innovations, discussed earlier, embedded state power into localities, and brought the state into a relationship with the peasantry in a way that did not happen in other countries. It also led to a tax structure that set Sweden apart from its European counterparts. Although later than most states in experiencing industrialization and introducing modern taxes, the cumulative effect of centuries of experience taxing the broad base of the population enabled the state to make this transition more rapidly and comprehensively than other states who lacked this experience.

Until the latter half of the nineteenth century, the main source of tax revenue in Sweden came from a variety of direct taxes that had been in place in some cases for centuries (Schön 2010: 162; Stenkula 2015: 305). These non-modern direct taxes included: the *grundskatter* ("basic tax")— based on land, the oldest existing tax at the time; the *bevillning*, originally an extraordinary surtax that was assessed and raised heterogeneously across the provinces and only in 1862 had become based on appropriations of either land or income; and the *mantalspenning*, a poll tax "introduced in 1625 during a period of intense warfare, and it was not abolished until 1938" (Stenkula 2015: 306). The *indelningsverket* was also still operating, only being abolished in 1904, just after the introduction of compulsory military service. Thus, until the mid-nineteenth century Sweden was collecting most of its revenue from the same taxes that had been established for centuries, and which were forms of direct tax that fell mostly on the broad bulk of the population.

This reliance on pre-modern direct taxes became increasingly unsustainable during the nineteenth century, especially after industrialization eventually arrived in Sweden. Between 1800 and 1860 a large deficit emerged, with the existing taxes diminishing in yield but political resistance to tax reforms coming from landowning peasants (Neal 2010: 295). During the latter half of the nineteenth century the introduction of modern taxes was stalled due to political considerations rather than administrative incapacity, resulting in indirect taxes for the first time becoming the greater proportion of revenue (Stenkula 2014: 16). It was only in 1903, after political reform of parliament and decades of official investigations and political debate that a new system of progressive taxation of aggregated net income based on an annual personal declaration of income was introduced. Less than ten years later direct taxes were again the greatest proportion of revenue (Stenkula 2014: 16).

The speed with which the Swedish state was able to successfully transition from early modern to modern forms of direct taxes reflects the hard and soft capacity it had acquired for direct tax collection from a broad base of the population over the preceding centuries, and is in marked contrast to the experience of other European states. Other states whose predominant tax structure had been reliant on indirect taxes took longer to build up the capacity to collect direct taxes. For example, the English state was one of the first to start modernizing taxation early in the nineteenth century, introducing income tax temporarily for the first time in 1799 and permanently in 1842. However, by the end of the nineteenth century indirect taxes were still the greatest proportion of revenue (Daunton 2010: 30). By 1925 the figure for the number of tax units registered with the British tax authorities (Inland Revenue) as a percentage of the economically active population was 23 percent, while the figure for Sweden was 80 percent (Flora and Heidenheimer 1981: 193). In Britain, historically very dependent on indirect taxes, especially customs and excise, the modes of collecting direct taxes, especially the land tax, had relied on local commissioners, rather than central bureaucrats (Daunton 2007 and Chapter 6 in this volume). In England there was not the same level of direct state penetration of the locality, and it took a number of decades for this to develop. In Sweden, where the state had been collecting taxes directly from the peasants for centuries, this capacity was already in place.

In the twentieth century Sweden adapted and updated its fiscal capacity to correspond to the new structure of the economy, becoming one of the most effective modern tax states. It modernized its existing strength in monitoring capacity, deploying some new technologies and innovations such as unique identifiers (*personnummer*). There was also extensive fiscal policy experimentation based on the ideas of social and economic engineering, public sector expansion and distributional ambitions, and reform of the tax authority to instill an ethos of facilitating tax returns (Jansson, Chapter 3 in this volume; Stenkula 2014). The corporatist model of government served to deepen the vertical fiscal contract observable in previous periods through the creation of the welfare state.

Conclusion

Sweden became a strong tax state not because it had greater economic resources relative to other states—it did not—but by finding, through a process of experimentation and adaptation, innovative means of resource extraction from society. Cadasters, population registers, the institution of salaried royal bailiffs and *indelningsverket* formed the foundations of Sweden's formidable monitoring capacity that has contained fiscal free-riding. Several consequences of the new complex organization of the state, such as non-arbitrary ways of tax assessment and direct interaction between state agents and the peasantry, also contributed to the development of a strong tax state, by setting in motion a robust fiscal contract between taxpayers and the state. The emerging virtuous circle was facilitated by the absence of strong resistance from the Church and nobility, resulting from both the structure of the Swedish economy and society, but also from proactive policies of the Crown either to eliminate or to co-opt opposition.

The developments of the twentieth century reinforced rather than created the underlying strengths of the Swedish fiscal state. The improvements in monitoring capacity were the latest in a long history of innovation to provide the state with the information it needed to solve the collective action problem of taxation. The welfare state that was built to provide services in return for high taxes continued the tradition of a robust vertical fiscal contract between state and subjects, now that they had become citizens. The egalitarian emphasis in social democratic politics resonated with the long history of a strong peasantry who negotiated their relationship with the state directly.

The modern Swedish tax state has proven itself to be as exceptional as the early modern tax state, and in the same ways. The modern tax state has maintained high fiscal monitoring capacity and strong vertical and horizontal fiscal contracts. While it is no longer driven primarily by war, the modern tax state has benefited from and continued the legacy of its early fiscal exceptionalism. "Getting to Sweden" was a four-hundred-year process.

Notes

1. A key moment of tax state formation in Britain was the late seventeenth-century development of the administration of excise taxation—taxes on the producers of commodities, especially beer—which would generate the revenue necessary to transform Britain into an imperial power in the eighteenth century (Ogborn 1998).
2. Figure 2.3 depicts a page from the tithe register from Hjärnarp parish in Skåne, southern Sweden, for the years 1766–83. It contains information on the farm (name and size) and the farmer (Påhl Rasmusson, replaced by his son Rasmus Påhlsson in 1779), the harvest (in sheaves for summer-rye, winter-rye, spring-rye, barley, oats, wheat, buckwheat, and beans). The columns to the very right contain information on the number of foals, calves, lambs, and geese born cumulatively.
3. The existence of a fiscal bargain at the heart of the relationship between citizens and rulers has been demonstrated in contemporary settings using a variety of methods: cross-country regression analysis (Ross 2004), citizen surveys (Fjeldstad 2004), and experimental methods (Cummings et al. 2009).

References

Åberg, Alf (1973), "The Swedish Army, from Lützen to Narva." In Michael Roberts (ed.), *Sweden's Age of Greatness, 1632–1718*. London: Macmillan, 265–87.

Axelsson, Per and Maria J. Wisselgren (2016), "Sweden in 1930 and the 1930 Census." *The History of the Family* 21(1): 61–86.

Baigent, Elizabeth (1990), "Swedish Cadastral Mapping 1628–1700: A Neglected Legacy." *The Geographical Journal* 156(1): 62–9.

Berman, Sheri (1998), *The Social Democratic Moment: Ideas and Politics in the Making of Interwar Europe*. Cambridge, MA: Harvard University Press.

Bordignon, Massimo (1993), "A Fairness Approach to Income Tax Evasion." *Journal of Public Economics* 52(3): 345–62.

Bregnsbo, Michael and Pasi Ihalainen (2011), "Gradual Reconsiderations of Lutheran Conceptions of Politics." In Pasi Ihalainen, Michael Bregnsbo, Karin Sennefelt, and Patrik Winton (eds.), *Scandinavia in the Age of Revolution: Nordic Political Cultures, 1740–1820*. Farnham: Ashgate, 107–20.

Buisseret, David (ed.) (1992), *Monarchs, Ministers and Maps: the Emergence of Cartography as a Tool of Government in Early Modern Europe*. Chicago, IL: Chicago University Press.

Burg, David F. (2004), *A World History of Tax Rebellions: An Encyclopedia of Tax Rebels, Revolts, and Riots from Antiquity to the Present*. London: Routledge.

Carruthers, Bruce G. (1996), *City of Capital: Politics and Markets in the English Financial Revolution*. Princeton, NJ: Princeton University Press.

Cummings, Ronald G., Jorde Martinez-Vazquez, Michael McKee, and Benno Torgler (2009), "Tax Morale Affects Tax Compliance: Evidence from Surveys and an Artefactual Field Experiment." *Journal of Economic Behaviour and Organization* 70: 447–57.

D'Arcy, Michelle (2011), "Why Do Citizens Assent to Pay Tax? Legitimacy, Taxation and the African State." Afrobarometer Working Paper No. 126.

D'Arcy, Michelle and Marina Nistotskaya (2017), "State First, then Democracy: Using Cadastral Records to Explain Governmental Performance in Public Goods Provision." *Governance* 30(2): 193–209.

Daunton, Martin (2007), *Trusting Leviathan: The Politics of Taxation in Britain, 1799–1914*. Cambridge: Cambridge University Press.

Daunton, Martin (2010), "Creating Legitimacy: Administering Taxation in Britain, 1815–1914." In Jose Luis Cardoso and Pedro Lains (eds.), *Paying for the Liberal State: The Rise of Public Finances in Nineteenth Century Europe*. Cambridge, MA: Cambridge University Press.

Dovring, Folke (1951), *De stående skatterna på jord 1400–1600* (With a Summary: Annual Land-Taxes in Sweden during the Fifteenth and Sixteenth Centuries). Lund: C. W. K. Gleerup.

Downing, Brian (1992), *The Military Revolution and Political Change: Origins of Democracy and Autocracy in Early Modern Europe*. Princeton, NJ: Princeton University Press.

Du Rietz, Gunnar, Dan Johansson, and Mikael Stenkula (2015), "Swedish Labour Income Taxation (1862–2013)." In Magnus Henrekson and Mikael Stenkula (eds.), *Swedish Taxation Development since 1862*. New York: Palgrave Macmillan, 35–122.

Ertman, Thomas (1997), *Birth of the Leviathan: Building States and Regimes in Medieval and Early Modern Europe*. Cambridge: Cambridge University Press.

Fjeldstad, Odd-Helge (2004), "What's Trust Got To Do With It? Non-Payment of Service Charges in Local Authorities in South Africa." *The Journal of Modern African Studies* 42(4): 539–62.

Flora, Peter and Arnold J. Heidenheimer (eds.) (1981), *The Development of Welfare States in Europe and America*. New Brunswick, NJ: Transaction.

Forssberg, Anna Maria (2014), "The Final Argument: War and the Merging of the Military and Civilian Spheres in 17th-Century Sweden." *Scandinavian Journal of History* 39(2): 170–84.

Gille, H. (1949), "The Demographic History of the Northern European Countries in the Eighteenth Century." *Population Studies* 3(1): 3–65.

Glete, Jan (2002), *War and the State in Early Modern Europe: Spain, the Dutch Republic and Sweden as Fiscal-military States, 1500–1600.* London: Routledge.

Glete, Jan (2006), "The Swedish Fiscal–Military State in Transition and Decline, 1650–1815." Unpublished manuscript. Paper presented at the XIV International Economic History Congress, Helsinki, August 21–25.

Hallenberg, Mats (2003), "Kungen, kronan eller staten? Makt och legitimitet I Gustav Vasas propaganda." In Börje Harnesk (ed.), *Maktens skiftande skepnader: studier i makt, legitimitet och inflytande i det tidigmoderna Sverige.* Umeå: Umeå University, 19–41.

Hallenberg, Mats (2012), "For the Wealth of the Realm: The Transformation of the Public Sphere in Swedish Politics, c. 1434–1650." *Scandinavian Journal of History* 37(5): 557–77.

Hallenberg, Mats, Johan Holm, and Dan Johansson (2008), "Organization, Legitimation, Participation: State Formation as a Dynamic Process – the Swedish Example, c. 1523–1680." *Scandinavian Journal of History* 33(3): 247–68.

Higgs, Edward (2001), "The Rise of the Information State: The Development of Centralised State Surveillance of the Citizen in England, 1500–2000." *Journal of Historical Sociology* 14(2): 175–97.

HM Revenue & Customs (2014), *Measuring Tax Gaps 2014 Edition. Tax Gap Estimates for 2012–13.* An Official Statistics Release, October 16. http://webarchive.nationalarchives. gov.uk/20150612044958/https:/www.gov.uk/government/uploads/system/uploads/ attachment_data/file/364009/4382_Measuring_Tax_Gaps_2014_IW_v4B_accessible_ 20141014.pdf.

Hoffman, Philip T. (2015), *Why did Europe Conquer the World?* Princeton, NJ: Princeton University Press.

Kain, Roger J. P. and Elizabeth Baigent (1992), *The Cadastral Map in the Service of the State—A History of Property Mapping.* Chicago, IL: University of Chicago Press.

Kiser, Edgar and Joshua Kane (2001), "Revolution and State Structure: The Bureaucratization of Tax Administration in Early Modern England and France." *American Journal of Sociology* 107(1): 183–223.

Levi, Margaret (1988), *Of Rule and Revenue.* Berkeley, CA: University of California Press.

Lext, Gösta (1968), "Mantalsskrivningen i Sverige före 1860." *Meddelanden från Ekonomiskhistoriska instituten vid Göteborgs universitet,* 13. Gothenburg: Gothenburg University.

Liliequist, Jonas (2015), "Laughing at the Unmanly Man in Early Modern Sweden." In Anna Foka and Jonas Liliequist (eds.), *Laughter, Humor, and the (Un)Making of Gender: Historical and Cultural Perspectives.* London: Palgrave Macmillan, 229–48.

Lindkvist, Thomas (1987), "Fiscal Systems, the Peasantry and the State in Medieval and Early Modern Sweden." In Jean-Philippe Genêt and Michel Le Mené (eds.), *Geneèse de l'Etat moderne: preéleèvement et redistribution: actes du colloque de Fontevraud, 1984.* Paris: Editions du Centre National de la Recherche Scientifique (CNRS).

Moore, Jr., Barrington (1978), *The Social Bases of Obedience and Revolt.* London: Macmillan.

Munck, Thomas (2011), "Preface." In Pasi Ihalainen, Michael Bregnsbo, Karin Sennefelt, and Patrik Winton (eds.), *Scandinavia in the Age of Revolution: Nordic Political Cultures, 1740–1820*. London: Routledge.

Myrdal, Janken (2011), "Farming and Feudalism, 1000–1700." In Janken Myrdal and Mats Morell (eds.), *The Agrarian History of Sweden: From 4000 BC to AD 2000*. Lund: Nordic Academic Press, 72–117.

Neal, Larry (2010), "Conclusion: The Monetary, Fiscal and Political Architecture of Europe, 1815–1914." In José Luís Cardoso and Pedro Lains (eds.), *Paying for the Liberal State: The Rise of Public Finance in Nineteenth-Century Europe*. Cambridge: Cambridge University Press.

Neveux, Hugues and Eva Österberg (1997), "Norms and Values of the Peasantry in the Period of State Formation: A Comparative Interpretation." In Peter Blickle (ed.), *Resistance, Representation and Community*. Oxford: Oxford University Press, 115–82.

Nilsson, Karl-Johan (1979), "System of Identity Numbers in the Swedish Population Register." Bethesda, MD: International Institute for Vital Registration and Statistics. Technical Papers No 3. www.cdc.gov/nchs/data/isp/003_System_of_Identify_Number_in_the_Swedish_Pop_Registers.pdf.

Nilsson, Sven (1982), "Krig och folkbokföring uder svenskt 1600-tal." *Scandia* 48(1): 5–29.

Nordin, Jonas (2011), "The Monarchy in the Swedish Age of Liberty (1719–1772)." In Pasi Ihalainen, Michael Bregnsbo, Karin Sennefelt, and Patrik Winton (eds.), *Scandinavia in the Age of Revolution: Nordic Political Cultures, 1740–1820*. Farnham: Ashgate, 29–40.

Oden, Birgitta (1972), "Historical Statistics in the Nordic Countries." In Val R. Lorwin and Jacob M. Price (eds.), *The Dimensions of the Past: Materials, Problems and Opportunities for Quantitative Work in History*. New Haven, CT: Yale University Press, 263–99.

OECD (2014), "Tax revenue" (indicator). doi: http://dx.doi.org/10.1787/d98b8cf5-en.

Ogborn, Miles (1998), "The Capacities of the State: Charles Davenant and the Management of the Excise, 1683–1698." *Journal of Historical Geography* 24(3): 289–312.

Olson, Mancur (1965), *The Logic of Collective Action: Public Goods and Theory of Groups*. Cambridge, MA: Harvard University Press.

Österberg, Eva (1977), *Kolonisation och kriser. Bebyggelse, skattetryck, odling och agrarstruktur i västra Värmland ca. 1300–1600*. Lund: CWK Gleerup/Liber.

Österberg, Eva (1990), "Compromise Instead of Conflict? Patterns of Contact between Local Peasant Communities and the Early Modern States: Sweden in the Sixteenth to Eighteenth Centuries." In Mats Lundalh and Thommy Svensson (eds.), *Agrarian Society in History: Essays in Honour of Magnus Mörner*. London: Routledge, 263–81.

Ostrom, Elinor (1990), *Governing the Commons: The Evolution of Institutions for Collective Action*. Cambridge: Cambridge University Press.

Poulsen, Bjørn (1995), "Kingdoms on the Periphery of Europe: The Case of Medieval and Early Modern Scandanavia." In Richard Bonney (ed.), *Economic Systems and State Finance*. Oxford: Oxford University Press, 101–22.

Retsö, Dag and Johan Söderberg (2015), "The Late-Medieval Crisis Quantified: Real Taxes in Sweden, 1320–1550." *Scandinavian Journal of History* 40(1): 1–24.

Riches, Daniel (2005), "Early Modern Military Reform and the Connection Between Sweden and Brandenburg-Prussia." *Scandinavian Studies* 77(3): 347–61.

Roberts, Michael (1953), *Gustavus Adolphus: A History of Sweden 1611–1632, Vol. I 1611–1626*. London: Longmans, Green and Co.

Roberts, Michael (1958), *Gustavus Adolphus: A History of Sweden 1611–1632, Vol. II 1626–1632*. London: Longmans, Green and Co.

Roberts, Michael (1968), *The Early Vasas: A History of Sweden 1523–1611*. Cambridge: Cambridge University Press.

Rodriguez, Enrique (1981), *Den svenska skattehistorien*. Lund: Liber Läromedel.

Ross, Michael L. (2004), "Does Taxation Lead to Representation?" *British Journal of Political Science* 34(2): 229–49.

Rothstein, Bo and Jan Teorell (2015), "Getting to Sweden, Part II: Breaking with Corruption in the Nineteenth Century." *Scandinavian Political Studies* 38(3): 238–54.

Schön, Lennart (2010), "The Rise of the Fiscal State in Sweden, 1800–1914." In Jose Luis Cardoso and Pedro Lains (eds.), *Paying for the Liberal State: The Rise of Public Finance in Nineteenth-Century Europe*. Cambridge, MA: Cambridge University Press, 162–86.

Scott, James C. (1998), *Seeing Like a State: How Certain Schemes to Improve the Human Condition Have Failed*. New Haven, CT: Yale University Press.

Sköld, Peter (2004), "The Birth of Population Statistics in Sweden." *History of the Family* 9: 5–21.

Spicer, Michael W. and Lee A. Becker (1980), "Fiscal Inequity and Tax Evasion: An Experimental Approach." *National Tax Journal* 33(2): 171–5.

Spicer, Michael W. and Scott B. Lundstedt (1976), "Understanding Tax Evasion." *Public Finance* 31(2): 295–305.

STA, Swedish Tax Authority (2013), *Taxes in Sweden: An English Summary of Tax Statistical Yearbook of Sweden*. https://skatteverket.se/download/18.77dbcb041438070e0398279/1389876671503/10414.pdf.

Steinmo, Sven (1993), *Taxation and Democracy: Swedish, British and American Approaches to Financing the Modern State*. New Haven, CT: Yale University Press.

Stenkula, Mikael (2014), "Swedish Taxation in a 150-year Perspective." *Nordic Tax Journal* 2: 10–42.

Stenkula, Mikael (2015), "Taxation of Real Estate in Sweden (1862–2013)." In Magnus Henrekson and Mikael Stenkula (eds.), *Swedish Taxation Development since 1862*. New York: Palgrave Macmillan, 303–27.

Teorell, Jan and Bo Rothstein (2015), "Getting to Sweden, Part I: War and Malfeasance, 1720–1850." *Scandinavian Political Studies* 38(3): 217–37.

Tilly, Charles (1992), *Coercion, Capital and European States AD 990–1992*. Malden, MA: Blackwell Publishing.

Willigan, Dennis J. and Katherine A. Lynch (1982), *Sources and Methods of Historical Demography*. New York: Academic Press.

Wisselgren, Maria J., Sören Edvinsson, Mats Berggren, and Maria Larsson (2014), "Testing Methods of Record Linkage on Swedish Censuses." *Historical Methods: A Journal of Quantitative and Interdisciplinary History* 47(3): 138–51.

Zhang, N., G. Andrighetto, S. Ottone, F. Ponzano, and S. Steinmo (2016), "Willing to Pay? Tax Compliance in Britain and Italy: An Experimental Analysis." *PLOS ONE* 11(2). https://doi.org/10.1371/journal.pone.0150277.

3

Creating Tax-Compliant Citizens in Sweden

The Role of Social Democracy

Jenny Jansson

As discussed by Nistotskaya and D'Arcy in Chapter 2 on Sweden, a long tradition of generally high-quality institutions has paved the way for excellent state capacity. This chapter focuses on the twentieth century, a time when Sweden developed into a high-tax-rate country with extraordinary tax compliance—a unique combination. Sweden underwent a profound trans-formation in the middle of the twentieth century: The Social Democratic Party (Socialdemokratiska arbetarpartiet, or SAP) won the 1932 election and stayed in office for forty-four consecutive years. High union density and corporatism introduced in the postwar period gave extensive powers to the union movement and to employers' organizations. The "golden age" of social democracy—the 1950s and 1960s—was characterized by full employment, an expanding welfare state system that included benefits such as comprehensive all-inclusive social insurance schemes, and diminishing wage inequality. It was in this context that Sweden transformed from a country with low tax rates to a country with high tax rates. Swedes are today among the most heavily taxed people in the world. Interestingly, Sweden also has the highest level of tax compliance, an unexpected combination. How was such a transition possible?

This chapter focuses on the *sense-making* of the tax system. More specific-ally, I examine how the SAP tried to create and reproduce tax morale while upholding the state's capacity to collect taxes. In democracies, governments need the electorate's support for their policies, regardless of the capacity of the state; of course, how citizens *perceive* politics is also important for winning elections. The political elite can play a crucial role by making sense of policies and acting as mediators to raise awareness. This is particularly important when a government pursues policies that may be unpopular among its citizens, such as raising taxes.

Perceptions of Fairness and Tax Compliance

Taxes can be understood as a contract between the citizens and the state: Citizens pay taxes in return for security and social services (Scholz 2003). Margaret Levi calls this contract one of *quasi-voluntary compliance*: An individual will cooperate with the government only if he or she perceives that the government is fulfilling its part of the contract. It is *quasi*-voluntary because the state possesses coercive means to make people pay (Levi 1988: 52–3). This does not imply that the state can do as it pleases. In democracies, unlike authoritarian states, dissatisfaction with the government's actions in fulfilling its part of the contract is expressed through elections. Citizens who are dissatisfied with taxation policy can vote for someone else, and thereby pursue changes in the contract. Therefore, if governments wish to raise taxes, citizens must be persuaded to approve such policies. Under these circumstances, the sense-making of the tax system becomes very important because it affects how citizens perceive taxes. For instance, if the common understanding of taxation is that it leads to free healthcare, citizens ought to be more willing to pay than if the common perception is that taxes are used to finance war.

There are two preconditions for upholding a tax contract between the state and its citizens: the state's capacity to collect taxes, and the state's ability to deliver something in return for the tax money (Levi 1988). These two factors—ability to collect and ability to deliver—are important for an understanding of tax compliance because they trigger ideas of fairness among the citizens. Research has demonstrated that perceived fairness is decisive for tax compliance; if citizens perceive the tax system or the government's use of tax money as fair, it is more likely that they will comply. A perception that the fiscal contract is just and that others are fulfilling their part has been proven to be important (Roosma, van Oorschot, and Gelissen 2015; Scholz 2003).

Previous research on tax compliance indicates that fairness can take on at least two different dimensions: It can be linked either to the state's capacity to collect taxes (i.e. does the tax-collecting process treat everyone fairly?) or to the redistribution of the taxes collected (i.e. is the state using the money in a fair and acceptable way?). The collecting process, which I refer to here as the *perceived state capacity to collect taxes*, refers to how the tax system and tax agencies work. In particular, two parts of the collecting process affect how citizens perceive tax collection. The first part is related to the effectiveness of the tax system and to *who* pays. If citizens perceive that only parts of the population actually pay taxes due to non-functioning institutions, there is likely to be a negative impact on compliance. Likewise, if the tax rules are very complicated, with numerous deduction possibilities, there is always a risk of tax avoidance. Tax planning tends to create a sense of unfairness; some people get away with paying less because they have the economic means or knowledge to do tax planning. If citizens perceive that others are "getting away with something" and not fulfilling their part, compliance will deteriorate (Levi 1991; Scholz 2003: 196). A sense of injustice impacts citizens' perceptions of the tax system negatively; no one wants to be the "sucker" who pays more than other citizens. The second part of the collecting process that ought to have an impact on tax compliance centers on the simplicity of the system: Is it difficult to pay taxes? If institutions are designed in a way that demands considerable effort from citizens, there is a risk that paying taxes becomes a burden to the citizens in a double sense. Making it difficult to pay taxes reminds citizens of their "sacrifice" to the state, which may well lead to a closer evaluation of how the money is spent and whether the process is fair. Hence, their experience of paying taxes will impact citizens' willingness to pay (see Table 3.1).

The second dimension of fairness focuses on the state's ability to deliver services in return for taxes: *the perceived fairness of the redistribution of resources.* Within the field of tax research, it has long been claimed that citizens who perceive that they receive good services in return for their tax money will be more compliant (Levi 1988; Levi and Kiser 2015: 8; Timmons 2005). Tax compliance depends on citizens' perception of the output from the tax system—the redistribution of resources. If the state does not deliver sufficient services in return for tax money, its citizens will object. In the same way, if the fiscal contract is perceived to be unjust, in the sense that the state takes more than the citizens get back, this will impact compliance (Levi 1988; Roosma, van Oorschot, and Gelissen 2015; Scholz 2003: 153–4). Finally, if citizens perceive that they are paying for others but do not get much in return themselves, this perception tends to trigger a feeling of unfairness; hardly anyone wants to pay for others. Combined with efficient tax-collecting

Table 3.1. Mechanisms of compliance

	Fair redistribution	Unfair redistribution
Perceived state capacity: Good	"Of course I'll pay!" (i.e. you get what you pay for)	"License to retrench" (i.e. you pay for more services than you receive)
Perceived state capacity: Bad	"A bit of fudging prevents you from being the sucker" (i.e. you may be paying more than others)	Coercion (i.e. you may be paying more than others and receive too little in return)

institutions, perceptions of unfair redistribution ought to make it easy for politicians to make cuts in the welfare state (compare Stanley, Chapter 7 in this volume, on the UK, and David Cameron's retrenchment politics).

I use these two dimensions—state capacity and fair redistribution—to analyze the policies of the Social Democrats in the postwar period.

The two dimensions of fairness support an understanding of why citizens comply, but how are citizens' perceptions of the tax system formed? I argue that a perception of fairness comes from the *personal experience* of paying taxes and the *public sense-making* of taxation.

Personal experience of the tax system strongly depends on how the tax-collection process is designed. The tax return procedure is of particular interest here, since tax returns are the most obvious contact that citizens have with a tax agency. Thus, tax returns play a major role in citizens' perceptions of the tax system and ultimately impact their perception of its fairness. Technology can improve institutions (North 1990: 131–40), so examining the techno-logical development of the tax system in Sweden during the SAP's time in office is one way of examining how the SAP tried to uphold state capacity.

The second factor, the sense-making of taxation, refers to how the tax policy is justified by the political elite and, in this case, the SAP. The way in which political issues are framed by the political elite impacts how citizens perceive policies. Political perception is a result of discursive struggle. Political actors can frame issues in different ways; hence, different meanings can be assigned to the same issue. For this reason, it is interesting to examine the actions of political actors in creating, maintaining, and reforming a perception of the tax system as being fair and just.

The analysis contains the following steps. I identify two time periods since World War II when the tax system was particularly debated. These two crucial periods constitute moments that could have impacted tax compliance but did not: the period of welfare state expansion, 1945–60, and the period of reform of the tax system, 1970–90. Within both these time periods, I examine the SAP's actions to create and reproduce tax morale, both rhetorically and in terms of actual reforms that were made. The two dimensions of fairness presented above guide this analysis. This study is built upon an analysis of minutes from the party board, internal documents, newspaper articles, parlia-mentary debates, and documents from the public administration.

Raising Taxes and Constructing the Welfare State: 1945–70

In modern states, redistribution takes place through the welfare state. Scholars have claimed that the Swedish national identity is tightly intertwined with the Swedish welfare state (Berggren and Trägårdh 2006; Trägårdh 2010). The modern connection between national identity and the welfare state originates from the notion of "the People's Home" (*Folkhemmet*), a concept that materialized after the SAP won the election and came into power in 1932. The result was a welfare state for *the people*, not only for the working class. Thus, the contract between the state and its citizens became a contract of social security in return for taxes. To enable such politics, taxes had to be raised.

State capacity to collect taxes

The development of the tax system in the postwar period had roughly two characteristic features: Income taxes increased steadily, as did progressivity in the tax system (Schön 2007: 487). Households' share of direct taxes increased during this time, whereas corporate taxes remained more or less at a steady (comparatively low) percentage throughout the 1950s and 1960s (Bergström 1969: 68–9). Progressive taxation on income was established in 1910 and this progressivity increased until the 1980s (Henrekson and Stenkula 2015: 12–16; Löwnertz 1983: 24).

Its massive electoral support in the postwar era created opportunities for the SAP to employ radical redistributive policies. Better preconditions hardly existed anywhere to construct a tax system in which the working class, and employees in general, were spared from high taxes, while capital was forced to pay a larger share of the costs of the welfare state. Yet corporate taxes were quite modest in comparison with the taxes paid by households (Bergström and Södersten 1994: 247).

One explanation for this situation is the arrangement of the labor market. Wages have always been negotiated by labor market parties without the meddling of the state. Wage negotiations were centralized in the 1950s; in other words, the umbrella organizations for employers' organizations and trade unions negotiated wages for all occupational groups. Moreover, the collective agreements covered most Swedish employees, and created strong organizations. In addition, in order for the SAP to gain sufficient and broad support for its reforms, an institutionalized relationship between the state and the labor market parties was established in the 1950s. Implications of corporatism included, for example, that organizations had representatives on agencies' boards, participated in investigations, and held regular meetings with the government. The system not only ensured that labor market parties could impact politics; these arrangements also had implications for the taxation policy (Steinmo 1993: 125–6). For example, the corporate tax rate was one part of this arrangement: Low corporate taxes would ensure that production costs would not impact the employment rate. Moreover, corporate taxes were designed in a way that made it very beneficial for employers to reinvest profits into their businesses in Sweden (Bergström 2007: 229–30) and thus also ensure high employment in the future. In addition, changes in the tax rate were always taken into consideration in wage negotiation rounds, which became a problem in the 1970s and 1980s, when raised taxes led to raised wage demands and subsequently to inflation. Because of corporatism and centralized wage bargaining, taxes, welfare, and wages have been treated as a single system by labor market parties and the state (Lindberg 2016; Partistyrelsen 1973; 1974).

I now turn to the SAP's policy to develop tax institutions and, more specifically, the procedure of paying taxes. Perhaps the most important reform in the postwar decade was the introduction of the withholding tax system in 1947. This reform made taxes preliminary: The employer would pay the taxes of an employee according to a table of wage levels (Peralta Prieto 2008: 30). If the employee had paid too much or too little, the tax agency would either make a refund or charge more after a review had been undertaken. Of course, this reform was important in preventing discontent among citizens; the simplification not only made it easier to pay taxes, but it also made the actual payment less obvious for the citizen.

The introduction of the withholding tax demanded new technology for printing tax return forms, and the so-called "citograf system" was introduced. In the citograf system, the tax authorities made one metal sheet for each taxpayer. The sheet contained his/her information and was used to print that individual's tax return form (Å. Johansson 2003; Peralta Prieto 2008: 29–30). Social security numbers, or *personnummer* (Å. Johansson 2003: 99), were established at the same time. These numbers had an important impact on tax collection and were eventually used in all registers. For that time period, this system (including both the technical solution and the social security number) was at the forefront of governmental handling of information on citizens' income and property ownership. Of course, there were limits on what sort of information could be preprinted on a tax return form.

The government made several attempts to simplify the tax return in the 1950s. However, the regulation of tax deduction remained complicated (Ekman 2003: 14), which in turn made the tax return complicated. The SAP's party board repeatedly expressed concern about the tax return procedure: If it was too complicated, it could impact the elections.

Another feature of the Swedish tax system that might have had an impact on citizens' perceptions of taxes was the administrative system. Control of the tax return was decentralized and held by a local committee, the *taxeringsnämnd* (TN). The TN was introduced in 1907 and consisted mostly of volunteers and laymen—the so-called *fritidsgranskare*, literally "spare-time reviewers" (SOU 1933: 27). Before 1951, Sweden had approximately 2,500 municipalities, a number that was reduced to 1,037 in 1951 through amalgamations. After the great municipal reform from 1971 to 1974, only 277 municipalities remained

(Erlingsson et al. 2015). Many of these municipalities had less than 3,000 inhabitants; consequently, local politicians or civil servants, who were often known by the local taxpayers (at least in small cities and in the countryside) monitored whether these taxpayers had filled in their tax return form correctly. This system had similarities to the scheme developed by Gustav Vasa in which local clergymen's knowledge about taxpayers was used to control tax collection (see Nistotskaya and D'Arcy, Chapter 2 in this volume). The arguments for this system, which used laymen instead of civil servants, were legitimacy (the gap between taxpayers and the monitoring authority was small), efficiency (taxable income was partly based on contextual knowledge among tax collectors), and the low cost of having people performing tax control voluntarily in their spare time (Malmer 2003). However, this system resulted in regional differences in the control function. More importantly, due to this controlling procedure, most of the people who were convicted for cheating were ordinary people who had committed small mistakes or who were cheating a little; meanwhile, advanced tax evasion and avoidance were not detected (Malmer 2003: 38; SOU 1969.42). It became clear over time that the downside of using laymen as monitors was that they did not have sufficient knowledge to detect advanced tax planning or cheating, but were only able to identify the "small cheats." Of course, this outcome had an impact on people's perceptions of the tax authorities and also, eventually, on the process of tax collection. The TN system was phased out in the 1970s. In 1951, *Riksskattenämnden* was established as the first national authority responsible for controlling tax collection (Malmer 2003: 36) and the first step toward a centralized tax agency.

The SAP put efforts into making the institutions of the tax system work as smoothly and efficiently as possible. There seems to have been an attitude within the party that raising taxes needed to be combined with making the payments as easy as possible. The party board expressed concern about how complicated systems could impact its popularity: "If you want people to pay high taxes, do not make it hard for them to pay" was the signature feature of the SAP's tax policy.

Justifying taxes: the precondition of the welfare state

Many of the big and costly social reforms, such as free healthcare, the pension system, free and inclusive schools, and a universal child allowance, were introduced during the 1940s and 1950s. As a result, taxes became a recurring issue that was discussed by the party board (see, for instance, Partistyrelsen 1950; 1954; 1956a). Raising taxes was perceived as a problem for the SAP. As in many other countries, taxes were increased during World War II. Once the war was over, the citizens seem to have expected the tax burden to be reset to prewar levels, but instead they were made permanent (Henrekson and

Stenkula 2015: 13; Steinmo 1993: 91–5). As a result, the 1950s became the "decade of the tax reduction debate" (Elvander 1972). There was little overall consensus among political parties on taxes, although the agendas of the right and the Liberals both promoted their reduction in election campaigns and parliamentary debates, thereby forcing the Social Democrats to develop a strategy for handling tax debates.

The party had two options when choosing a strategy for the election campaigns in the 1940s and 1950s. The first option was to meet the criticism on a detailed level and dig into the minor changes and reductions that had been made during the past term (because the tax system was often and gradually changed). However, this strategy risked focusing the election campaigns on technical taxation issues, which was probably not to the advantage of the SAP (Partistyrelsen 1950). The other option was to choose an aggressive strategy and go for social reforms and higher taxes: If the party proposed several new social reforms, the other political parties would be forced to relate their campaigns to the Social Democrats' proposals, and not the other way around. Such a strategy was developed by the party—attention was diverted away from taxation and instead focused on new social policies (Partistyrelsen 1950).

Every time the party board discussed taxation, it expressed concern about voters' reactions: How would voters react to increased taxes, or to the other political parties' proposals to reduce taxes? Each time, the solution to this problem was the same: enlightenment and propaganda. The main opinion of the party board in the early 1950s was that "if we only enlighten the working class about how the government is using the taxes, the fact that we are not reducing taxes further will be accepted" and "people will come to terms with the tax levels." As long as the party could show how taxes were being used, Social Democrat voters would not mind the tax levels. It was also important to communicate this message to voters in a way that would appeal to them. Thus, education and enlightenment became the strategy to win support for the tax policy (Partistyrelsen 1950; 1952; 1956c). Enlightenment is a recurring theme throughout the history of the Swedish labor movement. Whenever the leadership wanted to conduct policies that the rank and file disapproved of, the party board and the management of the Trade Union Confederation (Landsorganisationen or LO) used internal education and enlightenment of the members (Jansson 2012; Partistyrelsen 1942). Taxes were no different than the other issues that needed to be discussed among the members.

Another recurring theme for the party board was the importance of connecting social reform with their funding: "Enlightenment activities are needed to make clear that we have a choice between reducing taxes and more social reforms. One cannot eat the cake twice" (Erik Fast, Partistyrelsen 1952). In particular, propaganda and enlightening activities were focused on explaining to voters—especially workers—that the state and society were not enemies: "The state is the means that enables freedom for individuals through social reforms," Erlander stated during one meeting with the party board in 1952. Social reforms, Erlander concluded, were expensive and had to be funded (Partistyrelsen 1952).

The message conveyed in propaganda material produced by the SAP during the 1940s, 1950s, and 1960s can be summarized as "taxation is the foundation of the welfare state."

Most of the propaganda material produced in the 1950s starts by describing recent developments of the welfare state in Sweden. Recently implemented reforms are described and the beneficiaries of these reforms are listed. The propaganda then continues by explaining that a precondition for all the reforms made by the Social Democrats is the tax system. The concepts of "taxes" and "taxation" are often used together with those of "child allowance," "sickness insurance," and "education" (SAP 1950a; 1950b; 1954; 1960). The material also presents a clear connection between the state and its citizens. In a newspaper article on tax evasion, Prime Minister Erlander stated that "one must understand that the state is not an anonymous actor, we are the state. If you deceive the state, you are stealing from your neighbors and friends" (*Aftonbladet* 1959).

One famous election film from 1954 that was produced by the party, titled "Skattefria Andersson" (Tax Evader Andersson), clearly demonstrated the connection between paying taxes and the output of the welfare state. In the film, the main character, Andersson, tries living as a self-reliant man (*står på egna ben*). He does not pay taxes; instead, he has to pay for everything himself, such as schooling for the children, roads, hospital costs, and so forth. The film ends when Andersson wakes up from this nightmare and expresses how grateful he is for everything the state provides for its citizens. The message of the film is simple, and explicitly spelled out at the end: Citizens are co-dependent, and cooperation has made it possible to build a welfare state that sets the average citizen free (Socialdemokraterna 1954).

Passages in the material describing taxes very often connect taxes with the concept of "security." Taxes are the foundation of and the guarantee for a working social security system. The party board specifically discussed the meaning of the concept "security," and a board member concluded that the concept had been redefined during the 1950s from "security from mass poverty" to "including everyone in the improved standards of living" (Partistyrelsen 1956b). Thus, security was no longer mere survival; it also included the right to take part in the welfare state system—that is, social citizenship.

In 1960, the election campaign very explicitly stated that the welfare state costs money. In a pamphlet used in the campaign, the SAP listed the costs of different levels of education, such as high school, college, and university education. Hence, the SAP concluded, the suggested tax reductions proposed by the Liberals and the Right Party would endanger all the educational reforms SAP had brought in during the previous ten years (SAP 1960). The main message was that social reforms and social security were not compatible with tax reductions. Instead, taxes were described as "our common money" and the SAP stressed that taxes belonged to everyone (*Aftonbladet* 1959).

The SAP's framing of taxes during the phase of welfare state construction thus focused on establishing a link between taxes and the outcome of the welfare state (i.e. if you pay taxes, you will also get free social services). The party's attempts to impact citizens' perceptions of the tax system used fair redistribution as their point of departure: The tax money would be used in such a way that everybody would benefit.

Defending a Challenged Tax System: The 1970s and 1980s

During the 1950s and 1960s, the expansive phase of the welfare state, the SAP discursively connected taxes to the outcome of the welfare state. This period was characterized by low unemployment, increased wages, peaceful labor market relations, the individualization of income tax in 1971 (which made it more profitable for married women to work) and, in short, a higher standard of living for the Swedish people. This period, which was successful in many ways for the SAP, came to an end in the 1970s. The SAP, and its welfare state construction, was thoroughly challenged for the first time.

Sweden went through several economic, social, and political changes in the 1970s and 1980s that impacted its tax politics. For the first time in the postwar era, unemployment rose. Moreover, the "expand-the-welfare-system" strategy employed by the party to win elections had its flaws. Erlander called the problem "the discontent of rising expectations": Even though the social reforms had considerably improved citizens' lives, the citizens kept expecting more. If the citizens always expected comprehensive social reforms, sooner or later the party would have problems delivering such reforms. The radicalization of the trade union movement in the 1970s should be understood in this context.

The "other" branch of the labor movement, the LO, became another challenge to the party in the 1970s. In order for Sweden to take the next step toward an equal and classless society, the LO pressured the SAP to legislate on workplace democracy (increasing employees' influence on working conditions) and wage earners' funds (meant to distribute the profits of Swedish industry between employers and employees). From the trade unions' perspective, redistribution of wealth was not solely a tax issue; redistribution also took place through wage negotiations. In the 1970s, it became obvious that wages had not increased at the same pace as the profits made by businesses. Neither were reinvestments into Swedish industry proportionate to profits (Bergström 2007: 171–5; Hedborg 2016). Thus, according to the LO, there was a "profit surplus" that was neither being taxed nor redistributed through wage negotiations. The aim of the wage earners' funds was to seize control of this surplus. Thus, the funds can be interpreted as embodying widespread discontent regarding the redistribution of wealth in Sweden. The funds came to be very controversial, even among Social Democrats (Johansson and Magnusson 2012: ch. 6; Lewin 2002: ch. 9).

In this context, upholding the social democratic model turned out to be difficult, and the tax system quickly became a focus of criticism. Several tax reforms in the 1960s and 1970s had increased progressivity (Partistyrelsen 1971). However, the combination of rising marginal tax rates and inflation resulted in increasing numbers of middle- and working-class employees having to pay marginal taxes, which had never been the aim. Meanwhile, the innumerable, gradual changes that had been made to the tax system had turned it into a patchwork of different rules that opened up the possibility of tax planning for those who had the knowledge or the money to hire professionals to help them avoid taxes (Agell, Englund, and Södersten 1998: 8–9). This created opposition to the tax system, not only among the center and right parties but also within the left.

In 1976, the famous author Astrid Lindgren published the article 'Pomperipossa in Monismanien', a satirical fairy tale about the witch Pomperipossa, who was forced to pay a marginal tax rate of 102 percent because she did not have any loans that would entitle her to deductions (Lindgren 1976). Lindgren's fairy tale was written as a response to her own marginal tax rate. The story was published in the spring of 1976, and fueled criticism toward the system. Shortly after, in 1978, Gunnar Myrdal wrote another famous article in which he claimed that the tax system had turned Swedes into a "people of cheats." The poorly constructed tax system created incentives for everyone to try to cheat and avoid taxes. For Myrdal this was a failure for social democracy (Myrdal 1978: 500). He was not accusing rich people of evading taxes; rather, he was accusing the *system* of being wrongly constructed. The importance of Myrdal's and Lindgren's articles should not be underestimated. Until then, the Liberals and the right had been the main opponents of the system; however, their arguments could always be dismissed on ideological grounds. Astrid Lindgren's absurd marginal tax rate clearly demonstrated that the system had unintended consequences.

After the SAP lost the elections in 1976, an internal debate began within the party. The point of departure of this debate was not to make the system less progressive—the main principle for taxation would still be the "ability to pay," which implied that people with higher income could and consequently *should* pay a larger share. Taxes were an issue of solidarity (Palme 1976).

The message transmitted by the Social Democrat press in the 1970s continued to stress taxation as "justice" and "redistribution from the wealthy to the poor" (Andersson 1976; Therner 1974). At the same time, however, the media started to report on tax planning and the immorality of people who avoided and evaded taxes. Considerable attention was directed toward tax cheats and evaders; these were people who were trying to get a free ride on the welfare system, which was morally wrong (see, for instance, *Aftonbladet* 1979; Lindström and Nordin 1979; Nordin and Lindström 1977; Thalén 1979; a simple search in the National Library of Sweden's database of digitalized newspapers points in the same direction).

Were the taxation problems really as big as they were made out to be? Sträng commented on that particular question in 1980. His position was that the system had problems because of inflation and the deduction regulation, but that the situation was nowhere near as bad as the media was portraying. However, the rest of the party board did not agree. Instead, they seemed to have already been convinced in 1980 that the system caused injustices (Partistyrelsen 1980).

Questioned state capacity to collect taxes

The government's first reaction to the unfairness of the system was to make small adjustments to it; in the long run, this only contributed to making the tax system even more difficult to oversee and created even more possibilities for tax planning. The changes made by the center-right government that seized power in 1976 included some tax reductions at first. However, it turned out to be very difficult to reduce taxes, since this could only be done by making cuts in the welfare state system—which the party in power was reluctant to do (Blyth 2001; Steinmo 1993: 133). The center-right party's inability to lower taxes indicates how deeply embedded the welfare state was in the minds of Swedish citizens. It also indicates that the problem with the tax system was not the *redistribution* dimension of fairness; rather, the problems that occurred in the 1970s came from the *state capacity* dimension of fairness: The system was inefficient. In 1981, during the final year of the center-right government, the Liberals, the Center Party, and the SAP agreed on a major tax reform aimed at solving the problems with the system.

The Social Democrats won the elections in 1982 as well as in 1985 and 1988, and thus governed Sweden until 1991. The 1981 tax reforms were gradually implemented during these nine years in power; however the reforms did not manage to rectify the shortcomings of the system with regard to tax deduction possibilities and subsequent tax planning (Feldt 1991: 385). Marginal income tax rates decreased at first, but were raised again in the second half of the decade (Stenkula, Johansson, and Du Rietz 2014).

During the 1980s, concerned voices in the party stated that the system did not have the redistributing effects that its designers had intended. Swedish voters had accepted a high marginal tax rate because of the progressivity: The fairness of the system was that the richest paid most. This justice-based argument had always been very important in winning support for the redistribution policy. However, when the system did not in fact redistribute—which some claimed to be the case because the richest had ways of avoiding taxes through tax planning—then the whole foundation of the social democratic welfare state project came into question. This mobilized a segment of the party that wanted reform (see K.-O. Feldt's speech, Partistyrelsen 1986).

Reforming the system was, however, a difficult task. Kjell-Olof Feldt, who became the Minister of Finance after the election victory in 1982, was convinced that the funding of the welfare state was not sustainable. Feldt's first move was to suggest that cuts should be made to the welfare state immediately and that, in general, it should be scaled back. For most Social Democrats, Feldt's suggestion was simply unthinkable (Feldt, Ahlqvist, and Engqvist 1984; Lindberg 2016). Consequently, Feldt directed his attention toward the tax system.

During the 1980s, the government conducted three investigations that eventually led to a proposal. The proposed system was a shift of logics regarding justice and taxation. Ever since Ernst Wigforss' tax reform in 1948, the SAP had advocated a progressive tax system. The party had continually argued that "ability to pay" was the most just system because of its obvious redistributive features: Rich people pay more. Contrary to this understanding of justice, the proposed reform sharply reduced progressivity. Its main aim was to simplify the system, reduce both income and corporate taxes, and broaden the tax base (Riksrevisionen 2010: 11). The idea of a steeply progressive income tax was abandoned; instead, a proportional income tax set at 30 percent was introduced. Some progressivity remained, with incomes exceeding a certain break point paying an additional 20 percent; however, in the new system, marginal taxes could never exceed 51 percent, which was a considerable change from the old system (Agell, Englund, and Södersten 1996). This reduction of income tax and corporate tax was to be financed through a broadened tax base.

Why did the Social Democratic Minister of Finance become the main proponent for an almost flat-rate system? There are several explanations. In her book, *Högervåg*, Kristina Boréus analyzes how the concepts of "taxation" and "taxes" were used in the 1970s and 1980s and how Swedish public debate in the 1980s began to be entrenched in neoliberalism. With the growth of neoliberalism, these words were placed in a negative frame: taxation came to be framed in the public debate as a burden to citizens (Boréus 1994: 178, 258–69). This perspective coincides with an active neoliberal movement in

Sweden during the 1980s, directed by the Swedish Employers' Confederation (Svenska arbetsgivareföreningen (SAF)) and by think-tanks sponsored by the SAF (Blyth 2002: ch. 7; Boréus 1994: ch. 3; Johansson 2000). Another factor that may have influenced the design of the reform is the composition of the committees. In 1980, Sträng had already shown an interest in making the tax system less progressive, albeit with a proportional 45 percent tax rate for everyone (Partistyrelsen 1980), so the idea was not completely new. The architects behind the reform seem to have consisted of a group of relatively young men who came to be known as "Feldt's lads" (*Feldts grabbar*). They were well-educated economists—party members, but not people who had worked their way up through the party, which was the ordinary recruiting procedure. The group, also called the "right wing" of the party (*kanslihushögern*), was allowed great influence over the formulation of economic policy.

The logic of fairness and a new understanding of taxes

The tax reform required a new discourse on taxes and justice. Until the late 1980s, justice in the taxation discourse had been based on the principle of "ability to pay" (*skatt efter bärkraft*), which always implied progressivity; indeed, most party people would have claimed that the problem with the taxation system was *too little* progressivity (Steinmo 2002). This principle had its roots in the class struggle: Different classes have different economic preconditions. The goal of the labor movement was to reduce those economic cleavages, which could only be done if the rich paid more. However, since the redistributive effects of the tax system were being questioned, advocates of reform started to talk about justice as a situation where "everybody contributes." Setting limitations on tax deductions and simplifying the system would create a fair, transparent system in which no one could escape paying taxes. In other words, the party emphasized the horizontal contract between taxpayers and the state. It was argued that the prevalent tax system had suspended horizontal justice because the same type of income could be taxed in two very different ways (Riksdagen Prot. 1989/90.47: 26–7), creating injustices. Meanwhile, vertical justice, or redistribution between different classes, was de-emphasized by the party; naturally, the reform would in fact reduce corporate and income tax for high-income earners. It was implied, however, that since everyone would contribute at least 30 percent of their income, rich people would still pay larger sums.

The strategy to explain the new principle of taxation to voters contained three steps. First, the party and, above all, the Minister of Finance had to convince the public that the prevalent system was not working (Feldt 1991: 386). During the late 1980s, several brochures with this message were produced, both for internal party discussions and aimed toward citizens in general (see, for instance, SAP 1988a; 1988b).

Second, earlier reforms in the tax system had been pursued through extensive internal debates in the party. The ambition had been to establish reforms among the rank and file first, giving party members good insight into the politics, sometimes at the expense of quick decisions. Gunnar Sträng particularly advocated such a procedure (Partistyrelsen 1980; 1981). Feldt and Prime Minister Ingvar Carlsson chose a different strategy; they made sure they had *sufficient* support among the labor movement elite, trusting that the rank and file and activists would come to terms with their decision.

Finally, the reform was framed as a "whole new system." In his memoirs, Feldt emphasizes that the reform was not an improvement of the current system; it was a *new* system (Feldt 1991: 386, 422–6). This was another strategically important maneuver. During most of the twentieth century, the SAP had been the party that initiated big, tough reforms. Some of these reforms were contested, such as the pension reform in the 1950s, but most eventually became popular. The party's self-image contained a glorious past; it had enacted reforms that no other party could have made. The party "made *the big* reforms and took responsibility for Sweden" (Feldt 1991). Thus, the tax reform of the century restored the party's self-image as a central political actor: When needed, the SAP still had the ability to make changes that might be unpopular but that would be beneficial in the long run, and that would improve state capacity (Feldt 1991: 386). These revisions thus went well with the party's image as the responsible reformer.

Technical progress and improved state capacity

I now turn to the technical development of the tax system, which, in many ways, can be described as remarkable. Some important institutional reforms to simplify the system were initiated by the Minister of Finance, Gunnar Sträng, in the 1970s. Raising taxes, which the government had been doing incrementally for decades, required an effective tax administration (Peralta Prieto 2008: 35).

The tax agency was early in adopting an electronic data-processing system (EDP); in the 1970s, this technology started to have an increasing importance for tax collection. EDP facilitated preprinted tax return forms that could contain much more information than the citograf system or the punched card system, and assisted reform processes that made it easier to collect and pay taxes. However, the transition to EDP in the 1960s became a struggle between different interests: Some parties wanted an IBM solution while others claimed that the Swedish system developed by SAAB was preferable.

The government decided to buy both formats, resulting in two parallel systems being used to administer taxation in Sweden (Å. Johansson 2003). Of course, this decision created inefficiencies; however, it also forced the tax agency to invest in human capital such as programming, which became an asset for the tax agency in the long run.

Thanks to the EDP system, the tax return form could be designed with more preprinted information. This transformation to EDP was possible because the Swedish public administration had good computer knowledge and had adopted the latest technology early on. The registers that already existed were very good; however, above all, Sweden was a small country. The computer power required for similar system transformations in Germany or Britain did not exist in the 1970s, but it was sufficient for Sweden because of the limited amount of data (Peralta Prieto 2008: 28). The technological possibilities and limitations in making the tax system effective were known and discussed by the party board (Partistyrelsen 1980).

In 1971, the tax return form was simplified; the language used and the information sent to taxpayers was made more accessible to citizens (Peralta Prieto 2008: 41). Several investigations on how to simplify the tax system, including the tax return system, were conducted in the 1980s (Ds Fi 1983.16; SOU 1985.42). There seems to have been a parliamentary consensus that the system was too complicated, a factor that could annoy taxpayers and impact tax morale.

The tax agency also produced a booklet, "Dags att deklarera" (roughly, "It is Time to Do Your Taxes"), which was sent to every taxpayer along with the tax return form. The booklet still exists, and contains detailed information on how to fill out the form. According to one of the initiators, the intention was to make it easier for citizens to pay their taxes (Ekman 2003: 14–15). Information campaigns about the tax system, and about the tax return procedure in particular, continued throughout the 1970s and 1980s. This information was translated into different languages that mirrored the immigrant population. Popular educational organizations arranged study circles, and the tax agency even made seven programs about the tax return that were broadcast on one of Sweden's two national TV channels (Thärnström 2003: 120). An evaluation of the information campaign in 1971 indicated that a majority of taxpayers perceived the information as easy to understand, and "Dags att deklarera" became a prototype for other public information booklets (Thärnström 2003: 121). Moreover, the tax agency produced free information material with exercises that were handed out to schools with the aim of teaching all children about taxes (Thärnström 2003: 122).

However, even as the tax agency tried to simplify the tax-collecting process, the myriad of rules that existed before reform in 1990 ensured that a majority of the population needed help to do their taxes. This continued to be the case until 1987, when the first "simplified income tax return" was introduced (Riksdagen Prop. 1984/5.180: 121). With further reform in 1990, when most of the deductions were removed, the system changed even more. In 1991, the tax agency was made responsible for the census (until then it had been administered by the Church). This reform, together with increased computerization, led to the "simplified tax return form" in 1995. Under this new system, the tax agency collected information from all available sources about the income of every individual in Sweden, resulting in a very detailed preprinted tax return form. The taxpayer simply agreed or disagreed with the sum calculated by the tax agency. There was consensus among the political parties in parliament that the new tax return procedure was a natural development of previous simplifications to the tax return procedure. The less complicated procedure would not only be cheaper for the state, but citizens also appreciated its simplification. The only party that disagreed was the populist New Democracy (Riksdagen Prot. 1992/3.47). This simplification of the tax return procedure has continued ever since. In 2002, a tax return form on the Internet was introduced (Riksskatteverket 2003: 16), a service that has been supplemented with texting (the taxpayer simply approves the tax agency's calculations of his/her income through an SMS) and an app for smartphones.

These technical developments and the transition of administration from laymen to civil servants in the tax authority facilitated a transformation to a "service agency." The first steps were taken in the 1980s; however, the major transformation has occurred in the first decades of the twenty-first century (O. Johansson 2003; Stridh and Wittberg 2015). From the mid-1990s onward, the tax agency employed language consultants to work on improvements to instructions on the tax forms in order to make it as easy as possible for Swedes to complete returns and pay taxes (O. Johansson 2003: 117). Today, the Swedish Tax Agency is one of the most trusted authorities in Sweden (Medieakademin/Sifo 2015).

Conclusions

Fairness is the mechanism most commonly used to explain tax-compliant citizens. A precondition for the social contract is the perception of being treated fairly by the state. In this chapter, I have suggested that fairness can take two forms: fairness in the tax collection procedure, and fairness in the redistribution of collected taxes. The first decades after the war were a time of establishing good state capacity and framing the redistribution of taxes as fair. The SAP spent a great deal of time explaining the outcome of the social contract to citizens: Taxes led to free education, free healthcare, and so forth. Making sure that citizens understood how tax money was spent, combined with simplifying the tax system and making it efficient, placed Sweden in the upper left box of Table 3.1: the citizens got what they paid for. During the time period examined here, once the party had established the dimension of redistribution, it was hardly challenged in public debate. On the other hand, the dimension of state capacity was challenged.

Despite continuous work to improve and simplify the tax return procedure, the tax collection part of the social contract brought attention to the tax system during the 1970s and 1980s. The flaws of the system, which were debated in the 1970s, mainly concerned the unfair collection procedure. Perceptions within the party and, as far as I can tell, also in the public debate, asserted that the financing of the welfare state was unfairly distributed between different groups in society. The same type of income could be taxed in different ways depending on what specific deductions could be made. The vitally important dimension of fairness—that everybody was treated equally by the system—was questioned. Sweden moved into the lower left box of Table 3.1 during this period. The tax reform of the century set out to reset the fairness of the system. Whether the problems with the system were actually as severe as critics suggested, or whether the tax reform really solved all the system's problems remains uncertain. The reform undoubtedly broadened the tax base; however, the main critique against the reform was that it lowered taxes for high-income earners.

The SAP carefully considered how taxes were framed. The first decades after the war were mainly devoted to establishing a discourse in which taxation was connected to the welfare state. Thus, the party spent a lot of time making sure that the output of the welfare system was evident to the population. The taxation contract was made clear to citizens in terms of redistribution, which did not change during this time. In fact, the strong support for the welfare state made it difficult for the center-right government in the 1970s to lower taxes. The public sector became a debated issue within neoliberal and conservative groups in the 1980s (Boréus 1994: ch. 4); however, for the SAP, redistribution was not considered to be the problem, even though some critical voices were raised within the party. The public debate did not indicate that citizens perceived redistribution as unfair either; on the contrary, most research demonstrates that support for the welfare state was very strong in the 1980s (Svallfors 1989; 1996).

It is possible, however, to discern such tendencies in recent times. In the election campaign in 2006, the center-right parties launched the concept of "the outsiders" (*utanförskapet*) (Dahlberg and Sahlgren 2014), those excluded from the labor market, and claimed that this growing group constituted a major problem for Sweden. On the other hand, they pointed out, the labor force, those *included* in the labor market, should be better rewarded for their labor. Thus, after winning the election, the center-right parties implemented several tax credits for earned income (*jobbskatteavdrag*) between 2006 and 2014, and simultaneously made cutbacks in social insurance programs. Pitting one group against another in this way raised the question of fair redistribution: Why should those who work pay for those who do not? Even if support for the welfare state is still very strong, the center-right government of 2006–14 provided evidence that it is possible to win elections on tax reductions and cutbacks in the welfare state (cf. the upper right box in Table 3.1).

Within the SAP, taxes are still regarded as an act of solidarity. From a financial perspective, it is necessary to include everyone in tax payments in order to finance the welfare state; however, this principle is also a way of building solidarity in society. If everybody pays, then everybody is also entitled to the fruits of the welfare state. Research indicates that paying taxes is tightly connected to contributing to society; without the ability to pay taxes, people do not perceive themselves as fully worthy citizens (Jacobsson and Björklund Larsen 2010). From this point of view, taxes have become more than just a means to finance the welfare state.

References

Primary Sources
Ds Fi (1983.16), *Vissa ändringar i taxeringsförfarandet: delbetänkande.* Stockholm: Liber-Förlag/Allmänna förl.
Hedborg, A. (2016), Interview in Stockholm, March 4.
Lindberg, I. (2016), Interview in Stockholm, January 13.
Palme, O. (1976), *Anförande vid Handelsanställdas kongress i Malmö*, SAP, May 12, 1889/ B/08/048 Arbetarrörelsens arkiv och bibliotek, ARAB (Labour Movement's Archives and Library), Stockholm.
Partistyrelsen (1942), *Cirkulär. Kampanj för kollektivanslutning*, SAP 1889/B/05/A/03 ARAB, Stockholm.
Partistyrelsen (1950), *Protokoll fört vid socialdemokratiska partistyrelsens extrasamman-träde*, June 13, Sveriges socialdemokratiska arbetareparti/Protokoll partistyrelsen microfilm 1939–1951, ARAB, Stockholm.
Partistyrelsen (1952), *Protokoll fört vid socialdemokratiska partistyrelsens sammanträde*, October 22, Sveriges socialdemokratiska arbetareparti/Protokoll partistyrelsen microfilm 1952–1959, ARAB, Stockholm.
Partistyrelsen (1954), *Protokoll fört vid socialdemokratiska partistyrelsens sammanträde*, August 4, Sveriges socialdemokratiska arbetareparti/Protokoll partistyrelsen microfilm 1952–1959, ARAB, Stockholm.

Partistyrelsen (1956a), *Protokoll vid Partistyrelsens sammanträde i Socialdemokratiska Riksdagsgruppens förtroenderum*, April 27, Sveriges socialdemokratiska arbetareparti/ Protokoll partistyrelsen microfilm 1952–1959, ARAB, Stockholm.

Partistyrelsen (1956b), *Protokoll fört vid sammanträde med socialdemokratiska partistyrelsen*, May 8, Sveriges socialdemokratiska arbetareparti/Protokoll partistyrelsen microfilm 1952–1959, ARAB, Stockholm.

Partistyrelsen (1956c), *Protokoll fört vid sammanträde med Socialdemokartiska Partistyrelsens*, September 25, Sveriges socialdemokratiska arbetareparti/Protokoll partistyrelsen microfilm 1952–1959, ARAB, Stockholm.

Partistyrelsen (1971), *Protokoll fört vid sammanträde med socialdemokratiska partistyrelsen*, June 4, Sveriges socialdemokratiska arbetareparti/1889/A/2/A/21 ARAB, Stockholm.

Partistyrelsen (1973), *Protokoll fört vid sammanträde med socialdemokratiska partistyrelsen*, June 18, Sveriges socialdemokratiska arbetareparti/1889/A/2/A/22 ARAB, Stockholm.

Partistyrelsen (1974), *Protokoll fört vid sammanträde med socialdemokratiska partistyrelsen*, May 21, Sveriges socialdemokratiska arbetareparti/1889/A/2/A/22 ARAB, Stockholm.

Partistyrelsen (1980), *Protokoll fört vid partistyrelsesammanträde*, March 28, Sveriges socialdemokratiska arbetareparti/1889/A/2/A/27 ARAB, Stockholm.

Partistyrelsen (1981), *Protokoll gemensamt möte Riksdagsgruppen-Partistyrelsen-Landssekretariatet*, October 29, Sveriges socialdemokratiska arbetareparti/1889/A/2/A/28 ARAB, Stockholm.

Partistyrelsen (1986), *Protokoll fört vid extra sammanträde med socialdemokratiska partistyrelsen*, August 22, Sveriges socialdemokratiska arbetareparti/1889/A/2/A/33 ARAB, Stockholm.

Peralta Prieto, J. (2008), *ADB i folkbokföring och beskattning: transkript av ett vittnesseminarium vid Tekniska museet i Stockholm den 17 januari 2008*. Stockholm: KTH, Avdelningen för teknik- och vetenskapshistoria.

Riksdagen Prop. 1984/5.180, available at www.riksdagen.se.

Riksdagen Prop. 1989/90.47, available at www.riksdagen.se.

Riksdagen Prop. 1992/3.47, available at www.riksdagen.se.

SAP (1950a), *Med samlad kraft mot samma mål*, SAP 1889/B/08/018 ARAB, Stockholm.

SAP (1950b), *Rapport om vårt hushåll*, SAP 1889/B/08/018 ARAB, Stockholm.

SAP (1954), *Hur ska det bli för oss?*, SAP 1889/B/08/021 ARAB, Stockholm.

SAP (1960), *Tänk först… Välj sen*, SAP 1889/B/08/024 ARAB, Stockholm.

SAP (1988a), *Ett samtal kring den nya skatten*, SAP 1889/B/08/091 ARAB, Stockholm.

SAP (1988b), *Fiffel och båg eller skatt efter bärkraft?*, SAP 1889/B/08/091 ARAB, Stockholm.

Socialdemokraterna (1954), Skattefria Andersson, election film, www.youtube.com/watch?v=2_EWFlqDwdw.

SOU 1933, Betänkande med förslag till ändrade bestämmelser angående förbättrad deklarationskontroll och till förstärkt taxeringsorganisation m. m. Stockholm: Nord. bokh.

SOU 1969.42, *Skattebrotten*, Stockholm: Kungl. Boktryckeriet P A Norstedt & Söner.

SOU 1985.42, *Förenklad taxering: principförslag om taxering, omprövning, process m. m.: betänkande*. Stockholm: Liber/Allmänna förl.

Secondary Sources
Aftonbladet (1959), "Tre frågor till partiledarna om skatteskojet." February 15.

Aftonbladet (1979), "Skattepolitik för rika." April 10.

Agell, J., P. Englund, and J. Södersten (1996), "Tax Reform of the Century: The Swedish Experiment." *National Tax Journal* 49(4): 643–64.

Agell, J., P. Englund, and J. Södersten (1998), *Incentives and Redistribution in the Welfare State: The Swedish Tax Reform.* Basingstoke: Macmillan.

Andersson, J. G. (1976), "Budgetministerns närmaste man som vill sänka skatterna för de högavlönade." *Aftonbladet,* October 12.

Berggren, H. and L. Trägårdh (2006), *Är svensken människa?* Stockholm: Norstedts.

Bergström, V. (1969), *Den ekonomiska politiken i Sverige och dess verkningar.* Stockholm: Almqvist and Wiksell.

Bergström, V. (2007), *Rättvisa, solidaritet och anpassning: Landsorganisationens ekonomiska politik under fem årtionden.* Stockholm: Atlas.

Bergström, V. and J. Södersten (1994), "Kapitalbildningens politiska ekonomi." In B. Holmlund (ed.), *Arbete, löner och politik.* Stockholm: Publica/Fritzes, 241–62.

Blyth, M. (2001), "The Transformation of the Swedish Model: Economic Ideas, Distributional Conflict, and Institutional Change." *World Politics* 54(1): 1–26.

Blyth, M. (2002), *Great Transformations: Economic Ideas and Institutional Change in the Twentieth Century.* New York: Cambridge University Press.

Boréus, K. (1994), *Högervåg: nyliberalismen och kampen om språket i svensk debatt 1969–1989.* Stockholm: Tiden.

Dahlberg, S. and M. Sahlgren (2014), "Issue Framing and Language Use in the Swedish Blogosphere." In B. Kaal, I. Maks, and A. van Elfrinkhof (eds.), *From Text to Political Positions: Text Analysis Across Disciplines.* Amsterdam: John Benjamins, 71–92.

Ekman, G. (2003), "Några drag i den svenska skatteförvaltningens utveckling." In Riksskatteverket (ed.), *Deklarationen 100 år och andra tillbakablickar: en jubileumsbok.* Stockholm: Riksskatteverket, 7–20.

Elvander, N. (1972), *Svensk skattepolitik 1945–1970: en studie i partiers och organisationers funktioner.* Stockholm: Rabén and Sjögren.

Erlingsson, G. Ó., J. Ödalen, and E. Wångmar (2015), "Understanding Large-Scale Institutional Change." *Scandinavian Journal of History* 40(2): 195–214.

Feldt, K.-O. (1991), *Alla dessa dagar.* Stockholm: Norstedt.

Feldt, K.-O., B. Ahlqvist, and L. Engqvist (1984), *Samtal med Feldt: Berndt Ahlqvist och Lars Engqvist intervjuar finansministern.* Stockholm: Tiden.

Henrekson, M. and M. Stenkula (2015), "Swedish Taxation Since 1862: An Introduction and Overview." In M. Henrekson and M. Stenkula (eds.), *Swedish Taxation.* New York: Palgrave Macmillan, 1–33.

Jacobsson, K. and L. Björklund Larsen (2010), *Känslan för det allmänna: medborgarnas relation till staten och varandra.* Umeå: Boréa.

Jansson, J. (2012), *Manufacturing Consensus: The Making of the Swedish Reformist Working Class.* Uppsala: Acta Universitatis Upsaliensis.

Johansson, Å. (2003), "Från bläckpenna till datorhjärna." In Riksskatteverket (ed.), *Deklarationen 100 år och andra tillbakablickar: en jubileumsbok.* Stockholm: Riksskatteverket, 95–110.

Johansson, A. L. and L. Magnusson (2012), *LO: 1900-talet och ett nytt millennium.* Stockholm: Atlas.

Johansson, J. (2000), *SAF och den svenska modellen. En studie av uppbrottet från förvaltningskorporatismen 1982–91*. Uppsala: Acta Universitatis Upsaliensis.

Johansson, O. (2003), "Från undersåte till kund." In Riksskatteverket (ed.), *Deklarationen 100 år och andra tillbakablickar: en jubileumsbok*. Stockholm: Riksskatteverket, 111–18.

Levi, M. (1988), *Of Rule and Revenue*. Berkeley, CA: University of California Press.

Levi, M. (1991), "Are there Limits to Rationality?" *European Journal of Sociology/Archives Européennes de Sociologie* 32(01): 130–41.

Levi, M. and E. Kiser (2015), "Spend and Tax: Why and When States Underprovide Public Goods." http://cpd.berkeley.edu/wp-content/uploads/2015/01/Spend_and_Tax_Jan_25_2015.pdf.

Lewin, L. (2002), *Ideologi och strategi: svensk politik under 130 år*. Stockholm: Norstedts juridik.

Lindgren, A. (1976), "Pomperipossa i Monsimanien." *Expressen*, March 10.

Lindström, S. and S. Nordin (1979), "Betalade ingen skatt på sina inkomster." *Aftonbladet*, January 18.

Löwnertz, S. (1983), *De svenska skatternas historia: [en artikelserie av Susanne Löwnertz tidigare publicerad i RSV Info åren 1982–83]*. Stockholm: Riksskatteverket (RSV).

Malmer, H. (2003), "Granskningen av inkomstdeklarationer under 100 år." In Riksskatteverket (ed.), *Deklarationen 100 år och andra tillbakablickar: en jubileumsbok*. Stockholm: Riksskatteverket, 21–58.

Medieakademin/Sifo (2015), *Förtroendebarometer 2015*. Stockholm.

Myrdal, G. (1978), "Dags för ett bättre skattesystem!" *Ekonomisk debatt* 7.

Nordin, S. and S. Lindström (1977), "Barnen som äger aktier." *Aftonbladet*, April 22.

North, D. C. (1990), *Institutions, Institutional Change and Economic Performance*. Cambridge: Cambridge University Press.

Riksrevisionen (2010), *Enhetlig beskattning?* Stockholm.

Riksskatteverket (2003), *Deklarationen 100 år och andra tillbakablickar: en jubileumsbok*. Stockholm: Riksskatteverket.

Roosma, F., W. van Oorschot, and J. Gelissen (2015), "A Just Distribution of Burdens? Attitudes Toward the Social Distribution of Taxes in 26 Welfare States." *International Journal of Public Opinion Research* 28(3): 376–400.

Scholz, J. T. (2003), "Contractual Compliance and the Federal Income Tax System." *Washington University Journal of Law & Policy* 13: 139–203.

Schön, L. (2007), *En modern svensk ekonomisk historia: tillväxt och omvandling under två sekel*. Stockholm: SNS förlag.

Steinmo, S. (1993), *Taxation and Democracy: Swedish, British and American Approaches to Financing the Modern State*. New Haven, CT: Yale University Press.

Steinmo, S. (2002), "Globalization and Taxation: Challenges to the Swedish Welfare State." *Comparative Political Studies* 35(7): 839–62.

Stenkula, M., D. Johansson, and G. Du Rietz (2014), "Marginal Taxation on Labour Income in Sweden from 1862 to 2010." *Scandinavian Economic History Review* 62(2): 163–87.

Stridh, A. and L. Wittberg (2015), *Från fruktad skattefogde till omtyckt servicemyndighet*. Solna: Skatteverket.

Svallfors, S. (1989), *Vem älskar välfärdsstaten?: attityder, organiserade intressen och svensk välfärdspolitik*. Lund: Arkiv.

Svallfors, S. (1996), *Välfärdsstatens moraliska ekonomi: välfärdsopinionen i 90-talets Sverige*. Umeå: Boréa.

Thalén, L. (1979), "Nu måste det bli arbetarnas år." *Social-Demokraten*, September 12.

Thärnström, B. (2003), "Broschyren Dags att deklarera under 30 år." In Riksskatteverket (ed.), *Deklarationen 100 år och andra tillbakablickar: en jubileumsbok*. Stockholm: Riksskatteverket, 119–28.

Therner, B. (1974), "Det fattiga får betala de rikas skatteavdrag." *Aftonbladet*, October 18.

Timmons, J. F. (2005), "The Fiscal Contract: States, Taxes, and Public Services." *World Politics* 57(4): 530–67.

Trägårdh, L. (2010), "Rethinking the Nordic Welfare State Through a Neo-Hegelian Theory of State and Civil Society." *Journal of Political Ideologies* 15(3): 227–39.

Part III
Italy

4

Tax Evasion in Italy

A God-Given Right?

Josef Hien

Introduction

In 1814, an angry mob stormed Giuseppe Prina's house in Milan (Grab 1998). The mob threw Prina out of the first-floor window and dragged him, heavily injured, through the city streets. Outraged people lining the streets stabbed him to death. Prina was the finance minister and first tax collector of the Kingdom of Italy, a satellite state that Napoleon created in Northern Italy after conquering the country. In 2012, almost exactly two centuries later, two bombs exploded in front of the Agenzia delle Entrate in Livorno, the state agency responsible for tax collection. Later in the same week a mob attacked another Agenzia delle Entrate facility. Building and staff had to be protected by a massive deployment of riot police.[1] It was a violent reaction to Mario Monti, the new prime minister, announcing a crackdown on tax evaders.

With an estimated €200 billion evaded in 2013 (27 percent of GDP), Italy is at the top when it comes to tax evasion in Western Europe.[2] Eighty percent of Italians believe that their fellow citizens evade taxes, a number that is only surpassed in Western Europe by the Greeks. In fact, "Italians from all social groups often describe themselves as a people of cynics, extreme individuals who do not care about the public good, opportunistic with clientelistic propensities, untrustworthy if not altogether liars" (Patriarca 2010: 4). Scholars such as Robert Putnam and Edward Banfield have described this as *amoral familism* and cultural arguments of this type have become ever more popular amongst students of tax evasion.[3] The low tax compliance rate of Italians is attributed to their lack of tax morale.

The "Willing to Pay?" experiments raised doubts about explanations in line with the amoral familism thesis. In experimental settings Italians are less likely to cheat with their taxes than citizens of other countries and they are less likely to cheat one another. Furthermore, if they cheat, they "fudge"; they only cheat a little, not wholesale like their British and Swedish counterparts.

To explain this, the chapter rethinks the cultural argument about tax morale in Italy. It focuses on religion, a constitutive item of culture. Despite declining church attendance and affiliation, the Catholic Church is still the most powerful moral institution in Italy. The chapter argues that the predestination model embodied in Catholicism (in contrast to Protestant and reformed Protestant models) has some inbuilt features, like forgiveness, indulgences, and repentance, that make fudging morally acceptable. Through a historical-sociological analysis the chapter shows that these religio-sociological features of Catholicism became especially accentuated in the Italian case due to the severity of the Church–state conflict during Italian unification in the nineteenth century. The negative perception of Italians of their state has been formed by the deep conflict between Church and state that emerged during the Napoleonic occupation of Italy and reached its peak with Italian unification in the late nineteenth century. To the Vatican, territorial integration of the Italian nation state posed an existential threat, both at the political level (loss of territory) and at the spiritual level (diffusion of liberalism). From unification onwards the Vatican did all it could to harm the legitimacy of the Italian state.

This chapter follows this process from the Napoleonic invasion to the end of World War II and shows that the Vatican was highly successful in delegitimizing the Italian state and with it its right to tax. The Italian experience stands in sharp contrast to the Swedish and the UK cases where the Church entered into symbiosis with the state during the nation-building process. In Sweden and the UK the Church's legitimacy, social anchoring, and information were used to extract taxes, sometimes even with priests as tax collectors. None of this happened in Italy. In contrast, in Italy priests sometimes legitimized evasion. The willingness of Italians to pay their taxes still suffers today from the Church–state conflict.[4]

The chapter will first give an insight into the magnitude of tax evasion in Italy and show how national discourse connects it to the centuries-old debate about the Italian character. The second part discusses the connection between religion and tax morale, and sketches out the evasive tendencies of different Christian denominations. The third part analyzes the interaction between doctrine and Church–state conflicts and how they strengthened in Italy, first during the Napoleonic occupation and later during the nation-building process in the late nineteenth century. The fourth part examines the partial relaxation of Church–state conflict during the fascist dictatorship and in the immediate postwar period, and discusses its impact on tax morale. The Conclusion provides a brief summary of the chapter.

Tax Evasion in Italy

Yearly tax evasion in Italy throughout the 2000s varied between €170 billion and €240 billion. This is ten times higher than the US evasion rate (Bame-Aldred et al. 2013: 390; Chiarini, Marzano, and Schneider 2009: 279). In international rankings Italy is usually found at the top, surpassed in Western Europe only by Greece (Zhang et al. 2016).

Putting tax evasion in Italy into historical perspective is hard. Comprehensive timelines on evasion have existed only since the 1980s and the historiography on taxation in Italy is thin.[5] Tax evasion was high during the liberal period (1871–1922) and during fascism (1922–43). This we can derive from the frequency of tax revolts and tax protests across the peninsula (Riall 2008). Evasion rates declined at the beginning of the first republic (1945–92), but started to increase in the 1970s and reached a peak in the 1980s (Marigliani and Pisani 2006: 13, 16). Rates decreased in the 1990s but increased again during the early 2000s (Santoro 2010: 31).

In percentage terms this means that during the 1970s between 15 and 20 percent of Italians evaded taxes while the rate climbed to 26 percent in the 1980s. In the 1990s, tax evasion fell again, hovering between 15 and 20 percent. Workers employed in manufacturing evade very little, whereas the highest evasion rates can be found among the self-employed (Chiri and Sestito 2014: 38, 41; Marino and Zizza 2010). Little evasion can be observed in the construction and industrial sectors. The severity of evasion becomes obvious when we consider that the Italian state annually collects only a total of €350 billion while losing €250 billion through evasion (D'Attoma 2016).

What makes tax evasion such a widespread phenomenon in Italy? The discourse on this subject follows the general debates on the determinants of tax evasion. Economists argue that the reasons lie in the lax controls and the soft legal penalties for evaders in Italy (Manestra 2010; Santoro and Fiorio 2011: 103). Psychologists think that Italians evade because they perceive taxation as unfair since they do not get much in return for their payments to the state (Cannari and D'Alessio 2007: 31; Chiarini, Marzano, and Schneider 2009: 275). Behavioral economists point to strong social multiplier effects.

If one asks Italians why they evade taxes, they primarily say that they evade because everyone else does so (Cannari and D'Alessio 2007: 31; Galbiati and Zanella 2012). A distant second is the reason that Italians would be more likely to pay taxes if they had the feeling that the state would spend their money more wisely. Much lower in the ranking come issues such as the soft penalties for evasive behavior, the complexity of the tax rules, and the unlikeliness of being caught. A total of 87.1 percent of all Italians think that their fellow citizens evade taxes (Cannari and D'Alessio 2007: 37).

Cultural approaches have become ever more frequent in the literature on tax evasion in recent years (Torgler 2006). Scholars have identified diverging national "tax morals" across countries. Summing up a series of experiments Lewis and his collaborators conclude that "given the similarities between the tax systems of the UK and Italy" the differences can be attributed "at least partly" to cultural factors (Lewis et al. 2009: 438). In the literature on tax evasion it has become ever more commonplace that "culture envelopes attitudes towards tax compliance and evasion" (Bame-Aldred et al. 2013: 434).

Culture also seems to explain evasion in the Italian case. If we look at the centuries-old debate about the Italian character, we find a negative consensus prevailing that describes Italian civic culture as "far from flattering" (Patriarca 2013: 4; see also Bollati 1972). Italians themselves are convinced that "their character is faulty, and that this faultiness even explains much of the social and political problems of their country today" (Patriarca 2013: 5). As early as the eighteenth century travelers passing through Italy on their Grand Tour described the Italian character as "morally corrupt" (Patriarca 2013: 20). They were frequently seconded by Italian observers. Carlo Pilatini wrote in 1770 that his people were "lazy, timid, full of vices, and inclined to superstition" (cited in Patriarca 2013: 21).

This negative framing of the Italian character intensified in the run-up to unification in the nineteenth century. It was adopted by Italians of all political colors. The clerico-nationalist Vincenzo Gioberti wrote in 1846 in *Del Primato Morale E Civile Degli Italiani* that "[t]he greatest of all evil in Italy, I repeat, is the voluntary decline of national genius, the weakening of patriotic spirits, the excessive love of money and pleasure, the frivolity of customs, the slavery of intellects, the imitation of foreign things, the bad ordering of education, of public and private discipline" (cited in Patriarca 2013: 25). Giuseppe Mazzini, the famous leftist national revolutionary, described in 1832 "our mortal plague" as "the innate distrust of leaders, and the perennial suspicion of betrayals" (cited in Patriarca 2013: 34) and the liberal conservative nationalist icon Massimo D'Azeglio saw his fellow citizens as "a people heavily corrupted" that needed to be "reeducated" (cited in Patriarca 2013: 56). In 1878, eight years after Italy had been unified, Antonio Reale reflected that "it became fashionable to assert that the Italians [were] a people of little character, indifferent, slothful, skeptical, corrupt, dissimulating" (cited in Patriarca 2013: 67). The British journalist Tobias Jones assesses in his popular book *The Dark Heart of Italy* (2003: 17) that "[f]ew countries have citizens with such an 'each to his own' mentality, or so much *menefreghismo*, I don't careism (signaled with the back of the fingers thrown forward from the throat to the chin)."[6] Social scientists like Putnam and Banfield coined terms such as *amoral familism*, *generalized*, and *limited morality* to describe the Italian character.

The findings of the European Research Council (ERC) project, "Willing to Pay?", go against the above-described ascriptions. "Willing to Pay?" conducted experiments with more than 531 participants across Britain (Oxford, London, Exeter) and Italy (Milan, Bologna, Rome). Both countries have similar tax systems but differ in their tax evasion rates. Britain has an intermediate evasion rate, compared to other OECD countries, while Italy's evasion rate is extraordinarily high (twice the British rates). The expectation was that Italians would be also less willing to pay taxes in the experiments.

Surprisingly, "Willing to Pay?" found that in the laboratory setting British participants were more likely to cheat with their taxes than Italian subjects. While Italians cheat the state more in the real world, they cheat less in the experiments. This finding remained constant even when the tax rate, the severity of punishment, the probability of being audited, and the redistribution of the collected tax money were varied. In the experiment, Southern and Northern Italians displayed almost identical behavior when confronted with the same institutions. The findings go against the thesis of *amoral familism* and against the traditional negative foreign and domestic ascriptions of the Italian character. The findings suggest that Italians have a moral problem with their state rather than a moral problem with one another.

The great Italian social theorists, anthropologists, and philosophers such as Benedetto Croce (2004), Antonio Gramsci (2010), or Carlo Tullio-Altan (2000) pin the reasons for the screwed relation between Italians and their state in the incomplete national revolution at the end of the nineteenth century. Recent historiography suggests that at the heart of the problematic relation of Italians and their state institutions lies the rampant Church–state conflict, which "dealt a devastating blow" (Riall 2008: 9) to the legitimacy of Italian state institutions from the very beginning.

In the nineteenth century a conflict over citizens' loyalty between state institutions and the Church erupted that arguably re-enforced doctrinal positions within Catholicism that facilitated evasive behavior. Religion influences individual behavior through doctrinal prescriptions that vary between different Christian denominations. However, the basic principal doctrinal provisions for individual behavior are re-enforced through Church–state relations. Doctrine and Church–state relations co-evolve (Steinmo 2010) and leave an imprint on one another. In Sweden, the state-centrism of Lutheranism became positively re-enforced through the early fusion of Church and state in the eighteenth century (Nistotskaya and D'Arcy, Chapter 2 in this volume). Subsequently, the information, social networks, personal resources, and social disciplining power of the Church could be used for tax collection. In Italy, the situation was the opposite. A bitter conflict alienated Church and state throughout the nineteenth century and led to a codification of anti-statist Catholic doctrine whose effects can still be felt today in the tax morale of Italians.

Surveys published by demos & Pi confirm that contemporary Italians trust the Church in Italy, even after a sharp decline of religious practice since the 1960s and a series of pedophilia and fiscal scandals, more than most of their state institutions. Throughout the 2000s the Church came out in the top group of institutions that Italians trust most. In 2013, the Church claimed second place, surpassed only by the police force. In a list of seventeen institutions the government occupies fifteenth place, while parliament is in fourteenth place. Political parties are bottom in seventeenth place (Diamanti 2014). Since 2013, the Pope has also been included in their surveys. He came out on top both in 2013 and 2014; 88 percent and 87 percent of Italians (Diamanti 2013; 2014 respectively) trusted the Pope, while the highest-placed political institution, the president of the Republic, could only achieve half of the consensus that he received (44 percent and 49 percent, respectively).

That the persuasive power of the Church and its historically hostile relation to the state has had an effect on the tax behavior of Italians becomes even more compelling after a look into a special feature of the Italian tax system. It confirms that Italians are more willing to give to what they identify as communitarian institutions (e.g. the Catholic Church) than to the state. Since a reform in 1985 (amended in 1998), Italians can indicate on their tax form whether they want to pay the former church tax to another religious community, to the state or continue to pay it to the Catholic Church. The so-called *"otto per mille"* (eight per thousand) law indicates that the money should be used by state or religious communities for the provision of social services. The sum stemming from the *otto per mille* tax amounted in 2012 to €1.148 billion. Despite the newly introduced freedom of choice over to whom to allocate this sum, 82.24 percent of Italian taxpayers who made use of the *otto per mille* option continued to attribute the money to the Catholic Church. In contrast, only 13.35 percent of Italians gave their money to the state. The percentage of contributions to the state has fallen (1990: 22.31; 2000: 10.28; 2014: 13.35), while the Church share has increased (1990: 76.17; 2000: 87.25; 2014: 82.24).[7]

Not only surveys and tax data but also individual accounts point toward a connection between the Italians' tax evasion and the relationship between Church and state: During the *Tangentopoli* corruption scandals of the early 1990s the journalist Pino Nicotri disguised himself as a corrupt Christian Democratic politician and visited several priests in different parts of Italy in order to ask for advice whether to collaborate with the magistrates and tell them about systematic corruption and tax evasion of politicians. Despite the general call of the Milanese Cardinal Martini to collaborate with the state authorities most priests advised "in terms which emphasized private repentance over public justice, private and family duties over public ones" (Ginsborg 2001: 134). In Naples a priest told the journalist, "there is the justice of men, but there is a superior justice! . . . And then think of the consequences of what it [the exposure of his corrupt practices] would mean for your family" (Ginsborg 2001: 134). Tax evasion was a private matter in which the state had no say.

Religion and Tax Morale

The literature on tax morale argues that "religiosity has a significant positive effect on tax morale, even if other determinants such as corruption, trustworthiness, demographic and economic factors are controlled for" (Torgler 2006: 83). The higher the religiosity, the smaller is the propensity to evade taxes.

What the empirics show on the individual level does not seem to hold on the aggregated level. In continental Europe the countries with the highest religiosity—Greece, Italy, and Romania—are those with the highest evasion rates (Table 4.1). There is also a denominational split: in Protestant countries such as Sweden and the UK evasion is low; in Catholic countries such as Italy it is high. Evasion is highest in Orthodox countries like Greece and Romania.

This is surprising considering that from a Weberian perspective Orthodox Christianity is considered to be the most solidarity-oriented branch of Christianity, followed closely by Catholicism, considered to be strongly communitarian. In mainline Lutheranism and Calvinism the incentives for individualistic behavior are much stronger. Weber (1988: 96) sees a "deep suspicion towards the best friend" embedded in ascetic Protestant doctrine because "only God should be the man of confidence." We would expect ascetic Protestants, whose faith provides incentives for individualistic behavior, to be more inclined

Table 4.1. Country, confession, and belief in God as a percentage of population (2005) and size of the shadow economy (1999–2010)

Country (confession)	Belief in God (%)	Size of the shadow economy (% of GDP)
Romania (Orthodox)	90	28.4
Greece (Orthodox)	90	27
Italy (Catholic)	74	26.9
Sweden (Lutheran)	23	18.6
UK (Anglican)	38	12.5

Sources: Eurobarometer (2005) and Schneider and Enste (2013).

toward evasive behavior. However, in Catholic and Orthodox nations evasive behavior is far more widespread.

The answer might be that the individualism of ascetic Protestantism was countered by rigid morals and social disciplining mechanisms. These disciplining techniques were not only individual and inward looking but were also pushed for the congregation as a whole. Calvin ordered that each congregation should have a consistory to supervise "the morals of the congregation." The consistory "interviewed individual church members several times a year in order to ascertain whether they were fit to receive communion. Errant members—for example, drunkards, adulterers, wife beaters, and *tax cheats*—were excluded from communion" (Gorski 2003: 21, emphasis added). Disciplining was not solely left to the consistory but "each individual was not only made responsible for his or her own conduct but was charged to keep a watchful eye over other members of the congregation and to remonstrate with those who strayed from the path of righteousness." However, this was not enough for Calvin. He also wanted to transmit discipline beyond the congregation. "If the ungodly could not be saved, he reasoned, then they could at least be compelled to obey God's laws. Together, church and magistrate were to work towards the establishment of a 'Christian polity' (*res publica christiana*) to affect a thoroughgoing Christianization of social life" (Gorski 2003: 21). In a similar vein, the skeptic view of the individual in mainline Protestantism led to an appreciation of the state and its institutions because humans are "saints and sinners at the same time, and that's why they need to be under an institutional order that disciplines the sinner" (Reuter 2010). Catholicism has such disciplining elements only within and for the hierarchy of the Catholic Church.

The success of Protestant states such as Prussia or the Netherlands that had imported reformed Protestant bureaucrats in the seventeenth century led to an emulation of "disciplinary revolutions" (Gorski 2003) in Catholic countries during the counter-reformation. However, these were arguably bound to fail, due to the softer take of Catholicism on discipline and inner-worldly asceticism. In Catholicism it is not discipline but doing good works that brings you closer to heaven. Donations and alms should go to civil society or church charities, not to the state. Furthermore, the Catholic sinner has the possibility to repent or to buy indulgences. Hence, being not entirely accurate on one's tax declaration (fudging) can be corrected through paying alms or confessing.

However, since individuals pay taxes to the state it is not only religious doctrine that provides the ethical frame for their actions but also how this doctrine perceives the state. This is reciprocal, however, since how a state is perceived by a religion is informed by the severity of the Church–state conflict. Hence, we can only understand the impact of religion on taxation if we analyze how state institutions and church doctrine co-evolve throughout history.

The state- and nation-building process sets the stage for the relationship between religion and state. In Sweden, the early fusion of Church and state led to a mutual reinforcing of the state-centric view of Protestantism. The state was seen as something good, priests were paid by the state, and they were used for tax collection. Priests became public servants and their payroll depended on the tax base of the state (Nistotskaya and D'Arcy, Chapter 2 in this volume).

In the Catholic world, things were different. The Vatican already had a state and a territory. The theocracy occupied one-third of the Italian peninsula. The nation- and state-builders took the territory and cut religious prerogatives. This alienated the Church. And there was a second problem: nation- and state-builders in Italy were Liberals, so all they stood for was anathema to the Catholic Church. The ideas of liberal state-builders and the Catholic Church co-evolved in response to one another in light of the heavy Church–state conflict and the outcome was detrimental for tax morale in Italy.

Church and State in Nineteenth-Century Italy

The alienation between Church and state, and state and citizens in Italy started with the Napoleonic occupation. Following the French Revolution, Napoleon crossed the Alps and occupied Northern Italy. Napoleon established two satellite states: the Kingdom of Italy in the North and the Kingdom of Naples in the South. The rest of the peninsula (the states around the Apennine spine) became *départements réunis* incorporated into French territory and under French rule (the former territories of the House of Savoy, Genoa, Parma, Piacenza, and Tuscany). In 1808, Napoleon occupied Rome and subsequently the main territories of the Papal States (Ancona, Macerata, Fermo, and Urbino).

With occupation Napoleon unleashed a "War on Religion" (Broers 2004). Napoleon eliminated ecclesiastical privileges. He confiscated and sold Church land, introduced civil marriage and divorce, introduced freedom of religion, dismissed religious orders, and claimed the right to nominate bishops (Grab 2003). In 1809, the Pope excommunicated Napoleon. For centuries, the Church had been a source of information and a tool for social control for Italian political leaders who collaborated with the Vatican. Now a French senior official commented that the Church's use of "the conscience to manipulate human passion" made it "ever more dangerous." After the excommunication of Napoleon "the rupture with the church turned into an active source of fear for the French" (Broers 2003: 707). The situation was exacerbated further when the Pope was taken into confinement. However, in Italy, unlike in France, Napoleon failed in taming the Church. The historian Broers called the relationship between Napoleon and the Pope a "story of a Napoleonic defeat to rival that of 1812 in Russia, or indeed Waterloo" (Broers 2004: 6).

Napoleon did not only have pope and clergy pinned against him but soon also the rest of the population, especially the lower social strata. A principal reason was Napoleon's regime of fiscal extraction. Napoleon needed money and resources for his extended European military campaigns. The satellite states and the *départements réunis* were used for financial extraction and for filling the ranks of the Napoleonic army. Between 1802 and 1811, Napoleon doubled the expenses of the Kingdom of Italy. In 1804, half of the budget went to the Italian army, which was integrated into the Napoleonic army, and these contributions increased steadily between 1804 and 1811.

To cover the rising costs and the increasing demands from France, Giuseppe Prina, the finance minister of the Kingdom of Italy, enacted a series of reforms to extract revenue and they proved highly successful. Italy, in comparison to other continental European countries, had one of the most modern tax and finance systems at the beginning of the nineteenth century (Grab 1998: 128).

However, the extraction of fiscal resources and the streamlining of the taxation and conscription apparatus had negative effects for the population. The selling of Church land had resulted in land concentration and the countryside became increasingly enclosed (Grab 1995: 42). The result was a huge landless proletariat of day laborers, cut off from their traditional subsistence farming.

The Napoleonic thirst for territorial conquest in Europe was forever increasing financial demands on the Italian satellite states. The "French financial pressure resulted in an increasingly heavy tax burden that threatened to alienate the Italian population and undermine political and social stability" (Broers 2001: 155; Grab 1998: 128).

Giuseppe Prina, the finance minister and Napoleon's man for tax collection, had to increase taxes but disproportionately targeted the lower social strata, as landowners were essential for the political backing of the regime (Grab 1998: 133). The *tassa personale* (an income tax paid by all male citizens between 15 and 60) was augmented and *dazio consume* (indirect consumption taxes) on products such as candles, flour, hay, and vegetables were introduced in walled cities. The prices for salt and tobacco, both state monopolies, were increased (Grab 1995: 43).

However, to fulfill Napoleon's needs it was not enough to increase taxation. Taxes also had to be collected. Giuseppe Prina reformed the collection system by creating the Guardia di Finanza and introducing a highly centralized and effective system with strong incentives for tax collectors to bring in taxes. Collectors were appointed through public tenders. They received renewable, three-year contracts with competitive remuneration, but had to leave a deposit at the beginning of their term. The tax collector was liable for any uncollected money at the end of his term; what he did not collect was subtracted from his deposit. After the reform, in 1808, only 1.3 percent of personal tax remained uncollected (Grab 1998: 140).

Landholders paid their taxes because they had a favorable fiscal contract with the regime: little taxation in exchange for political support. But personal taxes were a problem. Responsibility for the collection lay with the *comuni*, which often turned a blind eye to tax evasion. The result was that in 1811, "out of a population of 5,668,457 tax was paid by 1,542,998" (Grab 1998: 134).

The tax increases, the disproportionality of the tax burden on the lower social strata, and the rigid enforcement of tax collection made the Napoleonic reforms unpopular. In 1809 Prina introduced a new milling tax, but it was the straw that broke the camel's back. The milling tax was incredibly complicated and bureaucratic and people started to revolt—tax collectors' houses were ransacked and tax records burned. "The authorities also ordered the clergy to preach against crime" (Grab 1995: 48), but the regime had alienated the Church too much. Instead, "many lower clerics defied the authorities and supported law violators" (Grab 1995: 57), and sometimes priests were directly involved in the revolts. The Napoleonic regime answered with harsh repression and 2,000 people were killed in the year 1809 alone. The population was alienated from the tax system and the state by the ever-increasing tax burden; the low proportion of these tax revenues assigned to public expenditure (84.7 million lire of the budget was allocated to the army; see Table 4.2); the disproportionate taxation system (including low tax rates for landowners); and the increasingly coercive tax extraction apparatus. In 1814, Giuseppe Prina, the finance minister of the Napoleonic satellite regime and the mastermind behind the tax system and extraction apparatus, was thrown out of the window of his house in Milan by an angry mob and brutally killed.

Table 4.2. Budgetary allocations in millions of lire in 1811

Departments	Expenses
War and tax for the French Army	84.7
Interior	16.6
Finance	3.1
Treasury	2.0
Justice	7.6
Foreign Relations	0.8
Religion	0.2
Public debt	21.0

Source: Grab 1998: 130

Risorgimento and Anti-Risorgimento

The spiral of alienation between centralizing state authorities and the population did not end once Napoleon was defeated. After the fall of Napoleon, the Congress of Vienna restored the Papal States and the other eight pre-invasion states. Nevertheless, the Napoleonic legacy, as hated as it was for its repressive character, had also left an enduring modernizing imprint on Italy. The "Napoleonic administration provided a model to Italian states during the post-Napoleonic period" (Grab 1995: 64). Moreover, the spirit of the French Revolution that Napoleon had brought to Italy had left a mark on Italian society beyond his fall. Liberal ideas started to grow and flourish, first in debating clubs and later in preliminary political associations across the peninsula. The Risorgimento had started and the national-liberal movement grew rapidly. Even in the Papal States, Gregory XVI enacted a series of liberal reforms in the 1840s.

The spread of a series of revolutions across the peninsula in 1848 put a sudden end to the liberal tendencies within the Vatican. Piedmont enacted the Statuto Albertino, the first liberal constitution in Italy, which foresaw a separation of state and Church, and this forced the Vatican to embark on a wholesale counter-revolution. The Anti-Risorgimento started. It was a war over public opinion and moral high ground, supported by novels as well as sophisticated socio-economic treaties that even included provisions for a just Catholic taxation regime, to counter the appeal of the Statuto and delegitimize liberalism.[8]

Antonio Bresciani, a Jesuit novelist, was recruited to lead the literary attack on the liberal forces that had started to unify Italy. In the 1840s and 1850s he published a trilogy (*L'Ebreo di Verona*, *Della Repubblica Romana*, and *Lionello*) that established a wider discourse against secularist forces and framed the Church's fight against the national-liberal movement in an exciting liberal format (murder, rape, love, and betrayal were all central themes in the novels). Chapters from the books were published as preview and serial stories in *La Civiltà Cattolica*, a Jesuit periodical—at that time the paper with the widest circulation in Italy. The Risorgimento was portrayed as the result of a "satanistically inspired conspiracy by secret societies" (Dickie 2017). Liberals and nationalists would bring "moral corruption, political disorder and devil worship" (Dickie 2017: 3). The secularism and liberalism of the French Revolution and the Risorgimento were connected to Protestantism and pinned to the heinous motives of a foreign occupation and invasion (Logan 1997: 55).

Indeed, the Risorgimento was a very popular movement in Protestant nations. In the United States and Great Britain, Garibaldi, Mazzini, and other central figures of the Risorgimento were worshipped because they were perceived as heroes in a fight against the "tyrannical and corrupt power of the papacy" and "what they saw as the superstitious and non-Christian practices of the Roman Catholic Church" (Raponi 2011: 1186). In return, the Jesuits portrayed the Risorgimento as a foreign Protestant invasion, alien and unable to grasp the concept of the real Italian society and therefore bound to fail (Romani 2013: 30).

The liberal ideal state and nation was portrayed as a mechanistic, soulless "Moloch" (Romani 2013) made up of isolated egoistic individuals and juxtaposed to the organic interpretation of a Catholic Italy made up of "ascending conflations of cellular structures, with the family as the primary cell and local communities as intermediate components" (Logan 1997: 55), where everyone is connected through brotherhood, love, and the concept of charity (Romani 2013). The *paese reale* (the moral majority of Catholic citizens) was idealized against the *paese legale* (liberal rule of law and institutions). *La Civiltà Cattolica* called the new liberal regime a "guasto ideale permanente" (permanent idealist damage) of "edonismo" (hedonism) and "paganismo" (paganism) (Romani 2013: 7).

From the 1850s onwards a dense network of Catholic thinkers was working hard on delegitimizing the territorially growing liberal state of Piedmont. On the other side, moderate liberals tried to include Catholic symbols in their nation-building agenda and to formulate a symbiosis between *patria* and Catholicism.[9] This was encountered with fierce resistance by the extremist Catholic camp, the so-called *ultramontanes* and intransigents. Between the 1840s and 1870s these groups developed a state theory that included a decisive theocratic element. There could be no Italian state without supremacy of the Pope over it (Romani 2014).

The ecclesiastical reforms in Piedmont and in the territories that were subsumed by Piedmont from the 1850s onwards fueled the Church–state conflict. A series of wars between 1860 and 1870 took away ever more territory from the Pope. In 1870, the Papal States had shrunk from one-third of the Italian peninsula to the city walls of Rome. When territorial unification was finalized in 1871, the Pope had lost Rome and found himself confined to the walls of the Vatican City.

If the Church could no longer have its territory, then the Italian state should not have full control over Italians either. For his political counterstrike the Pope crafted powerful weapons that aimed to destabilize the new nation state. From the 1860s onwards the Catholic Church "did all it could to rob the Italian state of its legitimacy" (Kertzer 2000: 205).

To harm the state, two myths were crafted that still endure today. The new state was framed as an illegitimate usurper state (myth number one) and the Pope was portrayed as being held prisoner by the new state in the Vatican (myth number two) (Kertzer 2000: 410). The two myths were flanked by three sets of doctrinal reforms.

First, Pius IX issued the encyclical *Quanta Cura* in 1864 containing the *Syllabus of Errors*, which "upheld the temporal power of his Holiness, denounced liberalism as an anathema, and made Catholicism incompatible with nationalism" (Kelikian 2002: 46). The syllabus argued fiercely against the abolition of the "temporal power of which the Apostolic See is possessed" (Pope Pius IX 1864: 76) and declared it also wrong that "[i]n the case of conflicting laws enacted by the two powers, the civil law prevails" (Pope Pius IX 1864: 42). Pollard comments that "[g]iven the strictures of the Syllabus, 'Liberal Catholic' seemed almost a contradiction in terms" (Pollard 2008: 28).

The second step was the creation of papal infallibility. In an internally highly contested move, the Pope strengthened his grip on the Church apparatus. This did not only go against the liberal zeitgeist but also against the strong resistance of some of the approximately 600 cardinals that came to Rome. It gave Pius IX unprecedented centralized powers over Catholicism.

A third important doctrinal innovation of Pius IX was the *Non Expedite* (Kertzer 2000: 193; Pollard 2008: 22). The Pope instructed that Catholics should abstain from any political involvement. Catholics could neither run for public office, nor elect politicians in the Italian state.

In a society where Catholic religion encompassed virtually the whole population, which had hosted the power center of Christianity for over a millennium, and where it was still necessary to bring a recommendation letter from the local parish priest in order to get a job in the 1950s, the Pope's proclamations did not go unnoticed. No ordinary Italians would give the Italian state their loyalty, unless they wanted to risk excommunication. Italy witnessed the emergence of mutually exclusive identities and loyalties from which the willingness to pay taxes suffered.[10]

Just Catholic taxation

The Anti-Risorgimento was not only a popular war over hearts and minds but also led to a specific reformulation of Catholic socio-economic thinking in Italy. Central to this was the Jesuit Taparelli d'Azeglio, who developed an alternative to the liberal, rationalist, political economic thinking. In a series of articles published between 1850 and 1870 in *La Civiltà Cattolica*, the periodical with the widest circulation in Italy in the second half of the nineteenth century, he worked out a counterproposal to the liberal state in which a Catholic idea of taxation played a key role (Romani 2013).

The baseline of Taparelli's critique was that the new Italian state taxed too much and redistributed only to itself. Tax revenue was eaten up by the constant expansion of state tasks and by its administrative and political elites. Little was left for the people.

Excessive taxation without redistribution was not only a practical and administrative problem but also a theocratic problem. The excessive taxation of the liberal state, so Taparelli said, put the whole Catholic model of ascendance and social cohesion at risk. The rich, if taxed too much, would refrain from giving alms. This would lead to a collapse of the Catholic poor relief system (*opere pie*) which was based on alms-giving by the higher social strata (Ferrera 1993). It would forestall the classic Catholic reciprocal way to heaven where the rich go to heaven for good works (alms-giving) and the beggar assures his ascendance by praying for him.

Taparelli d'Azeglio discussed the negative effects of the centralization of the tax system in detail. Taxation should be locally administered and the tax burden should be locally assessed (Romani 2013: 19). He railed against the "limitless increase of imposts, enacted without scruples and payed by the lowest social classes."[11] New assessments of property that the new state wanted to introduce for taxation such as the cadaster were marked as the result of the "spirito geometrizzatore" (Romani 2010: 38) of the French Revolution. Taparelli pointed out that the "state of the church had lived easily without cadaster for a thousand years."[12] Instead, taxes should be assessed by "applying the book of nature" (Romani 2013: 23), by local authorities in line with the subsidiarity principle.

The Anti-Risorgimento did not only create a counterproposal to the Liberal state that went all the way down to the tax code but also railed officially against it. *La Civiltà Cattolica* never tired of "denouncing the systematic and illegitimate withdrawal from the public budget by politicians and administrators."[13] Taxation was framed as "state robbery" and for Liberatore, one of the top writers for *La Civiltà Cattolica*, "A government that robs from the church, makes its own subjects thieves" because "[t]he government says: the property of the church, belongs to the state, and therefore the citizen says the property of the state belongs to the people, and part of the people am I."[14] Leopardi, another editor of *La Civiltà Cattolica*, claimed that "[a] liberal is nothing but the slave to every guilty passion" (Romani 2014: 625). And for the Jesuit Ballerini, liberals were all "natural egoists" and therefore prone to evade and fill their pockets (Romani 2013: 34).

The domestic dispute over the right tax regime and the moral right to tax was even noticed on the international diplomatic stage. The British chargé d'affaires in Rome concluded in 1893 in a letter to the Foreign Secretary that "tax avoidance 'is not considered in this country to be dishonest action nor even an evasion of a patriotic duty'" (cited in Duggan 2007: 339). In post-unification Italy, approximately "75 per cent of all taxes went unpaid" (Duggan 2007: 339).

Reconciliation? State and Church from Mussolini to Democrazia Cristiana

Before coming to power, Mussolini was not fond of Catholicism. He was not religious, not married, and his children were named after two important heretics. He wrote a slightly blasphemous novel in his early days (*The Cardinal's Mistress*) and demanded in his first political program the confiscation of Church property (Mack-Smith 1997: 378). His major fascist ideologists—Gentile, Solmi, and Rocco—had more affinity with Catholicism but only insofar as they saw great potential in exploiting its legitimizing power for the regime (Logan 1997: 57–8).

Hence, in the early days of his rise to power, anti-clericalism prevailed within the fascist movement. The Lateran Treaties came about because Mussolini realized after 1922 that he could not govern the country without the backing of the Church (Duggan 2013: 207–8). From that point onwards he did everything to get on good terms with the Vatican (Mack-Smith 1997: 378). Mussolini married, baptized his children, and started to prepare the Lateran Treaties, which ended seventy years of diplomatic hostility that had continued since unification.

The Lateran Treaties between state and Church were enacted in 1929. They guaranteed the Church a number of strong prerogatives in religious education, the taxation of Church enterprises, and estates. The Treaties recognized the sovereignty of the Vatican and in return the Church accepted the existence of the Italian state (Mack-Smith 1997: 379).

However, when Mussolini dissolved the Catholic scout movement in 1927 against his former promise, and integrated it into the fascist youth movement, the Vatican became cautious (Mack-Smith 1997: 372). The Lateran pacts were still signed a year later but relations became frosty when Mussolini adopted German racial laws in Italy in 1938. The Vatican knew now that the regime was drifting toward totalitarianism and, following the developments in Germany, the Pope saw that the effects could become uncontrollable for the Church. The Vatican pulled the plug when a series of war defeats weakened Mussolini and led to a disassociation of the conservative Italian establishment. Mussolini was toppled and arrested, and with the Church pulling some of the strings in this operation, it positioned itself well for the coming post-regime and postwar order.

Pius XI had called Mussolini "the man sent by providence" (Clark 1996: 255). The Pope saw in the fascist dictator a man with whom the Church could reach beneficial agreements.[15] However, the relationship between fascism and Church did not go beyond self-interest. Once neither side needed the other, the relationship broke down. Catholicism did not embrace the fascist Italian state—it did not become a clerical dictatorship like Franco's Spain or Salazar's Portugal. Even with the Lateran Treaties in place the fascist state remained for Catholic thinkers only a *paese legale*, not organically anchored in the Catholic identity of the *paese reale* (Logan 1997: 55). Hence, there was no decisive drop in tax evasion (Santoro 2010: 35). Tax morale remained so low that Mussolini himself had to address the issue in a speech in 1928 where he referred to evaders as "the worst parasites of national society" (cited in Selmi 2013: 9).

The end of fascism and German occupation brought Italy its first long-lasting democratic regime.[16] The fascist experience and the World War led in Italy, as in many other continental European countries, to a steep resurgence in religiosity (Mammarella 1978). Having abandoned Mussolini early enough the Catholic Church had positioned itself well for the postwar era.[17] The newly formed Christian Democratic party (Democrazia Cristiana (DC)) became the central reference point in Italian politics. The Christian Democrats stayed in government without interruption for over fifty years, longer than any other party in a democratic state. Tax evasion rates dropped for twenty years or so, but from the 1970s onwards they started to increase again.

The party evolved out of the Catholic subcultures in the Italian North. In the white regions of Lombardy, Piedmont, and Veneto, over 80 percent of the population attended mass on a regular basis in the 1950s (in contrast to 50 percent as the national average). Social and economic life was centered around the local parish and "religion, social life and economic development all seemed closely intertwined" (Galli 1978). In the 1950s and 1960s, on literally every main square in Italian villages, a visitor would find the local office of the Christian Democrats next to the church, usually boasting an attached bar with a license to serve alcohol. Through its strong local roots, facilitated both through the Catholic clergy and the local party apparatus, the party was able to create a direct connection to Rome to make sure that local demands were met (Galli 1978). Thanks to the Christian Democrats, the Italian state was for the first time becoming locally tangible for its citizens and could achieve legitimacy (Galli 1978). This was a very different relationship between citizens and state than during the liberal period when political elites were constantly afraid of the Catholic rank and file and therefore did not extend the franchise beyond 4 percent. The DC party ensured that local Catholic communities had for the first time since Italian unification a reason to pay their taxes.

In the 1950s and 1960s tax evasion in Italy remained low, compared to the previous period. Through the DC, Catholics could hold the state accountable for what it did with their money and, given the party's coherent Catholic ideology, it could even be sure that what the state did was in line with their ethical values and political worldview. However, at the beginning of the

1970s, tax evasion rates started to climb again as the peaceful coexistence between Church and state that the Christian Democratic party had enabled came to an end.

During the 1960s traditional Catholic subcultures had already started to weaken, both through changes in society (secularization) and through a turbulent reform process in the Vatican itself (at the Second Vatican Council) (Melloni 2007), and the DC began to lose votes. To balance this, it started to shift its center of electoral gravity from the white Catholic zones in the North to Southern Italy. The weak territorial organization of the Italian Church in the South meant that the Christian Democrats here could not secure their votes through a clerico-political connection (Garelli 2007: 21). Having occupied the state for over two decades they now started to use it as a gigantic spoils machine to distribute resources to their voters in the South. The Christian Democrats changed from being a "church-sponsored party" to a "state-sponsored party" (Diamanti and Ceccarini 2007: 41; Katz and Mair 1995). The party shifted its "political array of choices on offer, from the realm of values to the domain of interests"—hence, from Catholicism to clientelism (Diamanti and Ceccarini 2007). The party quickly drifted into rampant corruption, which included deals with organized crime in the South (Guzzini 1995).

In the South, tax evasion skyrocketed as the Christian Democrats turned a blind eye to the evasive behavior of their electorate (Guzzini 1995). The consequence was a need for heavy fiscal transfers from North to South, resulting in a situation where Northern citizens became ever less likely to pay their taxes.

Conclusion

This chapter began with the findings of the "Willing to Pay?" experiments that conclude that Italians are inclined to cheat their state but not one another, but this assertion clashed with the thesis of amoral familism and other negative ascriptions of Italian character over the past century. The discussion followed up on the literature that identifies a connection between tax morale and religion, and refined its position for the Italian case. From a religious sociological analysis of Church doctrine, it followed that Catholicism, in contrast to Protestantism and Ascetic Protestantism, facilitates fudging, regarding tax evasion as only moderately immoral behavior when it comes to the state. The chapter then demonstrated how these doctrinal provisions were strongly reinforced through fierce Church–state conflict during the formation phase of the modern Italian state. The deep hostility that the unification of Italy created between state and Church led to a Catholic legitimization of cheating the state.

Notes

1. See " 'Bomba' alla sede di equitalia la procura apre un'inchiesta," *Corriere Del Veneto*, October 5, 2012, http://corrieredelveneto.corriere.it/veneto/notizie/cronaca/2012/ 5-ottobre-2012/bomba-esplode-notte-alla-sede-equitalia-2112114208054.shtml; "Tre ordigni scoppiano davanti alla sede di equitalia a Napoli," *Corriere Della Sera*, January 17, 2012, www.corriere.it/cronache/12_gennaio_17/tre-ordigni-sede-equitalia-napoli_ df7dbf88-4096-11e1-a5d2-75a8a88b1277.shtml; "Perugia, allarme bomba a sede equitalia," *Corriere Della Sera*, January 4, 2012, www.corriere.it/cronache/12_gennaio_ 04/perugia-allarme-bomba-sede-equitalia_b5fc291e-36c9-11e1-9e16-04ae59d99677. shtml; Guido Ruotolo, "Livorno, molotov contro equitalia gli inqurenti: 'Almeno Tre Autori,'" *La Stampa*, May 12, 2012, www.lastampa.it/2012/05/12/italia/cronache/livorno-molotov-contro-equitaliagli-inqurenti-almeno-tre-autori-F0vPKarjQz15cS92fs3IcM/ pagina.html.
2. Mona Chalabi, "Tax Evasion: How Much Does It Cost?," *Guardian*, September 27, 2013, www.theguardian.com/news/datablog/2013/sep/27/tax-evasion-how-much-does-it-cost-a-country; " 'Evasione Incompatibile Con La Democrazia.' Befera All'attacco (con Saccomanni)," *Corriere Della Sera*, December 10, 2013, www.corriere.it/ economia/13_dicembre_10/evasione-incompatibile-la-democrazia-befera-all-attacco-con-saccomanni-305e94be-617d-11e3-9835-2b4fbcb116d9.shtml. The estimate for 2016 is, however, considerably lower at €120 billion. See: repubblica.it, "Evasione Fiscale, per La Gdf Mancano 110 Miliardi L'anno," *Repubblica.it*, January 18, 2017, www.repubblica.it/economia/2017/01/18/news/evasione_fiscale_guardia_di_ finanza-156282734/.
3. The historical continuity of the tax revolts of the nineteenth and twenty-first centuries described above shake arguments that see the evasive behavior of Italians solely rooted in contemporary causes, such as high fiscal pressure (Chiarini et al. 2009: 273), soft legal penalization of tax evaders (Manestra 2010), lax controls (Santoro and Fiorio 2011: 103), or the feeling of most Italians that they do not get much in return for their taxes (Cannari and D'Alessio 2007: 31). A series of tax code reforms and a tightening of controls in the 2010s have not led to a decrease in evasive behavior.
4. Due to the absence of a historiographic debate on taxation and the very limited amount of historical work on taxation in Italy it is not possible to establish a direct link between tax behavior, Church behavior, and state behavior. This paper will therefore use the perception of the state and especially the perception of the state's legitimacy as a proxy for the willingness of Italians to pay taxes. Furthermore, the standoff between Church and state explains evasive behavior in contrast to other countries but it does not explain the huge disparities of evasive behavior between the North and the South of Italy where the Church is traditionally in a much weaker position. To come to a better understanding of evasive behavior in the South, we examine the role the state played during unification in the South.
5. For example, Paul Ginsborg's book from 1990, arguably the most important popular science contribution on Italian postwar history, only mentions the words taxes and taxation on nine of its 586 pages. I contacted the five most distinguished historians of contemporary Italian history and the Risorgimento and none knew of an account

on taxation. However, all of them were eager to point out that such an account would be very much needed. It took Italian scholars till the 1970s to build timelines on evasive behavior based on standardized statistical estimates and the state started to monitor tax evasion comprehensively only in the 1980s after strong pressure from the European Union. Before that period we have to rely on estimates scattered in different government documents, based on very different estimation techniques which are incomplete in their timeline and territorial coverage (Manestra 2010: 57). See also Santoro (2010: 31).

6. Can we connect these stereotypical ascriptions to the Italian tax morale? If it is true that "[n]ational culture creates a context that encourages or discourages different rates of tax evasion" then we can find reasons for high evasion rates in the country in the Italian character.

7. The payment of the *otto per mille* is mandatory. However, it is not mandatory to indicate to whom it should go. Around 50 percent of Italians allocate the money. The money from the 50 percent who do not allocate is paid out automatically in accordance with the 50 percent who do choose to allocate it.

8. For summaries of the most recent historiographic debates on the Risorgimento, see Banti (2004); Banti and Ginsborg (2007); Davis (2000); Isabella (2012); and Riall (1994; 2008). For a review of the historiography on the Church in Italy, see Kertzer (2000; 2004); and Pollard (2008).

9. However, the Napoleonic experience also showed that state-building could not be achieved with an anti-Church sentiment. This led to a spiritualization of liberalism in Italy and a short period of liberalization of Catholic thought (Isabella 2015: 559). Catholicism became enshrined as the state religion in most states and worship of other religions became limited to the private sphere because liberals "shared the heartfelt conviction that religion was the pillar of any form of civil life" (Isabella 2015: 567). This led to a softening of the *ultramontane* camp and the liberal turn of Pope Pius IX, who implemented a liberal reform agenda in the Papal States in the 1840s (Romani 2014: 621).

10. The harsh standoff with the Church had also a strong impact on Italian Liberalism, the foundational political movement of Italy, both as a political force and as an ideology. As a movement, liberal elites were so afraid of the structural majority of the Catholic rank and file that they never substantially enlarged the franchise (even in 1900 only approximately 4 million out of 25 million Italians had the right to vote). As a consequence, Liberals never built a mass party in Italy. Furthermore, the conflict with the Church on social policy (one that the state was unable to win) led to a laissez-faire transformation of liberal ideology in Italy. The result was an ideological transformation of a progressive liberalism during the run-up to Italian unification into a strange beast, a mix between authoritarian liberalism and laissez-faire liberalism. The eclipsing of a social policy component from Liberal nation-building (a social policy such as Bismarck had used to unify Germany) meant also that the state needed far fewer administrative resources and money, both factors that impacted negatively on taxation. Furthermore, a colonial regime emerged in the South that extracted resources and transferred them for state-building in the North. An Italian version of Bismarck's Rye and Iron coalition

between Southern large estate landholders (*latifondisti*) and Northern liberal bourgeoisie emerged (see Gramsci's 2010 interpretation of the Risorgimento). Giolitti marked the problem in a speech in September 1900:

> Sonnino is right in saying that the country is sick politically and morally, but the principal cause of its sickness is that the classes in power have been spending enormous sums on themselves and their own interests, and have obtained the money almost entirely from the poorer sections of society. We have a large number of taxes paid predominantly by the poor, on salt, on gambling, the dazio on grain and so forth, but we have not a single tax which is exclusively on wealth as such. When in the financial emergency of 1893 I had to call on the rich to make a small sacrifice, they began a rebellion against the government even more effective than the contemporary revolt of the poor Sicilian peasantry and Sonnino who took over from me had to find the money by increasing the price for salt and the excise on cereals. I deplore as much as anyone the struggle between classes, but at least let us be fair and ask who started it. (Mack-Smith 1997: 214–15)

The colonialization and extraction of the South by the North reached a pinnacle with the *brigantaggio*, a full-scale military operation during the first three years after unification that left approximately 14,000 Southern Italians dead. The Pope also had a hand in that as he heavily financed the insurgents in the South in a last, desperate attempt to hinder Italian unification.

11. "smisurato aumento delle imposte, che senza alcuno scrupolo si facevano pagare in gran parte alle classi sociali piu basse" (Romani 2013: 15).
12. "stato della Chiesa sussive tranquillamente senza catasto mille anni" (Romani 2013: 38).
13. "denunciare i sistematici e illiciti prelievi dale casse pubbliche compiuti da politici e amministratori" (Romani 2013: 33).
14. "Un governo ladro, rispetto alla Chiesa, fa I sudditi ladri rispetto all erario"; "I beni della Chiesa dice il governo, sono dello stato, I beni dello stato, dice il private, sono del popolo, e parte del popolo sono io" (Romani 2013: 34).
15. The Pope had even sacrificed the Catholic People's Party (Partito Populare) in order to come to terms with Mussolini and had therefore played a part in putting an end to the short experience of Italian interwar democracy.
16. The landing of the Allies in the Italian South did not bring a reinforcing of state institutions but fueled particularism. The Allies used local mafias and their ties to the USA to stabilize the liberated territories. This included the death of nearly fifty local mayors and political functionaries of the Communist Party. This certainly did not have a positive impact on Southern tax morale (see Ginsborg 1990; Lupo 1997).
17. The Catholic Church could present itself as one of the major driving forces of the resistance. Once it became obvious that the Allies would not tolerate another authoritarian regime on the Italian peninsula, the Church had to grudgingly accept that their preferred option, a Franco- or Salazar-like autocratic regime with strong clerical ties, was no longer available. The Vatican therefore took the second-best option and agreed to the creation of a Christian Democratic party in 1944.

References

Bame-Aldred, Charles W., John B. Cullen, Kelly D. Martin, and K. Praveen Parboteeah (2013), "National Culture and Firm-Level Tax Evasion." *Journal of Business Research* 66(3): 390–6.

Banti, Alberto Mario (2004), *Il Risorgimento Italiano*. Rome-Bari: Laterza.

Banti, Alberto Mario and Paul Ginsborg (2007), "Per una nuova storia del Risorgimento." In Alberto Mario Banti and Paul Ginsborg (eds.), *Il Risorgimento*, Vol. 22, *Storia D'Italia, Annali*. Turin: Einaudi, xviii–xxxiv.

Bollati, Giulio (1972), "L'Italiano." In *Storia d'Italia*, Vol. I. Turin: Giulio Einaudi Editore, 949–1002.

Broers, Michael (2001), "Cultural Imperialism in a European Context? Political Culture and Cultural Politics in Napoleonic Italy." *Past & Present* 170: 152–80.

Broers, Michael (2003), "The Myth and Reality of Italian Regionalism: A Historical Geography of Napoleonic Italy, 1801–1814." *The American Historical Review* 108(3): 688–709.

Broers, Michael (2004), *Politics and Religion in Napoleonic Italy: The War against God, 1801–1814*. London: Routledge.

Cannari, Luigi and Giovanni D'Alessio (2007), *Le Opinioni degli Italiani sull'evasione Fiscale*. Working Paper No. 618, Banca d'Italia.

Chiarini, Bruno, Elisabetta Marzano, and Friedrich Schneider (2009), "Tax Rates and Tax Evasion: An Empirical Analysis of the Structural Aspects and Long-Run Characteristics in Italy." *European Journal of Law and Economics* 35(2): 273–93.

Chiri, Salvatore and Paolo Sestito (2014), "Audizione nell'ambito dell'indagine Conoscitiva sugli Organismi della Fiscalità e sul Rapporto tra Contribuenti e Fisco, 6e Commissione del Senato della Repubblica." Rome, March 5.

Clark, M. (1996), *Modern Italy, 1870–1995*. London: Longmans.

Croce, Benedetto (2004), *Storia d'Italia dal 1871 al 1915*, Vol. 16. Naples: Bibliopolis.

D'Attoma, John (2016), "Divided Nation: The North–South Cleavage in Italian Tax Compliance." *Polity*. www.journals.uchicago.edu/doi/pdfplus/10.1086/689982.

Davis, John Anthony (2000), *Italy in the Nineteenth Century: 1796–1900*. Oxford: Oxford University Press.

Diamanti, Ilvo (2013), "Gli Italiani e lo stato—Rapporto 2013." www.demos.it/a00935.php.

Diamanti, Ilvo (2014), "Gli Italiani e lo stato—Rapporto 2014." www.demos.it/a01077.php.

Diamanti, Ilvo and Luigi Ceccarini (2007), "Catholics and Politics after the Christian Democrats: The Influential Minority." *Journal of Modern Italian Studies* 12(1): 37–59.

Dickie, John (2017), "Antonio Bresciani and the Sects: Conspiracy Myths in an Intransigent Catholic Response to the Risorgimento." *Modern Italy* 22(1): 19–34.

Duggan, Christopher (2007), *The Force of Destiny: A History of Italy since 1796*. London: Penguin Books.

Duggan, Christopher (2013), *A Concise History of Italy*. Cambridge: Cambridge University Press.

Eurobarometer (2005), Special Eurobarometer 225/Wave 63.1: Social values, Science and Technology. http://ec.europa.eu/commfrontoffice/publicopinion/archives/ebs/ebs_225_report_en.pdf.

Ferrera, Maurizio (1993), *Modelli di Solidarietà*. Bologna: Il Mulino.

Galbiati Roberto and Giulio Zanella (2012), "The Tax Evasion Social Multiplier: Evidence from Italy." *Journal of Public Economics* 96(5): 485–94.

Galli, Giorgio (1978), *Storia della Democrazia Cristiana*. Rome-Bari: Laterza.

Garelli, Franco (2007), "The Public Relevance of the Church and Catholicism in Italy." *Journal of Modern Italian Studies* 12(1): 8–36.

Ginsborg, Paul (1990), *A History of Contemporary Italy: Society and Politics 1943–80*. London: Penguin.

Ginsborg, Paul (2001), *Italy and its Discontents 1980–2001*. London: Penguin.

Gorski, Philip S. (2003), *The Disciplinary Revolution: Calvinism and the Rise of the State in Early Modern Europe*. Chicago, IL: University of Chicago Press.

Grab, Alexander (1995), "State Power, Brigandage and Rural Resistance in Napoleonic Italy." *European History Quarterly* 25(1): 39–70.

Grab, Alexander (1998), "The Politics of Finance in Napoleonic Italy (1802–1814)." *Journal of Modern Italian Studies* 3(2): 127–43.

Grab, Alex (2003), "The Napoleonic Legacy in Italy." In *Proceedings of the Consortium on Revolutionary Europe 1750–1850 Selected Papers, 2001*. Tallahassee, FL: Florida State University, 183–93.

Gramsci, Antonio (2010), *Il Risorgimento e l'Unita d'Italia*. Rome: Donzelli Editore.

Guzzini, Stefano (1995), "The 'Long Night of the First Republic': Years of Clientelistic Implosion in Italy." *Review of International Political Economy* 2(1): 27–61.

Isabella, Maurizio (2012), "Review Article: Rethinking Italy's Nation-Building 150 Years Afterwards: The New Risorgimento Historiography." *Past & Present* 217(1): 247–68.

Isabella, Maurizio (2015), "Citizens or Faithful? Religion and the Liberal Revolutions of the 1820s in Southern Europe." *Modern Intellectual History* 12(3): 555–78.

Jones, Tobias (2003), *The Dark Heart of Italy: Travel through Time and Space Across Italy*. London: Faber and Faber.

Katz, Richard S. and Peter Mair (1995), "Changing Models of Party Organization and Party Democracy: The Emergence of the Cartel Party." *Party Politics* 1(1): 5–28.

Kelikian, Alice (2002), "The Church and Catholicism." In Adrian Lyttelton (ed.), *Liberal and Fascist Italy*. Oxford: Oxford University Press, 44–61.

Kertzer, David I. (2000), "Religion and Society." In John Anthony Davis (ed.), *Italy in the Nineteenth Century*. Oxford: Oxford University Press, 181–205.

Kertzer, David I. (2004), *Prisoner of the Vatican: The Popes' Secret Plot to Capture Rome from the New Italian State*. Boston, MA: Houghton Mifflin Harcourt.

Lewis, Alan, S. Carrera, J. Cullis, and P. Jones (2009), "Individual, Cognitive and Cultural Differences in Tax Compliance: UK and Italy Compared." *Journal of Economic Psychology* 30(3): 431–45.

Logan, Oliver (1997), "Italian Identity: Catholic Responses to Secularist Definitions, c. 1910–48." *Modern Italy* 2(1): 52–71.

Lupo, Salvatore (1997), "The Allies and the Mafia." *Journal of Modern Italian Studies* 2(1): 21–33.

Mack-Smith, Denis (1997), *Modern Italy: A Political History*. Ann Arbor, MI: University of Michigan Press.

103

Mammarella, G. (1978), *L'Italia dalla Caduta del Fascismo a Oggi*. Bologna: Il Mulino.

Manestra, Stefano (2010), "A Short History of Tax Compliance in Italy." Bank of Italy Occasional Paper, no. 81, http://papers.ssrn.com/sol3/papers.cfm?abstract_id=1825982.

Marigliani, Massimiliano and Stefano Pisani (2006), "Le Basi Imponibili IVA. Aspetti Generali Prinicpali Risultati per Il Periodo 1982–2002." Documenti Di Lavoro Dell Ufficio Studi. Agenzia Delle Entrate.

Marino M. and Roberta Zizza (2010), "The Personal Income Tax Evasion in Italy: An Estimate by Taxpayer's Type." Banca d'Italia.

Melloni, Alberto (2007), "The Politics of the 'Church' in the Italy of Pope Wojtyla." *Journal of Modern Italian Studies* 12(1): 60–85.

Patriarca, Silvana (2010), *Italian Vices*. New York: Cambridge University Press.

Pollard, John (2008), *Catholicism in Modern Italy: Religion, Society and Politics, 1861 to the Present*. Oxford: Taylor & Francis.

Pope Pius IX (1864), "Syllabus of Errors Condemned by Pius IX." Rome: Vatican. www.papalencyclicals.net/Pius09/p9syll.htm.

Raponi, Danilo (2011), "Heroism, Vice, and the Risorgimento." *The Historical Journal* 54(4): 1185–95.

Reuter, Hans-Richard (2010), "Vier Anmerkungen zu Philip Manow die Soziale Marktwirtschaft als Interkonfessioneller Kompromiss? Ein Re-Statement." *Ethik Und Gesellschaft* 1.

Riall, Lucy (1994), *The Italian Risorgimento: State, Society, and National Unification*. London: Routledge.

Riall, Lucy (2008), *Risorgimento: The History of Italy from Napoleon to Nation State*. Basingstoke: Palgrave Macmillan.

Romani, Roberto (2010), "Economia Politica e Pensiero Sociale Cattolico nello Stato Pontificio, 1775–1850." *Rivista di Storia Economica* 1: 35–74.

Romani, Roberto (2013), "Fiscalità Cattolica e Fiscalità Liberale. Taparelli d'Azeglio e 'La Civiltà Cattolica' 1850–1876." *Contemporanea* 16(1): 7–37.

Romani, Roberto (2014), "Liberal Theocracy in the Italian Risorgimento." *European History Quarterly* 44(4): 620–50.

Santoro, Alessandro (2010), *L'evasione Fiscale*. Bologna: Il Mulino.

Santoro, Alessandro and Carlo V. Fiorio (2011), "Taxpayer Behavior When Audit Rules Are Known: Evidence from Italy." *Public Finance Review* 39(1): 103–23.

Schneider, Friedrich and Dominik H. Enste (2013), *The Shadow Economy: An International Survey*. New York: Cambridge University Press.

Selmi, Martina (2013), *How Did We Get Here? A Brief History of Tax Compliance in Italy*. Fiesole: European University Institute.

Steinmo, Sven (2010), *The Evolution of Modern States: Sweden, Japan and the United States*. New York: Cambridge University Press.

Torgler, Benno (2006), "The Importance of Faith: Tax Morale and Religiosity." *Journal of Economic Behavior & Organization* 61(1): 81–109.

Tullio-Altan, Carlo (2000), *La Nostra Italia: Clientelismo, Trasformismo e Ribellismo dall'unità al 2000*. Milan: Università Bocconi Editore.

Weber, Max (1988), *Gesammelte Aufsätze zur Religionssoziologie I, Photomechanischer Nachdruck der Erstauflage von 1920*. Tübingen: Mohr Siebeck UTB.

Zhang, Nan, Giulia Andrighetto, Stefania Ottone, Ferruccio Ponzano, and Sven Steinmo (2016), "Willing to Pay? Tax Compliance in Britain and Italy: An Experimental Analysis." *PLOS ONE* 11(2): e0150277, doi: 10.1371/journal.pone.0150277.

5

Explaining Italian Tax Compliance

A Historical Analysis

John D'Attoma

Ex-Prime Minister Silvio Berlusconi once famously claimed that the "evasion of high taxes was a God-given right" (Bhatti et al. 2012). Reports from Istat, Corte dei Conti, and l'Agenzia delle Entrate estimate that tax evasion in Italy costs the state €120 billion per year in lost revenue (Santoro 2010). Using data from the Istituto nazionale di statistica (Istat), Alessandro Santoro demonstrates that evasion of value added tax (VAT) averages about 34 percent across regions (Santoro 2010). Figure 5.1 shows evasion rates for the regional tax on production.[1]

One explanation for relatively sluggish and asymmetric development in Italy argues that Southern Italy is driving most of these ills. This line of inquiry depicts Southern Italians as less endowed with civic virtue and social capital, which is reflected in their lower levels of economic development and, as shown in Table 5.1, government performance (Banfield 1967; Bigoni et al. 2016; Cartocci 2006; Putnam, Leonardi, and Nanetti 1994; Sabatini 2005a; 2005b). Here civic virtue is defined as high civic awareness and a shared consensus regarding the legitimacy of political institutions and public policy, together with political competence and trust (Almond and Verba 1963). Social capital refers to features of social life, such as networks and trust, that facilitate civic participation (Putnam, Leonardi, and Nanetti 1994).

This line of research typically associates development to the cultural underpinnings of society. Edward Banfield followed by Robert Putnam and his colleagues suggest that Southern Italy is a region characterized by *amoral familism*. Societies tied by amoral familism (bonding social capital) "emphasize family relations to the exclusion of all others" (Fukuyama 1995).

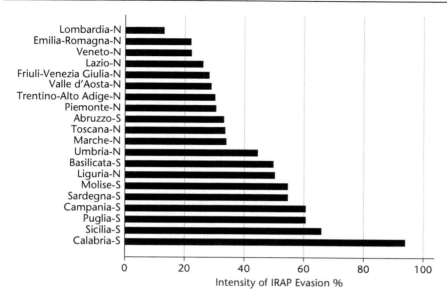

Figure 5.1. Rates of evasion of IRAP by region 1998–2002
Source: Istat in Santoro (2010).

Table 5.1. Quality of government: 14 Western European countries

Country	Quality	Impartiality	Corruption	Average
Finland	1.657	1.296	1.266	1.406
Netherlands	0.956	1.445	0.912	1.104
Denmark	0.723	1.004	1.560	1.096
Ireland	0.705	1.046	1.252	1.001
United Kingdom	0.507	0.797	0.871	0.725
Sweden	−0.030	1.128	0.897	0.665
Belgium	1.440	−0.229	0.054	0.422
Germany	0.265	0.322	0.651	0.413
Austria	0.320	0.133	0.359	0.270
Italy	**0.187**	**0.187**	**−0.634**	**−0.087**
Spain	0.083	−0.229	−0.115	−0.087
France	0.210	−0.758	0.074	−0.158
Portugal	−0.259	−0.848	−0.745	−0.617
Greece	−1.287	−0.655	−1.304	−1.082

Source: Nationally representative public opinion surveys were conducted by The Quality of
Government Institute about perceptions of local education, health, and law enforcement
institutions. Researchers asked participants to rate each of the three institutions on quality,
impartiality, and corruption. For more information, see Teorell et al. 2011.

A centuries-old debate about the Italian character would have us believe the
Italian "character is faulty, and that this faultiness even explains much of
the social and political problems of their country today" (Patriarca 2010: 5).
Indeed, Europeans perceive Italians as the least trustworthy of Western European nations (Mackie 2001).[2] In this framework, ethical behavior is thus

confined to the immediate family and closest friends. By *siphoning* money from the breadwinner, paying taxes, which benefits society at large, can be perceived as hurting the familial unit by imposing a cost coming out of their earnings that will indirectly benefit someone outside the familial unit, rather than directly benefiting themselves.

Nevertheless, the amoral familism argument has been met by a litany of critics, who argue that the social capital literature often confounds explanations with outcomes, which implies that public institutions and the elites that govern those institutions are somehow responsible for fostering a civic citizenry. For example, Levi suggests that a government's ability to protect property rights and a merit-based society (one opposed to the clientelism or nepotism found in Southern Italy) instill a generalized trust in society (Levi 1996). Even Putnam mentions in *Making Democracy Work* that the regimes prior to unification intensified distrust and vertical ties in the South, but he barely mentions how unification reduced the South to "semi-colonial status" and "its fragile commercial sector brutally merged with the North's more flourishing economy, a uniform tax system and customs union imposed on its vulnerable industries, and brigandage rooted out by a full-scale military campaign" (Tarrow 1996: 394). Filippo Sabetti contends that the growth of institutions and ecclesial infrastructure since the eighteenth century better explain the Italian political economy than the amoral familism stressed by Putnam.

Like these critics, I contend that the moralist argument fails to account for the institutional environment (such as a period of progressive politics, political competition, or strife between the Church and the state) from which behavior may manifest. While the vast majority of these scholars analyze economic and social development, I am concerned with why tax compliance is so low across Italy. Simply put, tax behavior reflects the quality of and perceptions about the government institutions to which a taxpayer is contributing. I argue that Italian tax compliance has evolved within a low-efficiency/low-trust equilibrium environment or what Bergman (2009) calls a low-compliance environment. There is ample evidence in the literature suggesting that individuals are more likely to pay taxes if they believe that their government is honest and efficient (Cummings et al. 2009; Edlund 1999; Frey and Feld 2002; Frey and Torgler 2007; Levi 1989; Levi, Sacks, and Tyler 2009; Pommerehne, Hart, and Frey 1994; Scholz and Lubell 1998; Smith 1992; Smith and Stalans 1991; Torgler and Schneider 2007). Taxation mobilizes citizens to demand accountability from their government, but on the other hand, a lack of government accountability can actually have the opposite effect, motivating individuals to evade their responsibilities (Huntington 2012; Paler 2013). According to Ross (2004: 234), "[b]oth the size of the tax burden, and the quality and quantity of government spending matter; citizens ultimately care about the 'price' they pay for the government services they receive."

It is no wonder that tax evasion is so rampant in Italy; Italy consistently ranks near the bottom on the Quality of Government index compared to other European nations (see Table 5.2). However, Italy's 44 percent tax burden (the ratio of tax revenue to gross domestic product (GDP)) is one of the highest in the European Union; only Denmark, Belgium, France, and Sweden have a higher tax burden (European Commission and Eurostat 2012). It is possible then that Italians live in an institutional environment that legitimizes tax evasion. If Europeans have come to think of Italians as dishonest and Italians themselves have come to agree, this may be a byproduct of this low-efficiency/low-trust equilibrium. Because confidence in public institutions is a direct reflection of the quality of those institutions, clearly Italians should have far less trust in their public institutions than Swedes (see Jenny Jansson, Chapter 3 in this volume). I suggest that, consequently, Italians are more likely to cheat on their taxes and avoid funding public institutions.

The particular tax compliance environment from which tax behavior is derived is one of government instability, bureaucratic complexity, and administrative inertia. Italian unification pitted the state against the Catholic

Table 5.2. Quality of government: Italian regions

Region	Quality	Region score	Rank
Trento	1.043	1.981	41
Valle d'Acosta	0.653	1.603	82
Friuli-Venezia	0.373	1.331	109
Veneto	−0.186	0.788	146
Emilia-Romagna	0.217	0.757	149
Umbria	−0.495	0.488	168
Toscana	−0.495	0.450	170
Marche	−0.535	0.448	172
Lombardia	−0.542	0.442	174
Piemonte	−0.652	0.335	182
Liguria	−0.848	0.144	190
Abruzzo	−1.097	−0.097	200
Sardegna	−1.307	−0.302	204
Basilicata	−1.423	−0.414	208
Lazio	−1.512	−0.500	211
Sicilia	−1.588	−0.575	213
Puglia	−1.604	−0.590	216
Molise	−1.6609	−0.645	220
Calabria	−1.687	−0.671	222
Campania	−2.242	−1.210	232

Source: Nationally representative public opinion surveys were conducted by The Quality of Government Institute about perceptions of local education, health, and law enforcement institutions. Researchers asked participants to rate each of the three institutions on quality, impartiality, and corruption. For more information, see Teorell et al. 2011. Southern regions are in bold.

Church and the North against the South. After a relatively short period of asymmetric state-building, Italians found themselves fighting in World War I for a country that was still greatly divided. Citizens' disaffection with the political system and a sharp economic downturn led to the rise of Benito Mussolini, Italian Fascism, and another world war. Since World War II, Italy has sustained a relatively high level of prosperity, despite major political turmoil such as right- and left-wing political terrorism in the 1970s; a large corruption scandal in which half of parliament was charged with corruption in the 1980s; and sixty-three governments since the "First Republic." The political and institutional instability in Italy has led to a profound distrust of government, and alongside that, an unwillingness to contribute to the state through taxation.

In the following sections, I examine these issues, focusing on the ways in which specific timing and institutions have shaped this low-efficiency/ low-trust equilibrium. I trace the ways in which unification pitted the North against the South, providing a different experience with the state in the two regions and hence different preferences regarding taxation. Furthermore, I argue that post-unification (1900–22) political instability fostered a deep distrust amongst Italians toward their political institutions, shaping a general political ideology that saw excessive taxes as an infringement of individual rights. This overarching political ideology curtailed the ability of successive administrations to create efficient and effective tax regimes.

This was then followed by a series of short-lived prime ministers, which led to the rise of Fascism (1929), followed by World War II, furthering Italian political discontent. Following World War II, a deep distrust of government shaped the new constitution, making tax collection an arduous task for the administration. Although the 1960s and 1970s can be characterized by unprecedented economic growth in Italy, much of it was fueled by clientelism and corruption, which in many ways contributed to tax evasion. Moreover, many in a series of major tax reforms implemented in 1972 to support the modern state were undermined by an overburdened judicial system, followed by a reliance on tax amnesties. Finally, the 1990s tax reforms attempted to address Italy's extremely large small-business and self-employed sector—one of the largest drivers of evasion. But those reforms were also watered down by the immense power of that sector weakening the administration's ability to collect taxes. In sum, I argue that unstable political institutions, such as a weak parliament unable to garner confidence and a constitution that protects the taxpayer at the expense of efficient administrative capabilities, beginning with unification, fostered a profound distrust of the state, which hindered the state's ability to collect taxes.

The Risorgimento and Italian Politics

In this section, I argue that the Risorgimento resulted in deep divides between the North and the South, which greatly affected citizens' willingness to pay taxes. Elites extracted a disproportionate amount of tax from the South to fund the development of the North, engraining a deep-seated distrust of the newly formed nation state in the South. The dominant ideology shaping the fiscal apparatus of the state reflected a great distrust in state power and intrusion. Tax collection thus was perceived to be a form of encroachment on individual rights, dampening the ability of the administration to collect taxes. By the end of the nineteenth century, interplay between the major political parties further shaped the tax environment. The Catholic Church and right-wing liberals joined forces in the North, where there was a strong industrial labor base, to organize mass political engagement in direct competition to the socialists. Catholic, right-wing, and socialist organizations made conscious efforts to build effective and efficient public institutions in order to garner support for their political movements; these institutions promoted a high-compliance environment in the North. On the other hand, the South, populated by mainly peasants, lacked any kind of industrial base and became disengaged with civic and associational life, leading to a low-compliance environment.

The Risorgimento (Resurgence) refers to a period of political consolidation in Italy from 1815 to 1871, ultimately culminating in Italian unification. Although the Risorgimento led to formally ratified political unification, it left the country divided between North and South, economically and politically. As Clark notes, the state imposed an unprecedented tax burden in the South at the time of unification, which funded the development of the North. The South made up only 27 percent of GDP, but 32 percent of the tax base, while the North generated 48 percent of national wealth and paid only 40 percent of the nation's taxes (Mack Smith 1997: 81).[3] Due to a much larger agricultural base in the South, higher taxes on grain disproportionately affected the South, while the North benefited the most from public spending. Since bread was a staple of the Southern Italian diet, increased taxes on grain also hit Southern peasants the hardest (Carter 2010: 211). The North's political dominance meant that it controlled decisions on taxation and public spending, which favored citizens in the North and extracted important resources through taxation from the South, exacerbating the North–South economic divide. For example, between 1862 and 1897, 455 million lire was spent on landfills in Northern and Central Italy, while only 3 million lire was spent on such resources in the South. The majority of school and railway

Figure 5.2. GDP per capita in the Mezzogiorno as a percentage of Northern GDP per capita

Source: Bianchi et al. (2011). Note: the vertical line represents unification.

spending was also concentrated in the North. Development in the South certainly suffered after unification, and, as a result, so did the Southerners' relationship to the newly formed state. Figure 5.2 illustrates the rapid decline in Southern (Mezzogiorno) per capita income as a percentage of Northern per capita income after the Risorgimento. These differences in economic development, investment, and taxation led to a sense of unfairness and distrust in the South, and hence to less willingness to pay taxes.

As the South was becoming further separated from the North economically, there was an important debate taking place regarding the fiscal state. Italy's history with foreign occupation instilled a sense of distrust of state power, which shaped the structure of fiscal institutions. It was thought that the government should never collect more than 5 percent to 10 percent of gross national product in taxes; the fiscal system would be based upon private rights, not public, and a system of laws, not authority; furthermore, the tax system would first and foremost respect the fundamental right of property. This last idea severely hampered the administration's ability to put together a land registry and has had long-lasting effects on the capacity of revenue officials to collect taxes, especially from the self-employed and entrepreneurs (Manestra 2010).

However, claims that the tax burden was too high were not solely the result of a liberal environment, but also an excessive tax burden. The early foundations of the Italian state exerted a massive tax burden on a population that was cautious of the state and citizens of neighboring regions. According to Manestra (2010), the tax burden was approximately 10 percent higher than in Great Britain as a result of a series of wars that did not have wide consensus among Italy's diverse population.

Toward the end of the nineteenth century, the Giolitti government set out to reform the tax system, but in the end the administration was unsuccessful, leaving federal, regional, and local taxes relatively unchanged. This was a problem not only at the legislative level; problems existed at the administrative level as well, largely related to difficulties in implementing the new national cadaster (compare this to the situation described by Marina Nistotskaya and Michelle D'Arcy in Sweden, Chapter 2 in this volume). Furthermore, local administrations were reluctant to update their lists of taxpayers, given that their organizations were made up of taxpayers themselves (Manestra 2010). Tax authorities also found it difficult to sanction taxpayers, as tax commissions were often biased in favor of the taxpayer, largely as a result of the excessive tax burden, exceeding 50 percent. In addition, the tax administration had difficulty proving the incomes of the self-employed and other professionals (Manestra 2010). Taken together, this three-dimensional relationship between administration (tax burden), the state (structure), and ideas such as distrust and caution amongst the populace, fostered tax non-compliance very early on. Corrado Gini (1962) echoes this when he claims that poor economic conditions, an inherent lack of respect for the state, low administrative salaries, inconsistencies in tax law, and an interpretation of private law were all drivers of low tax compliance.

In addition to administrative difficulties, I suggest that the dynamics between political parties also had an important impact on taxpayer behavior. By the turn of the twentieth century, rising fears of socialism and a large labor movement in the North made Catholics and right-wing liberals strange bedfellows. The Catholic Church and right-wing liberals, after the turn of the century, made a conscious effort to build civic associations as an alternative to a socialist workers' movement. This played an important role in driving civic consciousness and institutional development in Northern and Central Italy in the years immediately after World War I. By contrast, the lack of any significant industrial labor force in the South hampered political competition and inhibited the formation of efficient public institutions or a civic-oriented populace. Tarrow (1967: 168–9) argues that at the time of unification, "so ingrained was the clientele system that the mass of new voters, most of them rural and all of them dependent economically on the political elite, were easily integrated into the existing system." In other words, rather than having a political choice, poor Southern peasants became dependent on their clientelistic relationships with local elites. The provision of individualized goods from patrons to clients inhibited the foundation of a civic-oriented populace. Here we begin to see the beginnings of two separate equilibria. I characterize the North as moving toward a high-trust/high-efficiency equilibrium shaped by political competition and a strong industrial base, while the South's low-trust/low-efficiency equilibrium was formed by the state's neglect of the South and consequential clientelistic relationships.

The rise of a Catholic political party (the Italian People's Party, Partito Popolare Italiano) after 1914 marked the beginning of Catholic mainstreaming in Italian politics and challenged the dominance of the ruling party in the North. Because the state had almost completely dismantled organized Catholicism in the South in the early twentieth century, support for the Italian People's Party came mainly from the Northern regions of Italy. Pope Benedict XV, Pope Pius' successor, immediately reversed his predecessor's anti-modernization policies, such as banning Catholic trade unionism, while improving the Church's relationship with the Italian government and the Italian people. While anti-Italian stigma had been attached to the Catholic Church since the Risorgimento, Italian-Catholic politicians and the patriotism of the Catholic clergy during the war changed the prevailing feelings about Catholicism in Italy, bitterly dividing the old ruling class and paving the way for outside parties such as the People's Party and the Socialist Party (Partito Socialista Italiano). These two parties took a combined total of more than half of the legislative seats in the election of 1919. Only in the South did the "old government" parties (Liberal Democrats, Partito Liberale Democratico) win more than half the votes. This was largely the result of the practice of *trasformismo*, in which ruling parties won over the opposition party in return for political and, often, financial favors. The old-guard liberals, especially in the South, made use of public resources for both individual and political gain.

Political strife in Italy only further divided the North and South along party lines. As a result of the 1919 election, 146 of the 156 Socialist deputies came from the North and central regions; 76 of the 100 People's Party deputies were also from the North; and 162 of the 239 deputies from the Liberal Party and the Radical Party (Partito Radicale), who had previously dominated parliament, were elected in the South. Although this election resulted in the first "Radical" government, led by Francesco Nitti, political turmoil between the Radicals, Socialists, and Fascists led to Nitti's resignation and the return of the Liberal Democrat Giolitti as prime minister in 1920. When elections were called again in 1921, the Giolitti government's hegemony was tenuous. To solidify his control, he made certain concessions to the Fascists, including adding them to the government's party list. The disparate governing coalition Giolitti put together was doomed from the outset, which resulted in his immediate resignation, to be followed by a string of short-lived prime ministers and the eventual rise of Fascist leader Benito Mussolini.

In sum, the early twentieth century in Italy was marked by deep divisions between the North and South. These divisions were economic as well as political. The government extracted high taxes from the South to address its debts from the Risorgimento and develop the North. Political parties competed for the burgeoning industrial labor movement in the North by providing and building effective public services. The South, on the other hand, was ruled by the old ruling partly (liberals), who enjoyed a large political monopoly. By providing public jobs and financial favors to the landed elite through *trasformismo*, the ruling party maintained its hegemony in the South, marginalizing Southern citizens from the political process.

The Fascist Period

Here, I argue that the rise of Fascism reversed the Northern progress toward a high-efficiency/high-trust equilibrium, and even furthered Southern resentment toward the state. The Fascist period can be characterized by two main approaches to building effective administrative capabilities and public services across Italy: an attempt to modernize the tax system with a series of uniform tax reforms and a series of public investments that had the unintended effect of increasing the North–South economic divide. To dampen some of the more negative consequences of the administration's policies, the government funneled money through quasi-state organizations, strengthening clientelism in the South. Whereas in the North, the high-compliance environment began to unravel due to an authoritarian state and a second world war, clientelism hardened the low-compliance environment in the South.

Tax reform during the Fascist period involved three separate methods. The first, liberal tax reform in the early Fascist period (1922–5), provided preferential tax treatment to productive industries with the misguided expectation that these industries would then comply with existing tax law. After this reform failed, Mussolini shifted from liberal tax policies to an authoritarian model, where he would stigmatize and penalize evaders. He declared tax evaders "the worst parasites in the nation" and increased tax enforcement between 1926 and 1929 (Manestra 2010: 29). However, the corporatist economic model and increased foreign commitments, such as the Italian–Ethiopian War in the 1930s, which diverted administrative resources, led him to restrain the more authoritarian aspects of the administration's tax policy, which demanded a large amount of administrative oversight. This led the administration back to the more liberal, cooperative model of the 1922–5 period, especially with respect to businesses. Mussolini's industrial policy further accentuated economic divisions.

Although tax and administration reform are important aspects of any successful attempt to increase tax compliance, Mussolini's complete disregard for the South exacerbated the economic divisions between the North and South and therefore the differences in their tax compliance environments. Economic asymmetries and disproportional public investment generated a feeling of unfairness and distrust in the economic system, both of which reinforced the low compliance. Mussolini's industrial policy accentuated economic divisions between the North and the South by concentrating economic development in engineering, steelworks, chemicals, and hydro-electricity supply—all industries located in the industrial triangle of the Northwest. Almost half of industrial workers and two-thirds of engineers worked in Lombardy, Liguria, and Piedmont, while the majority of workers from the South were farmers and artisans (Clark 1996). The state also increased the extent of the welfare state in the Fascist period, making Northern industrial workers eligible for generous benefits not available to Southern workers—an imbalance that continues to this day. Because of the North's large industrial base, unionized workers were able to lobby for and win larger pensions than the average Southern Italian peasant. This contributed to patronage and clientelistic practices as a means of income supplementation in the South. Clients would directly exchange their votes for public employment and favorable tax treatment (Ferrera 1996).

Moreover, Mussolini's push to project Italy as an international power had adverse consequences for the Southern economy. Mussolini implemented a revaluation of the lira in 1926 to project Italy's position, which reduced wages and sharply increased unemployment, largely in the agricultural South (Neville 2014). In the late 1920s through the early 1930s, Mussolini increased tariffs on wheat, which amounted to a large concession to landowners, who gained the most from the government policies, whereas Southern peasants were hit the hardest. To lessen the damage in the South, the administration funneled jobs through *parastati*, quasi-governmental agencies that dealt with health, welfare, and pensions. Distribution through quasi-governmental agencies then became the most important criterion for resource distribution (Walston 1988).

Fascism only enlarged the economic and social disparity in Italy, and especially in Southern Italy. Moreover, Fascism's antidemocratic foundation and its overwhelming reliance on the state as the center of individual life reversed the virtuous circle in the North, while increasing discontent in the South due to the state's general neglect of that region. This had the effect of generating low trust and low compliance across the peninsula.

The First Republic

The period after World War II brought great, but asymmetric, prosperity to Italy. Just as during the previous period, political competition among the Christian Democrats, the Socialists, and the Communists (Partito Communista Italiano) led to major public works and investment in Northern Italy, while the Christian Democrat political monopoly in the South intensified clientelistic networks. Although the central government invested heavily in the South beginning in 1950 with a Fund for the South (*Cassa per il mezzogiorno*), the implementation of the fund was greatly affected by clientelism. In 1970, regional governments were established, further exacerbating the underlying issues in the South. Regional governments were granted more autonomy and discretion in the distribution of resources, especially financial resources, which they could then funnel to private interests. While clientelism became stronger in the South as a result, one of the largest corruption scandals in Italian history unfolded in the North. Widespread distrust in the governing parties brought down the government and led to the Second Republic.

After World War II, Italian citizens were polarized both economically and ideologically. In the period 1944–6, Sicilian farmers formed a movement aimed at secession from the North, which led to a June 2, 1946 popular vote pitting the Italian dynasty (the monarchy ruled by Humbert II of Savoy) against the Republic. The North, led by the Communists, Socialists, and Christian Democrats, favored the Republic; the majority of the South voted to uphold the dynasty (Gilmour 2011; Pollard 1998). In 1946, tensions between the Communists and the Christian Democrats presented another challenge to national unity: while the Communist Party was closely tied to the Soviets, aid and investment from the US government and US firms influenced the Christian Democrats and the Alcide De Gasperi government.

The 1947 Italian Constitution, however, showed remarkable levels of compromise between the parties, reflecting also a deep distrust in the state. The Italian Constitution, first and foremost, protects the individual from the state, which has unintentionally hindered the ability of the tax administration to collect taxes. Article 53 states: "all shall contribute to public expenditure in accordance with their means." Consequently, assessing an individual's means accurately is an arduous process. The intended effect, however, was to associate taxes with an individual's moral sensibilities. Referring to the tax reforms, Vanoni elegantly stated in the House of Deputies (Resoconti parlamentari 1948: 3744):

> In our country there is often the feeling that tax evasion has become a way of life ... the individual almost considers it a legitimate form of defense against an imposition he considers detrimental to their sphere of individual action ... tax

evasion takes on the characteristics of real and substantial anarchy, a negation of the first requirements of social life and is precisely why it seems irrepressible to get to a system in which there is neither justification, nor moral, nor techniques for evasion, and that leads to more open condemnation, moral rather than legal, for the evader.

Vanoni thus sees tax evasion within this context-specific equilibrium. The legitimate fear that the state will infringe on individual rights reflects the historical circumstances specific to the Italian taxpayer.

Between the new Finance Minister Enzio Vanoni and his colleagues there was wide consensus that administrative reform was the most pressing issue regarding taxation. Cesare Cosciani (1950) argued that the history of the tax system was plagued by irrationality perpetuated by a legislature that created an overabundance of laws that only specialists could understand. With past failures in administration in mind, Vanoni implemented broad, but incremental, tax reform, emphasizing taxation as a democratic responsibility. On January 11, 1951 under Finance Minister Vanoni the Republic passed the largest tax reform since the Fascist period, known as the *Legge Vanoni* (Vanoni Law). The law had four main features: (1) taxpayers—both employees and the self-employed—had to fill out annual tax returns; (2) greater progressivity combined with lower income taxes overall; (3) a series of consumption taxes; and (4) business taxes on items such as stamps and licensing (Ambrosetti 2004).

Vanoni's measures, especially those addressing mutual trust between taxpayer and administration, did not outlive his term, however. Audits actually became more inefficient and tax investigators were increasingly underpaid compared to private tax accountants (Manestra 2010). In 1959, the administration began raising rates on everything from capital gains to self-employed income. As a result, taxpayers increasingly came to disrespect the administrators or tax collectors. Therefore, highly paid tax accountants, who are paid to keep taxes low for their clients, were in direct conflict with an underpaid and under-appreciated tax administration. Administrators were at a clear disadvantage.

Though the 1950s marked the beginning of approximately two decades of great prosperity, data provided by Clark (1996: 357) depicts Southern Italy as similar to many underdeveloped countries, but much larger in population and territory than most. The disparities between the North and the South were so considerable and evident that the state instituted the Fund for the South, a rural spending agency providing roads, housing, and water to rural areas. Although the "Italian Economic Miracle" led to a convergence of incomes, with Southern income reaching approximately 70 percent of the national average, the Fund also established large fiscal transfers from North to South and significant migration flows from South to North. This fueled cultural stereotypes and out-group resentments.

The "economic miracle" and a massive injection of state spending on welfare (education and healthcare) significantly increased the living standards of the average Italian individual in the early 1960s. However, by 1967 the Italian economy was showing signs of crisis. A large migration of unskilled Southern workers successfully supplanted highly skilled factory workers in the North, which led to major factory floor protests throughout Northern Italy. Subsequently, Southern factory workers took to the shop floor to demand better pensions, social security, housing, and health services. By 1976, the trade union movement had become a major force in Italian politics encompassing nearly 50 percent of workers (Clark 1996: 377). Large pay raises, however, exponentially increased overall labor costs in Italy, causing a considerable downturn amongst Italian firms. With labor costs exceeding by 39 percent those experienced by British and German firms, profits tapered off significantly by the end of the decade. Both the extreme right and left responded to the crisis with political terrorism, including assassinations and kidnappings.

Weak public institutions, such as an unstable parliament and a constitution that severely hampered administration, the resilience of strong informal institutions, such as clientelism, and economic downturn reinforced this low-trust/low-efficiency equilibrium. From unification to Fascism, followed by the First Republic through the end of the economic miracle, we can observe several recurring themes in which the administration attempts to address low tax compliance by reorganizing tax administration, but without addressing the underlying defects of the tax system. New laws were stacked upon old laws, and new taxes were introduced to pay for wars and social programs. The tax system became increasingly more complicated and incomprehensible to the vast majority of taxpayers, further decreasing trust in a severely underfunded administration. Not only was there a lack of trust between taxpayers and the administration, but strong regional resentment stemming from longstanding cultural stereotypes lingered, and even proliferated, as a result of migration patterns, economic insecurities, and fiscal transfers. And once again, Italians were concerned about political crises and, consequently, political terrorism. These institutional and political dynamics structured the way in which Italians viewed their state and fellow citizens, consolidating the low-compliance environment.

From the Tax Reform of 1972 to the Present

Two decades after regional governments had been enshrined into the constitution, the state introduced regional governments in the spring of 1970. By the mid-1970s, Italian regions could provide subsidies, fund and staff welfare agencies, draw up regional development plans, and organize their own cooperatives. However, as Clark writes, these regional governments fed the Calabrian Mafia (*ndrangheta*) and the Neapolitan *camorra*, with local barons supporting particularism, rather than creating more efficient, democratic institutions. "There may," he notes, "have been little popular enthusiasm for the regions, but many of the organized interests-groups thought they were splendid" (1996: 392). Further unsuccessful attempts to curb tax evasion led to tougher sanctions on taxpayers and large tax reforms. However, a large aspect of these reforms concerned tax amnesty programs and a new Sector Studies program, both of which only furthered the low-compliance environment. Finally, in the early 1990s large-scale corruption was uncovered, bringing down the government and ushering in the era of Silvio Berlusconi—a renowned tax evader himself.

After the introduction of regional governments in 1970, important legislation was introduced to reform the tax system. Tax reform introduced in 1973 by the Minister of Finance, Luigi Preti, forced Italy to construct a more modern tax system to match the demands of a developed nation. It further had to complement a burgeoning public deficit and a far more uncertain situation than the preceding decade. The basic foundation of these reforms rested on the same principles as previous tax reforms: administrative changes, especially reducing a bloated bureaucracy and the numerous superfluous laws; and improving how the administration calculated taxable income. This included the establishment of a variety of new taxes such as the IRPEF (national progressive income tax), IRPEG (corporate income tax, replaced by IRES), ILOR (local income tax), INVIM (capital gains tax), and VAT.

The state even attempted to revert to a more authoritarian regime—tough sanctions and stigmatization—to enforce tax compliance. Provincial newspapers throughout Italy published the names of famous people who had evaded their taxes as well as 200,000 tax evaders between 1979 and 1981. Law 516/ 1982, the so-called *manette agli evasori* (handcuffs for evaders), designated a number of tax behaviors as revealing an attempt to evade taxes, making them serious criminal offenses with increased penalties. Prior to *manette agli evasori*, a judge could not indict an offender before there was undeniable proof of evasion (Santoro 2010), which, as I noted above, was an arduous process since the burden of proof was the responsibility of the investigators. *Manette agli evasori* resulted in an overburdened judicial system and a series of amnesty programs. As Manestra (2010: 42) states, "handcuffs for all, became handcuffs for no one." The courts found many of the provisions of *manette agli evasori* unconstitutional, and only a small fraction of accused transgressors were convicted under the law (Santoro 2010: Kindle location 951–2).

Additionally, tax amnesties and the inability to punish decreased compliance by influencing the compliance environment and social norms (Alm, McKee, and Beck 1990). Nonetheless, the Italian tax administration has relied heavily on amnesties since unification. According to Manestra (2010), there were eighty-three separate amnesties between 1900 and 2002, and between the 1970 tax reform and 2002 a form of tax amnesty was used every year. One of the major defects of repeated amnesty is it decreases the amount of risk associated with evasion. If potential evaders foresee an amnesty in the future, they will likely underreport their income. The use of amnesty was so common that tax evasion became a safe way to increase one's income, as illustrated by the responses from the 2004 Bank of Italy Survey of Household Wealth. When asked about their opinion on tax amnesties, 50 percent of respondents said they were unfair, compared to 36 percent who said they were a good policy. In another question participants were asked what they believed the outcome of amnesty to be; 32 percent responded, "tax evasion increases because the amnesty rewards tax evaders and discourages honest taxpayers" and 30 percent said, "tax evasion doesn't change because once tax evaders have regularized their past position, they begin to evade tax again until the next amnesty."[4]

Following the 1973 reform, there were three main approaches that shaped the 1990s tax reform bill, according to Manestra (2010). The most important aspect of these procedural changes was reforming the way in which small businesses fulfilled their accounting obligations. Structural changes attempted to fix the major sources of tax revenue, mainly VAT and direct taxes. Finally, quantitative reform set out to address the number of taxes, especially on sources of income. The less punitive Law 154/1991 and Law 74/2000 replaced *manette agli evasori*. As was common throughout the neoliberal era, tax reform in this period reduced tax rates while broadening the taxable base. However, income tax evasion actually increased after implementation of the tax reform through 1978, decreasing slightly in 1978–80, but never falling below 33.7 percent in this period.[5]

The most important feature of the 1990s tax reform was the adoption of *Studi di Settore* (Sector Studies) in 1998. Due to the large size of the self-employed and small-business sectors, focusing on this particular aspect of the economy was an important step forward for the administration. While most countries collect various data on individuals and companies, then place them into homogeneous populations based on those characteristics with minimum expected incomes, Italy is rare in that it actually makes this data available to the taxpayer before they file their taxes. Moreover, published minimum expected incomes are first negotiated between the tax administration and taxpayer representatives, such as the Consiglio Nazionale dell'Economia e del Lavoro (CNEL). Sector Studies came out of the recognition that the main driver of tax evasion in Italy was its particular economic structure, but the small-business sector's clout with government officials was so great that Sector Studies actually resulted in a more favorable situation for most taxpayers.

It is easy to predict the outcome of a policy that informs taxpayers of their expected minimum income level. As Bergman (2009: 10) elegantly argued, "People maximize utilities inasmuch as they pay as little taxes as they can. But the environment in which people operate fundamentally shapes how they frame the maximization benefits." Hence, those who make above the expected minimum will reduce their income to match the mandatory minimum, while those who earn below the minimum will either risk being audited, which is very likely, and bear those costs, or they will increase their income to avoid the legal costs of an audit. The societal effect of this is also significant. If it is known that small businesses and the self-employed can easily avoid taxes, the ripple effects will weigh heavily on the Italian tax system.

The continual unsuccessful attempts to fix the tax system, coupled with a series of corruption scandals that would eventually bring down Italy's national government, only exasperated the low-trust equilibrium. The largest corruption case, *Tangentopoli* (Bribesville), exposed a number of high-ranking public officials (half of parliament) for acts of bribery and led to the so-called "Second Republic" and the prominence of Silvio Berlusconi—a billionaire businessman who came in as a political outsider profiting from the lack of trust and promising to reduce taxes. He also was later convicted of tax evasion. The vicious circle that Steinmo discusses in the Introduction to this volume is evident throughout Italian history. An inefficient, corrupt, or a perceived-to-be-illegitimate state shapes a climate of distrust, rendering tax collection troublesome. Thus, the efficient provision of public goods becomes increasingly more difficult, reinforcing this low-trust/low-efficiency environment, and, in that, low tax compliance.

Discussion and Conclusions

Walk into any bar in Italy and you will likely hear someone lamenting their high taxes, poor public services, and corrupt politicians. The compliance environment is a direct reflection of this. Indeed, taxes are often a major topic of national conversation. The fight against tax evasion in Italy goes back long before Italy was a unified nation. In fact, aspects of Italian life that we often take for granted are often the result of some clever way of circumventing tax laws. For example, a salt tax in twelfth-century Pisa persuaded Florentines to stop using salt when baking bread—an unfortunate trend that continues to this day. It has also been suggested that the beautiful Triulli buildings in Puglia were built with dry walls and without mortar to allow settlers to easily dismantle them when the "taxman" came. Furthermore, tax evasion has historically been so rampant that Mussolini famously claimed that tax evaders are the worst parasites on earth. Similarly, former Prime

Minister Mario Monti asked his fellow citizens to stop referring to tax evaders as *furbi*, meaning clever. Unfortunately, these references tend to lend weight to the amoral familial approach.

However, the flaw in the amoral familialist argument leads us back to the complexities this study has sought to address in terms of tax evasion, compliance, and morale. By constructing a historical landscape dating back to the Risorgimento through the fall of the First Republic, I have identified several periods and institutions that have influenced the relationship between state and citizen.

The Risorgimento clearly had significant repercussions for Northern and Southern institutions and, in that, defined two different patterns of taxpayer behavior. I have argued that Southern Italians perceived the North as a distinct entity apart from themselves, and even as colonizers, while the North embraced calls from liberals for a unified nation state. Because the North was politically dominant, the South was expected to contribute a disproportionate amount of revenue to fund public works projects largely going to the North.

The rise of socialism and a socialist workers' movement in the North forced Catholics and right-wing liberals to join forces in direct competition to the socialists for the growing working class. While the South was left neglected by the political class, clientelism became deeply ingrained into the Southern way of life. In the North, political competition helped shape functioning public institutions and a thriving labor movement. This put the North on track to form a high-trust/high-efficiency equilibrium, while a low-trust/low-efficiency environment was established in the South.

The advent of Fascism altered the North's course, however. Unification, two world wars and Fascism shaped the compliance environment in both the North and South. After the fall of Fascism and the end of World War II, a deep distrust in the state was further reflected in the new Republic's constitution. An underlying fear that the government would infringe personal freedom and rights made tax collection increasingly difficult. This led to several tax reforms, most of which had very little effect on the compliance environment. Moreover, many of the more intrusive policies that would have resulted in increased controls were deemed unconstitutional. The administration thus felt handcuffed by certain institutional arrangements, rendering their only option a number of amnesty programs.

These amnesty programs merely deepened the low-compliance environment, making it increasingly difficult to enforce existing tax laws. The administration, realizing that the main source of evasion was the self-employed and small-business sectors, implemented a series of reforms called *Studi dei Settore* in the late 1990s. However, due to the political power of this particularly large sector of the economy, the reform ended up benefiting the taxpayer instead of the administration. Since then, the administration has attempted to fix some of the underlying problems with the tax system through pre-populated tax returns and a push to settle tax disputes out of court. Figures suggest that revenue as a result of these measures has increased.

Social norms and equilibria are sticky. Apart from major punctuations in the environment, change is usually incremental. Therefore, Italian policy-makers must address the underlying features of the low-trust/low-efficiency compliance environment. What is it that is driving this contagious behavior? How can policymakers address the metaphorical elephant in the room (the self-employed and small businesses) while at the same time fixing underlying economic issues? Vanoni had impeccable foresight when he said that administration reform must be implemented in a way that considers tax compliance as part of a holistic approach, accounting for not only the administration, but also the institutional (both formal and informal) environment. Benchmarking and learning from other European countries such as Sweden regarding these issues could be a step forward in creating a new taxpayer equilibrium.

Notes

1. In the Northern regions from Lombardy to Lazio, evasion of the regional tax on production (Imposta Regionale sulle Attivita Produttive, IRAP) ranges from about 13 percent to 54 percent; in the South (the Mezzogiorno), covering Molise to Sicily, it ranges from about 55 percent to 94 percent (see Figure 5.1). It is worth noting that both Liguria and Abruzzo do not conform to the expected North–South pattern. Abruzzo performs just slightly worse on The Quality of Government index (see Table 5.1) than Liguria, but the percentage of self-employed in Liguria is approximately one percent higher according to Istat (see http://noi-italia.istat.it/). The combination of lower-than-average quality of government and a high rate of self-employed individuals in Liguria could explain this unexpected result. In addition, Tuscany, Umbria, and Marche all have higher rates of self-employed individuals than Abruzzo.
2. Italians' perception of one another varies across regions. See Putnam, Leonardi, and Nanetti (1994); Tabellini (2010).
3. The center made up the remaining 28 percent of GDP.
4. www.bancaditalia.it/statistiche/tematiche/indagini-famiglie-imprese/bilanci-famiglie/documentazione/index.html.
5. The figures are cumulative figures of evasion and avoidance rates for employees, agricultural workers, manufacturing, and the self-employed, calculated by Bernardi (1989); Visco (1984a; 1984b; 1992); and Vitaletti (1984) using data on taxable incomes provided by Istat. A more detailed table, aggregated by type of employment, can be found in Manestra (2010).

References

Alm, J., M. McKee, and W. Beck (1990), "Amazing Grace: Tax Amnesties and Compliance." *National Tax Journal* 43(1): 23–37.

Almond, G. A. and S. Verba (1963), *The Civic Culture*. Princeton, NJ: Princeton University Press.

Ambrosetti, C. (2004), "Ezio Vanoni e la riforma tributaria in Italia." Siep Working Paper. www.siepweb.it/siep/images/joomd/1399115821325.pdf.

Banfield, E. (1967), *The Moral Basis of a Backward Society*. Glencoe: Free Press.

Bergman, M. (2009), *Tax Evasion and the Rule of Law in Latin America: The Political Culture of Cheating and Compliance in Argentina and Chile*. University Park, PA: Pennsylvania State University Press.

Bernardi, L. (1989), "Per un'introduzione al dibattito sul sistema tributario Italiano e alle proposte di riforma." In A. Pedone (ed.), *La questione tributaria*. Bologna: Banca d'Italia.

Bhatti, J., N. Apostolou, E. J. Lyman, and E. O'Regan (2012), "Tax Evaders in Greece, Spain, and Italy Better Beware." *USA Today*, January 29.

Bianchi, L., D. Miotti, R. Padovani, and G. Pellegrini (2011), "150 anni di crescita, 150 anni di divari: sviluppo, trasformazioni, politiche." *Rivista Economia del Mezzogiorno* 25(3): 449–516.

Bigoni, M., S. Bortolotti, M. Casari, D. Gambetta, and F. Pancotto (2016), "Amoral Familism, Social Capital, or Trust? The Behavioural Foundations of the Italian North–South Divide." *The Economic Journal* 126(594): 1318–41.

Carter, N. (2010), *Modern Italy in Historical Perspective*. London: A&C Black.

Cartocci, R. (2006), "L'unificazione fallita: Il sud e il capitale sociale." *Vita e Pensiero* 6: 105–13.

Clark, M. (1996), *Modern Italy 1971–1995*. New York: Longman.

Cosciani, C. (1950), *La riforma tributaria: analisi critica del sistema tributario italiano*. Florence: La Nuova Italia.

Cummings, R., J. Martinez-Vazquez, M. McKee, and B. Torgler (2009), "Tax Morale Affects Tax Compliance: Evidence from Surveys and an Artefactual Field Experiment." *Journal of Economic Behavior & Organization* 70(3): 447–57.

Edlund, J. (1999), "Trust in Government and Welfare Regimes: Attitudes to Redistribution and Financial Cheating in the USA and Norway." *European Journal of Political Research* 35(3): 341–70.

European Commission and Eurostat (2012), *Taxation Trends in the European Union*. Luxembourg: European Commission.

Ferrera, M. (1996), "The 'Southern Model' of Welfare in Social Europe." *Journal of European Social Policy* 6(1): 17–37.

Frey, B. and L. Feld (2002), "Deterrence and Morale in Taxation: An Empirical Analysis." CESifo Working Paper No. 760. www.cesifo-group.de/DocDL/760.pdf.

Frey, B. and B. Torgler (2007), "Tax Morale and Conditional Cooperation." *Journal of Comparative Economics* 35(1): 136–59.

Fukuyama, F. (1995), "Social Capital and the Global Economy." *Foreign Affairs* 74(5): 89–103.

Gilmour, D. (2011), *The Pursuit of Italy: A History of a Land, its Regions, and their Peoples*. London: Allen Lane.

Gini, C. (1962), *L'ammontare e la composizione della ricchezza delle nazioni*, Vol. 13. Turin: UTET.

Huntington, S. P. (2012), *The Third Wave: Democratization in the Late 20th Century*, Vol. 4. Oklahoma City, OK: University of Oklahoma Press.

Levi, M. (1989), *Of Rule and Revenue*. Berkeley, CA: University of California Press.

Levi, M. (1996), "Social and Unsocial Capital: A Review Essay of Robert Putnam's Making Democracy Work." *Politics & Society* 24(1): 45–55.

Levi, M., A. Sacks, and T. Tyler (2009), "Conceptualizing Legitimacy, Measuring Legitimating Beliefs." *American Behavioral Scientist* 53(3): 354–75.

Mack Smith, D. (1997), *Modern Italy: A Political History*. Ann Arbor, MI: University of Michigan Press.

Mackie, G. (2001), "Patterns of Social Trust in Western Europe and their Genesis." In K. Cook (ed.), *Trust in Society*. New York: Russell Sage Foundation, 245–82.

Manestra, S. (2010), "A Short History of Tax Compliance in Italy." Bank of Italy Occasional Paper No. 81. www.bancaditalia.it/pubblicazioni/qef/2010-0081/QEF_81.pdf?language_id=1.

Neville, P. (2014), *Mussolini*. London: Routledge.

Paler, L. (2013), "Keeping the Public Purse: An Experiment in Windfalls, Taxes, and the Incentives to Restrain Government." *American Political Science Review* 107(4): 706–25.

Patriarca, S. (2010), *Italian Vices: Nation and Character from the Risorgimento to the Republic*. Cambridge: Cambridge University Press.

Pollard, J. F. (1998), *The Fascist Experience in Italy*. London: Routledge.

Pommerehne, W., A. Hart, and B. Frey (1994), "Tax Morale, Tax Evasion and the Choice of Policy Instruments in Different Political Systems." *Public Finance* 49 (Supplement): 52–69.

Putnam, R. D., R. Leonardi, and R. Y. Nanetti (1994), *Making Democracy Work: Civic Traditions in Modern Italy*. Princeton, NJ: Princeton University Press.

Resoconti parlamentari (1948), Repubblica, Camera dei deputati, Assemblea, Discussioni, I legislatura, seduta del 21 ottobre, pag. 3744. http://legislature.camera.it/_dati/leg01/lavori/stenografici/sed0117/sed0117.pdf.

Ross, M. L. (2004), "Does Taxation Lead to Representation?" *British Journal of Political Science* 34(02): 229–49.

Sabatini, F. (2005a), "Social Capital, Public Spending and the Quality of Economic Development: The Case of Italy." FEEM Working Paper No. 14. www.econstor.eu/handle/10419/74038.

Sabatini, F. (2005b), "The Role of Social Capital in Economic Development: Investigating the Causal Nexus through Structural Equations Models." https://papers.ssrn.com/sol3/papers.cfm?abstract_id=901361.

Santoro, A. (2010), *L'evasione fiscale*. Bologna: Il Mulino.

Scholz, J. and M. Lubell (1998), "Trust and Taxpaying: Testing the Heuristic Approach to Collective Action." *American Journal of Political Science* 42(2): 398–417.

Smith, K. (1992), "Reciprocity and Fairness: Positive Incentives for Tax Compliance." In J. Slemroad (ed.), *Why People Pay Taxes: Tax Compliance and Enforcement*. Ann Arbor, MI: University of Michigan Press, 223–50.

Smith, K. and L. Stalans (1991), "Encouraging Tax Compliance with Positive Incentives: A Conceptual Framework and Research Directions." *Law & Policy* 13(1): 35–53.

Tabellini, G. (2010), "Culture and Institutions: Economic Development in the Regions of Europe." *Journal of the European Economic Association* 8(4): 677–716.

Tarrow, S. G. (1967), *Peasant Communism in Southern Italy*. New Haven, CT: Yale University Press.

Tarrow, S. G. (1996), "Making Social Science Work Across Space and Time: A Critical Reflection on Robert Putnam's *Making Democracy Work*." *American Political Science Review* 90 (June): 389–97.

Teorell, J., N. Charron, M. Samanni, S. Holmberg, and B. Rothstein (2011), "The Quality of Government Dataset." Gothenburg: The Quality of Government Institute, University of Gothenburg.

Torgler, B. and F. Schneider (2007), "What Shapes Attitudes toward Paying Taxes? Evidence from Multicultural European Countries." *Social Science Quarterly* 88(2): 443–70.

Visco, V. (1984a), "Disfunzioni ed iniquità dell'IRPEF e possibili alternative: un'analisi del funzionamento dell'imposta sul reddito in Italia nel periodo 1977–1983." In E. Gerelli and R. Valiani (eds.), *La crisi dell'imposizione progressiva sul reddito*. Milan: Franco Angelli.

Visco, V. (1984b), "Erosione ed evasione delle imposte sul reddito delle persone fisiche nel periodo 1975–1980." *Problemi di finanza pubblica* 6(18): 219–30.

Visco, V. (1992), *Fiscal System and Fiscal Reform in Italy in the 90s*. Bologna: Banca d'Italia.

Vitaletti, G. (1984), "Erosione ed evasione nel campo dell'imposizione personale: un'analisi quantitativa." *Rapporto CER*, No. 2.

Walston, J. (1988), *The Mafia and Clientelism: Roads to Rome in Post-War Calabria*. London: Taylor & Francis.

Part IV
United Kingdom

6

Creating Consent

Taxation, War, and Good Government in Britain, 1688–1914

Martin Daunton

It is not too much of an exaggeration to claim that England (or Britain from the union with Scotland in 1707) was the most successful tax state in late seventeenth- and eighteenth-century Europe,[1] combining a flow of tax revenues that was secured without serious political or economic crises, with large-scale borrowing from a sophisticated capital market, without default.[2] According to the estimates of Carmen Reinhart and Ken Rogoff for the period from 1300 to 1799, England defaulted on external debts in 1340, 1472, and possibly 1594—and never again. By contrast, its great imperial rival, France, defaulted in 1558, 1624, 1648, 1661, 1701, 1715, 1770, and 1788. In the nineteenth century, France secured a new reputation for probity, with only one more default in 1812 through hyperinflation, which wiped out most existing debts. The status of serial defaulter now passed to newly independent Greece with defaults in 1826, 1843, 1860, and 1893; and Spain in 1809, 1820, 1831, 1834, 1851, 1867, and 1882. Overall, the years of default and rescheduling between 1800 or independence and 2008 was nil in Britain and France, but 3.4 percent in Italy, 13.0 percent in Germany, 17.4 percent in Austria, 23.7 percent in Spain, and 50.6 percent in Greece (Reinhart and Rogoff 2009: 86–100).

A high degree of consent to paying taxes was achieved in the eighteenth century as Britain rose to be a major economic and imperial power. But this "compliance equilibrium" was not static, and was disrupted at the end of the wars with Napoleonic France, which led to a quarter-century of tension and weakened legitimacy of the tax system. The creation of a new equilibrium was a painstaking process of political innovation that drew in part on institutional systems that had been created in the eighteenth century, but also on new ways of formulating the relationship between the state and its citizens. This chapter therefore traces an arc from consent to loss to reconstruction.

Creating a Fiscal State

A commonplace of British historiography is the successful creation of a "fiscal–military" state in the later seventeenth and eighteenth centuries, which allowed the country to increase its tax revenue to a higher proportion of the national income than in other European countries, providing the basis for large-scale public borrowing at low interest rates without the risk of default, and allowing the creation of a powerful navy that secured the empire. Prior to 1688, taxes in England were in the range of 1.3 to 4.4 percent of national income, which was at the lower end of European extraction. The level rose with the accession of William III and wars with France from 1689 to 1697, to between 7.3 and 9.5 percent. The level remained at about 8 to 10 percent throughout the eighteenth century as a result of the frequent wars with France. During the French revolutionary and Napoleonic wars, taxation made a step change, from 12.3 percent of national income in 1790 to 18.2 percent in 1810; over the same period, government expenditure rose from 12 percent to 23 percent of GNP—a remarkably high figure that was not to be regained until World War I (Middleton 1996: 90–1; O'Brien 1988; O'Brien and Hunt 1993). Furthermore, Britain did not experience a major domestic tax revolt in the eighteenth century: the nearest was the excise crisis of 1733, which laid down clear limits of executive authority to raise taxes; and there was also the revolt of the American colonies beyond the shores of Britain. But the general picture is one of relatively harmonious collection of taxes within Britain (Brewer 1989; Mathias and O'Brien 1976).[3]

Why was the British state able to extract taxes without serious political crisis in the course of the long eighteenth century? The answer was partly a matter of timing. England in the seventeenth century avoided large-scale European land warfare and so did not need to find large sums of money in excess of the annual flow of tax revenues (Brewer 1989: 7–14, 24). Hence there was less need to sell offices or "farm" taxes on the same scale as in France, a contributory factor there to the lack of consent to taxation. The sale of offices meant that the bureaucracy was large, unaccountable, and exempt from taxes. Office-holders took their fees and salaries, and left the work to paid deputies. Why would taxpayers wish to pay in order to support a venal system of administration? Why would they willingly hand over their taxes to a "farmer" who retained the difference between the actual revenue and what he promised to pay the state? In England, tax farming was on a smaller scale and was generally ended in the late seventeenth century, and the relatively low number of offices sold meant that the English state escaped France's curse of "a sprawling, tentacular state apparatus made up of venal office holders" (Brewer 1989: 14–21, 23, 92–3; Doyle 1996).

The creation of consent was reinforced by the process of negotiating taxes with the subjects of the Crown. England/Britain had a political forum for negotiating changes in the system of taxation: acceptance of taxes was secured in Parliament which met every year after 1688 and controlled the taxing powers of the state. Spending and the authority to tax were integrated, for Parliament did not grant a permanent revenue to the king for additional expenditure, above all on war, but voted it on an annual basis (Reitan 1970).

Parliament was therefore a forum for negotiating an acceptable level of spending and the composition of taxes in Britain. Constraint on the central executive resulted in a high level of consent, and resistance to taxation was limited. Any changes in the structure of taxes or adjustment in duties were negotiated between different interests, whether north European merchants protesting against preference for timber from North America, woolen textile producers seeking to limit competition from Indian cotton cloth, or West Indian planters eager to secure markets for their sugar against East India Company pressure for a free trade in sugar and a monopoly for their China tea (Langford 1991; O'Brien, Griffiths, and Hunt 1991). The balance of custom and excise duties on different commodities was negotiated rather than imposed, and in the process economic interest groups were incorporated into the political system. Parliament was deeply jealous of its fiscal powers, and strict limits were set to the independence of the central executive from parliamentary control.

The ability of Parliament to control the executive and monitor spending rested on the availability of reasonably accurate accounts supplied to Parliament by the Treasury Commissioners. Britain was the first European state to compile a full statement of its financial position, which meant that its operations were visible. Representatives in Parliament could challenge waste, so that taxpayers had some confidence that their payments were being used for the intended purpose. Similarly, the state's creditors had confidence that the state was solvent and honest (Binney 1958; Brewer 1989: 129, 131). The costs of the American War of Independence did not lead to a fiscal crisis as in France, but to "economical reform" or a concern for administrative efficiency by improving financial administration, controlling expenditure, and preventing waste through the work of the Commission for Examining the Public Accounts of 1780 and parliamentary committees to examine expenditure and accounting methods in 1782, 1786, and 1792. The government's desire for efficiency in order to protect the creditworthiness of the state coincided with the demands of critics for reform (Brewer 1989: 85–7; Hoppit 2002; Reitan 1985; Torrance 1978).

Parliamentary scrutiny of spending meant that the British state was more public and accountable, and hence "stronger rather than weaker, more effective rather than more impotent. Public scrutiny reduced speculation, parliamentary consent lent greater legitimacy to government action. Limited in scope, the state's powers were nevertheless exercised with telling effect" (Brewer 1989: xix). The constitutional monarchy of Britain was stronger than the seemingly absolutist French state whose revenues were "owned" by others—the tax farmers and office holders—with many exemptions and privileges. Although the need for reform was obvious to French finance ministers, action was extremely difficult in the absence of representative institutions. The French Crown was not willing to adopt the British solution of a more formal constraint on its power in order to achieve greater effectiveness (Macdonald 2003: 258–61).

The method of collecting taxes was crucial to the relationship between subjects and the state. In Britain, opportunities for resistance and hostility between taxpayer and tax collector were reduced compared with most other European countries. There were no exemptions for nobles and clergy, no internal customs barriers and hence no need for paramilitary tax officials to intervene in the trade of the country (Brewer 1989: 128–9; Mathias and O'Brien 1976: 636–9). Above all, consent to taxation was increased by using the taxpayers themselves to assess and collect some taxes. Not only did local elites validate taxes through Parliament; they were also the local magistracy and commissioners for the land tax and assessed taxes. The commissioners were not paid and were not officials of the Crown; they were members of the landowning or urban elites. The pattern was very different from that in Sweden, where consent was created by a high level of monitoring by powerful institutions that created a precocious system to gather information. This "formidable monitoring capacity" (Nistotskaya and D'Arcy, Chapter 2 in this volume) is a striking feature of the Swedish system—yet in the case of England, consent was created by devolving collection to members of the local taxpaying public in order to reduce the need for government officials that would create resistance. The difference might be explained by the divergence in social structure. Sweden lacked a powerful landed aristocracy, and there was a direct relationship between the Crown and a free peasantry, which led to quasi-voluntary compliance between the state and the people. This relationship might be sustained by the Lutheran Church that created a sense of solidarity—an outcome that was only possible in the absence of major dissenting groups. The situation was somewhat different in England and Wales, where the Church of England was the established Church, and collected its own tax or "tithe" on the produce of farms, which was usually commuted to a fixed monetary payment. But its authority was also challenged by Catholics who survived the Reformation, and by the Dissenters or nonconformists such as the Baptists and Methodists. The Church of England did not fulfill the role of the Lutheran Church in Sweden as a major facilitator of consent. This role was instead undertaken by the local commissioners of taxes who reflected local social structures.

The case of local taxation is particularly instructive, for in England a large part of the tax revenue came from the rates—a property tax—levied by the parish. A distinction must be drawn between the parish as the ecclesiastical unit of the Church of England, and its role in civil government. In the Middle Ages, the parish was used by the Crown to raise revenue to finance war with France, and this capacity was then used for local purposes so that it became a civil as well as an ecclesiastical unit (Innes 1994). The parish vestry was not only responsible for running the church, but also for collecting revenue for the English Poor Law of 1601—the first tax-funded system of welfare in Europe. (In Scotland, the parish was used to finance schools more than to provide poor relief.) The existence of this unit of government and source of revenue meant that the central state was able to pass considerable responsibility to the locality. This parochial system of taxation could operate effectively because the small size of the unit meant that it was possible to monitor contributions and benefits; and it fitted with the demographic structure of nuclear families. In England, the age of marriage was high, so that married couples faced the prospect of supporting their own dependent children at the same time as their parents were in need of support. The solution to this so-called "nuclear family hardship" was to rely on parochial support for the elderly in the knowledge that the parish would support the married couple when they were in turn elderly. This inclusive system broke down under demographic pressure and economic change in the early nineteenth century, with concerns that benefits were being paid to an out-group or scroungers, and that income support was distorting a free labor market. The result was a "new poor law" in 1834 that attempted to restrict benefits, not only by changes in the rules governing payments but also a reform of the franchise. Instead of each ratepayer having one vote so that potential beneficiaries could overrule large taxpayers, a sliding scale was introduced to ensure that the poor rates were controlled by the largest contributors. Consent to taxation might therefore reflect group size and demographic structures (Prest 1990; Smith 1996).

The British system of taxation in the eighteenth century did have problems, for the land tax was granted by a Parliament of landowners in return for control over the finances of the Crown. Consent was achieved but adjustment to the land tax proved difficult. In theory, the land tax was levied at one of four rates, from 1s. to 4s. in the £. In reality, the rates were set to produce a yield of £500,000 to £2 million, with no adjustment to take account of the rising value of land in the later eighteenth century or the differential growth of regions of the country at a time of major structural change.

The agreement on the land tax of 1689 survived until 1799 when the pressures of the revolutionary war led to the introduction of a new income tax. Consequently, the landowners' contribution to the finances of the state fell over the eighteenth century (Beckett 1985; Ward 1963).

The lack of buoyancy in the land tax meant that the government turned to other sources of revenue. Assessed taxes were imposed on conspicuous signs of wealth such as male servants, hair powder, and riding horses. They were designed to fall on the rich, and were administered by the same local commissioners as the land tax. The result was a degree of tax evasion but a fair degree of consent and legitimacy. As we shall see, the commissioners administered the income tax between 1799 and 1816 with much the same trade-off between evasion and acceptance. By the early 1790s, the land and assessed taxes taken together had fallen to barely half their share of total taxation at the start of the eighteenth century. Landowners and the wealthy controlled Parliament and failed to maintain their proportion of the tax burden, yet without serious problems of financial collapse and default, or a loss of consent, for other sources of revenue were available.

Customs duties were a major source of revenue at the start of the eighteenth century, but fell by the end of the century. The customs service was an inefficient part of the state. Officials were appointed by the Treasury, often with more concern for political patronage than efficiency, and many had a life interest in the position. They were paid a modest salary and drew fees from the office, leaving the work to paid deputies who might supplement their income by offering advice to merchants on their payment of duties. The high level of duties on goods resulted in smuggling and evasion which was extremely difficult to police around the British coastline. Customs duties provoked resistance at the level of smuggling brandy or tea past customs officials rather than tax revolts and a collapse of revenues. There were no internal tariff barriers within Britain after the union with Scotland in 1707, so tensions between the population and officers were mainly confined to the coastal areas and ports rather than more generally through a paramilitary fiscal force. Revenue from customs duties failed to keep pace with the growth in British trade in the eighteenth century and reforming the structure of duties was difficult, both for strategic reasons and because change would provoke outcry from vested interests (Brewer 1989: 101–2, 130; O'Brien 1988: 23–6).

The major source of additional finance in the eighteenth century was the excise—a tax that was developed by Cromwell's government after the civil war. The mode of collection differed from both the local commissioners and the customs service in Britain, and the fiscal system of France. Officials or gaugers were appointed for their competence, which was ensured by a career ladder with promotion by merit and a pension on retirement. They were paid a salary so that they had an incentive to create efficient methods in order to reduce their workload, in contrast to customs officials who were paid fees and had an incentive to maintain existing procedures. Above all, the excise officials dealt with a relatively small number of large industrial production plants rather than the general public, and consequently tension did not permeate society (Brewer 1989: 69–87, 101–14; Coffman 2013; O'Brien 1988: 26–8).

The secure basis of tax revenues meant that the British state was able to borrow money on generous terms, at around a 2 percent lower interest rate than in France between 1746 and 1793 (Brewer 1989: 114–26; Stasavage 2003: 96–7; Velde and Weir 1992: 15–19, 36). The British state never defaulted on its debts and did not exploit currency debasement and inflation—a temptation that many other countries did not resist. An obvious reason for the absence of default is that Britain had representative political institutions so that a credible commitment was guaranteed by constitutional checks and balances, which prevented taxpayers from taking advantage of lenders. David Stasavage (2003: 24, 39, 99, 129, 154, 156, 172) is skeptical, arguing that checks and balances cannot prevent power falling into the hands of interests in favor of default. In his view, the answer lies in the nature of political divisions and the existence of parties. Where a society has "multiple political cleavages" and the choice of party affiliation was determined by non-economic issues, the division between creditors and taxpayers was buried within a wider coalition of interests and opinions. But Stasavage surely exaggerates the role of parties in preventing default compared with representative institutions. Can parties be separated from the existence of the representative institutions they were seeking to control? Representative institutions were also important in underpinning consent to taxation, which provided the flow of income for servicing loans. The implausibility of a sharp divide between creditors and taxpayers can be explained by factors other than the existence of parties. The strength of British finance rested on a collaboration of landed and moneyed interests in a patriotic alliance. Loans and the moneyed interest were seen as sustaining British liberties and prosperity by defeating French Catholicism and winning new markets in the colonies. Although financiers and the debt were potential threats to liberty, the solution was to contain them within a parliamentary system of close scrutiny of accounts and spending, in order to defend British liberties and Protestantism against external threat (Brewer 1989: 142–3, 161; Hoppit 1990: 316–17).

The commitment of the British state to pay its debts was linked with the credibility of any debtor in paying his debt—a serious consideration in such a highly commercialized society as Britain. Many taxpayers—merchants, industrialists, and traders—were not likely to support default given their own reliance on credit. They had a general concern to maintain the sanctity of credit, fearing that a loss of income might lead bond-holders to default on their own obligations and so threaten the fragile system of interlocking claims. Landowners shared their concerns, for they were deeply involved in the financial world through their use of mortgages. At the same time, the composition of bond-holders shifted in the second half of the eighteenth century so that their ranks were no longer dominated by foreigners and London moneyed interests. Bonds were held by insurance companies that dealt with a large number of policyholders; charities purchased bonds as a secure investment; and so did widows. A concern for the stability of government loans was widespread.[4]

During the Revolutionary and Napoleonic Wars, the British fiscal system continued to evolve to cope with the increasing demands for taxes and loans. The land tax and assessed taxes fell as a proportion of tax revenues, and the income tax was introduced in 1799 as a way of increasing the contribution from landowners and wealthy members of society. The land tax was fixed in the 1680s as part of the deal between the Crown and Parliament, which was dominated by the landed elite. This was not a serious issue in the early eighteenth century when land prices and rents were static or falling, but it did become a major issue in the later eighteenth century when land prices and rents rose sharply as a result of population growth, and this additional income was not taxed. The income tax was designed to tap this additional income. Initially, the income tax was collected by aggregating an individual's income from all sources—an intrusive and complex process. After 1803, the tax was collected on each source or "schedule" in a way that minimized intrusion by the state: tax was deducted automatically at source by the person paying rent or interest and dividends; and income from the profits of trade or business were assessed by local commissioners rather than by state officials. The commissioners were crucial to the legitimacy of the tax. Of course, payment of the income tax was not universally popular, yet it did produce considerable revenue. Britain was the most heavily taxed state in Europe, yet was able to extract revenue with fewer political difficulties.

Britain out-taxed, out-borrowed, and out-gunned the French during the Wars. The real problem for Britain came after the conflicts. The failure to renew the income tax in 1816, and the continued rigidity in the land tax, meant that the proportion of revenue from indirect taxes rose, and the legitimacy of taxation in Britain was under strain until the 1840s. A high proportion of revenue went on the service of the national debt, so that it was easy to argue that the fiscal system was a device to take money from the poor and industrious members of society and to transfer it to idle rentiers and the hangers-on at court and office. The external enemy was defeated, and in the view of many radicals the main threat to liberty came from within.

Losing Consent

The consent to taxation achieved in the eighteenth century was threatened after the defeat of Napoleon in 1815, and had to be recreated in the second quarter of the nineteenth century. There were a number of reasons for the emergence of deep political tensions over taxation. The income tax was a wartime measure, and was abandoned in 1816 despite the concern of the government for the problems that would follow in securing sufficient revenue to pay the massive costs of servicing the postwar debt, which had risen to over twice GDP.

The political difficulties were compounded by agricultural protection. Not only were the landed elite escaping their fair share of taxation, but they were protected by the Corn Laws, which limited the importation of grain unless prices rose above a certain level. Farmers and landowners were being protected as prices fell from the high wartime peaks, whereas other members of society were left to cope with economic difficulties—and were paying more taxes to cover the abolition of the income tax. The legitimacy of the fiscal system was called into question.

The problems of consent to taxation were exacerbated by two other factors. The first issue was the high level of debt service which seemed to radical critics to be a transfer payment from the industrious class to idle, parasitical rentiers.[5] The second issue was the unreformed parliamentary system. The proportion of the adult male population with the vote had declined since the eighteenth century, with some constituencies virtually uninhabited, whereas Manchester did not return a Member to Parliament (O'Gorman 1989). The Tory government was opposed to reform, and stressed the benefits of "virtual representation": a cotton manufacturer from Manchester could "buy" a parliamentary seat elsewhere. Of course, the Tories—largely drawn from the landed class—had a vested interest in not widening the franchise and thus giving more voice to northern industrial cities. Their response to complaints that they were pursuing self-interest was that landowners had leisure and a wider frame of reference to pursue the needs of the nation as a whole (Gambles 1999). This argument of "republican virtue" was challenged by a shift to a new discourse of responsibility, prudence, and self-control, exemplified by industrialists and traders (Pocock 1985).

A further reason to resist parliamentary reform was religious. In theory, England had a "confessional state" with the vote, higher education, and office-holding limited to members of the Anglican Church, so excluding Catholics, Jews, Methodists, and other "Nonconformist" Churches. Parliamentary reform would raise the specter of giving the vote to Catholics—above all in Ireland, which joined the Union in 1800. The Tory government's strategy was to show that an unreformed parliamentary system could reduce spending from its wartime heights and reduce the national debt. The Tory government did indeed make considerable strides, without convincing the skeptical radicals. The process of stripping out waste provided more evidence for the remaining problems rather than reassurance that they were being resolved (Harling and Mandler 1993). The result was a widespread political attack on the fiscal–military state that had lost its rationale with the defeat of France, and British manufacturers who had secured world markets so that they no longer needed government support through mercantilist protection (O'Brien, Griffiths, and Hunt 1991). In 1829, the vote was extended to Catholics and in 1832, the parliamentary system was reformed.

Of course, opponents of the fiscal–military state did not agree on either the diagnosis or the cure. The Anti-Corn Law League wished to abolish the Corn Laws and to reduce the level of government spending and taxation, which they saw as provoking warfare and militarism. However, the predominantly working-class Chartists saw repeal of the Corn Laws as cover for an attack on wages when food prices dropped. Where they could agree was in attacking landowners as Rent-seekers[6] whose massive wealth rested on the enterprise of others; and on a policy of retrenchment to sweep away the waste and corruption of a bloated state. Such an attitude blocked one way of resolving the fiscal problem: returning to the income tax, as proposed by some senior Tories (Hilton 1977: 260). The radicals and Anti-Corn Law League were doubtful, for they linked the income tax with war and militarism, and argued that it merely took back part of these ill-gotten gains from the Corn Laws, whereas other forms of income paid both higher foods prices as a result of the Corn Laws and the income tax.[7] A better solution, they argued, was retrenchment to liberate trade. Further, the income tax was unfair because it fell equally on income that arose "spontaneously" from permanent property in land that could be passed on to the next generation, producing an income regardless of character or age; and on transitory "precarious" income that depended on the hard work and character of the individual, and ceased on ill health, old age, or death.[8]

Restoring consent would be a major task, and it was one that was carried out with considerable success in the middle of the nineteenth century, above all by Robert Peel, who was a Tory of a different type from his predecessors as prime minister. His father was a wealthy cotton textile industrialist in Lancashire who bought a landed estate and sent his son to Harrow School and Christ Church, Oxford, where he mixed with members of the aristocratic elite. He started the process of recreating consent with the reduction in custom and excise duties in 1830, cutting taxes on "necessities of the people" in order "to excite a taste in the humbler classes of society for those comforts and those enjoyments—those luxuries he might add—of civilised society . . . the habitual possession of which, would form the best guarantee that the higher classes could have for the possession of their property and their power."[9] He restored the income tax in 1842 for an initial period of six years; it continued to face very strong opposition from free traders and radicals when it was renewed in 1848 and again in 1851. His ambition reached its apogee with the repeal of the Corn Laws in 1846.

Peel's strategy was largely successful, marking the demise of the Chartists at the very time of the outbreak of revolutions across Europe in 1848. The Great Exhibition of 1851 became a symbol of the new harmony in social relations, as the workers shared in the proceeds of industrialization and traveled to London in great numbers (Finn 1993; Stedman Jones 1983). The process took a further major step in 1853 with the great budget of William Gladstone, a disciple of Peel, who was, like him, from a background in both trade and land. His budget marks a turning point toward a high level of consent to taxation. This recreation of consent from the traumas of the three decades after the end of the Napoleonic Wars was carefully considered and not just an unexpected outcome of policies adopted for other reasons: there was fore-thought and explicit consideration of how to secure agreement to a new fiscal constitution.

(Re)creating Consent

A reduction in the level of taxation was not sufficient in itself to secure consent. Total government expenditure fell from around 23 percent of GNP at the end of the Wars to 12.4 percent in 1840, but criticism continued. Contemporaries had little sense of taxation as a proportion of national income, or any idea of the debt to GDP ratio: they focused on the *absolute* levels of spending and the size of any budgetary surplus or deficit. Regardless of the overall level of extraction, the fiscal system seemed biased and costly. We need to consider the process of legitimation on three levels: the political rhetoric developed by the ruling elite, the nature of the system of account-ability and surveillance of spending and taxing, and the particular relation-ship between the taxpayer and the state.

One factor that contributed to the legitimation of taxation was the nature of the British political elite. For all its attempts to develop a sense of public duty and integrity, the claims of the Tory government in the 1820s and 1830s flew in the face of the perception of corruption and self-interest. Peel and Gladstone were heirs to the Tory notion of public duty, but their achievement was to make it integral to their character as incorruptible public men, expressed through their sober dress, hard work, and general demeanor. The rhetorical strategy was helped by the fact that they straddled interests of land and trade. Their devotion to public duty was linked to a claim that they and the state were disinterested or neutral between class interests. Their ambition was conservative, but in a different sense from the postwar Tory ministries, which had aimed to preserve the rule of a narrow political elite within an unreformed constitution. Peel concluded that the best strategy for preserving the rule of the political elite and of protecting property was to adopt policies that were even-handed between those with property and those without. To Gladstone, fiscal probity was a means to create an integrated society and a source of morality (Matthew 1986: ch. 3). The attacks on a corrupt and repressive state by middle-class radicals and Chartists gave way to "constitutional radicalism" with a clear distinction between what was seen as continental despotism and British liberty. The concern became much less about the parasitical nature of the British state, and more about a new sense of patriotism that was open and plural (Biagini 1991; 1992; Finn 1993).

By constraining state expenditure and as far as possible excluding the state from involvement in economic interests, it was hoped to protect the political elite from challenge and to define the state as a neutral arbitrator. Politicians must rise above personal greed and self-interest; they must also rise above any temptation to use the state to favor one interest against another, whether a trade group in search of protection or a social group seeking tax breaks. This rhetoric of disinterestedness, of being even-handed between all types of property and the propertied and non-propertied, was central to Gladstone's budget of 1853, where he strongly dissented from criticism of the landed elite as Rent-seekers who did not pay their fair share of taxation. As we saw, many radicals and free traders opposed the income tax, and argued that landowners should make a greater contribution. At the very least, they argued, the income tax should be differentiated to fall more heavily on "spontaneous" or unearned incomes than on "precarious" earned incomes that involved the risks of trade and personal exertion. Gladstone was appalled, seeing differentiation as a means of defining classes in the tax code, undermining the integrative function of the fiscal constitution. It would also be interpreted by landowners in Parliament as yet another example of the privileged treatment of merchants and industrialists. It would turn taxation into the plaything of vested interests.

In his budget of 1853, Gladstone took another approach. Rather than automatically granting a lower tax rate to precarious incomes on the basis of what ought to be saved to provide for retirement and for dependents, he introduced a tax break on life insurance premiums, regardless of the source of income and according to actual savings. Furthermore, he "balanced" the fiscal constitution through a careful calculation of liability to all forms of tax, local and national, on income, and on assets at death so that real property paid its proper share of taxation. This was a way of avoiding differentiation and of removing the land question from "high" politics for a generation (Matthew 1979).

It is easy to assume that the income tax provided the state with a new source of revenue that would allow it to extract a higher proportion of national income, above all for war—precisely the concern of the radical and free trade opponents. Gladstone's strategy was instead to sell it as a means of constraining the state and preventing war, and in doing so he won over the radical opponents. The income tax was linked with the franchise: the property qualification for voting was closely aligned with the threshold for paying income tax. Both Peel and Gladstone stressed that the income tax was temporary, so that voters who were also taxpayers would vote for retrenchment and peace. Public choices would have immediate private consequences in tax bills, so that electors had an incentive to vote for cheap government (Matthew 1986: 125–8). This argument was threatened when the Conservatives opportunistically extended the franchise in 1867 in the hope of securing support. Even so, the franchise remained narrower than in most European countries—and working men who secured the vote in 1867 initially continued to see the state as something to keep in its place. However, the very success of presenting taxation and the state as neutral or disinterested in time led to a shift in attitudes. The result of constraining the state, creating a sense of even-handedness and incorruptibility, was to create a greater willingness to pay and to turn to the state for welfare. One aspect of neutrality was a shift away from anti-trade union policies to an approach that rested on the neutrality of the state between labor and capital (McKibbin 1984). Far from seeking to constrain trade unions, the British state was willing to utilize them and other working-class voluntary bodies to deliver welfare benefits. In the unemployment and health insurance schemes of 1911, the unions and friendly societies that provided sickness benefit and medical assistance became "approved" societies administering benefits on behalf of the state, receiving compulsory contributions from employers and employees and a subsidy from the state (Daunton 1996a). The notion of a "level playing field" might have been a spurious piece of rhetoric from the ruling elite to mask wider inequalities, but it did mean that they had to take care not to expose the claim as merely rhetoric, and it did mean that the Labour party was willing to turn to the state and to tax for the funding of welfare. Constraint gave way to consent, and a sense that the state was fair (Daunton 1996a).

The process of recreating consent did not only depend on political language and rhetoric, but more concretely on administrative or accounting rules that contributed to the high level of legitimacy and trust. In order to constrain the action of self-seeking politicians and the ambitions of spending departments, rules were needed, some of which go back to auditing principles introduced in the eighteenth century. The rules in themselves were not novel, but there was a much greater sense of moral commitment to them, and they hardened into Treasury dogma that continued into the interwar period and beyond.

The first rule was a rejection of hypothecation—that is, pledging particular revenues to particular purposes. In the eighteenth century, hypothecation was used as a means of creating trust, for particular taxes were earmarked to cover particular loans. By the mid-nineteenth century, different assumptions applied, for hypothecation implied an increase in the role of the state by treating it as a collection of services and functions, each of which was individually desirable with a protected source of revenue. Revenue should therefore be unified, treated as a single pool of money that was separate from the purposes for which it was raised. The ban on hypothecation was high on the list of the Treasury's constitutional principles for the fiscal system (Daunton 2001).

The second rule was the rejection of *virement* of funds. The danger of moving unspent balances that remained in one budget head to another was that money would always be spent up to the maximum, so ratcheting up spending. Whereas revenue was treated as a single sum without any ties to a particular purpose, spending was subdivided into annual "votes" of the House of Commons. A balance remaining on one vote could not be used to cover a deficit on another or to increase spending. Neither could a vote in one year be carried over to the future, with the danger that the present was placing burdens on the future. The ban on *virement* was therefore linked with a third rule: annual parliamentary votes and close scrutiny of accounts. Although Parliament was unlikely to refuse a request for money for a government policy, the freedom of the executive was constrained. Spending on any new venture had to be carefully argued, and annual votes and the ban on *virement* helped to constrain the state. At the same time, the need to obtain approval for every item of spending led to transparency and trust, for each item of spending had to be specifically sanctioned (Daunton 2001).

There was a strong emphasis on the need for constant vigilance by Parliament as a protection for the public against the spending plans of the executive. Radical reformers argued for an extension of the franchise in the early nineteenth century less as a means to create a more democratic political system than to change the composition of members of Parliament in order to purge it of "interest" and to make parliamentary control more effective in eliminating militarism and waste (Taylor 1995). Gladstone was very anxious that the principle of scrutiny by Parliament and Treasury control of spending departments should be maintained, and the rules were tightened after they were breached in the Post Office's purchase of the telegraph companies: in 1869, £7 million was approved in Parliament to carry out nationalization, but when this limit was reached, the official in charge simply continued without authorization. As a result, the Treasury appointed its own official within the Post Office to enforce accounting rules (Daunton 1985: 318–24). Similarly, Gladstone was horrified by a breach of the principle of annual votes in 1889 when the Conservative government created a Naval Defence Fund to pay for the construction of battleships, borrowing money that would be paid out of taxes for the next seven years. Gladstone saw a threat to the constitutional principle that the Commons should not pledge future revenue. When he returned to power in 1892, he undid this "great constitutional innovation" (Daunton 1996b). Crucially, the role of the Commons was to scrutinize spending; it was not to propose spending or to haggle over tax breaks. In Britain, the budget was presented by the Chancellor as a package, with limited scope for revision; if it were rejected—a very rare event—the government fell and an election followed. Consequently, the tax system was much less prone to explicit bargaining and special favors; it was usually drawn up by the Chancellor and a small group of advisers, and presented to the Cabinet as a more-or-less done deal (Steinmo 1988–9).

The ban on hypothecation and *virement*, and the insistence on annual votes, meant that there was the possibility of a surplus at the end of the year. A further rule was that this surplus should not be carried forward to the next year. The rule removed the temptation of politicians to build up a surplus and then cut taxation just before an election, or announce a politically popular program. The result would be "a gigantic system of jobbery." After 1829, the convention was that any surplus should be transferred to the sinking fund in order to reduce the national debt, so releasing funds that could be more effectively used by the private sector. Repayment of the national debt would also create confidence that the state was trustworthy, so maintaining British credit and ensuring that the public would lend to the state in times of war. In this way, the national debt was turned from a burden into the "war chest" to defend Britain (Daunton 2001).

Of course, the burden of the national debt fell because there was no major continental war, and because of unprecedented economic growth. The government published figures of the aggregate net liabilities of the state, showing a fall from £837.6 million in 1840 to £685 million in 1890; and debt charges fell from around 55 percent of the gross expenditure of central government in the second quarter of the nineteenth century, to under 20 percent at the start of the twentieth century. Contemporaries were aware of these figures, although they did not have our more recent calculations that the national debt fell from 260 percent of GDP in 1816 to 24 percent in 1914 (Daunton 2001; Neild 2012). Nevertheless, it was clear that taxation was less open to the accusation of being a transfer from active producers of wealth to parasitical rentiers.

These accounting and constitutional principles were important in establishing the legitimacy of the state and consent to taxation that allowed Britain to adapt to the new urban, industrial society with its demands on spending for infrastructure, welfare, and defense. Gladstone celebrated these principles in 1891 at Hastings—a location that was central to perceptions of English national identity as a fusion of the democratic principles of the defeated Anglo-Saxons and the centralizing tendencies of the Normans (Burrow 1981: 143). The existence of one without the other would lead to a weak, fragmented state or to autocracy, so it was vital to maintain balance through rigorous financial checks on the executive by local representatives in the Commons. As Gladstone put it,

> The finance of the country is intimately associated with the liberties of the country. It is a powerful leverage by which liberty has been gradually acquired. Running back into the depths of antiquity for many centuries, it lies at the root of English liberty, and if the House of Commons can by any possibility lose the power of the control of the grants of public money, depend upon it your very liberty will be worth very little in comparison. (Daunton 2001)

Here was one of the great myths of English national identity.

In addition to political rhetoric and the rules of Parliament and central government, consent was secured by the way in which taxes were collected. The explicit aim in Britain was to minimize direct contact between the central bureaucracy and the individual citizen—a principle that helped to secure consent. Many of the features of tax collection in Britain go back to the seventeenth and eighteenth centuries. As we have seen, the land tax and assessed taxes on external signs of wealth were administered in the locality by members of the taxpaying class who served as commissioners. When the income tax was introduced, a similar system was adopted: commissioners with an income qualification of £200 a year had responsibility for assessing and collecting the tax. These general commissioners had considerable discretion, and at the time of the introduction of the income tax, the prime minister said that they should be "persons of a respectable situation in life; as far as possible removed from any suspicion of partiality, or any kind of undue influence: men of integrity and independence" (Daunton 1998: 118). They selected assessors who in turn appointed collectors, often the same people: they were usually tradesmen or small farmers, and were similar to the local parish officers who were drawn from the residents of the parish and paid a commission of 1½d. in the pound collected. In 1860–1, there were about 54,000 assessors in the United Kingdom, not all of whom were efficient or conscientious. The general commissioners were themselves paid a small commission which was used to employ a clerk—usually a local solicitor who was not otherwise part of the state bureaucracy. There was a small central bureaucracy in London and some state officials in the localities—the surveyors, who checked that the system was working properly, and provided information on the rules to the lay commissioners and assessors (Daunton 2001).

The success of the income tax rested on keeping a balance between delegation to the localities and the taxpayers, and central oversight to prevent corruption and collusion. The general commissioners were widely seen as the protectors of citizens against oppression by the central state. One reason why the income tax was abandoned at the end of the Napoleonic Wars was the problem concerning its administration in London, with its conflicting jurisdictions and difficulty in assessing incomes from various commercial and financial activities. As a result, the state suspended the general commissioners in the City. This apparently dictatorial centralizing decision alienated the City of London, provoking a petition to abolish the income tax in 1816 (Hope-Jones 1939: 54–5). When the income tax was reintroduced in 1842, Peel was very careful to ensure that the commissioners retained their authority, above all in their appellate function. At various times, proposals were made to substitute government officials in collecting and assessing taxes but efficiency was usually overruled by concern for the rights of the taxpayers (Daunton 2001: 188, 194–7; Stebbings 1992; 2009).

This reliance on lay commissioners connected with another feature of the income tax: it was based on schedules. The idea was to collect as much tax as possible at source, so that a tenant farmer paid his rent to the landlord net of tax and handed the balance to the collector. The farmer's own income was difficult to estimate, so was fixed by the amount of rent paid. Similarly, interest on bonds and dividends was paid net of tax. The result of this system was to reduce intrusion into the personal affairs of a taxpayer whose total income was not known to officials or to the local assessors and collectors. It also minimized direct contact with the tax collector. The main problem was Schedule D, comprising profits from trade, industry, and the professions, which could only be estimated at the end of the tax year, and with considerable uncertainty. The lay commissioners were particularly important, for they came to an agreement with local trades over such matters as depreciation allowances, which relied on local interpretation of national legislation. The estimate of Schedule D profits relied on the honesty of the individual taxpayer, as it was difficult to check the accuracy of figures, and the assessors as small traders might themselves have a personal interest in underestimating the figure.

The officials in London at the Board of Inland Revenue explicitly accepted the trade-off between consent and avoidance. In 1870, the Board claimed that 40 percent of assessments were under-recorded, and in 1890 it was suggested that there was in effect a 20 percent reduction in the income tax from trade and professions. The alternative was officious intrusion into the affairs of individuals, which would lead to resentment. Indeed, industrialists were not above publicly defending their under-reporting of profits as a way around "unfair" rules on depreciation. Similarly, it was not easy to get returns from employers of the names of their employees who might be liable to tax on their earnings. Sometimes, they took a principled attitude that they were not informers for the state; often, they just failed to make a return in the knowledge that there were few if any sanctions. Parliament was reluctant to impose stronger controls that might serve only to alienate taxpayers. Attitudes only gradually changed as it was realized that compliance and consent were more likely to be called into question by the ability of some taxpayers to evade payment: the shift was apparent in the committee on the income tax of 1905, which argued that the issue was no longer the fear that the income tax was inquisitorial but rather that too many people avoided payment (Daunton 2001).

The schedular system meant that it was not possible to introduce a progressive income tax, for it was not based on the total income of any taxpayer. This was a major advantage in 1842 in securing consent, and it was reiterated by leading officials at the turn of the nineteenth century and again at the turn of the twentieth century, when the Liberal party was turning towards progressive taxation. The head of the Inland Revenue warned the Liberal Chancellor of the dangers of his proposal, pointing out that any attempt to discover the total income of taxpayers was too dangerous:

> we should be making 100 incidental enemies for every recalcitrant, or mendacious, plutocrat... [I]s the game worth the candle? Would this extra million a year not be dearly bought if it involved setting up a feud, so long happily avoided, between the public generally and the vast body of persons, often not very well-mannered or very literate, who are concerned in the collection of taxes.
>
> (Daunton 1996b: 160)

Might it not alienate the commissioners on whose cooperation the collection of the tax relied? A leading Treasury official argued against change in 1906 on the grounds that "the collection is one of the wonders of the world. It is the envy of other nations. We must do nothing to imperil this productivity" (Daunton 2001: 325). But a new generation of Treasury officials realized that administration could be reformed; and progression was supported by the marginalist revolution. The political context had changed, so that clinging to a non-progressive income tax that had been needed to secure consent might now threaten consent.

One context for the introduction of a graduated income tax was the limit to the existing structure of local taxation based on the rates. The costs of local government had been increasing in the later nineteenth century as a result of the higher levels of spending on public health, on education after the introduction of publicly funded schools in 1870, and on the development of the Poor Law as a system of institutional care for the elderly, orphans, and the sick. The rates were regressive, forming a higher proportion of the rent of smaller houses than large properties; and the rate base was not increasing as rapidly as demands for expenditure. The situation reached a crisis point after 1900: a boom in house building led to a fall in rent, and squeezed the profits of rental property. The limits to consent in local taxation had been reached—but what could be done? At the same time, the costs of fighting the Boer War were placing strains on central government taxation. One solution, favored by some Conservatives, was to switch to imperial preference. By imposing import duties on goods from outside the empire, the government could secure revenue and, so it was claimed, create steady employment that would reduce pressure on the Poor Law. This approach was defeated in the general election of 1906, which left the new Liberal government with a need to find an alternative way of securing revenue and dealing with the social problem. The answer was a shift to a progressive income tax, and also to differentiation between earned and unearned income. Differentiation and a radical attack on the "unearned increment" of higher land prices in the "people's budget" of 1909 were also ways for the Liberal party to respond to the growth of the Labour party by showing that it was sensitive to the demands of workers for a shift in the distribution of income and wealth. Of course, there were dangers in introducing differentiation and graduation of the income tax, for it might alienate middle-class voters and property owners. The result was a constitutional crisis when the budget was rejected by the unelected House of Lords composed mainly of aristocratic landowners, so challenging the principle that tax and spending were the responsibility of the elected House of Commons.

Taxation became a major political issue in the two general elections of 1910, but there was a crucial difference from the situation in other countries such as France, Germany, and the United States. The income tax itself was accepted and firmly entrenched, whereas in these countries its adoption was still a matter of deep division. It was not just that the income tax had a longer history in Britain, but also that the Liberals were careful to adjust the incidence on a crucial constituency: married men with children. As well as introducing graduation and differentiation, the Liberal Chancellor gave a tax break to married men with dependent children, so that the rate of taxation for family men actually fell. Britain entered World War I with a fiscal system that was reformed, with a high level of compliance and consent. What seemed in other countries a dangerous innovation was in the case of Britain more consensual. The income tax, despite its problems, was embedded within civil society, which helped to create a high level of compliance, trust in the fairness of the tax, and widespread acceptance of the legitimacy of the state. It was part of the wider context of the state and civil society in Britain—the delegation of responsibilities to charities and voluntary associations, and the high level of autonomy granted to self-governing professions. Furthermore, the excise and import duties were now limited to a very narrow range of goods, so that payment was presented as being voluntary: no one needed to drink wine or beer, smoke tobacco, or imbibe tea and coffee. There was no general sales tax that would alienate small shopkeepers who had to collect the duty, or consumers who would have to pay. During and after World War I, the Treasury firmly rejected such an imposition, which was seen as alienating taxpayers and threatening the carefully constructed consent to taxation (Daunton 2001). Britain was unique in surviving World War I without any serious threat to consent.

Consequences and Conclusion

The recreation of consent to taxation in the nineteenth century was designed to constrain the state, not to release it to spend more. The technique was successful, with government spending falling from a peak of about 23 percent of GNP in 1810 to 8 percent in 1890. A change soon started, with a rise between 1900 and 1914 as a result of the combined effect of rearmament and welfare spending to 12 percent of GDP in 1913. There was then a displacement with World War I to around a quarter of GDP (Middleton 1996: 9, 91). This rise was facilitated by the earlier constraints: by containing the radical critique of the "tax eater" state and the fear of placemen and sinecures, it was possible to establish new government agencies. It was necessary to "cleanse" and curtail the state before a more positive role was feasible. Labour was ready to turn to the state and taxation, moving away from the earlier radical fear that taxation would be used to sustain an idle class of aristocrats and courtiers. Indeed, they were ready to move away from their earlier stress on self-reliance in friendly societies and trade unions to state-funded welfare. The creation of consent and compliance in the nineteenth century therefore laid the foundations for the later growth of the state, without the sort of problems that were found in many other countries. The difference was very apparent at the end of World War I when the burden of debt repayment was negotiated with fewer strains than after the Napoleonic Wars or in other countries. Politicians and officials made explicit reference to the need to be even-handed between different interests so that the state could be portrayed as neutral or disinterested; and the need to retain compliance by avoiding the perils of a broad-based sales tax.

Understanding the processes by which consent and compliance were constructed needs to proceed on three levels. The first is political rhetoric, which is not necessarily about justifying high levels of state spending—that was not the aim of Peel and Gladstone—but of even-handedness, public duty, and incorruptibility. Secondly, auditing or accounting rules and transparency were needed to show that the money obtained by the state was accountable. And thirdly, modes of collection were required that did not intrude too much on the individual. The recreation of consent to taxation in the nineteenth century survived for much of the twentieth century but, for a wide variety of reasons, faced a growing challenge by the last quarter of the century.

Notes

1. This paper follows the argument of Daunton (2001; 2002). An early version of this material appeared in Daunton (1998; 2008).
2. See Ormrod, Bonney, and Bonney (1999), especially the chapter by Bonney and Ormrod, pp. 1–21; on the emergence of a loan market, see Dickson (1967).
3. Coffman (2013) pushes the origins of the excise and acceptance of higher levels of taxation back to the Civil War. On the excise crisis, see Langford (1975).
4. On credit, see Muldrew (1998); on the changing composition of bond holders, Dickson (1967); on the use of mortgages, Macdonald (2003: 230).
5. See Rubinstein (1983) for an exaggerated account.
6. "Rent" refers to the unearned increment received by the landowner for scarcity.
7. Parliamentary Debates, 3rd ser. 62, March 21, 1842, cols. 979–81.
8. I discuss this debate at length in Daunton (2001).
9. Parliamentary Debates, new ser. 23, March 19, 1830, col. 658.

References

Beckett, J. V. (1985), "Land Tax or Excise: The Levying of Taxation in Seventeenth- and Eighteenth-century England." *English Historical Review* 100: 285–308.

Biagini, E. F. (1991), "Popular Liberals, Gladstonian Finance and the Debate on Taxation, 1860–74." In E. F. Biagini and A. J. Reid (eds.), *Currents of Radicalism: Popular Radicalism, 1850–1914*. Cambridge: Cambridge University Press, 1–20.

Biagini, E. F. (1992), *Liberty, Retrenchment and Reform: Popular Liberalism in the Age of Gladstone, 1860–1880*. Cambridge: Cambridge University Press.

Binney, J. E. D. (1958), *British Public Finances and Administration, 1774–92*. Oxford: Clarendon Press.

Bonney, R. and W. M. Ormrod (1999), "Introduction: Crises, Revolutions and Self-Sustained Growth: Towards a Conceptual Model of Change in Fiscal History." In W. M. Ormrod, M. M. Bonney, and R. J. Bonney (eds.), *Crises, Revolutions and Self-Sustained Growth: Essays in European Fiscal History, 1130–1830*. Stamford, UK: Paul Watkins Publishing, 1–21.

Brewer, J. (1989), *The Sinews of Power: War, Money and the English State, 1688–1783*. New York: Alfred A. Knopf.

Burrow, J. W. (1981), *A Liberal Descent: Victorian Historians and the English Past*. Cambridge: Cambridge University Press.

Coffman, D. M. (2013), *Excise Taxation and the Origins of Pubic Debt*. Basingstoke: Palgrave Macmillan.

Daunton, M. (1985), *Royal Mail: The Post Office since 1840*. London: Athlone Press.

Daunton, M. (1996a), "Payment and Participation: Welfare and State Formation in Britain, 1900–1951." *Past & Present* 150(1): 169–216.

Daunton, M. (1996b), "The Political Economy of Death Duties: Harcourt's Budget of 1894." In N. B. Harte and R. Quinault (eds.), *Land and Society in Britain, 1700–1914*. Manchester: Manchester University Press, 137–71.

Daunton, Martin (1998), "Trusting Leviathan: British Fiscal Administration from the Napoleonic Wars to the Second World War." In Valerie Braithwaite and Margaret Levi (eds.), *Trust and Governance*. New York: Russell Sage Foundation, 102–34.

Daunton, Martin (2001), *Trusting Leviathan: The Politics of Taxation in Britain, 1799–1914*. Cambridge: Cambridge University Press.

Daunton, Martin (2002), *Just Taxes: The Politics of Taxation in Britain, 1914–1979*. Cambridge: Cambridge University Press.

Daunton, Martin (2008), "The Fiscal–Military State and the Napoleonic Wars." In M. Daunton (ed.), *State and Market in Victorian Britain: War, Welfare and Capitalism* Woodbridge: Boydell Press, 40–60.

Dickson, P. G. M. (1967), *The Financial Revolution in England: A Study in the Development of Pubic Credit, 1688–1756*. New York: St. Martin's Press.

Doyle, W. (1996), *Venality: The Sale of Offices in Eighteenth-Century France*. Oxford: Oxford University Press.

Finn, M. (1993), *After Chartism: Class and Nation in English Radical Politics, 1848–1874*. Cambridge: Cambridge University Press.

Gambles, A. (1999), *Protection and Politics: Conservative Economic Discourse, 1815–52*. Woodbridge: Boydell and Brewer.

Harling, P. and P. Mandler (1993), "From 'Fiscal–Military' State to Laissez-Faire State, 1760–1820." *Journal of British Studies* 32(1): 44–70.

Hilton, B. (1977), *Corn, Cash, and Commerce: The Economic Policies of the Tory Government, 1815–30*. Oxford: Oxford University Press.

Hope-Jones, A. (1939), *Income Tax in the Napoleonic Wars*. Cambridge: Cambridge University Press.

Hoppit, J. (1990), "Attitudes to Credit in Britain, 1680–1790." *Historical Journal* 33(2): 305–22.

Hoppit, J. (2002), "Checking the Leviathan, 1688–1832." In D. Winch and P. K. O'Brien (eds.), *The Political Economy of British Historical Experience, 1688–1914*. Oxford: Oxford University Press, 267–94.

Innes, J. (1994), "The Domestic Face of the Military–Fiscal State: Government and Society in Eighteenth-century Britain." In L. Stone (ed.), *An Imperial State at War: Britain from 1689 to 1815*. London: Routledge, 96–127.

Langford, P. (1975), *The Excise Crisis: Society and Politics in the Age of Walpole*. Oxford: Oxford University Press.

Langford, P. (1991), *Public Life and the Propertied Englishman, 1689–1798*. Oxford: Clarendon Press.

Macdonald, J. (2003), *A Free Nation Deep in Debt: The Financial Roots of Democracy*. New York: FSG.

McKibbin, R. (1984), "Why was there no Marxism in Great Britain?" *English Historical Review* 99(391): 297–331.

Mathias, P. and P. K. O'Brien (1976), "Taxation in Britain and France, 1715–1810: A Comparison of the Social and Economic Incidence of Taxes Collected for the Central Governments." *Journal of European Economic History* 5(3): 601–50.

Matthew, H. C. G. (1979), "Disraeli, Gladstone and the Politics of Mid-Victorian Budgets." *Historical Journal* 22(3): 615–43.

Matthew, H. C. G. (1986), *Gladstone, 1809–1874*. Oxford: Clarendon Press.

Middleton, R. (1996), *Government versus the Market: The Growth of the Public Sector, Economic Management and British Economic Performance c.1890–1979*. Cheltenham: Edward Elgar.

Muldrew, C. (1998), *The Economy of Obligation: The Culture of Credit and Social Relations in Early Modern England*. Basingstoke: Palgrave Macmillan.

Neild, R. (2012), "The National Debt in Perspective." *Royal Economic Society Newsletter*, issue 156 (January), 20–2. www.res.org.uk/view/article5jan12Correspondence.html.

O'Brien, P. K. (1988), "The Political Economy of British Taxation, 1660–1815." *Economic History Review* 41(1): 1–32.

O'Brien, P., T. Griffiths, and P. Hunt (1991), "Political Components of the Industrial Revolution: Parliament and the English Cotton Textile Industry, 1660–1774." *Economic History Review* 44(3): 395–423.

O'Brien, P. K. and P. Hunt (1993), "The Rise of the Fiscal State in England, 1485–1815." *Historical Research* 66: 129–76.

O'Brien, P. K. and P. Hunt (1999), "England, 1485–1815." In R. Bonney (ed.), *The Rise of the Fiscal State in Europe, c.1200–1815*. Oxford: Oxford University Press, 53–100.

O'Gorman, F. (1989), *Voters, Patrons and Parties: The Unreformed Electoral System of Hanoverian England, 1734–1832*. Oxford: Oxford University Press.

Ormrod, W. M., M. M. Bonney, and R. J. Bonney (eds.) (1999), *Crises, Revolution and Self-Sustained Growth: Essays in European Fiscal History, 1130–1830*. Stamford, UK: Paul Watkins Publishing.

Pocock, J. G. A. (1985), *Virtue, Commerce and History: Essays on Political Thought and History, Chiefly in the Eighteenth Century*. Cambridge: Cambridge University Press.

Prest, J. (1990), *Liberty and Locality: Parliament, Permissive Legislation and Ratepayers' Democracies in the Nineteenth Century*. Oxford: Clarendon Press.

Reinhart, Carmen M. and Kenneth S. Rogoff (2009), *This Time Is Different: Eight Centuries of Financial Folly*. Princeton, NJ and Oxford: Princeton University Press.

Reitan, E. A. (1970), "From Revenue to Civil List, 1688–1702: The Revolution Settlement and the 'Mixed and Balanced' Constitution." *Historical Journal* 13(4): 571–88.

Reitan, E. A. (1985), "Edmund Burke and Economical Reform, 1779–83." *Studies in Eighteenth Century Culture* 14: 129–58.

Rubinstein, W. D. (1983), "The End of 'Old Corruption' in Britain, 1780–1860." *Past & Present* 101(1): 55–86.

Smith, Richard (1996), "Charity, Self-interest and Welfare: Reflections from Demographic and Family History." In M. Daunton (ed.), *Charity, Self-Interest and Welfare in the English Past*. New York: St. Martin's Press, 23–50.

Stasavage, D. (2003), *Public Debt and the Birth of the Democratic State: France and Great Britain, 1688–1789*. Cambridge: Cambridge University Press.

Stebbings, C. (1992), "'A Natural Safeguard': The General Commissioners of Income Tax." *British Tax Review*: 398–406.

Stebbings, C. (2009), *The Victorian Taxpayer and the Law: A Study in Constitutional Conflict*. Cambridge: Cambridge University Press.

Stedman Jones, G. (1983), *Languages of Class: Studies in English Working-Class History.* Cambridge: Cambridge University Press.

Steinmo, S. (1988–9), "Political Institutions and Tax Policy in the United States, Sweden and Britain." *World Politics* 41(4): 500–35.

Taylor, M. (1995), *The Decline of British Radicalism, 1847–70.* Oxford: Clarendon Press.

Torrance, J. (1978), "Social Class and Bureaucratic Innovation: The Commissioners for Examining the Public Accounts, 1780–87." *Past & Present* 78(1): 56–81.

Velde, F. R. and D. R. Weir (1992), "The Financial Market and Government Debt Policy in France, 1746–1793." *Journal of Economic History* 52(1): 1–39.

Ward, W. R. (1963), *The English Land Tax in the Eighteenth Century.* Oxford: Oxford University Press.

7

"When We Were Just Giving Stuff Away Willy-Nilly"

Historicizing Contemporary British Tax Morale

Liam Stanley

Introduction

To what extent is the British population willing to take the Leap of Faith? The aim of this chapter is to contextualize the British population's willingness to pay tax, i.e. tax morale, in the political and social upheavals since the 1980s. Over this period, the Thatcher and New Labour governments in particular have transformed the British state away from the previous commitment to corporatism and compromise. Thatcher attempted to dismantle the social foundations of the welfare state on the basis that "there is no such thing as society," and the New Labour governments continued this through individualizing welfare provision. These reforms—often characterized, rightly or wrongly, as neoliberal—have gone hand in hand with the acceleration of inequality and a widespread distrust of politics. These social and institutional changes since the advent of Thatcherism have led to a shared sense that British taxpayers are getting less bang for their buck. The recent turn to fiscal austerity—the most salient British political issue from 2010 until 2016—has intensified these societal and political conflicts over the fairness of tax and spending.

This chapter argues that within this context, British taxpayers are increasingly unwilling to take that all-important leap of faith necessary for the contemporary state—enormous, by historical standards—to thrive and, to an extent, exist at all. But the story is not that simple, because, while morale may be decreasing, compliance is increasing. To make sense of this apparent tension, I draw on Albert Hirschman's (1970) famous concepts of exit, voice, and loyalty. In the context of powerful tax collectors and an efficient withholding system, the majority of British taxpayers have very few options to "exit" from paying tax if they decide that they are getting an unfair deal. With no exit open to them, many have decided to "voice" their concerns, including the election of the 2010 Conservative coalition and 2015 Conservative-majority pro-austerity governments. The implied message from these governments has been relatively clear: there will be pain for many, but if you are hardworking then you stand to benefit and, ultimately, have greater freedom to spend your own money as you see fit.

The chapter seeks to build on and engage with Martin Daunton's contribution in this volume (Chapter 6) and with the results from the associated "Willing to Pay?" project (see this volume's Introduction). Martin Daunton's chapter on the emergence of the British tax state argues that the preconditions for compliance and consent started to break down from the 1970s onwards. Britain has a marked history of clear, transparent, and good government—especially when it comes to taxation and revenue collection. Since the eighteenth century, the British tax state has been characterized by low levels of corruption, a commitment to clear rules that resonate with fairness, and the transparent negotiation of taxation by Parliament. In the modern day, the majority of UK tax collection is relatively straightforward and is strictly enforced by the powerful institution Her Majesty's Revenue and Customs (HMRC). This combination means that the majority of British citizens have little option to evade. The main sources of lost revenues are therefore the shadow economy and large-scale tax avoidance by the wealthy. These sources have been further scrutinized since the beginning of fiscal austerity in 2010, and are now central to social conflict over how the economy and society ought to be organized.

The "Willing to Pay?" project has made surprising findings about British tax compliance. Through the comparative laboratory tax compliance experiments, the study has shown that British participants (mostly young people at university) are the least willing to contribute to the public good among the five countries in the study. To put it another way, British participants are the most likely group to "cheat" on the tax compliance experiments—a finding that went against the initial hypotheses of the project. To supplement and hopefully shed light on this surprising finding, I draw on somewhat unorthodox evidence: focus groups. In 2012, at the height of fiscal austerity, I carried out a series of focus groups with British taxpayers in order to understand why fiscal austerity had not been as fiercely opposed as we might expect. This data provides unique micro-level evidence of British tax morale. Using this data, I highlight how there is an increasing *gap* between prudent normative expectations about how tax and spending ought to be organized, and—on the other hand—the actual lived experiences of engaging with the uses and abuses of "taxpayers' money." In short, the data highlights the decreasing tax morale of British taxpayers.

The chapter is organized into three sections. The first section reviews the contemporary British tax state, with a particular focus on illustrating the relative powers of the tax collection authorities. The second section provides an overview of recent trends in British tax morale. The third and final section draws upon the focus group data to provide micro-level evidence for the wider argument of the chapter.

The British Tax State

As Daunton's chapter demonstrates, the British tax state is characterized by its consent and compliance. Those twin pillars remain essentially in place, despite postwar changes. There is a conventional general narrative of British postwar fiscal change. The tax changes made during World War II—including the introduction of the withholding pay as you earn (PAYE) system—helped pave the way for the expansion of the welfare state. The population was willing to accept a degree of private austerity in exchange for the creation of, among other services, the National Health Service (NHS) as a just reward for a war-torn population (Fielding 1992). This led to the so-called "golden age" of the welfare state, whereby a Keynesian regime was maintained with a party-wide consensus (Wincott 2013). This regime partially unraveled in the late 1970s, but Thatcher never quite managed to live up to her rhetoric of rolling the state back in practice. New Labour then won three elections on the bounce from 1997 onwards with the implicit promise of Thatcherism "with a human face." In practice, New Labour invested heavily in public services and increased social protection. The resulting fiscal deficit widened severely following the global financial crisis, thus providing the raw materials for a resurgent Conservative government to announce the so-called "age of austerity": the largest cuts to public spending (with some mild tax rises) seen in postwar Britain. Amidst all this, there is a case to be made that tax morale, in general, has been declining—as Figure 7.1 indicates.

The structure of the British tax system has remained largely consistent throughout this period. The PAYE system—predictably introduced under the auspices of war in 1942 (Daunton 2002: 111–14)—means that personal income tax is withheld from salaries by employers and then paid directly to the state. Unlike the US system, there is no complex system of deductions in which a tax return is necessary for most income tax payers. As a result, the majority of British people do not file a tax return of any sort. Only around 15 percent of personal income tax is collected through self-assessment, which

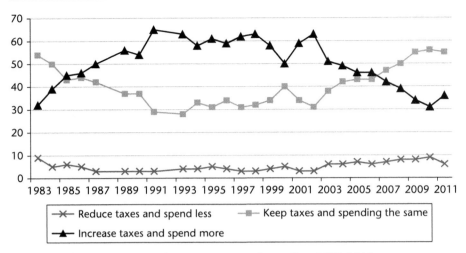

Figure 7.1. Attitudes to taxation and spending 1983–2011
Source: *British Social Attitudes Survey 2013* (NatCen Social Research 2014).

in the broader picture represents around 4 percent of total government receipts. Individual employees, who as a group represent the majority of taxpayers, therefore have no opportunity to cheat income taxes. National Insurance (the second largest source of state revenue) and student loan repayments are also organized through the PAYE system. This powerful withholding system is an important factor in securing tax compliance.

Other revenue sources are less straightforward. With the exception of business transactions, value added tax (VAT, a universal consumption tax that typically ranges between 15 and 20 percent) is automatically applied to all goods and services. Reflecting trends across most modern democratic tax states, the standard VAT rate has increased from 8 percent to 20 percent with the share of revenue flowing from VAT doubling since 1979 (Pope and Roantree 2014: 41). VAT is now the third largest revenue source. The most recent high-profile tax protests were organized by truck drivers against fuel duty in September 2000, and could suggest that "the move to indirect taxes has its limits" (Daunton 2002: 35).

There are more chances for individuals to cheat on council tax (i.e. local tax, which is based on property), which is collected by local government and requires a degree of self-declaration. And the same goes for inheritance tax and capital gains tax. Even with capital gains tax, there are a number of exemptions that greatly limit the chances for evasion. Cars, assets with a limited lifespan, owner-occupied housing, and items worth under £6,000 are all exempt from capital gains tax. As a result, only around 0.5 percent of total taxpayers incur the tax.

Compared to individual earners, businesses have more chances to evade. The shadow economy is by far the biggest source of the British tax gap (HMRC 2016). HMRC makes a clear distinction between the shadow (or hidden) economy, in which an entire source of income is not declared, and tax evasion, in which a declared source of income is deliberately underreported. Within that undeclared economic activity, HMRC make a further distinction between "ghosts" and "moonlighters." Ghosts are individuals who receive a taxable income but are unknown to HMRC and other authorities because no income is reported at all. Moonlighters, on the other hand, pay tax on some income through PAYE—but fail to declare earnings from a second job or additional income from self-employment. With regard to tax compliance, the issue is not whether ghosts or moonlighters accurately report their incomes, but whether they declare at all.

Research commissioned by HMRC has shown that there are a large variety of reasons why people enter the hidden economy, whether ghosts or moon-lighters (HMRC 2012a). They divide these into individual, social, and struc-tural reasons. Individual reasons include perceived need, lack of confidence in the ability to comply, and anger at the perceived misuse of public money (on which, see "Historicizing Contemporary Tax Morale: Micro-Level Analysis" below). Social reasons include family and cultural values, industry norms, and societal acceptance. Structural reasons include the fiscal and non-fiscal costs of complying, a sense that the system is geared against small and/or irregular amounts, and a low level of scrutiny from the government. All of the moon-lighters or ghosts participating in the research earned in excess of £15,000 per annum from their hidden income.

Very few of the moonlighters or ghosts that participated in the project were especially tactical about covering their tracks based on a nuanced understand-ing of how HMRC and the tax system works (HMRC 2012a: 10). This is hardly surprising given that many ghosts and moonlighters do not even identify themselves as businesses (HMRC 2012b: 5), and as therefore obliged to pay taxes. Many ghosts and moonlighters, for instance, do not keep accounts and are therefore unable to calculate their hidden incomes or even sense whether they are making a profit or not. It would be unfair and ineffective, the logic typically follows, to target "their little bit" of non-compliance. Many of those interviewed felt that they were making a net contribution to society and that they were therefore morally justified in their engagement in hidden economy activities. As a result, those interviewed did not typically self-identify their behavior as extreme or significant—a view that was typically justified by pointing to those who are "worse" than them, such as welfare benefit fraudsters, MPs implicated in the expenses scandal, those engaged in large-scale tax avoidance, and criminals. Taken as a whole, the way in which moonlighters and ghosts in the hidden economy *identify* themselves as non-business entities, when taken together with the clear benefits of hiding their income, is an important explanation for this form of non-compliance.

For those who do self-identify as taxpayers, the institutionalized power of HMRC is a very good reason to comply. Between April 2010 and March 2014, HMRC prosecuted 2,650 individuals for tax crimes, with very high profile barristers, accountants, and lawyers included among them (HMRC 2014). Indeed, HMRC have similar criminal investigation powers to other British law enforcement agencies. In particular, HMRC has the power to: apply for orders requiring information to be produced, apply for search warrants, make arrests, and search suspects and premises following arrest (HMRC 2015).

These powers are reflected in the experiences of people convicted of tax evasion, as reported in a qualitative research project commissioned by HMRC (Turley and Keeble 2015). While some participants expressed the view that HMRC and the police have behaved appropriately, proportionately, and with respect, others were more critical in reflecting the arrest process. These included stories of how homes were raided early in the morning; officers arrived wearing bulletproof vests; the use of police dogs; excessive numbers of officers; and so on. These participants considered such actions "aggressive," "intimidating," and ultimately disproportionate in terms of the offence committed and the likelihood of them evading arrest.

HMRC's "Compliance Perceptions Survey" provides further insights into tax compliance. The survey splits the sample into small- to medium-sized enterprises (SMEs), self-employed, and employees. Although the groups give similar answers to some questions in the 2014 edition—for instance, 95 percent of SMEs and 89 percent of the self-employed and employed stated that tax evasion was unacceptable—there were more stark differences in other respects. For instance, on whether they felt HMRC treated them fairly, 80 percent of SMEs, 76 percent of self-employed, and just 56 percent of employed agreed. The most illuminating divergence in results, however, is in questions relating to perceptions of tax evasion. Only 31 percent of SMEs believe that tax evasion is widespread, in comparison to 78 percent of self-employed and 78 percent of employed. Fifty-four percent of SMEs believe HMRC is putting in the right amount of effort to prevent tax evasion, in comparison to 28 percent of self-employed and 26 percent of employed. Finally, 68 percent of SMEs believe that regular tax evaders would be caught, compared to 47 percent of self-employed and 40 percent of employed.

These results suggest a number of different insights. For one, the differences in SMEs and self-employed/employed suggest that the more direct interaction with HMRC one has, the more optimistic one is about tax evasion. On the one hand, this may be because SMEs are highly targeted by HMRC for tax compliance, and are therefore more likely to have directly experienced HMRC's push for compliance. On the other hand, this divergence might be explained by different meanings of "tax evasion." Those involved in SMEs are far more likely to be aware of the differences between tax evasion and tax avoidance, for instance. For an employee with no particular interest in tax politics(!), this distinction is unlikely to be made. This is significant because of the salience of recent tax avoidance scandals. Tax evasion may mean one thing to SMEs and quite another to the employed.

Even before the Panama Papers and other related scandals, tax avoidance and tax havens have been of high relevance in the UK. There has been public outrage over the tax avoidance schemes used by a number of high-profile celebrities. For example, the well-known comedian and entertainer Jimmy Carr was forced to publicly apologize in June 2012 after using the legal but morally dubious K2 tax avoidance scheme (BBC 2012). Although not as salient in the popular press, a number of leaks and whistleblowers have helped reveal the way in which firms headquartered in the UK have avoided millions in tax. The so-called Luxembourg leaks, for example, revealed how major British companies, such as the vacuum cleaner firm Dyson, have used complex webs of internal loans and interest payments to avoid millions of pounds in tax (*Guardian* 2014). Given that the majority of these schemes are legal it is difficult to categorize these instances as cheating (Tax Research UK estimates that total tax avoidance is at least £19 billion). Tax avoidance nevertheless matters for the legitimacy of HMRC in particular and for the British tax state more generally.

In this context, the way in which HMRC offers so-called "sweetheart deals" to large-scale tax avoiders has come under particular scrutiny. Included within this are the high-profile deals that HMRC has struck up with the likes of Google and Starbucks. Although the £130 million tax deal with Google was lauded as a major success by Prime Minister David Cameron, MPs have since launched an inquiry into the UK's tax system after the government was accused of allowing Google to pay too little.

These sorts of favorable deal are not just found in high-profile tax avoidance scandals. Following the release of the "HSBC files" that contained the details of about 130,000 holders of secret Swiss bank accounts (at the time the largest banking leak in history), HMRC implied that it would be ramping up prosecutions for offshore evasion. As Jolyon Maugham (2015) has pointed out, in the 2014 annual report on tackling offshore evasion, "No Safe Havens," HMRC claimed to be making 2,962 actual and prospective charging decisions—implying in the process that these related to offshore tax evasion. Although HMRC presents its data on prosecutions as if some of those were for offshore tax evasion, their failure to provide a breakdown makes it impossible to tell one way or the other. Only through a parliamentary committee has the true data been revealed: eleven prosecutions (fifteen years' jail time collectively) in relation to offshore tax evasion over the last five years (PAC 2015).

Given the way in which HSBC handled its files, this is hardly surprising. As Richard Murphy (2015) the tax campaigner has pointed out, HMRC actively encourages those named in the HSBC files to take advantage of an amnesty (called the "Liechtenstein Disclosure Facility") offering very low penalties on unpaid tax and immunity from criminal prosecution. HMRC provides assurance that criminal proceedings will not be pursued if a full disclosure is made. Some campaigners raised questions over why an amnesty was required when non-compliance was already known about. Given HMRC's independence, there is very little scrutiny over how these deals and policies are made. This is in stark comparison to Daunton's emphasis on the importance of transparency and fairness in building a legitimate tax state.

Since tax compliance is best explained by the structure and institutions of taxation itself (excellently covered in Steinmo 1993 and Daunton 2002), I will focus the remainder of this chapter on understanding contemporary tax morale in the UK. The starting point in conceptualizing tax morale is the observation that most people are actually willing to pay taxes; so it is therefore important to analyze the *processes* (in addition to the *outcome* of compliance) in which people consent to and/or justify the extraction of tax revenues (Torgler 2007: 65). In the rest of this chapter, I plan on historicizing contemporary British tax morale: first, by presenting an overview of recent developments as a form of macro-level analysis; and second, by presenting focus group data as a form of micro-level analysis in support.

Historicizing Contemporary Tax Morale: Macro-Level Analysis

New Labour, who came to power in 1997, largely accepted the terms of the Thatcherite settlement and set out to build a more equitable society while maintaining a low interest rate, low inflation, and low tax regime. Mark Bevir (2007) makes the useful distinction between the "delivery stage" and the "tired stage" of the New Labour project. The first New Labour government (1997–2001) can be characterized as the delivery stage, in which they paid heed to the imperatives of contemporary global capitalism—most notably through their fiscal rules under the Code for Fiscal Stability (see Clift and Tomlinson 2006; Hay 2006)—resulting in a fiscal surplus. However, they increasingly tried to have their cake and eat it, by significantly increasing investment in public services without adequately raising more revenue. This "tired stage" (2001–5) involved giving up all pretense of "trying to keep the public finances on an even keel" (Watson 2013a: 18), thus leading to a serious deterioration of their previous surplus into a deficit (Thompson 2013: 6–10). New Labour nonetheless managed to generate a baseline economic and fiscal credibility throughout the majority of their administration by consistently meeting the self-imposed "sustainable investment rule" and "golden rule" from 1997/8 to 2006/7 (Chote et al. 2010). It should be pointed out, however, that they met these rules because rising expenditure was used to finance investment, particularly in the NHS, rather than funding the day-to-day running costs of the public sector (Chote et al. 2010: 1; Thompson 2013: 8).

From this there are two implications for tax morale. The first implication is the relationship between the ups and downs in public spending and tax morale. Increases in public spending (on health and education as well as various benefits and in-work tax credits) under Labour initially conferred a degree of legitimacy because they were largely deficit-fueled rather than revenue-fueled, coincided with a period of sustained economic growth, and followed a period of perceived underfunding. Second, despite claims by the then Chancellor Gordon Brown to have fixed the problem of boom and bust, New Labour left the UK in a precarious fiscal position. The global financial crisis widened the fiscal deficit further. As a result, the opposition Conservative party were able to convince many voters that the only answer to "Labour's Debt Crisis" was expenditure-based fiscal consolidation (Stanley 2016). That a majority of people believe that austerity is necessary is relevant for tax morale. This trend suggests that many people are committed to what is in effect a transformation of the fiscal constitution, whereby fiscal austerity will lead to fewer services being provided for roughly the same levels of revenue.

In this sense, changes in the practices and justifications of welfare policy have also contributed toward lower tax morale. More than anyone, Matthew Watson (2013a; 2013b) has picked up on the strange paradoxes of New Labour's welfare reform—which extended the logic of Thatcherite changes to the welfare state. New Labour's earlier welfare strategy focused upon tackling a perceived culture of irresponsibility around those who depended on welfare benefits. There was an emphasis upon ensuring that welfare no longer encouraged "something for nothing" but instead ensured that those in need received "something for something" (Watson 2013a: 11). In particular, New Labour's "welfare-to-work" strategy was based upon a rejection of traditional redistribution to ensure equality of outcome since this risked institutionalizing a culture of irresponsibility (which in turn poses a risk in regard to long-term fiscal pressures). An alternative justificatory framework was produced to signal this shift, in which welfare policy was increasingly geared toward delivering equality of opportunity by tackling social exclusion through investing in human capital (Lister 2003). Levitas (1998) argues that New Labour extended the Thatcherite move away from a view of social exclusion as intertwined with material poverty, and instead toward a view that distinguishes between those who are socially integrated (mostly in terms of labor market attachment and employment) and those who are excluded as a "moral underclass."

In effect, this reconfiguration of poverty as exclusion entailed treating unemployment as a cultural and/or behavioral problem rather than an economic one. If poverty is the result of a culture of worklessness that arises from losing contact with the labor market, then the logical solution is to provide people with "the personal wherewithal to improve their own lots" (Watson 2013a: 10). By realigning poverty with social exclusion and a culture of passivity, the poor were essentially divided into those who earned their relief through active behavioral change and those who were deemed undeserving for foregoing such activities. This also manifested itself in the rise of means-tested benefits. The paradox is that this ended up costing a lot of money.

New Labour's welfare reforms have dovetailed with important shifts in how British society generally understands and defines the nature of impoverishment. While it was previously associated with material and economic conditions, there is evidence that it is becoming increasingly individualized and stigmatized. Shildrick and McDonald's (2013) research into sixty men and women in northeast England caught up in the "low-pay, no-pay cycle" discussed poverty in respect of themselves and others. Paradoxically, they found that interviewees typically denied their own poverty despite living in material hardship. Others, however, were identified as poor—although this poverty was not linked to material hardship—but were judged for their irresponsible consumption and their failure to resiliently manage the situation they had been dealt (2013: 296). This process was, for Shildrick and McDonald, a process of identity formation:

> In presenting themselves as largely unremarkable, in rejecting the label of poverty, in stressing pride in coping with hardship, research participants constructed a self-identity in contrast to a (usually) nameless mass of "Others" who were believed, variously, to be work-shy, to claim benefits illegitimately and to be *unable* to "manage" and to engage in blameworthy consumption habits. (2013: 291)

The meaning of being poor has shifted away from hardship via material conditions toward the absence of an attitude of "bettering oneself"—another obligation welfare benefit recipients must fulfill to prove that they deserve taxpayer redistribution.

These trends in how poverty and welfare are understood in society evolved in tandem with a shift in values following the Thatcher (1979–90), Major (1990–7), and Blair (1997–2007) governments. The most recent and cutting-edge research on this question indicates that individuals who came of political age during Thatcher's premiership hold more right-wing and authoritarian attitudes compared to generations who came of age before (Grasso et al. 2017). Interestingly, the findings show that the New Labour generation is even more right-wing than its predecessors. Grasso and her co-authors argue that Thatcherism shaped public opinion and social values in the long term; the Major and

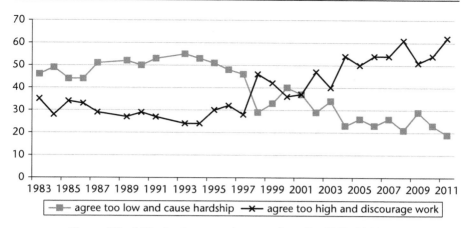

Figure 7.2. Attitudes to unemployment benefits 1983–2011
Source: British Social Attitudes Survey 2013 (NatCen Social Research 2014).

New Labour governments largely continued the Thatcherite agenda. On almost all measures relating to redistribution, welfare, and inequality, the findings demonstrate an upswing over the years of birth of Thatcher's Children, thereby reversing a trend toward greater support for redistribution and social egalitarianism observed among previous political generations. This rise of Thatcherite values also helps explain a shift in the way in which Britons relate to taxation: rather than providing a public good or fulfilling the obligations of society, there is a sense that tax merely reduces the freedom for individuals to choose how to spend their own money.

Taken together, these trends are reflected in public opinion. As Figure 7.2 shows, public attitudes to unemployment benefits have significantly hardened in recent times with 60 percent now agreeing that Jobseeker's Allowance is too high and therefore discourages work—which is a significant turnaround. Meanwhile, a 2012 YouGov poll surveyed public knowledge on the welfare budget, revealing the following:

- On average people think that 41 percent of the entire welfare budget goes on benefits to unemployed people, while the true figure is 3 percent.

- On average people think that 27 percent of the welfare budget is claimed fraudulently, while the government's own figure is 0.7 percent.

- On average people think that almost half the people (48 percent) who claim Jobseeker's Allowance go on to claim it for more than a year, while the true figure is around 10 percent.

It is therefore reasonable to hypothesize that changes in the practice and justification of welfare policy may have had a detrimental impact upon British tax morale.

In addition to shifts in public spending and welfare, the evolution of public sector governance is also an important factor in explaining declining tax morale. Most Western governments have reformed their public sector in recent decades in the name of new public management in order to improve efficiency. This has involved imposing benchmarking exercises, targets, performance-related pay, and short-term contracts; the creation of internal markets in which public sector organizations are encouraged to compete with one another; and public–private partnerships (PPPs) whereby private firms provide public services including the design, construction, maintenance, and operation of infrastructure assets traditionally provided by the public sector (Bell and Hindmoor 2009: 119). The NHS in the UK provides an exemplar of these sorts of practices. Reforms have given doctors more control over their budgets, with the expectation that doctors would send their patients to those hospitals that scored highly in performance measurements, and that therefore overall service provision would improve as hospitals responded to these new competitive pressures (Bell and Hindmoor 2009: 119).

I have three hypotheses about how the transformation of governance has impacted tax morale. First, the marketization of public services and, in particular, the proliferation of PPPs has muddied the distinction between the public and private sectors. If tax morale is based in part on an evaluation of the quality and quantity of the services people receive, then this muddying may be significant. This is even more so when we consider how relatively unaccountable the private sector is. Second, there is a sense that many of these reforms have led to both an increased bureaucracy and an expensive management culture that provide very little value for money. Paying for education or health is one thing, and paying for bureaucracy and management is another. Third, there is an increased sense of unfairness. With rising frequency, there are local or national controversies over the salaries of those in the public sector. For instance, in Birmingham, the chief executive of Birmingham City Council was revealed to have been paid £233,000 (US$338,926) in 2011. The prevalent justification for such salaries is that a public sector CEO needs to be paid at a similar rate to those in the private sector in order to attract and then retain "talent." However, people resent that their tax is going toward these very high salaries.

Finally, trust is an important factor in explaining tax morale (Torgler 2007: 23). Since tax politics "shapes and is shaped by patterns of public trust" (Martin, Mehrota, and Prasad 2009: 13) this is a very salient issue for our purposes. Experimental work has shown that more trust in the government, the tax administration, and the legal system, tends to increase tax morale and thus taxpayers' willingness to contribute with their taxes (Torgler 2007: 18). It is therefore reasonable to expect that people will resist tax rises if they do not trust the state to spend carefully their rightfully earned cash. As an illustration,

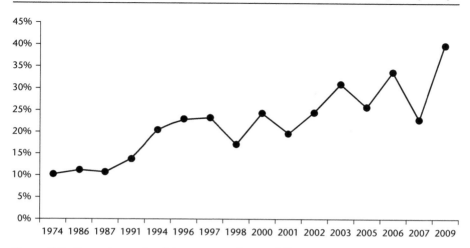

Figure 7.3. Percentage who "almost never" trust UK governments (of any party) to place the needs of the nation above the interests of their own political party
Source: Richards and Smith (2014: 2).

Figure 7.3 highlights how skepticism concerning whether the UK government serves the national interest over their party interests has risen over time.

A number of high-profile scandals and controversies have created a widely shared sense that the UK is host to a closely networked elite who, otherwise detached from normal society, use their privileges in morally dubious ways in order to further their own ends. In the introduction to an edited volume entitled *Institutional Crisis in 21st Century Britain*, David Richards and Martin Smith (2014) list many of the events that contributed to this feeling:

- The conviction of the BBC presenter Stuart Hall for child-sex offences following the arrest of other current or former BBC employees on similar charges in the wake of the Jimmy Saville affair. Many more establishment figures, including prominent politicians, are also alleged to have been involved.

- The investigation into British banks following allegations of manipulating the LIBOR (London interbank offered rate) interest rate.

- The "cash for honors" scandal concerning alleged links between political donations and life peerages.

- As already mentioned, the MPs' expenses scandal "exposed the pathology within Westminster of an embedded culture of self-regulation, secrecy and club-like government that rendered it, in the eyes of many, as not fit for purpose and further added muster to an existing debate over arguments concerning the lack of legitimacy engulfing the formal arenas of UK politics" (Richards and Smith 2014: 2).

- The "hacking scandal" to emerge from parts of the UK media, but most notably the News International organization, which revealed a set of "informal, insider, elite, networked relationships between the political class, the media and the Metropolitan Police" (Richards and Smith 2014: 2).

All these events have, in different ways, helped contribute to an anti-politics sentiment in the UK in which the "Westminster bubble" is the main target. We can therefore hypothesize that this is another factor in explaining the declining tax morale.

Historicizing Contemporary Tax Morale: Micro-Level Analysis

Claire: But you're saying that . . . there are differences [between now and before the crisis] . . . it's not so much of giving things away for free, like computers, and things. Laptops. For kids to use, but the adults were actually using them and the children were not. Taking them to shops and getting them chipped. All that business . . . there's none of that any more! But we're getting out of the recession, and we're not as bad as we was *when we were just giving stuff away willy-nilly*—d'ya know what I mean? [emphasis added].

Rose: But why haven't the state got any money? Why haven't we got any money? [. . .] We pay the highest taxes in the world. Why haven't we got any money left?

In general terms, the focus group participants I interviewed did not talk about the allocation and efficiency of public finances in particularly positive terms. It appeared at times as if participants were implicitly answering a question: assuming that we accept that the state must cut back to reduce the fiscal deficit, then we may naturally want to contemplate how and why the state managed to overspend in the first place. Throughout these discussions, it was notable that while participants sometimes had their individual "big" explanations for state profligacy (the armed forces, "too many people in the country," for example), it was the "little" explanations that stemmed from everyday life that were consistently drawn upon. The state, it seems, is experienced as a wasteful and inefficient body for allocating and spending public money. Participants made sense of this in two ways: through recalling stories of (what I will term) the "illogical banalities" of state spending, whereby public finances are used in unjustifiable, pointless but localized ways; and through telling stories that highlighted (as one participant put it) the "bonkers system," i.e. the systematic nature of state profligacy. I will outline each in turn.

The example below is particularly illustrative of "illogical banalities" because it was in response to a question about controversies regarding local spending cuts, which I asked every group toward the beginning of discussions. The participants in this group decided to interpret the question about controversies about spending cuts in a manner that is quite telling:

Nicholas: I would be the opposite. I would say my controversy is spending money round here on the roads, throwing money around—and I'm thinking, [why] are they doing that?

Duncan: On street lights ... or ...?

Nicholas: Well, just on ... that business down there towards Manor Road and towards your road, there's a bridge. [... And] they've extended the pavement. What have they done [that] for!? I've got no idea.

Whereas the excerpt above highlights the perverse incentives and institutions that encourage this illogical banality, the following excerpt gives a sense of a cultural sea change:

Caitlin: I still think there's probably a lot of money wasted. I mean, at the moment, we're having all new streetlights being put up on our road. And you look at the old ones and you think "Hmm, well, there's—"

Mandy: In lots of places—not in Moseley [interview location], but generally—to save money.

Caitlin: I'm sure they'd say that these ones are energy-saving or whatever. But I just think if times are sort of hard then I think you probably just leave that for another couple of years and think they'll last a bit longer, y'know. I just think that all the time there is money wasted on ... dunno. I dunno. Office furniture, and paperclips. And ... I dunno. I was brought up that you didn't replace something until it broke really, and things then lasted a long time and now they don't. I feel as if there's too much replacing of stuff because [Michael: you can], yeah. Whereas in these sorts of time we should be thinking, oh, that road doesn't need resurfacing, we could make that last another year.

While the discussions above tended to tell stories about everyday experiences of illogical banality of localized spending, there were also discussions that reflected wider views about the *systematic nature* of state profligacy.

The participants below shared numerous anecdotes that painted a picture of an almost tragicomedy of state incompetence:

Nicholas: It's shut that has [the swimming pool].

[...]

Linda: Ridiculous.

Kyle: Farce. It's just somebody is on the table, and it's just money after, money after, money after—how much have they spent on it? £350,000 was it? [...] And it's just rubbish isn't it. What they're doing with it. It's a hell-of-a-waste of money. But it's a great facility.

In other instances, however, the focus was on onerous and unnecessary bureaucracy, often emphasizing the one-size-fits-all nature of benefits or the impenetrability of official documents without necessarily making a point about the need for fiscal austerity:

> **Mandy:** It's the same with this incapacity benefit, or whatever it's called now, they change it all the time. The way they have this system, and it doesn't fit everybody. So you might fill in a form that doesn't apply to you, and there's so many people appealing—and I know some of these, because of my friend—and she won't know until September because there's so many appealing, even though she had a phone call saying she must appeal. So it's this crazy system.
>
> [...]
>
> **Michael:** Yeah, it's really a bonkers system.

Some of the most interesting anecdotes, however, came from those who worked within the public sector. Their position within the thick of it provided an interesting take on how the institutions that make up the state have been slowly transforming over the last few decades: the move to "new public management" (Dunleavy and Hood 1994), "modern governance" (Finlayson 2003), and other, related, practices. In particular, there was discussion of, as one participant put it, "the Suits," which referred to an abstract group of well-paid managers whose roles were, in some sense, unnecessary (and thus a waste of money):

> **Jerry:** ... but sitting right in the middle of the health service and watching it go on and I've previously worked in the local authority, so I watched it happen there a couple of decades ago. What kind of annoys me is when you have cutbacks, and they are terrible cutbacks, then they're done very badly, inasmuch as they say right you've got to save 10 percent, so the people who make the decisions about how we do this are the people who are on one hundred grand plus in really good director/management [...] Those people sit and discuss what should be done and how to make efficiencies with all the people who are making £15,000–£20,000 a time, and how we'll have to cut back on some of them, and some of them might have to work longer hours and all that, and I never see any reduction in the people who are earning one hundred grand, I've never seen one of them decide ... made redundant.
>
> [...]
>
> **Michael:** Things that we get most jarred off about is ... endless kinds of investigations, meetings, focus groups [laughter]. But on a scale that is ... keeping some bloke in a suit in a job. And you think that bloke in a

suit doesn't actually need a job, he could just . . . We don't need all this . . . It just seems a lot of "padding" in various levels above those people on the ground who do the jobs. I think . . . I dunno, that seems to be across the board.

Caitlin: There's too much talking, not enough action.

[. . .]

Michael: In many ways, most of us are kind of baffled by lots of decisions made. But I think that's common across any public sector working, y'know, the decisions that are made you just think, Christ, what's that about?

Mandy: It's the faceless people further up who have no idea what's going on.

Again, what makes this discussion distinctive is that complaints are directed toward abstract issues and what are regarded as systematic problems rather than individual managers. The "suits" were often contrasted with those who actually did the work, "those on the ground," with whom most participants implicitly identified. Although there were some counter-narratives that defended the role of the state in contemporary political life, the abiding direction of the discussions was toward airing grievances with wasteful state spending.

In addition to voicing their concerns about the inefficiency of state spending, the focus group participants also voiced concerns that they do not sufficiently benefit from public spending and redistribution. In Kidder and Martin's (2012) research on everyday fiscal discourse, they find that their interviewees (small business owners from Florida in the United States) produced a "sense of group position" whereby they typically self-identified as hardworking in contrast to those rich and poor undeserving types who unfairly benefit from the fiscal system. I found a similar sentiment in the focus group discussions, in which "the average" person was contrasted with the undeserving poor and rich. For example:

Caitin: I think we've got too much debt. And the cuts are being made in . . . for normal . . . normal? ["The average?"] Yeah the average person. And personally, I think it always hits the middle-income families. Always. Because you're either up there with your £29m bonus, or you're down there and you do get help—I'm not saying everyone—but you do get a lot of benefits and help. But if you're in this middle bit, you don't quite get your child benefit, you don't quite get help with your university fees, you don't get that . . . .

The focus group participants did not spend a great deal of time discussing the undeserving poor (which is most likely due to the unusual collective nature of the interview and the politeness of British society). Nevertheless, such discussions did take place, and when they did it was often in the context of *whom* "we" (i.e. taxpayers) pay for and whether they deserve it. This notion of "giving money away" was brought up in many groups. For example:

Rose: Yeah [sarcasm]—Vote Labour! They're giving money away left, right and centre. Let's give you some because you haven't got a job, and let's give you some because you've got five kids. And the next kid some too, because you've just arrived in the country and we feel sorry for you. You can't just go out giving money to everybody.

The undeserving aspect of being poor and on benefits is somewhat complicated by what some considered as the perverse incentives inherent in the welfare state:

Caitlin: There isn't much incentive for people to actually, sort of, get up and get on and feel that it is worthwhile for them really.

However, it becomes clear from the assumptions underpinning more detailed discussions that the perverse incentives of the welfare state do not necessarily excuse those that receive long-term benefits:

Rose: You've got to have a big incentive. It's no good...it's a shame, because it's the middle people who do go out and get the work, and I'm not saying that people are unemployed because they want to be, but what I'm saying is that there is a big sector of people who are in the middle—like I was a single-parent once, working. I was worse off than some single parents, not working. So where is my incentive? And then you've got families where it's my husband is working but I'm not at the moment. We struggle.

[...]

Michael: But you do get this stereotype, and you think well...if they can get more money sitting on their backsides on welfare or whatever they get, then you can't blame them, but they haven't got that inbuilt is it...pride? That you have to go and work for a living—do anything, rather than be on the dole....

The subtext to comments such as this is that incentives are an important contributory factor to an imagined life on welfare benefits, but that people of the correct moral fiber have the personal strength, willpower, and dignity to avoid it. It is important to note that these discussions were often contested. For example, participants sometimes highlighted the more "structural" impediments to work, such as a high national or regional unemployment rate, which occasionally led to reappraisals of the moral character of the unemployed.

Some of the groups discussed the unfairness of tax evasion: how rich taxpayers can lower or eliminate their burden through using clever and expensive accounting to exploit legal loopholes. In doing so, these discussions often served to reassert the moral authority of hardworking taxpayers. The following excerpt, although lengthy, is very illustrative of these concerns.

Kyle: And yeah, that's what the government suddenly thought, well, the best [inaudible] in the world, we already pay so much bloody tax in this country as a whole anyway, I don't know how much more you can squeeze out of people with taxes. So you've got to make cuts somehow. Y'know, but you almost feel sorry for Jimmy Carr, in the sense that if he was paying what he should have been paying then he would have had a lot more money.

Nicholas: There's been a couple of comments that I've noted that, on Jimmy Carr should pay for his own personal health, but he still drives down the road, he still uses the street lights, which everybody else is paying for. But somehow, these people don't seem to think that—"why should I pay for that?!" But they should do, shouldn't they? They should pay their fair share. Like everyone else does.

Kyle: Oh yes, I agree, they should pay their share . . . But at the end of the day you can only squeeze so much money out of people. That's the same across all levels, and that's why the cuts.

Nicholas: But it seems like it's the middle ground that's being squeezed. It's the softest, easiest target.

Kyle: Well yeah because the Jimmy Carrs and the clever accountants will . . . well they'll either vote with their feet and go elsewhere—which is the big danger because if you tax them too much they will do that, and when I say elsewhere, they won't go far, they might just go to the Channel islands.

But there were also specific discussions about two groups of undeserving rich in particular—bankers and politicians—who were often jointly categorized on the basis of shared characteristics: they are both perceived as culpable for the 2008 global financial crisis, and they are both seen as unfairly receiving state financial support. Blaming these groups for the financial crisis is important because it suggests that neither bankers nor politicians deserve to receive support through "taxpayers' money." There were two events in particular that brought attention to this public support: for politicians it was the MPs' expenses scandal,[1] and for bankers it was the state-funded bailout of the financial sector following the 2008 crash. Both of these events were consistently used to make a point about the unfairness of the fiscal system.

The discussion about undeserving others seemed to contribute to low tax morale: the bottom cannot pay; the top find loopholes; and so the middle therefore over-contributes while seemingly receiving less bang for their buck:

Kyle: But it is true though, isn't it? You can only squeeze out Middle England so much, because they're the ones who are paying it. 'Cos the bottom don't pay it, and the top . . . find . . .

Linda: . . . clever ways round it.

There were numerous examples in which the undeserving rich and poor were used to make a point about the existence of a middle ground that typically lost out in the fiscal order of things:

Caitlin: And you do get a bit resentful. I'm standing out here in the cold selling all this, and all my income tax is just going to someone who doesn't want to work, someone who is just sitting at home and going off on a holiday to Mallorca for two weeks. And I've stood out in the cold funding their holiday in the sun. And you do sort of get a bit . . .

Michael: And they think it's their right, rather than the . . . I think you hit the nail on the head—it's the middle ground that are squeezed. And those people—us, maybe—fit into the middle ground. Who will take the time to do that, who will do what we're told, because we respect authority and we think if we don't fill these forms in something bad will happen. But there are people out there who don't, and they exploit the system completely, and I think there's very much this society has changed a little bit.

The most explicit expression of this sense of group position in an explicitly fiscal sense is from Kyle:

Kyle: . . . and so you can't get it [tax to finance the fiscal deficit] off these guys because they [inaudible] or they'll find a way of being in the Channel Islands or wherever it might be, and you're not going to get if off the people at the bottom, because we don't ask for it half the time but we're certainly not going to get it from the bottom end, so it is Middle England who are having to pay more and more. And everybody, most British people, aspire to be moving up and up and up, the aspiration is that you get up there and then you're back down here again, and you're back up there and the next thing you know you're back down. How do you do it? And we all struggle with that I think.

Conclusion

What does this micro-level analysis tell us about contemporary British tax morale, within the wider picture of explaining cross-national variation in willingness to pay taxes? There are two conclusions. First, the majority of the participants who were interviewed appeared to have low tax morale. In making a point about how the middle classes bear a disproportionate fiscal burden, participants told stories about the profligate state (which suggests that public funds were being wasted) and about how social groups who do not deserve help are otherwise benefiting (which suggests that public funds are being misdirected). Second, this suggests that there is a "gap" between, on the one hand, taxpayers' expectations for prudence and fairness and, on the other, the lived experiences of engaging with the uses and abuses of "taxpayers' money." However, given the structure of tax in the UK, this low morale does not translate easily into tax evasion. These findings must be placed in the context of the preceding sections—a strong British tax state, but a society characterized by increasing inequality and a widespread distrust of politics.

This chapter has painted a certain picture about tax morale in the UK: in response to taxpayer perceptions of the declining value of services that they receive from the state in relation to the tax that they pay, there are few "exit" routes to non-compliance for the majority of individuals. Those with extensive resources opt to exit through tax avoidance schemes. As a result, taxpayers must increasingly "voice" their grievances as their frustrations stew. In short, British taxpayers are increasingly unwilling to take the Leap of Faith, but many have little option but to comply.

Note

1. In 2009, the MPs' expenses scandal consumed British politics. Following a revelation by a major newspaper, detailed information from leaked documents demonstrated how some MPs had abused their parliamentary expenses—in particular, making personal financial gain from claiming the Additional Members Allowance. The scandal was seen as symbolizing everything that is wrong with the current political system: politicians who don't care about the average person, who are just in it for their own personal gain, and so on.

References

BBC (2012), "Comedian Jimmy Carr: I've Made Terrible Error over Tax." June 21. www.bbc.co.uk/news/uk-politics-18531008.

Bell, S. and A. Hindmoor (2009), *Rethinking Governance: The Centrality of the State in Modern Society*. Cambridge: Cambridge University Press.

Bevir, M. (2007), "New Labour in Time." *Parliamentary Affairs* 60(2): 332–40.

Chote, R., R. Crawford, C. Emmerson, and G. Tetlow (2010), "The Public Finances: 1997 to 2010." *2010 Election Briefing Note No. 6 (IFS BN93)*. www.ifs.org.uk/publications/4822.

Clift, B. and J. Tomlinson (2006), "Credible Keynesianism? New Labour Macroeconomic Policy and the Political Economy of Coarse Tuning." *British Journal of Political Science* 37(1): 47–69.

Daunton, M. (2002), *Just Taxes: The Politics of Taxation in Britain, 1914–1979*. Cambridge: Cambridge University Press.

Dunleavy, P. and C. Hood (1994), "From Old Public Administration to New Public Management." *Public Money & Management* 14(3): 9–16.

Fielding, S. (1992), "What Did 'The People' Want?: The Meaning of the 1945 General Election." *The Historical Journal* 35(3): 623–39.

Finlayson, A. (2003), *Making Sense of New Labour*. London: Lawrence and Wishart.

Grasso, M., S. Farrall, E. Gray, C. Hay, and W. Jennings (2017), "Thatcher's Children, Blair's Babies, Political Socialization and Trickle-Down Value Change: An Age, Period and Cohort Analysis." *British Journal of Political Science*. https://doi.org/10.1017/S0007123416000375.

Guardian (2014), "Luxembourg Tax Files: How Tiny State Rubber-Stamped Tax Avoidance on an Industrial Scale." November 5. www.theguardian.com/business/2014/nov/05/-sp-luxembourg-tax-files-tax-avoidance-industrial-scale.

Hay, C. (2006), "What's in a Name? New Labour's Putative Keynesianism." *British Journal of Political Science* 37(1): 187–92.

Hirschman, A. O. (1970), *Exit, Voice, and Loyalty: Responses to Decline in Firms, Organizations, and States*. Cambridge, MA: Harvard University Press.

HMRC (2012a), "Understanding the Hidden Economy: Qualitative Research with Ghosts and Moonlighters." *Research Report 207*. www.gov.uk/government/uploads/system/uploads/attachment_data/file/344828/report207.pdf.

HMRC (2012b), "Understanding Key Problems for SMEs: Hidden Economy Levers, Ghosts and Moonlighters. Identifying Effective Levers to Reduce Entrants into, and Encourage SMEs out of the Hidden Economy." *Research Report 208*. www.gov.uk/government/uploads/system/uploads/attachment_data/file/344827/report208.pdf.

HMRC (2014), *HMRC Fast Facts: Record Revenues for the UK*. www.gov.uk/government/publications/hmrc-fast-facts-record-revenues-for-the-uk–2.

HMRC (2015), *2010 to 2015 Government Policy: Tax Evasion and Avoidance*. Policy paper. www.gov.uk/government/publications/2010-to-2015-government-policy-tax-evasion-and-avoidance.

HMRC (2016), *Measuring Tax Gaps 2016 Edition: Tax Gap Estimates for 2014–15*. http://webarchive.nationalarchives.gov.uk/20170621230141/https://www.gov.uk/government/statistics/measuring-tax-gaps.

Kidder, J. L. and I. W. Martin (2012), "What We Talk About When We Talk About Taxes." *Symbolic Interaction* 35(2): 123–45.

Levitas, R. (1998), *The Inclusive Society? Social Exclusion and New Labour*. Basingstoke: Palgrave Macmillan.

Lister, R. (2003), "Investing in the Citizen-Workers of the Future: Transformations in Citizenship and the State under New Labour." *Social Policy & Administration* 37(5): 427–43.

Martin, I. W., A. K. Mehrotra, and M. Prasad (2009), "The Thunder of History: The Origins and Development of the New Fiscal Sociology." In I. W. Martin, A. K. Mehrotra, and M. Prasad (eds.), *The New Fiscal Sociology: Taxation in Comparative and Historical Perspective*. Cambridge: Cambridge University Press, 1–28.

Maugham, J. (2015), "How Many People has HMRC Prosecuted for Offshore Evasion?" November 4. https://waitingfortax.com/2015/11/04/how-many-people-has-hmrc-prosecuted-for-offshore-evasion/.

Murphy, R. (2015), "Did HMRC Abuse the Liechtenstein Disclosure Facility?" February 14. www.taxresearch.org.uk/Blog/2015/02/14/did-hmrc-abuse-the-liechtenstein-disclosure-facility/.

NatCen Social Research (2014), *British Social Attitudes Survey 2013*. UK Data Service, SN: 7500. http://doi.org/10.5255/UKDA-SN-7500-1.

PAC (2015), *House of Commons Committee of Public Accounts: HM Revenue & Customs Performance in 2014–15. Sixth Report of Session 2015–16. HC393* [November]. London: HMSO.

Pope, T. and B. Roantree (2014), "A Survey of the UK Tax System." IFS Briefing Note BN09. www.ifs.org.uk/publications/1711.

Richards, D. and M. Smith (2014), "Introduction: A Crisis in UK Institutions?" In D. Richards, M. Smith, and C. Hay (eds.), *Institutional Crisis in 21st Century Britain*. Basingstoke: Palgrave Macmillan, 1–14.

Shildrick, T. and R. MacDonald (2013), "Poverty Talk: How People Experiencing Poverty Deny their Poverty and Why they Blame 'the Poor.'" *The Sociological Review* 61(2): 285–303.

Stanley, L. (2016), "Legitimacy Gaps, Taxpayer Conflict, and the Politics of Austerity in the UK." *British Journal of Politics & International Relations* 18(2): 389–406.

Steinmo, S. (1993), *Taxation and Democracy: Swedish, British and American Approaches to Financing the Modern State*. New Haven, CT: Yale University Press.

Thompson, H. (2013), "UK Debt in Comparative Perspective: The Pernicious Legacy of Financial Sector Debt." *British Journal of Politics & International Relations* 15(3): 476–92.

Torgler, B. (2007), *Tax Compliance and Tax Morale: A Theoretical and Empirical Analysis*. Cheltenham: Edward Elgar.

Turley, C. and J. Keeble (2015), *Qualitative Research with People Convicted of Tax Evasion*. Research report. www.gov.uk/government/uploads/system/uploads/attachment_data/file/459617/Qualitative_research_with_people_convicted_of_tax_evasion.pdf.

Watson, M. (2013a), "New Labour's 'Paradox of Responsibility' and the Unravelling of its Macroeconomic Policy." *The British Journal of Politics & International Relations* 15(1): 6–22.

Watson, M. (2013b), "The Welfare State Sources of Bank Instability: Displacing the Conditions of Welfare State Fiscal Crisis under Pressures of Macroeconomic Financialization." *Public Administration* 91(4): 855–70.

Wincott, D. (2013), "The (Golden) Age of the Welfare State: Interrogating a Conventional Wisdom." *Public Administration* 91(4): 806–22.

Part V
United States

8

The Not-So-Infernal Revenue Service?

Tax Collection, Citizens, and Compliance in the United States from the Eighteenth to the Twentieth Centuries

Romain Huret

Introduction

At the end of the 1960s, the *Reader's Digest* was still one of the most widely read magazines in the United States. From suburban houses to waiting rooms across the country, it was possible to read the *Digest*'s stories about the future of the nation. By then, many articles dealt with the methods of federal tax collection. With the help of information from readers, lawyers, accountants, and even Internal Revenue Service (IRS) employees, the associate editor of the *Reader's Digest*, John Daniel Barron, recounted the tragic case of John J. Hafer. In October 1958, this businessman from Cumberland, Maryland, was notified by an IRS agent that his books and records should be made available for a routine tax audit. According to Barron, the audit turned into a nightmare. "The IRS tactics ultimately had their effect. Hafer had long been known as a community leader, an 'honest, free speaking' man. 'One thing about John, he was never afraid to stand up and be counted,' recalled County Commissioner Lucile Roeder. But belief spread that Hafer had to be guilty of *something*," explained Barron. As a consequence, in the small town, Hafer's customers, even friends, shied away from him, and his business dwindled. "Eight years spent fighting the IRS to prove his innocence," concluded Barron, "consumed his life." A few days after having been cleared by the federal government, John J. Hafer died. Such narrative of tax martyrdom spread into mainstream media and found strong echoes in a country doomed by political scandals, the

Vietnam fiasco, and deindustrialization. Throughout the decade, the "Infernal Revenue Service," as it was called by its enemies, was targeted by angry conservatives to denounce the whole unfairness of the progressive tax system and the tyrannical methods of federal agents (Huret 2014: ch. 7).

This chapter describes the central issue of tax collection and the reasons why Americans still comply with the federal tax system. As in many countries, the tax collector and the IRS have suffered, and still suffer, from a very bad reputation that frequently emerges in pamphlets, newspapers, and books. Such literature conveys the idea that tax collection depends on the level of coercion imposed by statist authorities. In other words, it is supposedly imposed by "tyrannical tax-gatherers," as conservatives call them, who leave no space for bargaining. As a consequence, in such a coercive framework, resistance and revolt appear legitimate. In his passionate and posthumous investigation of IRS misdemeanors, John A. Andrew underlines the famous— and often misunderstood—quotation by Chief Justice John Marshall, "the power to tax involves the power to destroy." This coercive model implies that fear and enforcement officers are the main vehicles of tax compliance in a country so attached to the idea of freedom against tyranny. Memory of famous tax rebels such as Ronald Reagan's favorite Daniel Shays reinforces such popular understanding of the American creed of taxation (Adams 1998; Andrew 2002; Heaps 1971; Huret 2014: 274–8; Kornhauser 2002).

Interestingly for my purpose, such a framework is often used to emphasize tax collection in so-called "weak states," especially in Africa. For many years, the US federal government has been described as particularly "weak" in comparison to European states. Current reconsideration of this alleged weakness has led to a new vision of both the nature of the American state and its peculiar and progressive system of taxation. As I argue in my book, *American Tax Resisters*, tax resisters were until the 1970s a minority of taxpayers, and ultimately "tax resistance put the emphasis instead on the millions of individuals who have agreed to pay their taxes" (2014: 279). As a consequence, it is worth reconsidering the complex relationship between tax collectors, citizens, and the federal government to historicize the US "leap of faith" all the more since the level of compliance is historically particularly strong and progressive tax rates particularly high.[1]

In this chapter, I propose a triangular framework including citizens, civil servants, and institutions. This view is part of a current historiographic trend that goes beyond an antagonistic approach opposing society to the state or vice versa. Recent scholarship on the nexus between state and society stresses reciprocal interactions between institutions and various social groups. Everybody agrees that citizens are more likely to comply when they perceive institutions as procedurally fair in both decision-making and implementation processes. Neither citizens nor the state are abstract individuals and institutions.

Instead, they interact in spaces that render possible both tensions and compromise, resistance and compliance. The delicate equilibrium that Martin Daunton emphasizes on the British case (Chapter 2 in this volume) is the result of such antagonistic and sometimes complementary forces.[2]

Most of the time, books on US taxation revolve around either the incremental development of the fiscal apparatus or the mobilization of society against tax procedures and law enforcement. What is often missing is a careful study of the tax collection process itself and its impact on fiscal citizenship. In this chapter, I do not propose an analysis of tax collection per se, but in dynamic interaction with citizens and other institutions. Instead of a coercive model of compliance, I propose a common ground model based upon three elements that explain why Americans have accepted in the past and, generally speaking, still accept today the expansion of fiscal power: (1) social legitimacy of the state and its actors; (2) a reach-out consensus on the definition and measurement of incomes and wealth; and (3) the ability of taxpayers and tax collectors to find room for negotiation. A historical outlook on different tax regimes demonstrates how institutional and social actors have looked for common ground since the Early Republic to the present. Consent is not a static process, but something dynamic and renegotiated by each generation.[3]

Invisible Tax, Invisible Collection (1776–1913)

On June 2, 1864, a citizen named Joseph Karned, living in Steubenville, Ohio, charged some of the officers of the eleventh district with various irregularities and stated that the income of certain individuals and establishments had not been returned in full. In the same state, an impostor named Thomas H. Glanner pretended to be a tax collector and borrowed money on the strength of his alleged position. Local newspapers denounced such cases and hoped that federal authorities would soon launch investigations into the alleged misdemeanors. The new commissioner of the Bureau of Internal Revenue, Joseph Lewis, decided to improve tax collection and establish investigations in tax districts to limit cases of tax abuse. In a letter sent to many inspectors, he urged them to report all wrongdoings. Otherwise, they would contribute to undermining the credibility of the whole tax system. As these examples suggest, tax collection was an arduous task during the Civil War during which many new taxes were voted by congressmen in order to raise sufficient revenue to pay for the war. The fluid boundaries between private and public spheres were at stake. Furthermore, citizens felt that tax rates and taxable incomes were set somewhat arbitrarily. Such difficulties explain why policymakers turned to the tariff as the most convenient way of collecting revenues during the nineteenth century. By making both tax collectors and tax rates invisible, elites eased the process of consent among the population (Bensel 1990; Flaherty 2009; Huret 2014: ch. 1; Richardson 1997; Unger 1964; Wilson 2006).

Before turning to the tariff, it seems important to stress the fact that tax collection had been delegitimized by the Revolution itself. In the new republic, the building-up of a new fiscal contract implied the creation of new social and professional roles such as exciseman, gaugers, or customs officers. Their holders were perceived to have a direct personal interest in collecting taxes. They were suspected of corruption and were locally referred to as "invaders." As a matter of fact, the patronage system—which was the rule—reinforced the lack of legitimacy. At the end of the eighteenth century, for instance, Federalists sought to work through local channels of influence and power in order to combine a new source of political power with pre-existing sources of governance. The Treasury Secretary, Alexander Hamilton, turned to local elites to collect federal taxes. It became a strongly divisive job that sparked a major revolt—the "Whiskey Rebellion"—from 1791 to 1794. Acts of civil disobedience were supported by local elites who felt dispossessed by the Federalists' administration and feared losing their local powers. A sociological analysis has shown that non-compliance depended upon the level of political integration of elites and their positions in the network of patronage relations (Brown 1993; Edling 2003; Kohn 1972; Slaughter 1986).

Another difficulty that arose from tax collection derived from the very definition of taxable incomes and wealth. For example, when Alexander Hamilton, one of the Founding Fathers, chose a tax on dwellings because he believed that homes were a more accurate index for assessing individuals' wealth, he sparked another revolt—the John Fries rebellion. By focusing on properties, the tax became popularly known as the "the Window tax" and was largely rejected. In 1802, Congressmen repealed the tax and abolished the position of Commissioner of the Revenue and all offices having to do with the collection of internal taxes. The tariff therefore became the ideal tax that minimized racial, social, and political tensions. It was also easy and invisible to the general public, even though citizens paid it indirectly. In the South, as historian Robin Einhorn brilliantly explains, there was strong hostility among slave owners to taxing slave property. Hamilton had already acknowledged that customs offices that collected the tax formed a small and efficient cadre of officials. If he urged them to initiate suits against recalcitrant merchants, he was ignored. As Gautham Rao has recently shown, Hamilton's proposal was largely rejected, and a fruitful process of negotiations occurred at the discretion of customs houses. Rao (2016: 98) rightly explains that overseas merchants accepted paying taxes so long "as they essentially set the terms of customs officials' methods of tax collection and regulation."[4]

Until the end of the nineteenth century, tariff collection was perfectly suited to the legitimacy of the new American state, the uncontested definition of taxable incomes it conveyed, and the room for "relaxations" it provided, to use one officer's own words. All alternative regimes (Civil War income tax, internal taxes during the Reconstruction period) failed because they were seen as too coercive. In other words, from the Southern moonshiners who opposed the tax on whiskey to businessmen in the North who hated the income tax, collection of direct taxes was denounced as arbitrary, unfair, and unconstitutional.

Finding Common Ground (1913–1941)

In the modern nation that emerged at the dawn of the twentieth century, tax reform became a major issue, and taxation of both personal and corporate incomes was by then seen as a legitimate way to regulate the new industrial order. As a new white-collar middle class of urban professionals gained more political influence, progressive taxation became a popular response to the vast change that had overwhelmed the country. Due to the economic depression of the mid-1890s, fear gripped millions of citizens. As a consequence, more and more Americans adopted a broader view of the government's role in dealing with the social consequences of industrialization. In the new industrial nation, citizens agreed with the reallocation of the fiscal burden and claimed that they had a legitimate claim upon the profits and earnings capacity of business corporations (Brownlee 2004: 41–57; Goodwyn 1978; McGerr 2003; Mehrotra 2010; Postel 2007).

During public meetings, politicians from the South and the West lambasted the Supreme Court for the *Pollock* decision that in 1894 rendered taxation of incomes unconstitutional and they found that their audiences responded with enthusiasm. Democrats began to introduce constitutional amendments that would permit income taxation and a more equitable distribution of the tax burden. Support for direct taxation grew steadily over the next fifteen years. In 1906, the American Federation of Labor endorsed income tax for rich taxpayers. The progressive movement tapped into discontent felt for monopolistic businesses and corruption. In Wisconsin, Governor Robert La Follette Sr. initiated a multipronged reform program, including a new income tax. Tax reform was for him the best way to curb the power of corporations. Offended by corruption and immorality in business, "Battling Bob" promoted scientific reform based upon expertise and social sciences. Far from the invisible mechanism of collection that prevailed during the nineteenth century, a scientific system of collection would enable policymakers to implement fair tax reform and to give legitimacy to tax collectors (Brownlee 1974; Ellis 1940: 237; Keller 1990: 208–15; Mehrotra 2004; Thelen 1972).

External crises such as World War I and the Great Depression reinforced belief in the power of the federal government, even among elites. Lawyers from the Bureau of Internal Revenue tapped into such a favorable change to prove their efficiency and promised to implement a disinterested system of collection. As Ajay Mehrotra aptly explains in his book on the rise of progressive taxation, "a wide cross-section of Americans welcome the transformation from an antiquated system of disaggregated, hidden, politicized, indirect and regressive taxes to a centralized, transparent, professionally administered regime dedicated to direct and progressive taxation." From Herbert Hoover's idea of an "associative State" to Roosevelt's arduous experiments, all leaders endorsed the idea of scientific taxation, even though they disagreed on the boundaries of the state. In spite of resistance, especially against the withholding mechanism, the filing of an income tax return became part of Americans' sense of fiscal citizenship. April 15 became a special, but not dreadful, day (Mehrotra 2015; 2016; Zelenak 2013).

Citizens also reached a consensus on the perfect taxable revenue: income tax. In the early twentieth century, the tariff decreased as a source of revenue. In October 1913, after two-thirds of states had ratified the Sixteenth Amendment, the 63rd Congress instituted a new tax on individual incomes. From 1913 to the New Dealers' high progressivity agenda of the 1930s, the taxing of both corporate and individual revenues gained strong legitimacy in the country. President Franklin Delano Roosevelt not only increased federal tax rates, but also hoped to combat the "unjust concentration of wealth and economic power." Progressivity became the only game in town, and the soak-the-rich ideology turned into a mainstream way of thinking.[5]

In order to encourage tax compliance, the federal government presented itself as "open-minded" and proposed "even-handed administration of tax laws," to quote one of the most important lawyers of the Bureau of Internal Revenue of the 1910s, Daniel Roper. To enable taxpayers to express their grievances, Treasury Secretary Andrew Mellon created in 1924 the Board of Tax Appeals—a major step in the reform of tax litigation. Until then, the rule was "pay first, litigate later," which forced the taxpayer to pay the government before turning to the Bureau of Internal Revenue for appeal. The Board suffered from a problem of congestion. From its inception to December 1931, 270,894 letters of deficiency had been sent and 62,239 appeals had been filed with the Board. In March 1932, there were still 17,261 cases pending before the Board because its capacity was only 1,600 a year. In the eyes of the taxpayer, this congestion was less a problem than the symbol of an "even-handed administration" of tax law (Mehrotra 2013: 359). It enabled many taxpayers to obtain tax refunds with the help of tax lawyers (Kornhauser 2009).

One of the most contested issues of the new progressive tax regime was the publicity provision contained in different revenue laws. Each time—in 1913, 1924, and 1935—congressmen repealed it after waves of protests and petitions. For instance, the 1934 Revenue Law authorized public access to every taxpayer's name, address, gross income deductions, credits, and tax payments. All taxpayers were asked to submit an additional form, which was printed on pink paper. Many Progressives endorsed the measure as the best way to limit tax evasion. This publicity provision sparked a "pink-slip campaign"— thousands of letters were sent to Congress to protest against it. Congressmen decided to repeal the law in early March in order to protect the confidentiality of taxpayers' personal information (Huret 2014: 145–50; Kornhauser 2009).

A perfect example of the quest for common ground was the implementation of the so-called "pick-up" scheme in the 1920s. This was an answer to the double imposition of tax inheritance at both state and federal level. In 1916, most states already had a state death tax when a federal estate tax was adopted to finance war expenditures. In 1915, the states collected $29 million in death taxes; nine years later, $79 million. This double taxation led to a competition between states trying to attract wealthy taxpayers. In the early 1920s, Florida, Alabama, and Nevada became tax havens. In answer to such an unfair system, congressmen decided to implement the subtle "pick-up" mechanism that made inheritance taxation uniform. A state death credit was enacted that enabled the states to enjoy 25 percent (in 1924), then 80 percent (in 1926) of estate tax revenue (Advisory Commission on Intergovernmental Relations 1961; Cooper 2006).

To sum up, from the Sixteenth Amendment to World War II, legitimacy of the new regime was based upon consensus on the new scientific method of collection, acceptance of the income tax as the best tax, and room for negotiation between policymakers and citizens.

Withholding, Businessmen, and Mass Consent (1941–1960)

Under the new tax system adopted in 1942, the number of individual taxpayers grew from 3.9 million in 1939 to 42.6 million in 1945. In six years federal income tax collections leaped from $2.2 billion to $35.1 billion. The shift from a narrow-based income tax to a mass-based one was a peculiar challenge for the Roosevelt administration. By the end of the war, nearly 90 percent of the members of the labor force submitted income tax returns, and about 60 percent of the labor force paid income tax. If patriotism played a part in explaining the lack of resistance, one has to stress also the fiscal bargain between policymakers and citizens. The Revenue Act of 1942 encapsulates debates about consent and a fair tax system (Brownlee 2004; Leff 1984; Zelizer 1998; see also Jones, Chapter 9 in this volume).

In 1941, the Treasury was particularly concerned with both the nature of collection and the reaction of would-be taxpayers to mass taxation. A survey conducted by a young economist named Milton Friedman described the way ordinary Americans viewed the new tax system and the collection of taxes by withholding from paychecks. Opponents represented only 10 percent of the sample. According to Friedman, they could be "classed as rugged individualists" and "are typified by such comments as 'I don't like to have my pay check touched' and 'I prefer to manage my own affairs.'" Only four people objected to the compulsory nature of the plan, arguing that it represented a form of regimentation and was the first step toward dictatorship. Six respondents expressed their concerns about further burdens on their already precarious situation. As one person put it, "Pretty soon there won't be anything left in the pay envelope." As Friedman noted, the attitude toward taxation varied according to the taxpayer's occupation and gender. While only two-fifths of the people interviewed were white-collar workers, three-quarters of the unfavorable answers came from this group. Women also tended to react less favorably than men. Other taxpayers contended that they preferred the withholding system to direct assessment and collection by the federal government. The withholding system, it was felt, would mean considerably less hardship. "You will hardly miss a little at a time" or "it would be a lot easier than paying it out in a lump sum," argued some of those interviewed. However, Milton Friedman urged policymakers to be cautious and concluded that "while only very few people opposed the plan on the ground that it was a form of regimentation, it was conceivable that this argument could assume larger proportions." Citizens who were aware that the withholding system would mean double payments in 1943 seemed anxious about their ability to save enough money.[6]

In May 1943, the popular magazine *Life* published a stunning editorial that criticized the tax "mess," citing in particular the withholding system envisioned by the Treasury Department. "Collecting two years in one is old Chinese custom," mocked the editorial, referring to the government's intention of asking citizens to pay for two years of taxes in 1943. Why did the government not accept the idea of tax forgiveness for all taxpayers, the op-ed continued? The chairman of the New York Federal Reserve Bank and treasurer of R. H. Macy and Company, Beardsley Ruml, made a name for himself by objecting in harsh terms to the Treasury Department's plan. A former professor of education, Ruml became an expert and a prolific writer in the field of taxation. As debates revolved around the tax system, he accepted the withholding mechanism but proposed a forgiveness of 1942 taxes to ease the pinch in 1943. After passionate debates and discussions, the Roosevelt administration accepted the bargain.[7]

Although after 1945 most Americans paid their income and corporation taxes by the deadline, as they were asked in the song written by Irving Berlin ("I Paid my Income Tax Today") at the request of the Treasury, they had found room for negotiations with the Bureau of Internal Revenue and the Treasury. Throughout the war, Roosevelt and his tax advisers were reluctant to impose a highly coercive system of assessment and collection either for ordinary citizens or businessmen. The new collection system based upon withholding gave businessmen—not Internal Revenue agents—the task of implementing the new tax code. In other words, the withholding system was a way to minimize face-to-face encounters between citizens and federal officers. Designed to allay taxpayers' fears, the implementation of the withholding system in 1943 made it more difficult to criticize taxes that citizens paid each month out of their paychecks. Economist Milton Friedman even contended that it was "enthusiastically favored by a large majority of people," as it would be a "sound business procedure, insuring maximum collection."[8]

Through this clever system, the Roosevelt administration gained the support of middle-class taxpayers and big corporations. During those years, hundreds of American companies enjoyed massive tax refunds, which had the effect of erasing most of their reconversion losses after World War II. According to Carl Shoup, a Columbia University economics professor and leading tax expert, the 1945 law gave "corporations all, if not more than they could have hoped for in a quick tax reduction bill." The Revenue Act of 1942, which sparked the era of easy finance, crystallizes the common ground model in action. No coercive action was necessary to implement the mass-based income tax. Consent was obtained through a clever process of compromise and compulsion by the state. In spite of high tax rates, tax dodgers remained a minority, and were presented as unpatriotic citizens. At the end of the 1960s, however, such common ground was attacked in different parts and social groups of the country (Kruse and Stuck 2012; Ruml 1946; Shoup 1945: 487; Wilson 2012; Zelenak 2013: 72–7).

Chain Reaction, Eroding Consent (1970–2010)

At the end of the 1960s, consent to taxation was threatened for one main reason: progressive tax architecture was then seen as neither scientific nor fair. On January 20, 1969, even Treasury Secretary Joseph warned of a taxpayer's revolt among the middle class. The unfairness of the whole tax system was criticized in many parts of the country as the number of tax loopholes increased. In 1967, Barr deplored, no income taxes were paid on 155 tax returns with gross incomes of $200,000 or more. Accumulation of tax loopholes and exemptions transformed the tax code into a long and complex legal

189

treaty. In a span of twenty years, all elements that cemented the fiscal equilibrium were shaken, and consent lost ground in the United States (Balogh 1991; Steinmo 1993; Zelizer 1998: 298).

In the 1970s, movements for tax justice gathered together different kinds of people, from single men and women to angry conservatives in the West and the South. Unmarried people wondered why singles paid more taxes than couples with the same total income. In some cases, the tax burden could be as much as 42 percent higher. The gap between norms of taxation and the social transformation of American society reinforced the process of chain reaction. Citizens scrutinized the tax code and questioned its most unfair parts. Even presidents deplored the unfairness of tax collection in the country. Republican President Gerald Ford explained that "the people are fed up with the petty tyranny of the faceless federal bureaucrats today as they were with their faraway rulers in London in 1776." President Jimmy Carter called the tax code a "national disgrace." Even sitcoms, such as *All in the Family*, *The Honeymooners*, and *Roseanne*, showed a deterioration of Americans' attitudes toward compliance (Huret 2014: 218; Zelenak 2013: 86–91).

Distrust of the IRS became one of the defining characteristics of the 1970s, and paved the way for the erosion of the progressivity embedded in the tax system through tax cuts favoring capital income and wealthy taxpayers. When Donald Crichton Alexander was sworn in as commissioner in mid-1973, he inherited an agency whose prestige was rapidly sinking. The new revenue commissioner had to face growing criticism of the IRS and acknowledged that maintaining public confidence in the agency was his "No. 1" task. Revelations about the IRS's Special Services staff then appeared in the national press. In August 1973, *Time* learned that an IRS branch had been set up in 1969 at the White House's request and had collected files on 3,000 organizations and 8,000 individuals—not all of them radical, though clearly left-wing. While many of the persons and groups listed had tax violations on record, others had nothing substantial lodged against them. A top-level memo indicated that "a great deal of material had not been evaluated." The functions of the Special Services group were described in a January 12 memo written by John J. Flynn, the North Atlantic regional commissioner, to the directors serving under him. Noting that the group worked closely with other federal investigative agencies, Flynn called it a "central intelligence-gathering facility within the IRS." The purpose of the group was to "receive and analyze all available information" on organizations and individuals promoting extremist "views or philosophies"—whether right- or left-leaning. Suspects were included "without regard to the philosophy or political posture involved." 'ABC News' aired an hour-long documentary on national TV accusing the IRS of being too willing to share confidential tax returns with other government agencies and of occasionally using heavy-handed tactics to collect money (Andrew 2002: 278–80; Johnson 2009: A-19; *Time* 1973).

Such attacks were not isolated. In 1985, tapping into traditional anti-tax rhetoric, conservative president Ronald Reagan derided the inept federal system, provoking easy laughs from his audience during the numerous meetings he held in 1985. In early June, during meetings in Virginia, Wisconsin, and Pennsylvania, he assailed a tax code that ran "roughshod" over Main Street America, calling for an end to "unproductive tax shelters, so that no one will be able to hide in the havens privilege builds." He derided the complexity of the existing tax code by frequently reeling off the incomprehensible last sentence of Section 509(a): "For purposes of paragraph (3), an organization described in paragraph (2) shall be deemed to include an organization described in section 501(c) (4), (5), or (6), which would be described in paragraph (2) if it were an organization described in section 501(c) (3)." By repeating such strikingly memorable examples of the complexity of the tax code, he undermined the expertise of tax agents and citizens' trust in the system of tax collection. Ten years later, William Reynolds Archer Jr., the new chairman of the Committee on Ways and Means, decided to put on display in Congress the original nineteen-page law establishing the income tax. "This small 19-page baby," explained Archer "was the original document that grew up to become today's monster." Archer found many receptive ears among the middle class and the wealthy, major beneficiaries of the prosperity of the 1990s, which was fueled by the dizzying rise of the stock market. Denounced as both absurd and monstrous by prominent leaders of the nation, tax collection lost its legitimacy (Huret 2014: 255, 256, 258).

Furthermore, a powerful assault against the progressive tax system and its pillar—the income tax—was organized by supply-side economists and grassroots organizations such as Grover Norquist's Americans for Tax Reform. During debates in Congress and due to budgetary constraints, many conservatives proposed to enact regressive taxes in lieu of the income tax. House Majority Leader Dick Armey and presidential candidate Senator Arlen Specter of Pennsylvania both sponsored a proposal for a flat income tax. The idea came from Robert Hall and Alvin Rabushka, two economists from the conservative Hoover Institution. In a 1981 article in the *Wall Street Journal*, Hall and Rabushka had offered many hints of the virtue of a flat tax for both businesses and individuals at a 19 percent rate. All income would be taxed at source, and the simplicity of collection would enable the federal government to save taxpayers' money. To convince Americans, Armey used the same argument as Archer, contending that the tax return would fit on a postcard and could be completed in only fifteen minutes. He added that the effect would be "tremendous" for taxpayers. A married couple filing jointly, for example, would reduce their taxable income through a $26,200 personal exemption and subtract an additional $5,300 for each dependent child. A family of four with an income below $36,800 would owe no income tax under the Armey plan, as opposed to the $3,100, or 8.4 percent, that such families paid on average. Referring to the rule of uniformity and tapping into the conservative ideology of common sense, Armey explained that the flat tax "was based on the idea of fairness we learned in grade school: *Everyone should be treated the same*" (Kornhauser 1995: 612). The Treasury, however, announced that such a flat tax would cost $244 billion in lost receipts annually, and it would be necessary to find other sources of revenue (Hall and Rabushka 1995).

Is it a coincidence that physical and verbal opposition to tax collectors reappeared in the country in the 1980s? Violent actions by Midwestern libertarians such as Gordon Kahl made the news. Although such radical actions remained few in number, the fear of contagion was prevalent in the Reagan administration. "The mind-set of America has changed since World War II," warned Roscoe Egger Jr. In an interview with *Time* magazine, the IRS commissioner voiced his conviction that tax evasion was on the rise, and that evasion was not seen to be as antisocial as it used to be. The American Institute of Certified Public Accountants helped propagate the idea that more and more taxpayers were "not paying their full tax." According to the figures given by the Treasury, the number of taxpayers claiming that they were not liable for income taxes had increased dramatically over the previous several decades. In 1982, Congress responded to this increase by enacting provisions, including Number 6702 imposing a $500 civil penalty on frivolous income tax returns, and Number 6673 permitting courts to punish taxpayers who filed frivolous complaints. Such an increase in coercive power to collect taxation is more a signal of the weakness of the state than a symbol of its "tyrannical power" (Huret 2014: 241–73).

As today's Tea Partiers suggest, the legitimacy of the federal government to collect taxation has suffered from continuous attacks since the 1970s. When asked what they were angry about, Tea Party supporters stated three main issues that debunked the postwar common ground: government expansion, the unfairness of the definition of taxable income that plagued the middle class, and the lack of room for negotiation. The federal bargain implemented during World War II has been challenged in a way that has questioned both the centrality of the income tax and the right of federal agents to collect taxes. Both inheritance tax and the "pick-up" tax have been attacked. Many believe that the whole architecture of federal taxation has to be rebuilt in order to eradicate citizen distrust and state competition (Carter 2010; Skocpol and Williamson 2012).

Conclusion

The main goal of this chapter has been to propose a model to analyze the social and political fabric of consent in the United States. Historical evidence helps us minimize anti-tax rhetoric that occupies such a central role in today's political discourse in the United States. Even though more studies need to be done—especially around the Treasury Department—I have identified three main factors that posit the ineffectiveness of the coercive model. Each tax regime reveals the bargaining process between citizens and the federal government. Far from describing tax collection as a life-or-death process, this article describes reciprocal interactions between individuals and their institutions. While in other countries secrecy rules, institutional procedures enabled American citizens to influence the design of the tax code and the form of tax collection. Publicity of taxpayers' forms has been rejected, while withholding has been seen as a way to minimize face-to-face encounters with federal agents. In other words, the mass-based income tax, that made the country a champion of progressivity, was carefully negotiated during World War II. Fear was not the main vehicle that pushed people to pay their taxes. By contrast the current crisis of the US system rests upon a delegitimization process of the state, an ever-growing attack on the progressivity of taxation and a worsening of the reputation of the IRS. By playing with fears and emotions, politicians have contributed to the demise of the federal power to tax and paved the way for the debt crisis that plagues the nation's finances. The very sense of fiscal citizenship has to be rebuilt. In 2014, President Obama deplored the fact that the US tax code was "riddled with wasteful, complicated loopholes that punish business investing here, and reward companies that keep profits abroad" (Mehrotra 2015: 971). As taxes always define the economic duties that come with citizenship, it is probably the whole American social contract that needs to be refined in the Trump age in order to restore consent (Michelmore 2012).

Notes

1. For the weak state/coercive model, see Fjeldstad (2001). For an attempt to reconsider the traditional interpretation on the weakness of the state, see Balogh (2008). See also the special issue of the *Journal of Policy History* (vol. 25, no.3) I co-edited with Nicolas Delalande in 2013.
2. For further discussion, see Bergman (2003); Daunton (2001); Delalande (2011); Kwass (2000); Levi (1988); Lo (1990); Martin (2008); Martin, Mehrotra, and Prasad (2009: 1–27); Scholz and Lubell (1998); Slemrod (1992); Tilly (1992).
3. See Martin (2013); Paul (1954); Philipps (2002); Ratner (1942); Slemrod and Bakija (2008); Steinmo (1993); Thorndike (2013); Witte (1985). The idea of the "middle

ground" comes from Richard White's classical study on the Midwest, *The Middle Ground: Indians, Empires, and Republics in the Great Lakes Region, 1650–1815* (New York: Cambridge University Press, 1991). His middle ground is a network of fluid relationships, held together by its own language, rituals, and patterns of behavior that enabled Indians, Europeans, and Americans to coexist.

4. See also Huret (2014: chs. 1 and 2); Newman (2004).
5. Quotation in Mehrotra (2013: 356). See also Brownlee (1996: 81–106); Leff (1984); Mellon (1924); Murnane (2004); Thorndike (2013).
6. For the survey, "Attitudes Toward Payroll Deductions. The Proposed Withholding Tax and Increased Social Security," 230 people were interviewed in Baltimore and Minneapolis from August 7 to August 20, 1942. All were employees in establishments where the payroll deduction plan for war bond purchases was in effect: 1, 2, 7. See Burgin (2012: 164–5).
7. Editorial, *Life*, April 26, 1943: 22. See also Reagan (1992).
8. Talk by the Secretary on the American Taxpayers' March 15, 1944 Income Tax Problem, Secondary Draft, January 10, 1944, Folder G4–1/44–4, Questions and Answers on Tax Simplification, January 4, 1944, National Archives, RG 56, www.archives.gov/. See also Sparrow (2008).

References

Adams, Charles (1998), *Those Dirty Rotten Taxes: The Tax Revolts that Built America*. New York: Free Press.

Advisory Commission on Intergovernmental Relations (1961), *Coordination of State and Federal Inheritance, Estate, and Gift Taxes*. Washington, DC: ACIR.

Andrew, John A. III (2002), *Power to Destroy: The Political Uses of the IRS from Kennedy to Nixon*. Chicago, IL: Ivan R. Dee.

Balogh, Brian (1991), *Chain Reaction: Expert Debate and Public Participation in American Commercial Nuclear Power 1945–1975*. Cambridge: Cambridge University Press.

Balogh, Brian (2008), *A Government Out of Sight: The Mystery of National Authority in Nineteenth-Century America*. Cambridge: Cambridge University Press.

Bergman, Marcelo (2003), "Tax Reforms and Tax Compliance: The Divergent Paths of Chile and Argentina." *Journal of Latin American Studies* 35: 593–624.

Bensel, Richard Franklin (1990), *Yankee Leviathan: The Origins of Central State Authority in America, 1859–1877*. Cambridge: Cambridge University Press.

Brown, Roger H. (1993), *Redeeming the Republic: Federalists, Taxation, and the Origins of the Constitution*. Baltimore, MD: Johns Hopkins University Press.

Brownlee, W. Elliot (1974), *Progressivism and Economic Growth: The Wisconsin Income Tax, 1911–1929*. Port Washington, NY: Kennikat Press.

Brownlee, W. Elliot (1996), *Federal Taxation in America: A Short History*. Cambridge: Cambridge University Press.

Brownlee, W. Elliot (2004), *Federal Taxation in America: A Short History*. New York: Cambridge University Press.

Burgin, Angus (2012), *The Great Persuasion: Reinventing Free Markets since the Depression.* Cambridge, MA: Harvard University Press.

Carter, Jimmy (2010), "1970s Saw a Tea Party-like Wave." *USA Today*, September 29.

Cooper, Jeffrey A. (2006), "Interstate Competition and State Death Taxes: A Modern Crisis in Historical Perspective." *Pepperdine Law Review* 33(4): 835–82.

Daunton, Martin (2001), *Trusting Leviathan: The Politics of Taxation in Britain 1799–1914.* Cambridge: Cambridge University Press.

Delalande, Nicolas (2011), *Les batailles de l'impôt: Consentement et résistance de 1789 à nos jours.* Paris: Le Seuil.

Edling, Max (2003), *A Revolution in Favor of Government: Origins of the U.S. Constitution and the Making of the American State.* New York: Oxford University Press.

Ellis, Elmer (1940), "Public Opinion and the Income Tax." *Mississippi Valley Historical Review* 27: 225–42.

Fjeldstad, Odd-Helge (2001), "Taxation, Coercion and Donors: Local Government Tax Enforcement in Tanzania." *The Journal of Modern African Studies* 39(2): 289–306.

Flaherty, Jane (2009), *The Revenue Imperative: The Union's Financial Policies during the American Civil War.* London: Pickering & Chatto.

Goodwyn, Lawrence (1978), *The Populist Moment: A Short History of the Agrarian Revolt in America.* New York: Oxford University Press.

Hall, Robert and Alvin Rabushka (1995), *The Flat Tax.* Washington, DC: Hoover Institution Press.

Heaps, Willard A. (1971), *Taxation U.S.A.* New York: Seabury Press.

Huret, Romain D. (2014), *American Tax Resisters.* Cambridge, MA: Harvard University Press.

Johnson, David C. (2009), "Donald C. Alexander, 87, Who Resisted Nixon at I.R.S., Is Dead." *New York Times*, February 8, A-19.

Keller, Morton (1990), *Regulating a New Economy: Public Policy and Economic Change in America, 1900–1933.* Cambridge, MA: Harvard University Press.

Kohn, Richard H. (1972), "The Washington Administration's Decision to Crush the Whiskey Rebellion." *Journal of American History* 59(3): 567–84.

Kornhauser, Marjorie (1995), "Equality, Liberty and a Fair Income Tax." *Fordham Urban Law Journal* 23: 607–61.

Kornhauser, Marjorie (2002), "Legitimacy and the Right of Revolution: The Role of Tax Protests and Anti-Tax Rhetoric in America." *Buffalo Law Review* 50: 819–924.

Kornhauser, Marjorie (2009), "Shaping Public Opinion and the Law: How a 'Common Man' Law Ended a Rich Man's Law." *Law and Contemporary Problems* 73: 123–47.

Kruse, Kevin M. and Stephen Stuck (eds.) (2012), *Fog of War: The Second World War and the Civil Rights Movement.* New York: Oxford University Press.

Kwass, Michael (2000), *Privilege and the Politics of Taxation in Eighteenth-Century France.* Cambridge: Cambridge University Press.

Leff, Mark (1984), *The Limits of Symbolic Reform: The New Deal and Taxation, 1933–1939.* Cambridge: Cambridge University Press.

Levi, Margaret (1988), *Of Rule and Revenue.* Berkeley, CA: University of California Press.

Lo, Clarence Y. H. (1990), *Small Property versus Big Government: Social Origins of the Property Tax Revolt.* Berkeley, CA: University of California Press.

McGerr, Michael (2003), *A Fierce Discontent: The Rise and Fall of the Progressive Movement in America 1870–1920*. New York: Free Press.

Martin, Isaac W. (2008), *The Permanent Tax Revolt*. Palo Alto, CA: Stanford University Press.

Martin, Isaac W. (2013), *Rich People's Movement: Grassroots Campaign to Untax the One Percent*. New York: Oxford University Press.

Martin, Isaac W., Ajay K. Mehrotra, and Monica Prasad (eds.) (2009), *The New Fiscal Sociology: Taxation in Comparative and Historical Perspective*. New York: Cambridge University Press.

Mehrotra, Ajay (2004), "More Mighty than the Waves of the Sea: Toilers, Tariffs, and the Income Tax Movement, 1880–1913." *Labor History* 45(2): 165–98.

Mehrotra, Ajay (2010), "The Public Control of Corporate Power: Revisiting the 1909 U.S. Corporate Tax from a Comparative Perspective." *Theoretical Inquiries in Law* 11: 491–532.

Mehrotra, Ajay K. (2013), *Making the Modern American Fiscal State: Law, Politics, and the Rise of Progressive Taxation, 1877–1929*. New York: Cambridge University Press.

Mehrotra, Ajay K. (2015), "Reviving Fiscal Citizenship." *Michigan Law Review* 113(6): 943–71.

Mehrotra, Ajay K. (2016), "From Contested Concept to Cornerstone of Administrative Practice: Social Leaning and the Early History of U.S. Tax Witholding." *Columbia Journal of Tax Law* 7: 144–69.

Mellon, Andrew W. (1924), *Taxation: The People's Business*. New York: Macmillan.

Michelmore, Molly C. (2012), *Tax and Spend: The Welfare State, Tax Politics, and the Limits of American Liberalism*. Philadelphia. PA: University of Pennsylvania Press.

Murnane, Susan (2004), "Selling Scientific Taxation: The Treasury Department's Campaign for Tax Reform in the 1920s." *Law and Social Inquiry* 29(4): 826–9.

Newman, Paul Douglas (2004), *Frie's Rebellion: The Enduring Struggle for the American Revolution*. Philadelphia, PA: University of Pennsylvania Press.

Paul, Randolph E. (1954), *Taxation in the United States*. Boston, MA: Little, Brown.

Philipps, Kevin (2002), *Wealth and Democracy: A Political History of the American Rich*. New York: Broadway Books.

Postel, Charles (2007), *The Populist Vision*. New York: Oxford University Press.

Rao, Gautham (2016), *National Duties: Custom Houses and the Making of the American State*. Chicago, IL: University of Chicago Press.

Ratner, Sidney (1942), *American Taxation: Its History as a Social Force in Democracy*. New York: W. W. Norton.

Reagan, Patrick D. (1992), "The Withholding Tax, Beardsley Ruml, and Modern American Policy." *Prologue* 24: 19–31.

Richardson, Heather Cox (1997), *The Greatest Nation on Earth: Republican Economic Policies during the Civil War*. Cambridge, MA: Harvard University Press.

Ruml, Beardsley (1946), "Taxes for Revenue Are Obsolete." *American Affairs* 8(1): 35–9.

Scholz, John and Mark Lubell (1998), "Trust and Taxpaying: Testing the Heuristic Approach to Collective Action." *American Journal of Political Science* 42(2): 398–417.

Shoup, Carl S. (1945), "The Revenue Act of 1945." *Political Science Quarterly* 60: 481–91.

Skocpol, Theda and Vanessa Williamson (2012), *The Tea Party and the Remaking of Republican Conservatism*. New York: Oxford University Press.

Slaughter, Thomas P. (1986), *The Whiskey Rebellion: Frontier Epilogue to the American Revolution*. New York: Oxford University Press.

Slemrod, Joel (1992), *Why People Pay Taxes: Tax Compliance and Enforcement*. Ann Arbor, MI: University of Michigan Press.

Slemrod, Joel and John M. Bakija (2008), *Taxing Ourselves: A Citizen's Guide to Debate over Taxes*. Cambridge, MA: MIT Press.

Sparrow, James (2008), "'Buying Our Boys Back': The Mass Foundations of Fiscal Citizenship in World War II." *Journal of Policy History* 20(2): 264–86.

Steinmo, Sven (1993), *Taxation and Democracy: Swedish, British and American Approaches to Financing the Modern State*. New Haven, CT: Yale University Press.

Thelen, David (1972), *The New Citizenship: Origins of the Progressivism, 1885–1900*. Columbia, MO: Missouri University Press.

Thorndike, Joseph J. (2013), *Their Fair Share: Taxing the Rich in the Age of FDR*. Washington, DC: Urban Institute Press.

Tilly, Charles (1992), *Coercion, Capital, and European States, 1990–1992*. Cambridge, MA: Blackwell.

Time (1973), "The Nation: Keeping a Little List at the IRS," August 13.

Unger, Irwin (1964), *The Greenback Era: A Social and Political History of American Finance, 1865–1879*. Princeton, NJ: Princeton University Press.

Wilson, Mark R. (2006), *The Business of Civil War: Military Mobilization and the State, 1861–1865*. Baltimore, MD: Johns Hopkins University Press.

Wilson, Mark R. (2012), "The Advantages of Obscurity: World War II Tax Carry-Back Provisions and the Normalization of Corporate Welfare." In Julian Zelizer and Kim Philipps-Fein (eds.), *What's Good for Business: Business and Politics since World War II*. New York: Oxford University Press, 16–44.

Witte, John F. (1985), *The Politics and Development of the Federal Income Tax*. Madison, WI: University of Wisconsin Press.

Zelenak, Lawrence (2013), *Learning to Love Form 1040: Two Cheers for the Return Based Mass Income Tax*. Chicago, IL: University of Chicago Press.

Zelizer, Julian (1998), *Taxing America: Wilbur D. Mills, Congress, and the State 1945–1975*. New York: Cambridge University Press.

9

Seeing Taxation in the Mid-Twentieth Century

US Tax Compliance

Carolyn C. Jones

A Visionary Notion

An understanding of tax compliance begins by asking why should Americans pay taxes? Progressive economists in the late nineteenth and early twentieth centuries rejected or minimized a benefits-received theory in their writings. The most prominent economist in the development of federal taxation, E. R. A. Seligman, wrote that the success of progressive taxation in America depended on "the state of social consciousness and the development of the feeling of civic obligation" (Seligman 1894: 193).[1]

In one of the most interesting passages on taxation and citizenship ever written, Seligman argues for the rejection of benefits taxation:

> It is now generally agreed that we pay taxes not because the state protects us, or because we get any benefits from the state, but simply because the state is a part of us . . . He does not choose the state, but is born into it; it is interwoven with the very fibers of his being; nay, in the last resort, he gives to it his very life . . . We pay taxes . . . because, in short, the state is an integral part of us.   (Seligman 1895: 72)

With regard to the federal government, middle income Americans' tax contributions were largely in the form of indirect consumption and excise taxes before the 1930s. A clear connection between taxes paid and their consequences was not clear to payers and was contested among various economic, regional, and political groups. Tariffs might protect American industries and workers from foreign competition or those same taxes might increase the cost of living for the poorer ordinary citizen, and enhance monopoly and corporate power.

After the Civil War, the federal government, using its tariff and excise tax regime and land sales, was able to finance debt repayment, military operations such as the Indian Wars and the Spanish–American War of 1898, a large program of Civil War pensions for Union veterans and their dependents, land grant colleges, and public works such as transcontinental railroads and the Panama Canal (Brownlee 2016).

As the country became more urbanized and industrialized by the end of the nineteenth century, more taxpayers began to question the fairness of the system. The inability of property taxation to reach the intangibles of the rich provided fuel for a restive and progressive response to the Republican tax scheme.

Various groups (populists, farmers, Democrats, those outside the Northeast) began to advocate for a progressive federal income tax aimed at the rich. Congress passed such a tax in 1894, only to have it overturned by the United States Supreme Court as unconstitutional in *Pollock v. Farmers' Loan and Trust Co.*[2] By 1913, a new Sixteenth Amendment to the US Constitution allowed for a tax on incomes without apportionment according to the census. The income tax enacted in 1913 was one aimed at the wealthiest citizens. In 1914, the tariff and excises were the major sources of federal revenues; the income tax constituted 10 percent of revenues, paid by just 2 percent of the labor force (Mehrotra 2013: 299). In 1918, the last year of the Great War, only about 7.7 percent of the total population was covered by taxable returns (Seltzer 1968: 62). By 1919, however, income and profits taxes comprised about half of federal revenues. These taxes were designed with the new estate tax and excess profits taxes to "soak the rich."

Legibility for Citizens

In 1909, a decision was taken to make public excise tax returns on corporate income. It was felt that making returns public could prevent stock fraud while also providing accurate financial information. In the days before the Securities and Exchange Commission, it was hoped also that this sort of transparency would make markets more honest and more efficient. Opponents raised privacy concerns, fears of base and envious snooping by malefactors and business competitors, and worries about how publicity could lead to "undue governmental control" (Kornhauser 2010: 126). Objections from the business community resulted in the repeal of disclosure in 1910, while giving the president discretion to disclose tax information (Kornhauser 1990).

In the scandal-ridden mid-1920s, Congress enacted limited income tax publicity with respect to individuals in the 1924 Revenue Act. Names, addresses, tax paid, and refund amounts were subject to disclosure. This information was published in newspapers, creating a backlash against the publicity project. In 1925, in *United States v. Dickey*,[3] the US Supreme Court struck down indictments against a Kansas City newspaper owner and editor for publishing income tax information.

The Supreme Court's blessing did not end criticism of income tax publicity. Citing privacy, "Anglo-Saxon fair play," fears of "Prussianiz[ing] our Government," facilitation of interspousal investigations and criminal opportunists, opponents continued to inveigh against publicity. This was despite the fact that less than 10 percent of Americans needed to file an income tax return (Seltzer 1968: 62). In 1926, Congress softened publicity requirements by making only names and addresses public (Kornhauser 2010: 127–9).

Congressional investigation of the 1929 stock market crash and the minimal amounts of tax paid by very wealthy Americans such as J. P. Morgan led to a reinvigorated version of tax publicity in 1934: the infamous "pink slips" required by that year's Revenue Act. All income tax payers needed to submit a pink form detailing their name, address, gross income, taxable income, and amount of tax liability (Kornhauser 2010: 130).

This public information, its proponents said, would prevent tax evasion, keeping taxpayers and administrators honest. Paying taxes was "public business" and publicity would deter people from cheating on taxes if others could discover it, and would instill trust as citizens saw that others were paying their fair share (Kornhauser 2010: 130).

At this point, Congress reversed course and repealed income tax publicity before it became law in response to (at least in part) anti-tax publicity campaigns by a variety of groups. Efforts at tax publicity were intended to serve both the government and taxpayers in making tax collection more transparent. For the government, publicity of tax information could be used to elicit additional information from close associates, neighbors, colleagues, or others, data that could reveal more untaxed income or various arrangements designed to obscure assets and income from the government.

For taxpayers, it was hoped that long lists of taxpayers, taxes due (and the more detailed information on the pink slips) would assure those paying taxes that they were in the company of many who were also paying their fair share. For the more than 90 percent of citizens not subject to income tax in the 1930s and before,[4] seeing the lengthy newspaper supplements listing the rich and mighty would provide the average citizen with a catalog of those in a position to pay federal taxes, and the "common man" with the pleasure felt in knowing he was not on the list.

Even during World War I, relatively few Americans were direct taxpayers. The soak-the-rich regime of the early decades of the twentieth century treated most Americans as observers to taxpaying rituals and responsibilities. In this period, at different times, Congress provided publicity as a way of demonstrating to those paying indirect federal consumption taxes that the wealthy were paying their progressive income taxes. Most Americans had little control over whether they complied with these taxes—that was in the hands of vendors.[5] The reporting on payment by the rich was intended to advertise a fairer, more progressive aspect of the federal tax system.

Tax Evasion in the 1930s

As the Great Depression set in, contrasts between the rich and the rest of Americans became an important theme for President Franklin D. Roosevelt. The president faced opposition from the right and from a variety of populist programs such as those from Huey Long and Father Coughlin, who promised massive government transfers to the economically disadvantaged. In the summer of 1935, Roosevelt attacked tax laws as having "done little to prevent an unjust concentration of wealth and economic power":[6]

> Whether it be wealth achieved through the cooperation of the entire community or riches gained by speculation—in either case the ownership of such wealth or riches represents a great public interest and a great ability to pay.[7]

In this period, the role of federal income tax was clear. It was to be used as a weapon against those Roosevelt called "economic royalists" (Rosenman 1938: 232). He highlighted the contrast between "the vast majority of our citizens" (who owed no federal income tax) and "a small, but powerful group which has fought the extension of [the] benefits of democracy, because it did not want to pay a fair share of their cost" (Rosenman 1938: 524–5).

The "vast majority" might be satisfied to see the Roosevelt administration go after those who contrived to avoid paying their "fair share." Those not subject to the income tax could see the government go after the 10 percent who were. This was obvious with respect to a campaign against tax avoidance by the wealthy. Tax avoidance techniques were on the rise in 1937 (Paul 1954: 202). J. P. Morgan, fresh off the boat from a trip to Europe, is reported to have said, "Congress should know how to levy taxes, and if it doesn't know how to collect them, then a man is a fool to pay the taxes" (Paul 1954: 203).

Following hearings detailing tax avoidance and evasion by sixty-seven wealthy families, Congress responded with the Revenue Act of 1937. Foreign and domestic personal holding companies, hobby losses, incorporated yachts and country estates, and personal service corporations were just a few of the devices resorted to by the well-to-do. For Roosevelt, plutocratic tax evasion and avoidance focused income tax reform upon the very small group of Americans already subject to income taxation instead of upon measures that would have broadened the tax base and the role of the income tax as a source of federal revenue.

Social Security

As the economic depression lingered through the 1930s, Americans began to ask more from their federal government in terms of a social safety net. The Social Security Act of 1935 authorized a program of old age insurance, unemployment compensation, aid to the needy, and aid to dependent children. It was ambitious in scope for the US federal government at the time. Developed by the Roosevelt administration, in part in response to Huey Long's Share Our Wealth plan and the broad popular interest in Dr. Francis Townsend's Plan, the program was financed by nominally equal taxes on employers and employees on the basis of an employee's wages or salary. Old Age Assistance was sold as insurance "yours by right when your working days are over" (National Archives 1939). From August 1935 to the end of December 1936, more than 30 million Americans needed to be enrolled in the program. The payroll taxes were slated to begin January 1, 1937. The Social Security Board had to devise a numeration scheme, eventually choosing a nine-digit system that meshed with the technical capacities of other departments. To get everyone enrolled, the US Postal Service was deployed to sign up citizens (National Archives 1939; Social Security 2013).

Once those to be included in the system were identified, a reliable way to collect and record payroll taxes had to be devised. Here employers and taxpayers themselves were relied upon to report employee compensation and remit both employer and employee taxes. Identifying and enumerating taxpayers (even assigning last names as in the case of Inuit people in the Alaska Territory), collecting taxes, and recording information on which benefits would be paid, was an enormous challenge.

While postal assistance and newsreel footage may have encouraged participation (if one's employers did not do their duty), social security system planners seemed aware of the need to assure the public that their earnings and payments into the system would be accurately recorded, a mammoth undertaking considering that, in 1939, there were 44 million separate wage accounts. As the program was being devised, one proposal was to have stamps that could be affixed to pass books to record payments. Instead, the social security board commissioned a series of short films and newsreels, demonstrating the large number of professionally dressed employees at work in the Candler Building, an old Coca-Cola bottling warehouse in Baltimore. Viewers could see the massive visible index in alphabetical order. There was also the 13,000-volume numerical register of social security numbers. IBM machines turned earnings records into punch cards for tabulation and calculations (Social Security 2013). The film shows the procedure for error checking—inserting a needle through a stack of punch cards (Social Security n.d.). The government film, *Social Security for the Nation* (National Archives 1939), praised the workers with "nimble fingers" and "alert minds," who were "always checking, controlling and rechecking."

Registering for social security exposed citizens to taxation, but also allowed them to receive the benefits of the social insurance programs, sold by Roosevelt as insurance to which taxpaying citizens were entitled. As Roosevelt recalled, "we put those payroll contributions there so as to give the contributors a legal, moral and political right to collect their pensions and their unemployment benefits. With those taxes in there, no damn politician can ever scrap my social security program."[8] This was a tax that could be popularly conceived as based upon individual benefits to be received, its redistributive features not apparent. There was, therefore, a benefit in being known to the social security agency and some reassurance in knowing how one's information was recorded, manipulated, and preserved. Despite this depiction of a paid-for benefit, the government also portrayed the social security system as "pooling the risk for joint protection [as] the method of our democracy" (National Archives 1939).

There was, however, a less positive aspect to the social security narrative. Under social security, benefits were based upon wage work, and, in the 1930s, 85 percent of families had a single male breadwinner. As historian Alice Kessler-Harris summarizes, "Casual laborers, the unskilled and untrained, housewives, farm workers, mothers and domestic servants all found themselves on one side of a barrier not of their own making. Their own benefits not earned, but means-tested, classified as relief, not rights" (Kessler-Harris 2001: 4). Those exclusions from the social security system were not accidental. Agricultural workers and domestic servants were often African Americans or other racial minorities. For Franklin Roosevelt, legislative enactment required appeasing white southern legislators who would not consent to economic rights for most black citizens (Quadagno 1996: 20).

Without ties to a covered wage earner, social insurance (with federal rules and some state variations) became welfare collected by "welfare queens" viewed more negatively and, often, seen in racial terms (Levin 2013).[9]

The Voluntary Regime

During the 1930s, about 5 percent of Americans were required to file federal income tax returns. With war concerns heightening toward the end of the 1930s, Congress lowered exemptions to bring more citizens into taxpaying status (Seltzer 1968: 62). As the United States edged toward war in the late 1930s, and then was immersed in total war by the end of 1941, the role of income taxation and the identities of those paying changed. The Roosevelt administration fairly skillfully used patriotism as the rationale for the new bargain.

Polls from 1938 to 1939 show a lack of public support for reductions in taxes "on people with high incomes," and a plurality of support for publicity of the income tax returns "of rich men" (Cantril 1951: 317). Public surveys from 1938 and 1939 supported exemption of over three-fourths of the American population from income taxation. As America seemed more likely to be drawn into the war that was engulfing Europe and Asia at the close of the 1930s, income tax remained essentially, as Hoover's Treasury Secretary described it, a tax "with high exemptions and very low rates on the smaller taxable incomes," a tax that was "as a practical matter" very difficult to alter.

By fall of 1939, the Treasury (with the president's blessing) considered a three-pronged approach: an excess profits tax, an income tax to fight inflation, and finally, as a defense-industry-fueled recovery occurred, Secretary Morgenthau "believed it would be just and feasible to increase taxes on middle and lower income groups" (Blum 1967: 279). In the Revenue Acts of 1940 and 1942, Congress responded by increasing the income tax class from 7.4 million to 27.6 million (Paul 1954: 318). Once the United States entered the war in December 1941, revenue demands spiked. The Revenue Act of 1942 increased the number of taxable returns on net income by over 45 percent. Professors Surrey and Warren aptly noted that income tax had "changed its morning coat for overalls" and had "spread from the country club group district down to the railroad tracks and then over to the other side of the tracks" (quoted in Paul 1954: 318).

The 1942 Act also included a Victory Tax, a 5 percent gross income tax on all income over $624. The Victory Tax promised a partial postwar credit. Taking the Victory Tax into account, the income tax rolls increased from 13 million to 50 million in one year. By 1943, 68.9 percent of the total population was covered by a taxable return as compared with 2.6 percent of the population just ten years earlier. The fledgling mass income tax faced two large compliance challenges. First, income tax had been so clearly identified as a tax on the rich that its application to middle-income and working-class taxpayers could be seen as illegitimate. Second, the Treasury Department and Internal Revenue Service did not have in 1942 the ability to collect taxes on current year incomes, nor had withholding by employers been enacted. While the new mass income tax was law, the administrative capacity to collect it was frighteningly low. In fact, the Commissioner of Internal Revenue publicly doubted that a withholding system could be implemented because of adding machine and office supply shortages.[10] More Internal Revenue agents were needed.[11] With inadequate capacity, the public's willing self-assessment was essential until the enactment of withholding and the transition to tax collection on current incomes.

The Quest for Legitimacy

So how did the Treasury and other wartime propaganda agencies seek to address the question of the legitimacy of a mass income tax, a tax very vulnerable to avoidance and evasion? Treasury Secretary Henry Morgenthau Jr. was a great supporter of war bonds. His idea was "to use bonds to sell the war, rather than vice versa" as the spearhead for getting people interested in the conflict. War bonds were said to be the "voluntary," "democratic" way to finance the war. After meeting at the White House in April 1942 Morgenthau reported:

> This is what the President dictated. He said, "Give me something like this . . . the Volunteer tax plan is working so well that it is believed not essential to change at this time to compulsory savings until we have had a chance to step up the volunteer plan to make it include practically everybody in the country."[12]

The Roosevelt administration's support for the "voluntary" tax program was often based on a belief that bond purchases resulting from free choice were accomplished in the "American" or "democratic" way. Compared to taxes that were levied by an elected Congress with the president's signature, the individualized assessment involved in a truly voluntary bond purchase was portrayed as more emblematically American. The support these purchases suggested could be seen as creating a sense of participation in the defense effort. For top Treasury officials, particularly for Secretary Morgenthau, this "psychological" or "morale" effect was of great importance. The achievement of these effects, however, was seen as dependent on true voluntarism and lack of coercion. As one Treasury aide said, "[w]hen a person buys a bond now, that is a chance for him to make a voluntary patriotic contribution to his Government, and there isn't any amount of money you can get out of a legally enforced contribution that is going to make up for the morale that goes along with that voluntary contribution." The "voluntary tax program" could be viewed as a test of Seligman's view that the state was a part of citizens. "The duty of supporting and protecting it is born with us." Treasury officials were concerned about effects on "world morale" if the "voluntary" tax program failed (Jones 2007: 437).

Further, Treasury "mass psychology" expert Peter H. Odegard praised the voluntary program as offering "a flexibility of adaptation to the individual's varying circumstances." Compulsory programs might, he suggested, yield less as "millions...would feel that they had discharged their duty in full when they paid the imposed levy" (Jones 2007: 437).

This appeal for voluntary contributions from rational and patriotic actors proved to be a failure. The government moved with some qualms to a program with more coercive features. As one aide commented:

> You see, we have been going on all these months opposed to quotas. That is, that was our stated policy rejecting quotas. We have made our program one that people could participate in or not as they chose, one in which the people could determine how much they were to invest with not even a suggestion from the Treasury as to what the dimensions of the program were.[13]

By pressuring employers, union officials, nonprofit groups, and other intermediate groups, 10 percent of payroll was to be set aside for war bond purchases. State quotas were established. These quotas signaled a socially acceptable level of support if not a progressive one. In a radio program, Morgenthau tried to preserve a commitment to progressivity:

> All of us who get a regular income should set aside at least ten percent of it every pay day for War Savings Bonds, and those who have been earning especially high pay in the war industries are going to set aside even more.[14]

The coercive features of the bond campaign could be seen in some of the promotional materials. A 1944 promotion described:

> Police summons' distribution on all cars. "Summons" form leaflet required the person to appear at nearest War Bond issuing office headed "War-time Violations" or "Please Report Immediately" or "Fine" and went on to explain value of War Bonds and importance of investing during campaign.[15]

During 1944, "the Committee" sent a memorandum to "everyone in the New York Office" of advertising firm BBDO. The memo reported that "up-to-date 83% of the 420 BBDOers in New York have announced their intention of joining the Drive. We had hoped that we might even do better than this. No doubt many of those who haven't come along with us this time have their good reasons for not going so. We do feel that there are a few who need just a little more urging and perhaps this announcement will help them make up their minds." The memorandum invites everyone to a draw for ten free $25.00 War Bonds. "P.S.—to the Ladies—Bring your pocketbooks with you."[16]

Market research by the Treasury revealed that people bought bonds to invest safely, to help a family member in the armed forces, to combat inflation, and to save for life after the war. Equally telling were reasons that did not elicit many takers—fear of national peril, or enthusiasm for the New Deal, or the Four Freedoms (Blum 1976: 20).

In the midst of total war and massive deployments, the "voluntary" program failed in reaching its goals. These lessons were transferred to the "compulsory" world of taxation where persuasion could attempt to legitimate mass income taxation, and where the enactment of withholding would take compliance decisions out of citizens' hands.

Legitimacy of Mass Income Tax

Through World War II, the argument for mass taxation was founded on the extraordinary claims of the war itself. In a Group Meeting in November 1943, the following colloquy took place between Secretary Morgenthau and one of his chief aides in a discussion of selling increased taxes to Congress:

H. M. Jr.: [T]his fellow Lee Wiggins, I thought, made an excellent suggestion. He said he thought our whole psychological approach had been wrong. Every time we asked for increased taxes instead of talking excess profits, and so forth—every time use war taxes. I want ten and a half billion dollars of additional war taxes. Keep driving that thing home to the people. You say that you don't want to pay war taxes? Say it is only for the war. All the way through say war taxes.

Mr. Gaston: That is pretty close to what Dave Lawrence told me, that if they could have some assurance that these taxes were only for the duration of the war it would be very reassuring.

H. M. Jr.: Right. I ought to say about a hundred times, "war taxes."[17]

If bond purchasers did not cite New Deal programs as reasons for their action, the Roosevelt administration was committed to portraying tax revenues pouring directly into winning the war. The mass income tax was sold as a way of assuring victory in the existential struggle that was World War II. In *The New Spirit*, a Disney animated short commissioned by the Treasury in 1942, the radio, appropriately, informs Donald Duck that it is "your privilege, not just your duty, but your privilege to help your government by paying your tax and paying it promptly." The irascible duck gathers the supplies necessary to fill in his return, including a bottle of aspirin, and finds the job easier than he had anticipated. As an actor with an income of $2,501, Donald used dependent credits for Huey, Dewey, and Louie, and found that his taxes came to $13. After Donald races from Hollywood to Washington, the film shows how tax revenues (stacks of gold coins) are transmuted into guns, planes, and ships. Taxes were needed to beat the Axis. At the end when the American flag is formed by clouds around a setting sun, the narrator intones, "Taxes will keep democracy on the march."

In the controversial pamphlet *Battle Stations for All*, issued in February 1943, the Office of War Information pamphleteers sought to defuse accusations that the unprecedented level of taxation was in some way benefiting the New Deal social agenda. In a box set off from the rest of the page and headlined "Non-War Expenditures Reduced," the pamphlet asserted that "Under the new budget submitted by the President, ninety-six cents of every dollar spent by the Government will be for war costs and interest on the public debt and only four cents for so-called 'non-war' purposes."[18] In later radio messages, the percentage of the federal budget going to the cost of war was set between 93 and 95 percent. And the federal budget was at unprecedented levels. The Office of War Information in 1944 described the enormity of the costs. "Direct war expenditures for fiscal 1943 were 12 billion dollars [...] a figure totally beyond human comprehension. But that incomprehensible sum figures down to $2,894 every second of the day [...] an amount equivalent to about a year's wages for perhaps half of the persons who are expected to file income tax returns by March 15."[19]

By making the argument that taxes went to defeating the Axis and not to Dr. New Deal, the administration tried to legitimate a mass income tax as a very clear payment for war. If small-time taxpayers had not had to pay before, it was the war that was responsible. The "real authors of our tax burden" were "in Berlin and Tokyo" (Jones 1988–9: 721). As Eddie Cantor pointed out on his radio show in February 1944:

> We want all you Axis countries to know that we in America are busy right now making out our income taxes. We know this must frighten you, because it's these taxes that paid for the ships that brought our men to your shores this year and we'll continue to pay our taxes so that we can beat you, Mr. Hitler and so that we can beat you, Mr. Tojo, and you, Mr. Mussolini [...] Musso—Whatever happened to you, Mr. Mussolini?[20]

If it was the war (and just the war) that was being financed by new income tax payers, the legitimacy of the tax depended on assurances that everyone (particularly the wealthy) were paying their fair share. In late 1941, Irving Berlin submitted a song entitled "I Paid My Income Tax Today" to Treasury Secretary Henry Morgenthau Jr. A lower income tax payer is the voice in the song—glad to be newly subject to the income tax along with millions of other new taxpayers. Seeing an airborne bomber, the singer claims he helped to build them just as "Rockefeller" did.[21]

A December 30, 1941 letter from Morgenthau to Berlin suggests that the Treasury commissioned the song:

> The more I think about your new song, the more I wonder how you ever managed to do the job so well. It wasn't an easy assignment to make people sing about taxes, but you have done it beautifully, and also hit the nail on the head as far as Treasury policy is concerned.[22]

In early 1942, the Treasury Department sent the Barry Wood recording of "I Paid My Income Tax Today" to 872 radio stations with a letter asking for frequent air time. Four days later, the Danny Kaye recording of the same song was sent out as well. Sheet music was sent to sponsors of musical programs and the networks were asked to play the song as often as possible until the March 15 deadline (Jones 1988–9: 714).

The government also sought to insert appropriate wartime messages into movies that were largely for entertainment. The Office of War Information's Government Information Manual for the Motion Picture Industry suggested that movies show uncomplaining taxpayers. David O. Selznick's *Since You Went Away* followed up on this hint by showing a wealthy man claiming that it "suits me if they tax me 100 percent!" (Jones 1988–9: 718). Assurance that the wealthy were willing to pay their fair share apparently was intended to make income tax payments by the less well-to-do more palatable.

Those who did not meet their tax obligations were treated as "others" and, most assuredly, un-American. In a second Donald Duck tax film, *The Spirit of '43* (Disney 1943), Donald's paycheck is the subject of a debate within Donald's conscience between a spendthrift and a Scrooge McDuck-like character. This was before current payment or withholding, when Americans needed to save to ensure tax payments. Disney's McDuck reminds Donald that "every dollar you spend for something you don't need is a dollar – to help the Axis." The spendthrift is clad in a zoot suit and transmutes into Hitler. Mr. McDuck in his kilt, interestingly, is all-American. The zoot suit emerged as a symbol of un-American outsiders in another context. In June 1943, sailors in downtown Los Angeles dragged Mexican American youths from their seats in the Orpheum Theater, beat them, and destroyed their zoot suits. The Zoot Suit Riots demonstrated the marginalized societal status of Latinos in wartime (Sparrow 2011: 227–37). The Disney tax film made use of these racial stereotypes in encouraging adherence to the tax laws.

Making Tax Payments Less Voluntary

With the income tax's application to average Americans, it was clear to federal tax officials that the infrastructure of tax collection was "poorly adapted to the budgets and flow of income of 44 million taxpayers" (Paul 1954: 333–4).

At the time, income taxes were not collected. Instead, they were paid in quarterly installments in the following year. As incomes rose with rising employment and wages, failure to tax concurrently with income was an expensive defect in tax design.

Placing the income tax on a current basis found an outspoken champion in Beardsley Ruml, Treasurer of R. H. Macy & Company and Chairman of the Board of the Federal Reserve Bank of New York. Ruml professed concern for retirees and enlistees or draftees who experienced declining incomes, yet were expected to pay income taxes for a previous year out of more meager incomes. The solution was for the federal government to require income tax payments currently, but a problem lay in creating the transition to this method. Under the existing tax system, Year 1's tax liability was paid in Year 2. If, in Year 2, the tax payments were made current, a taxpayer would be required to pay Year 1's and Year 2's taxes in Year 2. This was seen as an unacceptable situation. In essence, Ruml's plan was to forgive Year 1 tax liability, but require the taxpayer to make his Year 2 tax payments. For Ruml, this was the "daylight savings" approach to government finance; a proposal under which the Treasury would lose only when "the books would finally be closed [on Judgment Day]." The Treasury objected to the greater benefits the wealthy would receive by reason of Year 1 forgiveness under the Ruml Plan. While some forgiveness was necessary to make the system current, the Treasury Department was disappointed by Congress' eventual solution in the Current Tax Payment Act of 1943—essentially a 75 percent forgiveness of the lower of 1942 or 1943 tax liabilities. Unforgiven tax liabilities could be paid over the following two years.[23]

Most importantly, the Act established the now familiar withholding system for tax collection. The withholding system was a significant advance in administration of the income tax. Elimination of delay in payments made the income tax much more responsive to wartime revenue expansion. As wage earners had become used to periodic deductions from their paychecks for Social Security and unemployment taxes, income tax payment also became less detectable. The advent of withholding ensured the income tax's place as a major and massive revenue source.

The problem faced by income tax propagandists during World War II was legitimating the imposition of that tax on average citizens when it was formerly targeted exclusively at the wealthy. In seeking to justify mass income taxation, public officials struggled with the recent history of the tax as a class tax and with the reluctance to implement President Roosevelt's domestic and social agenda. While seeking to make reasons for taxpaying legible and persuasive to average citizens, Congress succeeded to a great extent in placing the tax beyond justification; to make it so routine that rationalization was not as necessary. The withholding system, by placing responsibilities for reporting and payment on third parties, removed critical aspects of the taxpaying process from the majority of taxpayers who were employees and transferred them to their employers. This trend was furthered by the opportunity to file a return by answering a few questions on one's withholding receipt (Form W-2) and sending it to the Bureau of Internal Revenue where the tax due or refund owed would be computed (Jones 1988–9).

The Postwar Period

It is interesting to note that during much of World War II, there is little mention of tax evasion, avoidance, or penalties. This is in stark contrast to prosecutions and investigations of the wealthiest taxpayers (including, unsuccessfully, former Treasury Secretary Andrew Mellon) during the 1930s. The Treasury understood its very limited wartime capacity. As Secretary Morgenthau said in March 1943, "Suppose we have to go out and try to arrest five million people?" (Jones 1996: 139). The war itself, as the project funded by tax revenues, was a point of near consensus for the public. What would become of the tax system and compliance programs after VJ Day?

In an undated "Report on Postwar Taxation," the conclusion was evident. "The individual income tax . . . must be kept a mass tax, because after the war very large amounts of revenue will still need to be raised for many generations to come." This was the most flexible and important revenue source for the federal government. Dropping rates would be preferable to higher exemptions. "It would be bad for tax morale to drop millions of taxpayers from the tax rolls one year and in another year to bring them again under the income tax, only to drop them again as revenue requirements change."[24]

The highest rates from the World War II years stayed with little modification, dropping from a top rate of 94 percent to 92 percent during the 1950s.[25] There was demand for a tax cut after the war and it took the form of a surrender on a tax compliance issue and a means of recognizing and encouraging marriage. As marginal rates crept up and more citizens became federal income tax payers, attention began to turn to the individually based nature of the federal income tax. Some states including Oklahoma, Oregon, Nebraska, Michigan, and Pennsylvania switched from Anglo-American common-law marital property systems to community property. This was because marital rights under the common-law system were seen as inchoate and insufficiently robust to support division of (usually) a husband's earnings or income from property owned by him. By contrast, in community property states, originally Southern and Western states, a husband and wife would each have an equal, undivided interest in income earned by a spouse and in income from community property acquired during marriage. A 1930 US Supreme Court case,

Poe v. Seaborn held that in community property states, each spouse should be taxed on one-half of the community income, whether that income arose from labor or from capital.[26]

Because of steep progressive rates, a married couple would, as a couple, pay the least tax if they could divide income between them equally. This was relatively easily accomplished in community property states. It was more difficult to accomplish in common-law states. Husbands tended to be primary breadwinners and joint spousal ownership of property was not engrained in property titles as yet (Hines 1966). Average citizens in non-community property states resented their disfavored tax position. An Iowan wrote to his senator, Bourke B. Hickenlooper: "I wish you would do all you can to inact [*sic*] a law, so that husband and wife can split their income and thereby reducing their income tax. It isn't right that some states are able to do so and others are not...I have a brother-in-law [in California] that has much larger net income than I have and yet we have to pay more income taxes than they do."[27] In common law states, the Bureau of Internal Revenue and the courts were called upon to assess the tax validity of a new proliferation of family partnerships—attempts to split income among family members. The Bureau took a relatively hard line on these partnerships often finding that wives made no capital or labor contributions, or using gendered measures of the value of women's work to the business. In many of these cases, the partnership agreements were not viewed as a sufficient basis for income-splitting between spouses or among family members (Jones 1988).

With more states converting to the "foreign" community property system (which afforded women somewhat increased legal ownership of marital income and property) and with an explosion of family partnerships, pressures to reduce taxes after the war and to deal with asymmetrical family taxation resulted in the federal adoption of the joint return in 1948. This original joint return computed the tax on one-half of the couple's income, and then doubled the tax—reaching roughly the same split income result as community property achieved. The difference was that state legislatures could offer tax reductions only by altering married people's legal rights to income and property. Congress enacted tax reduction without any change in the legal rights between spouses (Jones 1988).

The joint return came at a propitious time and was aligned with changes in American culture. During the war, many women took jobs outside the home, sometimes in family businesses, sometimes as clerks and secretaries, sometimes as the iconic Rosie the Riveter in defense industries. Once the war had been won, over two million women left the labor force in 1946. Women represented 35.4 percent of the civilian labor force in 1944, but that figure fell to 28.6 percent in 1947, although it was still higher than it was before the war (Hartmann 1982: 168).

For some women, the war's end meant a return to domesticity and social and gender stability. As tax legislative counsel and (later) Harvard law professor Stanley S. Surrey said in 1948:

> [One implication of the split-income plan is that] [w]ives need not continue to master the details of the retail drug business, electrical equipment business, or construction business, but may turn from their partnership "duties" to the pursuit of homemaking. (Surrey 1948: 111)

The return to postwar domesticity and the production of a generation of baby-boomers was also consonant with Cold War ideology. American domestic life with a wife working at home was seen by many Americans as superior to the factory and other work performed by Soviet women. The 1959 "kitchen debate" between Vice President Richard Nixon and Soviet Premier Nikita Khrushchev illustrated this contrast. Nixon claimed that "diversity, the right to choose, [...] is the most important thing. [...] We have many different manufacturers and many different kinds of washing machines so that the housewives have a choice. [...] What we want is to make easier the life of our housewives" (May 2008: 422). Khrushchev rejected that "capitalist attitude toward women" (May 2008: 432). In the United States, Nixon was viewed as prevailing even if his characterization of domestic life in postwar America was not entirely accurate. Adopting the joint return served as a legal expression for the postwar nuclear family—culturally expressive, not disruptive of the familial status quo, and easier to enforce than the earlier individually based regime. In addition, it solved an apparent unfairness in the income tax system from the point of view of many Americans.

Once the atmosphere and imperative of total war was removed, what was it that taxpayers were paying for in its absence? For the Truman administration, World War II quickly morphed into a cold war with the USSR and other communist movements. Just as World War II was configured as a war against evil, godless communism came to be seen as the antithesis of the American way.

After World War II and during the Cold War, the United States—containing Protestants, Catholics, Jews, and secularists—began to adhere to what Jewish theologian Will Herberg called a "civic religion of the American Way of Life" (Marty 1996: 294). A rather abstracted religion was seen as foundational. President Dwight Eisenhower stated that "a democracy cannot exist without a religious base. I believe in democracy" (Marty 1996: 302). Godliness was seen as the cause of America's growth. Americans were to battle communism, in the words of Democratic presidential candidate Adlai Stevenson, "for [the new enemy's] aim is total conquest—not merely of the earth, but of the human mind. He seeks to destroy the very idea of freedom, the concept of God Himself" (Marty 1996: 306). Yet in a country with many faiths and many denominations within those faiths, historian Daniel Boorstin stressed the importance of "nondenominationalism" and an "ability to produce a kind of elixir, sometimes vapid and always unpungent, a blended distillate of all our different religions" (Marty 1996: 308). The signal achievement of this civic religion may be the addition to "one nation" of "under God" to the Pledge of Allegiance in 1954 and "In God We Trust" as the national motto in 1956. It expressed a providential faith in American exceptionalism, strength, and superiority. The high point of this civic religion was the late 1940s to the early 1960s. Tax revenues were tithes to that project.

In the postwar period, church membership and church construction experienced enormous growth (Ahlstrom 2004: 949–63). The alignment of civic religion and the federal government in the fight against communism seemed to support defense outlays and, for some, increased foreign aid.

For much of the first part of the twentieth century, the Protestant Federal Council of Churches and its successor, the National Council of Churches (NCC), presumed to take a leading role in articulating a Christian ethic for the United States. Formed during the height of the progressive social gospel movements, the Federal Council of Churches sought to institutionalize the social gospel—"the application of the teaching of Jesus and the total message of the Christian salvation to society, the economic life, and social institutions . . . as well as to individuals" (Hopkins 1967: 98). Individual charity was seen as inadequate to the challenges of modern society. "Stewardship was then applied in a sense to the state, which, as guardian of God's gifts to the people, should oversee their just distribution" (Hopkins 1967: 98).

Ties to government were especially visible after World War II as President Eisenhower placed the cornerstone for the new National Council of Churches building in New York and as prominent figures with political ties such as Allen Foster Dulles and Charles P. Taft were active in its affairs.

Nevertheless the postwar period saw the NCC come under attack from more conservative business-allied groups. The NCC formed a Lay Committee and J. Howard Pew, a retired Sun Oil executive, became its leader. Pew viewed the NCC as comprised of "ministerial economic illiterates." Dupont executive Jasper Crane wrote in 1948 that economist Friedrich Hayek had told him that "it was the Church of England that led Great Britain into socialism. Must we admit that the Federal Council of Churches is leading the United States on the road to serfdom?" (Jones 2002: 95).

A survey by libertarian religious group Spiritual Mobilization found that 88 percent of ministers found nothing morally wrong with a progressive income tax, and 59 percent felt it was just to tax the wealthy at rates as high as 80 percent. Only 23 percent of clergy felt that "taxing the rich to help the poor through government welfare is against Christian (ethical) principles, because it removes the voluntary aspect of true charity" (Jones 2002: 106).

Pew and his allies, the National Association of Manufacturers and Spiritual Mobilization, battled NCC liberals during the 1950s with both sides employing schools on economics for ministers, book reviews, and publications of various sorts. Rev. John Bennett saw two warring factions within Protestantism: a Social Gospel emphasis "rather uncritical of collectivist answers" against "a very extreme type of individualism which wants to go back to an absolutely unreconstructed capitalism" (Jones 2002: 162). Conservatives accused the NCC leadership of communist sympathies, distributing a pamphlet entitled "How Red Is the Federal/National Council of Churches?" Some NCC leaders did have socialist ties. As Senator Joseph McCarthy began to move against NCC leaders in 1956, President Eisenhower condemned such attacks as "irresponsible" and "against American principles of freedom and democracy." The attacks were defused, but left a weakened NCC in its wake.

Polling in the 1950s showed Americans were supportive of progressive taxation. In their famous 1952 essay, "The Uneasy Case for Progressive Taxation," Professors Walter Blum and Harry Kalven Jr. identified the reduction of economic inequality as the strongest case for progression. They, too, cited the survey of Christian ministers.

If the case for progressive taxation was uneasy as a matter of economics, celebrated theologian Reinhold Niebuhr saw taxation as coercion, but "also a method of supporting his own long-range sense of duty toward the community as against a short-range disinclination to do so." Laws, Niebuhr wrote, provided an "approximation of a loving community [...] under conditions of sin" (Niebuhr 1953: 244).

In the postwar period, the NCC faced a vigorous and new level of opposition from evangelical Christians and conservative businessmen arguing for a Christian libertarianism.[28] Much of the critique from this branch of Protestantism was directed at the welfare state. As one minister wrote in his sermon contest entry, "The growing acceptance of the philosophy of the Welfare State is a graver peril to freedom in America today than the threat of military aggression" (Kruse 2015: 32). James W. Fifield Jr., head of the anti-NCC Spiritual Mobilization, called out minimum wages, price controls, social security pensions, unemployment insurance, veterans' benefits and a wide range of federal taxation as "tyrannical" and violative of "natural law." For the NCC and its ilk, there was contempt: "Unclothed, their gospel is pure socialism— they wish to employ the compulsion of the state to force others to act as the social gospelers think they should act."

The conflicts over race, the Vietnam War, and President Lyndon B. Johnson's War on Poverty and Great Society programs, expanded divisions among American citizens. Mainline ecumenical NCC and allied local leaders were instrumental in the passage of the Civil Rights Act of 1964 giving greater rights to African Americans (Risen 2014). It was an attack on the Jim Crow South (and Northern practices as well). To fundamentalist and evangelical Protestants, this coerced integration was unacceptable. Many Southerners left the Democratic Party (which was in part responsible for the Civil Rights Act), enrolled their children in religiously based unintegrated private academies and became more rejectionist toward the federal government and its taxes. It was this rejection of big government taxation and power that fueled the election of Ronald Reagan in 1980.

Superficially, civil religion was no longer even united. Religion came increasingly to mean evangelical religion, while the mainline NCC churches lost members and political influence. For fundamentalist and evangelical Christians, the Republican Party became, in the words of Daniel K. Williams, God's Own Party.

Secular conservative movements also began to organize and resist federal taxation. From Ayn Rand to household employers in Texas to Vivien Kellems, protests about the level and techniques of federal taxation received a fair amount of publicity. Even some popular children's books were not supportive of the federal government. *The Little House on the Prairie* books by Laura Ingalls Wilder do not paint a positive picture of the government. In one of the books in the series, *The Long Winter*, Mr. Edwards, a former neighbor, shows up in South Dakota escaping eastern territories that are "too settled-up." Mr. Edwards is portrayed very positively in the series as the savior of the Ingalls' homestead and the bringer of presents from Santa Claus. Mr. Edwards' visit this time, however, is comprised almost entirely of a passionate complaint against taxation (Ingalls Wilder 1971: 112–13).

Without a compelling and unifying cause for taxation, tax compliance propaganda in the postwar era morphed from the wartime celebrity and nongovernmental voices urging patriotic support for the war effort. During the Truman administration, the shift in public relations emphasis was to anecdotes about government apprehension of ordinary people. In a *Collier's* article, "They Can't Fool the Revenue Man," Undersecretary of the Treasury A. L. M. Wiggins told of a friend's challenge to him. "Oh yes, I know you get most of the big boys. But how about the little fellows? There must be thousands of them who get away with murder every year." Wiggins went on:

> Well, my friend was wrong. Take the case of the man who ran a filling station and lunch counter on the outskirts of a sizeable city [. . .] He figured that he could chisel a few hundred dollars in income taxes without running any risk. He operated on a cash basis; how could anyone know how much he took in? [. . .] I estimated that it cost this man about $1,000 to try to evade $300 in taxes.
>
> (Wiggins 1947: 68)

Wiggins did not discuss what it cost the Treasury to pursue this small-time evasion. The Commissioner of the Internal Revenue Service warned tax-cheating farmers in Minnesota, paperboys, and a delicatessen owner feeding his family from inventory: "You see, it's almost impossible to deceive our investigators, because most of them are generally familiar with every type of tax dodge ever attempted, and if they run across what appears to be a new one, they can look into the files and find it's been tried before" (Schoeneman 1949: 126). Tax evaders could be tripped up by "disgruntled or underpaid employees," "unusual currency transactions," "sudden displays of wealth," "hat-check receipts, tips to waiters," an "estranged and angry wife," even success stories in newspapers and magazines (Wiggins 1947: 71). The Treasury's boasts about compliance could be seen as assuring ordinary taxpayers that everyone would pay taxes under the federal income tax. Of course, it was withholding and third party reporting that did the heavy lifting for the mass income tax.

Conclusion

The earlier emphasis on the wealthy targets of a class tax allowed ordinary Americans to see a part of the federal revenue system as aimed at those most able to pay. The establishment of Social Security taxes enabled the government to tax average citizens, who, it was thought, would receive direct payments in exchange for their contributions. During Roosevelt's New Deal, the income tax was a class tax directed at the wealthiest Americans. With the advent of World War II, the image presented was one of Americans' consent and unanimity in support of the war effort. Propaganda stressed that taxation was for this purpose and not for less popular New Deal programs. This story of purpose was part of the Roosevelt administration's compliance program—linking the purpose of taxation to the war and making it clear that all were paying their fair share.

In the meantime, citizens became more legible to the federal government. With the introduction of withholding by employers for social security and bond purchases, the government was able to use third parties to collect taxes before workers got their "take-home pay." The expansion in 1943 to withholding of income taxes made a mass income tax possible. The amount of income known to the government and accounts were reconciled on annual income tax returns with taxpayers identified by social security numbers. For decades, this very ordinary compliance device has been a foundation of federal revenues.

As the mass income tax was launched during World War II, agreement on the aims of taxation supported the transition from class tax to mass tax. During the immediate postwar period, a period of consensus seemed to be operating within popular culture with respect to anti-communism and civil religion, and regarding tax policy. Some of this "convergence" could be viewed as the result of the Democratic Party's de-emphasis on class politics and its support for a variety of tax cuts (Brownlee 2016).

Beneath this "consensus" were the beginnings of deep divisions about the size and purposes of federal government, and the role of government as opposed to other societal institutions. The 1960s exposed societal rifts on race, gender, sexuality, and America's role in the world that have continued to the present day. Evangelical churches have emerged as the most perceptible religious voices in debates about government, federalism, and morality. The denominations comprising the social gospel-based NCC are on the decline in members, in political power, and in budgets. Historian David A. Hollinger in his Presidential Address to the Organization of American Historians has argued that the NCC's support for racial equality and against American adventurism abroad created alliances with secular organizations and attitudes that continue to have societal influence. As Hollinger wrote:

> This sympathetic engagement with diversity that has become so visible and celebrated a feature of the public life of the United States is the product of many agencies, but prominent among them are the egalitarian impulses and the capacities for self-interrogation that ecumenical Protestants brought to the great American encounter with diversity during the middle and late decades of the twentieth century... Our narrative of modern American religious history will be deficient so long as we suppose that ecumenical Protestantism declined because it had less to offer the United States than did its evangelical rival. Much of what ecumenical Protestantism offered now lies beyond the churches, and hence we have been slow to see it. (Hollinger 2011: 48)

The unifying themes of total war and One Nation Under God may be seen as diminishing as America fights non-state actors, terror, and itself. Today a variety of enforcement problems threaten to erode public trust in the competence and fairness of the Internal Revenue Service. The structure of income taxation is seen by many to be unfair. The World War II and postwar era did establish the federal government's power to collect income and social security taxes from the waged and salaried masses. But corporations and hedge fund managers seem to be able to use international entities and to exploit the lower rates on capital gain income to reduce their effective tax rates in ways not available to average Americans.

In addition to questioning the fairness of the income tax system, Americans are divided, in truth very divided, on the purposes to which tax revenues should be put. The level of social insurance from Social Security, Medicaid, Medicare, and the Affordable Care Act is under active Congressional debate, let alone contests over domestic spending, military expenditures, and outlays for "soft power" abroad. The perceptions of fairness in taxation and a lack of consensus on the role of government will persist in plaguing the American tax system as it continues to collect a majority of its revenues by means that take many choices about compliance away from wage-earning and salaried citizens.

Notes

1. See also Mehrotra (2013). In one of the most memorable passages of his writings, Seligman (1895: 72) argued for a notion of fiscal citizenship.
2. 157 U.S. 429 (1895). https://supreme.justia.com/cases/federal/us/157/429/case.html.
3. 268 U.S. 378 (1925). https://supreme.justia.com/cases/federal/us/268/378/.
4. Seltzer (1968: 62) shows that under 10 percent of the population were covered by taxable returns, with the exception of 1920.
5. Most American state sales taxes were adopted during the 1930s and required retailers to collect the tax from customers (Pomp 2015: vol. 1, 6–5).
6. 79 CONG. REC. 9657 (1935). www.gpo.gov/fdsys/pkg/GPO-CRECB-1935-pt9- v79/content-detail.html.
7. 79 CONG. REC. 9657–8 (1935). www.gpo.gov/fdsys/pkg/GPO-CRECB-1935- pt9-v79/content-detail.html.
8. www.archives.gov/exhibits/treasures_of_congress/text/page19_text.html.
9. In 1976, Ronald Reagan told a memorable story:

   > In Chicago, they found a woman who holds the record. She used 80 names, 30 addresses, 15 telephone numbers to collect food stamps, Social Security, veterans' benefits for four nonexistent deceased veteran husbands, as well as welfare. Her tax-free income alone has been running $150,000 a year.

   While not all of Reagan's stories would survive fact-checking, this one was based on Linda Taylor, officially listed as "white as a child, but could pass as black." www.slate.com/articles/news_and_politics/history/2013/12/linda_taylor_welfare_queen_ronald_reagan_made_her_a_notorious_american_villain.html.
10. Paul to the Secretary (May 19, 1942), 529 (in Blum 1967: 262); Cann to the Secretary (July 28, 1942), 554 (in Blum 1967: 285); Memorandum to Assistant Secretary Sullivan from Acting Commissioner Cann (July 29, 1942), 555 (in Blum 1967: 64); Mr. Sullivan to the Secretary (July 30, 1942), 555 (in Blum 1967: 220).
11. Paul to the Secretary (May 19, 1942), 529 (in Blum 1967: 262); Cann to the Secretary (July 28, 1942), 554 (in Blum 1967: 285); Memorandum to Assistant Secretary Sullivan from Acting Commissioner Cann (July 29, 1942), 555 (in Blum 1967: 64).
12. Meeting on President's Speech (April 23, 1942 10:10 a.m.), 520 (in Blum 1967: 11).
13. Inflation Group Meeting (April 8, 1942, 4:00 p.m.), 514 (in Blum 1967: 197, 201–2).
14. Dollars in the War (April 23, 1942, 10:00–10:30 p.m. EWT, Blue Network), 520 (in Blum 1967: 40, 51).
15. Preliminary 6th War Plan Advertising Press and Radio Plan (prepared for August 8, 1944 meeting), Bruce Barton Papers, State Historical Society of Madison, WI, 70–3.

16. "To Everyone in the New York Office" (December 11, 1944), Bruce Barton Papers, State Historical Society of Madison, WI, 70–3.
17. Group Meeting—Taxes (November 27, 1943, 9:30 a.m.), 680 (in Blum 1967: 1160).
18. Pamphlets 1942–3, Records of the Office of War Information, Record Group 208, National Archives, College Park, MD.
19. Fortnightly Budget for Wartime Editors of Women's Pages (March 4, 1944) Taxes—Radio, Program Guides and Publicity Materials for the Economic Stabilization Campaign, Records of the Office of War Information, Record Group 208, National Archives, College Park, MD.
20. Eddie Cantor Program, (OWI Plug) (February 23, 1944) Taxes—Radio, Program Guides and Publicity Materials for the Economic Stabilization Campaign, Records of the Office of War Information, Record Group 208, National Archives, College Park, MD.
21. I. Berlin, "I Paid My Income Tax Today" (December 26, 1941), 480 (in Blum 1967: 83).
22. Letter from Henry Morgenthau Jr. to Irving Berlin (December 30, 1941), 480 (in Blum 1967: 82).
23. Current Tax Payment Act of 1943, Pub. L. No. 78–68, § 6, 57 Stat. 126, 145–9 (1943). http://legisworks.org/congress/78/publaw-68.pdf.
24. Department of Treasury, "Report on Postwar Taxation" (n.d.), 37–8, Blough Papers, Harry S. Truman Presidential Library & Museum, Independence, MO.
25. Historical Highest Marginal Income Tax Rates. www.taxpolicycenter.org/statistics/historical-highest-marginal-income-tax-rates.
26. *Poe v. Seaborn*, 282 U.S. 101 (1930). https://supreme.justia.com/cases/federal/us/282/101/.
27. Letter from George Werning to Bourke B. Hickenlooper (January 6, 1948), (Tax, Income, 1948) Bourke B. Hickenlooper Papers, Herbert Hoover Presidential Library, West Branch, IA.
28. This is well documented in Kruse (2015).

References

Ahlstrom, Sydney E. (2004), *A Religious History of the American People* (2nd edn.). New Haven, CT and London: Yale University Press.

Blum, J. (1967), *From the Morgenthau Diaries*. (Available in Franklin D. Roosevelt Library, Hyde Park, NY.)

Blum, John Morton (1976), *V Was for Victory*. San Diego, CA: Harcourt Brace Jovanovich.

Brownlee, W. Elliot (2016), *Federal Taxation in America: A History* (3rd edn.). New York: Cambridge University Press.

Cantril, H. (ed.) (1951), *Public Opinion, 1935–46*. Princeton, NJ: Princeton University Press.

Disney (1942), The New Spirit. US Government Film Collection, Motion Picture Collection FAA 188, Library of Congress.

Disney (1943), The Spirit of '43. US Government Film Collection, Motion Picture Collection FAA 256, Library of Congress.

Hartmann, Susan M. (1982), *The Home Front and Beyond: American Women in the 1940s*. Boston, MA: Twayne Publishers.

Hines, N. William (1966), "Real Property Joint Tenancies: Law, Fact and Fancy." *Iowa Law Review* 51: 582–625.

Hollinger, David A. (2011), "After Cloven Tongues of Fire: Ecumenical Protestantism and the Modern American Encounter with Diversity." *Journal of American History* 98(1): 21–48.

Hopkins, Charles Howard (1967), *The Rise of the Social Gospel in American Protestantism, 1865–1915*. New Haven, CT: Yale University Press.

Ingalls Wilder, Laura (1971 [1940]), *The Long Winter*. New York: Harper & Row.

Jones, Carolyn C. (1988), "Split Income and Separate Spheres: Tax Law and Gender Roles in the 1940s." *Law and History Review* 6(259): 274–93.

Jones, Carolyn C. (1988–9), "Class Tax to Mass Tax." *Buffalo Law Review* 37: 685–737.

Jones, Carolyn C. (1996), "Mass-Based Income Taxation: Creating a Taxpaying Culture, 1940–1952." In W. Elliot Brownlee (ed.), *Funding the Modern American State, 1941–1995*. New York: Cambridge University Press, 107–48.

Jones, Carolyn C. (2002), "Hard Shells of Community: Tax Equity Debates within the National Council of Churches after World War II." In Joseph J. Thorndike and Dennis J. Ventry Jr. (eds.), *Tax Justice: The Ongoing Debate*. Washington, DC: Urban Institute Press, 95–122.

Jones, Carolyn C. (2007), "Bonds, Voluntarism and Taxation." In John Tiley (ed.), *Studies in the History of Tax Law*, Vol. 2. Oxford: Hart Publishing, 427–43.

Kessler-Harris, Alice (2001), *In Pursuit of Equity: Women, Men, and the Quest for Economic Citizenship in 20th Century America*. New York: Oxford University Press.

Kornhauser, Marjorie E. (1990), "Corporate Regulation and the Origins of the Corporate Income Tax." *Indiana Law Journal* 66(1): 53–136.

Kornhauser, Marjorie E. (2010), "Shaping Public Opinion and the Law: How a 'Common Man' Campaign Ended a Rich Man's Law." *Law and Contemporary Problems* 73 (Winter): 123–48.

Kruse, Kevin (2015), *One Nation Under God: How Corporate America Invented Christian America*. New York: Basic Books.

Levin, Josh (2013), "The Welfare Queen." *Slate*, December 19. www.slate.com/articles/ news_and_politics/history/2013/12/linda_taylor_welfare_queen_ronald_reagan_made_ her_a_notorious_american_villain.html.

Marty, Martin E. (1996), *Modern American Religion: Under God, Indivisible, 1941–1960*. Chicago, IL: University of Chicago Press.

May, Elaine Tyler (2008), *Homebound Bound: American Families in the Cold War Era*. New York: Basic Books.

Mehrotra, Ajay (2013), *Making the Modern American Fiscal State: Law, Politics and the Rise of Progressive Taxation, 1877–1929*. New York: Cambridge University Press.

National Archives (1939), Social Security for the Nation. Record Group 47, Records of the Social Security Administration 1934–ca. 1992, Assorted Motion Picture Archives 1953–ca. 1980. National Archives, College Park, MD.

Niebuhr, Reinhold (1953), "Coercion, Self-Interest and Love." In Kenneth Boulding (ed.), *The Organizational Revolution*. New York: Harper, 228–44.

Paul, Randolph E. (1954), *Taxation in the United States*. Boston, MA: Little, Brown and Company.

Pomp, Richard D. (2015), *State and Local Taxation* (8th edn.). Dallas, TX: Pomp/Primedia E-launch LLC.

Quadagno, Jill (1996), *The Color of Welfare: How Racism Undermined the War on Poverty*. New York and Oxford: Oxford University Press.

Risen, Clay (2014), *The Bill of the Century: The Epic Battle for the Civil Rights Act*. New York: Bloomsbury Press.

Rosenman S. (ed.) (1938), *The Public Papers and Addresses of Franklin D. Roosevelt*. New York: Random House.

Schoeneman, George (1949), "Tax Cheaters Beware!" *American Magazine*, February.

Seligman, E. R. A. (1894), "Progressive Taxation in Theory and Practice." *The Economic Journal* 4(14): 301–5.

Seligman, Edwin R. A. (1895), *Essays in Taxation*. New York and London: Macmillan & Co.

Seltzer, Lawrence H. (1968), *The Personal Exemptions in the Income Tax*. New York: University of Columbia Press.

Social Security (2013), A Hope of Many Years: A Brief History of Social Insurance. Video available at www.ssa.gov/history/video/.

Social Security (n.d.), The Systems Story. Video available at www.ssa.gov/multimedia/video/SystemHistory/#more-content.

Sparrow, James T. (2011), *Warfare State: World War II Americans and the Age of Big Government*. New York: Oxford University Press.

Surrey, Stanley (1948), "Federal Taxations of the Family—The Revenue Act of 1948." *Harvard Law Review* 61: 1097–164.

Wiggins, A. L. M. (1947), "They Can't Fool the Internal Revenue Man." *Collier's*, September 20.

Part VI
Romania

10

Tax Collection without Consent

State-Building in Romania

Clara Volintiru

In Romanian folklore tax collectors are often portrayed as predators. For example, Mihail Sadoveanu wrote in his historical novel, *Dimineți de Iulie*, of 1927: "There was a time when great was the surprise that this people had not totally disappeared. Like birds of prey, the tax collectors would hover over them at all times."[1] This is not surprising, as in pre-modern times the level and use of collected duties tended to have nothing to do with the citizens' wants or needs. In response, evading taxes is equally poignant in popular culture, as the expression for running away literally means escaping taxes (*a da bir cu fugiții*).

Romanians' cognitive framing of paying taxes sheds light on why there is a low fiscal collection rate to this day. Inefficient and ineffective administration characterizing this country is traceable to a weak state capacity in early modern times. In short, Romanian citizens seem to be traditionally "unwilling" to pay their duties to the state. Nevertheless, the puzzle that this case study addresses is how this can be, given that our experimental research clearly shows the opposite. Romanians are in fact inclined to be highly compliant; but, they do so when the social context involves cooperation mechanisms such as sharing the money, or acquiescing to the use of the collected sums.

The historical analysis of the Romanian case allows us to look at Romanian institutions and the behavior of Romanian people, but we cannot trace a single Romanian state per se in early modern times, given that its territory was split. Romanians have historically inhabited three main regions: Wallachia, Moldavia, and Transylvania. 2018 marks the one hundredth anniversary of the unification of all these regions. Given foreign influences and the subsequent development of the state in each of these provinces, this case study presents us with a natural experiment of sorts. Austro-Hungarian rule and influence in Transylvania developed an early bureaucratic system, while the institutional environment of the Principalities of Wallachia and Moldavia was modeled in the periphery of the Ottoman Empire. These differences informed the relationship citizens have with administrative authorities and, to a certain extent, even after the institutional homogenization of the past century, we can observe a higher compliance in Transylvania than in the Principalities.[2]

Both the legitimacy and the authority of fiscal collectors were poor. Two factors affected their legitimacy: they were representing foreign (i.e. Austro-Hungarian or Ottoman) powers, and there was a complete lack of correlation between collection and redistribution. Monetary and in-kind taxes were collected under obligations toward an external beneficiary, while internal suppliers such as ecclesiastical units or local noblemen supplied care or security functions. This uncoupling of fiscal functions is also reflected in the deficiencies of authority: regulations were inconsistent or superfluous, given that they were designed for a quasi-colony or a periphery state. Overall, the authorities' capacity to monitor was weak; enforcement was not undertaken in a systematic or institutional manner, but rather was discretionary, under the contextual burden of external fiscal pressures.

To resolve deficits of legitimacy and institutional capacity, tax collection in Romanian territories was largely conducted through local intermediaries. What stands out in this case study is that the Romanian rulers' main involvement in foreign affairs was paying taxes to foreign powers. The sequencing and the manner in which fiscal revenue was collected (i.e. after it was paid by the ruler) established a patrimonial system. As such, informal rules and practices emerged and consolidated over time, especially with regard to the provision of a basic redistributive system (e.g. hospitals, policing, and dispute settlement).

An institution whose authority is firmly rooted in informal practices is the Church. It has acted as an intermediary of administrative and political affairs since pre-modern times. The Romanian system of redistribution was developed around the ecclesiastical institutions. Both the Orthodox and the Catholic Churches were able to extract their own revenues from the general population and noblemen. Whereas the Catholic Church was much more heavily assimilated in the Austro-Hungarian administrative apparatus, the Orthodox Church has worked in parallel with any formal administration up until modern times. It has legitimized rulers and provided cultural, social, and religious services to the population.

Under a quasi-colonial developmental path, Romanian authorities have not developed a proper social contract with the people. The tax collection process has been one of enforcement (to the extent possible), with little rights or privileges granted in return. This was especially true in pre-modern times, but also largely applicable to the administrative reforms of the monarchy, or those of the authoritarian communist regime, throughout the twentieth century. While redistribution significantly increased over the modern period, the internalization of cooperation logic between taxpayers and the state did not occur. As far as general social norms go, we find Romanians, much like Italians, presenting strong personal values of honesty and compliance, but poor trust in institutions.[3]

Why Use Historical Analysis in the Romanian Case Study?

A large amount of literature exists on the contemporary failures of the Romanian state. In addressing the quality and legitimacy of state authorities in Romania, several studies have explained contemporary state incapacity in terms of post-communist transitional legacies (Ban 2014; Light and Phinnemore 2001; Pop 2006; Stan 2009; Stan and Vancea 2015).

In this field of studies, some authors have looked at the political actors and the institutionalization of the party system (Light and Phinnemore 2001; Mungiu-Pippidi 2002; Stan 2009; Volintiru 2012). Others have focused on disruptive shifts in the Romanian political economy (Ban 2014; Gabor 2010; Pop 2006). Such studies reflect a process of post-transitional consolidation framed by a wider comparative literature on new democracies (Ban 2016; Dimitrov, Goetz, and Wollmann 2006; Kitschelt et al. 1999; Linz and Stepan 1996). They reveal the formation of poor contemporary expectations from the state, and implicitly, citizens' low tax morale (see Todor's analysis of the post-communist tax system in Chapter 11 in this volume).

Given this wealth of arguments on why Romanians are unlikely to trust their state, and consequently pay their taxes, the question is why we should look further back to pre-modern times to explain this behavior. The answer is because Romanians have faced an uncoupling of the functions of collection and redistribution since early modern times. As I show here, this historical separation between collection and redistribution has made people less willing to take "the leap of faith" even when circumstances improve. Furthermore, the historical variation in institutional capacity between regions informs people's behavior to this day. If anything, the most systematic statist redistribution of public goods and services occurred in the twentieth century. This has not managed, though, to change Romanians' perception of administrative institutions as extractive bodies (and just that).

The historical analysis pursued in this chapter provides us with several key insights into why Romanian institutions never managed to build contingent consent—a close connection between taxpaying and public goods or services. As foreign powers have directly or indirectly ruled the Romanian territories, developing a systematic tax collection capacity was not a priority. Consequently, Romanian citizens did not get much back from the state, and the Church intervened to provide much-needed welfare goods. This situation contrasts with the Swedish case where the Church intervened to consolidate the collection capacity of the state (see Nistotskaya and D'Arcy, Chapter 2 in this volume). The balance of power between administrative and ecclesiastical authorities in Romania is more like the competition logic of the Italian Church (see Hien, Chapter 4 in this volume), even though it was not competing for collected resources (as in the Italian case), but just for legitimacy or moral authority.

Much like everywhere else, the tax collection process in Romania has been linked to the dynamics of international power relations. Throughout their history the Romanian Principalities have been ruled or dominated by larger regional powers. Since pre-modern times, the duties and obligations shared between national elites (i.e. local rulers and notables) and foreign powers (e.g. the Hungarian Kingdom, Ottoman Empire, Austro-Hungarian Empire, and Russian Empire) have had a decisive effect on the manner in which revenues were collected.

More importantly, the dynamic of these power relations had a determining role in how the extracted revenues were to be spent: they were not redistributed. This in turn affected the expectations of taxpayers. As the Romanians harbored low expectations of redistribution and negative perceptions of tax collectors, a vicious circle of low compliance (given the opportunity) has been formed and has persisted to the present day. Furthermore, low expectations of redistribution, although engineered by foreign administrators, have been maintained in later years by domestic elites.

We thus find the emergence of a patrimonial system that was being supported by the international balance of power. Foreign powers, which did not wish to engage in the direct administration of Romanian territories, encouraged a bilateral relationship with rulers, while formally recognizing the rights and privileges of the citizens (mostly as a leverage against the rulers). Consequently, there was only a marginal preoccupation with systematically collecting taxes from citizens, as rulers relied predominantly on their own personal fortunes and foreign creditors. Secondly, the historical setting of Romanian territories allowed for a consolidation of informal practices, especially in terms of redistribution. There were few regulatory provisions, most of which in turn derived from foreign systems (e.g. Ottoman law). Extended regulatory provisions on the systematic delivery of public goods and services were introduced later, tentatively in the eighteenth and more specifically in the nineteenth century (see, for example, the Organic Statute, discussed below in *"Taxes, intermediaries, and bureaucratic genesis"*). The Church provided informally most of such services as medical care (*bolniţe*), education, and dispute settlement.

In the Romanian case study we find little evidence of a direct relationship between citizens and the state as we would define it under a social contract rationale. Instead, we find a high reliance on intermediaries to ensure administrative processes. Throughout the early modern period, most administrative institutions have been constructs of foreign powers, based on diplomatic relations or contextual interests. This "captive" status of the Romanians, in between semi-colonial and autonomous rule, consolidated the power of informal practices as constant benchmarks of conduct and practice. Acquiring the consent of taxpayers, or convincing them to cooperate with the state to solve collective problems was not the framing upon which tax collection was developed here (as opposed to Sweden, for example; see Nistotskaya and D'Arcy, Chapter 2 in this volume). Instead, a pyramidal system of enforced collection was the prevalent practice.

Both state capacity to extract resources and the availability of resources are relevant in the process of fiscal collection. Historical sources tend to showcase Transylvania as having a higher administrative capacity and more (taxable) resources, while the Romanian Principalities lacked both. This is not entirely so. The economic development of the regions varied extensively over pre-modern times, which means that institutional evolution played a major role in the tax collection capacity of each region.

When looking at urbanization levels as a measure of economic development there is no distinguishable developmental pattern for the Ottoman-controlled Romanian Principalities of Wallachia and Moldavia on the one hand, and Transylvania on the other.[4] If anything, both in the sixteenth century and as late as the eighteenth century, Moldavia was more like Transylvania than Wallachia, which had a higher urbanization rate, similar to that of other European countries such as Denmark or Ireland (Murgescu 2010).

Transylvania did indeed grow, but slowly and steadily on a basis of gradual urbanization, and in such communities monitoring and administrative reach was easier. In the case of Wallachia, like other European economies of the time, the main economic driver was an increase in agricultural productivity (e.g. the introduction of corn crops) (Murgescu 2010: 94–9). In Moldavia, the sharp increase in urbanization in the eighteenth century can be attributed to a preferential fiscal regime from the Ottomans, given the Russian Empire's expansion in the area. It is therefore a story of institutions and not one of economic endowment.

Legitimacy and Social Expectations on Redistribution

Romanians had a shifting image of the state throughout pre-modern times. Autonomy alternated with dependency; the conditions of dependence alternated as well. The Ottomans, for example, provided no clear, predictable expectations of the relationship between center and periphery, as they treated each province differently (Barkey 2008). Hungarian rule was more institutionalized, but it gave way to Ottoman domination in the sixteenth and seventeenth centuries in Transylvania. Whether it was through military action, fiscal compliance, or strategically developed trade relations, the Romanians have been in a perpetual process of redefining the limits of authority and the duties owed.

While enduring a prolonged state-building process, Romanians experienced a steady development of informal institutions and social norms (e.g. feudal relations, ecclesiastical community norms). These were consolidated by iterations and confirmations through practice. Because of the constancy and predictability of such community-based norms of sharing and creating public goods and services, along with the legitimacy of their promoters (e.g. local lords or priests), Romanian behavior was shaped by the (ever-changing) regulations of informal rather than formal institutions. Gretchen Helmke and Steven Levitsky assert that informal institutions can often have a profound and systematic effect on political outcomes, and scholars "who fail to consider these informal rules of the game risk missing many of the most important incentives and constraints that underlie political behavior" (2004: 725).

Romanian systems of collection and redistribution were mentioned in formal decrees, but the manner in which the duties were fulfilled was not. An extensive, carefully detailed literature covers the Ottoman fiscal system (Darling 1996; Fischer-Galati 1959; Karaman and Pamuk 2010; Panaite 2013), and through this we can find important details on collection (not so much redistribution) in Romanian Principalities (e.g. how much was owed and on what basis, frequency, to whom and by whom the payments were delivered).

It is, however, a mirrored perspective, as we find out from Ottoman sources how things (were supposed to have) happened. When we look at fragments of domestic historical records in Romanian territories, the regulatory image becomes blurred by domestic, ad hoc practices and means of implementation (e.g. monetary approximations, in-kind compensations, substantial annual variations, and off-the-books payments).

Similarly, while we can find detailed accounts of fiscal administration in Hungary (Bonney 1999), it is much less clear how resilient administrative practices were in Transylvania after it fell under Ottoman influence, or how rural areas compared to urban centers.

For example, Richard Bonney raises the question of informal consolidation of practices in tax collection, as he asserts: "fiscal systems have always been with us, but...the 'fiscal state' was not" (1999: 2). If we look at the historical formal and informal institutions shaping fiscal compliance (or lack thereof) in Romanian territories, we need look no further than the legitimacy and authority of tax collectors. A domestic fiscal state (see Levi 1988; Migdal 2001; Skocpol 1979; Tilly 1992) was not characteristic of the Romanian collection system, the extractive role being fulfilled by foreign states. As such, the effectiveness of fiscal collection relied on the degree to which domestic agents or intermediaries were recognized themselves as legitimate or authoritarian.

Romanians' perceptions on the legitimacy of fiscal duties were significantly influenced by the fact that these were external impositions. The Romanian Principalities of Wallachia and Moldavia were politically dependent on the Ottoman Empire throughout the entire pre-modern period.[5] Transylvania had been annexed to Hungary in the eleventh century and fell under Ottoman rule in the sixteenth century, under similar conditions to the other Romanian territories. It was not until the eighteenth century that the Austro-Hungarian administration model became systematically implemented in Transylvania.

Some of the main historical Romanian studies treat the territories under Austro-Hungarian influence separately from those under Ottoman influence (see e.g. Murgescu 1996; 2012). I am, however, resisting this approach, as the fiscal system bears similar limitations (with lasting effects): foreign authority (i.e. an external collector), lack of correlation between tax collection and redistributive benefits (i.e. national suppliers) and an overall poor institutional capacity—both for monitoring and enforcement, especially in the predominantly rural areas. The distinguishing element that is of main interest to the present analysis is that the administrative capacity of monitoring and systematic enforcement, as well as the delivery of public services (i.e. contingent consent) were implemented sooner in Transylvania via Austro-Hungarian influence than they were in the Principalities. This in turn shaped citizens' perceptions and expectations.

Taxes, intermediaries, and bureaucratic genesis

When looking at the early modern period, "due to high shares of intermediaries, Ottoman revenues lagged behind those of other states in the seventeenth and eighteenth centuries" (Karaman and Pamuk 2010: 593). Obviously, using intermediaries was not restricted to Ottoman practices. England, for example, used appointed commissionaires to collect and evaluate taxes in exchange for a fee or commission, while Sweden used the Lutheran Church as agents of tax collection and monitoring. The latter was more successful on grounds of legitimacy and territorial penetration. According to historical records, the rulers of the Romanian Principalities were seen as tax intermediaries themselves.

Land tax was the predominant fiscal revenue up until modern times. In the eighteenth and nineteenth centuries the village was still a "collective fiscal unit," meaning that the entire community was responsible for land taxes, called *cisluire* (Lupan 1937: 11). Beyond limited collection capacity, other drivers of this indiscriminate approach were the high capacity of community leaders to maintain order, and a sense of equity. The small, agrarian communities had a high level of informal monitoring or self-regulation driven by local authority figures (e.g. priests, local lords). Furthermore, because the land tax was one of the main sources of fiscal collection, the Ottomans would frequently use the status of "protected lands" for the Romanian principalities to ensure their territorial integrity. This in turn implied the safeguarding of the property rights of nobles and churches with large land holdings, paying their taxes in a predictable manner. An incipient social contract was formed between domestic elites and foreign powers.

As weak as monitoring was in comparison to Western European countries of the time, there were some administrative instruments of oversight worth acknowledging. Given the Western influence, Transylvania started to develop bureaucratic monitoring in pre-modern times (e.g. cadastral records, life events, judicial decisions on debts and duties). With the frequent administrative changes in Wallachia and Moldavia Principalities, and the high level of illiteracy, the Church's census records here were much more reliable than the administrative ones. Most of the peasantry would be highly compliant with ecclesiastical procedures of life events such as birth, marriage, and death.

The lasting effect of this largely informal overseeing of tax payments is that neither the state's monitoring capacity (e.g. cadaster records, census data) nor the overall approach to tax enforcement has improved significantly in modern times. We can see the interpretative nature of the evaluation of taxpayers' income for fiscal purposes, even on the eve of the contemporary statist structure: "when the lifestyle of a taxpayer shows a discrepancy with known incomes, fiscal authorities can recur to evaluation according to *hints and assumptions*" [in Romanian, emphasis in the original text] (Madgearu 2014: 88).

Most of the administrative constructs of the Romanian state were "improvisations based on random practices in Europe" (Rădulescu-Motru 2012 [1937]: 6; see also Janos 1989). In the early twelfth century, court positions occupied by local noblemen or boyars (*boieri*) were Slavonic constructs (e.g. *logofăt, pharnic, spătar, ban*), having a ceremonial role rather than an official function (such as responsibility for stocks, or the armory). They further became territorially bound in *judeţe* (the Latin term for county) after the

Orthodox alignment with the Western branch of Christianity. Following the Unification of the two Romanian Principalities of Wallachia and Moldavia in 1859, French administrative structures were imported as well (e.g. Prefectures).[6] In a noteworthy analysis in the early twentieth century, Constantin Dobrogeanu-Gherea (1910: 29) underlines the tensions between Western institutional imports and the socio-economic realities of Romania: "the peasants did not request the introduction of liberal capitalist institutions, but rather the suppression of serfdom; they would have been sooner satisfied with an absolutist monarchy or a ruler [*Vodă* in the original] liberating it from serfdom [*iobăgie* in the orginal]."

The dependency of administrative development upon contextual constraints continued during the seventeenth and eighteenth centuries. Legal Codes were introduced in Wallachia and Moldavia, integrating existing informal practices with former Byzantine concepts of law.[7] These state-building efforts brought all the Romanian territories to a more consistent level of institutional development. Still, these reforms were essentially driven by the rulers' desires to increase and extend tax collection as much as possible (Ghica 2014 [1880]).

Later, in the nineteenth century,[8] the Organic Statute (*Regulamentul Organic*) introduced the first common legislative framework for both Principalities, under the Russian protectorate. It built heavily on existing administrative and judicial practices, but under the direction of the Russian administrator Kiseleff they were formalized and homogenized, while "striving to prevent abuses."[9] The Statute delineated for the first time the internal engagement of the state to provide public goods and services such as roads, street lighting, cleaning and signage, fire stations, policing and prisons, medical personnel, healthcare centers, schools, regulation of pharmaceutical suppliers, and various judicial and administrative functions. More significantly to the present study, the Organic Statute specifically included the "establishment for the first time in the Romanian countries of a regulated centralized accountancy system that would ensure the checks over the duties collected by state agents, and create a formal framework for the provision of pension, as opposed to the discretionary decision of the ruler as before."[10]

While legal scholars argue that no constitutional foundations existed before the Organic Statute, historians point to the existence of approximately twelve versions of legal references framing the administration of rule of Wallachia and Moldavia, as well as the provision of "common good" (*binele obștesc*) that the rulers were supposed to safeguard (Barbu 2000).

Subsequently, increasingly fervent nationalist emancipation movements established international connections with neighboring organizations, such as the Greek Anti-Ottoman revolutionary society Etaireia. Nationalist Romanian movements imported many demands regarding citizens' rights and administration procedures from them, constructing the modern framings of state legitimacy.[11]

The Church as a redistribution agent

The Romanian case study shows that, over many centuries, most state and Orthodox Church functions have been interlinked (Stan and Turcescu 2011). One of the fundamental organizational principles derived from the Orthodox Church's Byzantine past is the theocratic notion of *symphonia*—taken to mean harmony between Church and state. This relationship developed steadily as the Church became an essential vehicle for nationalist movements serving "as an important transmission belt from state to society, implementing an agenda of domestic integration and homogenization" (Van Meurs and Mungiu-Pippidi 2010: xiii).

The existence of the Orthodox Church under the Ottoman Empire was readily encouraged by the Sultans. It was regarded as a means to control the vassal populations and to help in the collection of taxes (*tribut*), given the informal authority of the clergy and the already well-organized network of monasteries. Additionally, as non-believers, the South-Eastern European populations were charged a higher tribute or tax (*harac-i maktu*) to preserve the autonomy of their territories (Panaite 2013: 403). Collection of the annual per capita tax (*cizye*) owed by non-Muslims in Wallachia and Moldavia was overseen by the same Ottoman treasurer (*baş defterdar*) (Darling 1996: 75).[12]

While the Byzantine Empire subsidized the activity of all Orthodox clergy (Zachariadou 2006), revenue sources changed under Ottoman rule. In order to maintain its day-to-day activities, the Orthodox Church developed a taxation system, complementary to that of the state:

> The collection of these taxes was a privilege granted by the sultans, who apparently continued the Byzantine tax, known as the kanonikon, levied on the inhabitants, the priests and the monasteries of a region in order to cover the expenses of their metropolitan bishop. (Zachariadou 2006: 179)

Much like in Italy, competition was created at this stage between the Church and the administration in the collection of taxes (see Hien, Chapter 4 in this volume, on the Italians' contributions to the Catholic Church). Still, local nobility worked closely with the ecclesiastical elites as their legitimacy was codependent. Tax collection was thus not impeded but actually facilitated by this cooperation.

In exchange, the Church enjoyed a wide range of privileges. For example, records from the rule of Constantin Brâncoveanu in Wallachia show the numerous tax exemptions the Principality enjoyed (Zachariadou 2006).

As taxes in the seventeenth century were largely paid in kind, monasteries were not only exempted from giving a proportion of their production (e.g. wine, honey) to the state, but were also allowed to trade in these goods by establishing selling points, such as wine cellars.[13] These fiscal privileges coupled with the autonomy it enjoyed, generated significant wealth for the Church.

Fiscal burdens owed to foreign powers increased markedly at the beginning of the seventeenth century, especially in Wallachia. Consequently, many free peasants started to lose their status, selling off any property they might have had, and becoming "dependents" on the estates of some local lords, but predominantly on those of monasteries (Murgescu 2010: 40).

While the external fiscal burden on the Romanian Principalities increased, the number of new monasteries that were being established continued to grow. By the fifteenth century, all of the main Romanian territories had a similar number of monasteries, but in the following centuries many more monasteries were being established in Wallachia and Moldavia (Table 10.1). Historical records show the provision of public services in both Catholic and Orthodox monasteries. The latter increased their provision of social services significantly: hospitals (*bolniţe*), educational centers (from primary schools to academies, e.g. Sâmbăta de Sus), printing presses (e.g. at Trei Ierarhi), orphanages, elderly care centers, and the supply of food and clothing for the poor. Local churches would assume many informal care-giving functions, but did not possess the personnel and physical infrastructure (e.g. buildings, land) that the monasteries did.

After the Unification of the two Romanian Principalities in the nineteenth century, the state took over the wealth of the monasteries (*secularizarea averilor mânăstireşti*). Subsequently, much as in the aftermath of the Reformation in England and Sweden in the sixteenth century, the Church became an agent of the national state. Furthermore, it created a very important class for the years to come: the peasant landowner. This notion of property for the lower classes was quintessential in the subsequent exercise of tax collection.

Table 10.1. Number of newly established monasteries in Romanian territories

	15th century and earlier	16th century	17th century	18th century
Moldavia	12	23	21	13
Transylvania	14	0	15	12
Wallachia	20	28	35	18
Total	46	51	71	43

Source: Author's calculations based on the Romanian Orthodox Church (BOR) archival records, Archives of Hungary, www.archivportal.hu/en/archives-of-hungary/archives-of-the-romanian-orthodox-church/. Small ecclesiastical centers are excluded; both Catholic and Orthodox monasteries have been accounted for in the table.

The Romanian Principalities of Wallachia and Moldavia: Fiscal Responsibilities and Payment Mechanisms

Periphery status and contractual legitimacy

The entire economic exchanges of Wallachia and Moldavia in the sixteenth century were driven by their fiscal duties to the central government of the Ottoman Empire: "Romanian products were being exported south of the Danube, or towards Western Europe . . . through fiscal duties these trade networks were filling the coffers of the rulers who in turn used them to pay to the Ottomans" (Murgescu 1996: 313). Furthermore, while fiscal duties changed yearly (depending on the internal constraints of the Ottoman Empire) the responsibility of fulfilling them lay with the appointed ruler.

A reciprocal legal relationship existed between the core and semi-periphery: Romanian territories have been (at times) "tributary states" (i.e. owing tribute— both levies and gifts, military and foreign policy support) as well as "protected states" (i.e. Ottomans owed military and foreign policy support, and could interfere in internal matters in the interest of Romanians) (Panaite 2013). In order to safeguard their fiscal base in these territories, the Ottomans adopted "specific measures designed to ensure the protection and stability of the [vassal] population in Wallachia, but also other sources of revenues, like customs, salt mines and the taxation on the grazing of animals belonging to people south of Wallachia" (D. Panaitescu 2014: 60). The Ottoman Empire's central government used its protection responsibilities to confirm or redraw its support for the rulers' actions and property rights. It did so in Moldavia and Wallachia to a considerably greater extent than in Transylvania.

The Ottoman central government would thus provide a sense of legitimacy to the tax collection process: as long as subjects paid their taxes owed to the Sultan, their rights and property would be safeguarded, even against the oppression of their own ruler. To this end the official demands would "often invoke the fundamental role of the ruler to protect the life, the property, and the wellbeing of the inhabitants of Wallachia, Moldavia or Transylvania, as subjects of the sultan" (Panaite 2013: 419).

The common framing of taxes as "recognition gifts" (*tribut*) created an ambiguous framing of underlying contractual provisions due to fluid power relations between the Romanian Principalities of Wallachia and Moldavia on the one hand, and the Ottoman Empire on the other hand. Duties paid on time ensured that the Ottomans would not invade the "autonomous" Romanian Principalities' territories, but the latter were still heavily dependent in economic and diplomatic matters on the former. In turn, the Ottomans enjoyed minimal costs in administrating these territories, and no responsibility for developing institutions or enforcing compliance on a geographically dispersed population.

Tax collectors and duties owed

According to the system of appointment by the Sultan, the rulers were directly responsible for the payment of duties owed. They would thus, for their own sake, secure the annual payments, often taking out loans to top up the yearly collection. Some historical records refer to the rulers of Wallachia and Moldavia as "leaseholders of duties" (*arendași ai tributului*) (as in the chronicle of the Ottoman bureaucrat Tursun Beg in Panaite 2013: 403). The Principalities were consequently ruled in an openly patrimonial manner, whether by local lords (i.e. *voievozi* or *domni*) or Greek rulers imposed by the Ottomans.[14]

According to the seventeenth-century chronicler, Grigore Ureche, starting in the sixteenth century in Moldavia and the seventeenth century in Wallachia, governors were appointed to take on administrative duties, such as collecting taxes (Ureche 2011). This arrangement reflected the relative detachment rulers and *boieri* had towards this source of income. As Pippidi notes:

> The political organization of Moldavia and Wallachia appeared centralized and despotic, yet real administrative power was weak. The state was conceived as an extended household... Members of the ruling class, including hired foreign experts in fiscal matters and administration, were seen as servants of the prince and were promoted for reasons of nepotism or simple favouritism, not as free men who had consented to a contractually limited obligation to serve the state.
>
> (2010: 119)

Under the rule of Constantin Brâncoveanu, Wallachia enjoyed considerable freedom in international affairs, both in terms of trade and diplomatic relations with Transylvania and other Western countries, such as the Italian city states of the time. It was during this rule that the first systematic inventory of fiscal duties and debt was created—the "Registry of Wallachia's Treasury during the Time of Constantin Brâncoveanu."[15] This registry covered all types of tax and repaid loans, so that we can disentangle the mechanisms employed by rulers to pay their duties to the Ottomans. On average, a quarter of the duties were supplied on site, from local creditors in Istanbul, as the ruler or his representatives would arrive to pay the annual duties to the Sublime Porte (Table 10.2).

Even though he possessed a large personal fortune, Brâncoveanu still relied (like his predecessors) on Istanbul-based loan sharks. Some of them were Muslim guild leaders (e.g. the leader of the butchers' guild, Casap-bașa, or the leader of the furriers guild, Mehment Celebi Chirchiu-bașa[16]), while others were Orthodox noblemen and tradesmen. This dependency of Romanian rulers on third parties (i.e. lenders) to fulfill their fiscal duties to the Ottoman Empire illustrates clearly the lack of sustainability of the domestic fiscal collection system.

Given that the loans bore considerable annual interest, their proportion of 73.72 percent out of the total amount paid to the Sublime Porte in 1702

Table 10.2. Duties and loans in Wallachia (1694–1703)

Year	Repaid loans		Total duties paid to the Sublime Porte
	Sum in Thalers (silver coins)	Percentage of Total Payments	Sum in Thalers (silver coins)
1694	35,533	10.62%	334,554
1695	33,554	8.73%	384,478
1696	44,960	11.22%	400,574
1697	45,189	13.93%	324,484
1698	112,675	30.34%	371,422
1699	100,688	37.37%	269,447
1700	52,900	13.74%	385,134
1701	203,722	41.55%	490,342
1702	180,290	73.72%	244,570
1703	184,980	27.88%	663,591
Total	994,491	25.71%	3,868,596

Source: Based on data from the Registry of Wallachia Treasury, Berza 1958, quoted in Murgescu 2012: 118, adapted by the author.

reveals the fiscal burden as disproportionate. This high debt share is striking, especially since total duties were half of what they were the previous year. It confirms the wide variations of domestic collection capacity, as well as the level of spending by the ruler.

Brâncoveanu cut several taxes for tradesmen and Church duties. He invested at the same time in the development of many administrative and ecclesiastical centers. He pursued the development of a semi-autonomous state in Wallachia (with redistributive functions) by balancing increasingly stronger (economic) ties with the West with duties owed to the Ottomans. Ambitious as his reforms were, the contextual circumstances were not in his favor. Along with his four sons, he was decapitated in Istanbul in 1714 after all their fortunes had been confiscated. There was both domestic and foreign opposition to his endeavors to change the status quo of Wallachia at that time. Brâncoveanu's reforms are important because it was the first time that a social contract was tentatively developed between a Romanian ruler and his subjects.

From the early eighteenth century to the beginning of the nineteenth century, the Ottoman Empire appointed lords of Greek origin in the vassal Principalities of Moldavia and Wallachia called Phanar Lords. These were usually promoted from previous positions (*dragomani*) of interpreters (i.e. intermediaries) or officials, and as such were trusted by the Sultan to serve his pecuniary interests in these territories. They also had to pay for such appointments, with the highest bid usually successful. They would promote their own patronage networks of power, using lower ranking dignitaries whom they trusted, to the detriment of the more established local noblemen (*boieri*) of the Principalities.[17] Generally, such rulers used power to enrich themselves—given the predictably short timeframe, and serving at the pleasure of the Sultan. Some even absconded with most of the national budget (*visteria*) after finding out about their imminent dismissal. Ion Vodă Caradja emptied Wallachia's coffers when he ran away to Pisa in 1818, after tripling his personal fortune by selling noble titles and some of the national salt mines (Ghica 2014 [1880]).

Formal and informal systems of payment

Throughout the pre-modern period, formal records indicate that the Romanian Principalities (and Transylvania in the fifteenth and sixteenth centuries) owed three types of tax to the Ottomans. *Haraci* or *tribut* refer to the collective duties owed yearly by a given province via its ruler. *Peşcheş* or *plocon* refer to dedicated payments to the Sultan or various high dignitaries for personal use (e.g. securing the throne) or domestic interests (e.g. representing legal interests in international negotiations) of the ruler. Finally, there were payments in support of military campaigns that would go either to the Sublime Porte for subsequent distribution, or directly where they were needed (e.g. the Crimea). Under the rule of Brâncoveanu (1654–1714) the relative distribution was as follows: a third were the collective duties (*haraci*) and goodwill payments for the Sultan and his close circle (*plocon de bairam*); a third were formal bribes or payments to obtain favors from Ottoman officials (*plocon*); and a third were military support payments.[18]

Rulers were normally selected domestically, from amongst and by the dignitary boyars, but sometimes informal payments were made to ensure patronage from Ottoman officials (*ruşefet*) (Murgescu 1996: 215). While *peşcheş* or *plocon* were forms of bribe made transparently and recorded, *ruşefet* was made "under the table" in a personalized manner, bypassing domestic deliberations. Anecdotal accounts from the sixteenth century suggest a bid-like system, where one contender, Mihnea Turcitul, offered one million gold coins, while the other, Petru Cercel, offered 1.16 million coins (Murgescu 1996: 215). Considering that collective duties for that period ranged between 50,000 and 70,000 gold coins annually, we can see the disproportionate size of these informal payments for which we have no systematic coverage.

With a vast territory, predominantly agrarian land, and a small community social structure, the local noblemen or boyars (*boieri*) were important figures of authority in the Romanian Principalities, mediating the obligations of subjects with the responsibilities of the ruler. This can be traced to a patrimonial legal structure: the system of property rights over land and the people living on and working that land, as well as the benefits they were required to give in return, such as housing.[19] Noblemen thus realized the basic functions of a fiscal system: they collected the duties, and provided protection and benefits in return to the population.

More importantly still, the strong institutionalization of local authorities originates in local elites. The average rule lasted only about three years (Pippidi 2010: 19). In contrast, the boyars were more resistant to change, and managed to ensure their rights and privileges in an organized manner; it was from amongst them that Romanian rulers were usually selected.

Taxes paid to local dignitaries—whether administrative (i.e. delegated boyars) or ecclesiastical (i.e. the bishops and clergy in monasteries)—were mostly in kind. They in turn had to deliver both in-kind and monetary taxes to the representatives of the Ottoman Empire. An example of an annual duty to the Sultan would have been carried by the leading noblemen to Constantinople: "as a sign of our obedience, the ruler will make sure to send to the Sublime Porte, by way of two Moldavian *boieri*, 4,000 Turkish ducati, 11,000 piasters, 40 hawks, 40 gestate mares—all as a gift [original in Romanian]" (Ureche 2011).

Between the eleventh and eighteenth centuries frequent taxation systems on the population were joint labor (i.e. an extended family was collectively taxed) in exchange for working on the land (*clacă*) (e.g. for four days a week[20]) or a tenth of produce (*dijma*). The latter was often specific to each of the major production sectors (e.g. *vinărit* for wine producers or *oierit* for livestock). In the pre-modern period, bearing similarities to a tax farming system, various categories of collector were established based on the type of duties or levies they were charged with collecting. Historical records also show specialized collectors for products such as fruits (*găblari*), agricultural products (*găletari*), or hay (*fânari*). Along with labor contributions, in-kind levies were collected by people from local rural communities. In contrast, monetary levies collected by such appointees as *birari* or *dăbilari* were the responsibility of early versions of clerks, often situated in more affluent urban communities.

As experienced tradesmen, Greek rulers would often impose heavy duties on certain desirable imports from the Austro-Hungarian Romanian territories (e.g. strong liquor). They thereby ensured their own monopoly and maximized their personal profits. Previous Romanian rulers had gone out of their way to liberalize such trade across the borders of the Romanian territories; an example is Constantin Brâncoveanu's decision to lift taxes on wine traders from Braşov—a city on the border with Transylvania.[21] Trade liberalization was key to both the maximization of the fiscal base and the consolidation of links across Romanian territories.

Transylvania and the Early Development of Administrative Capacity

Collection and redistribution

Under Austro-Hungarian rule a public administration system was developed in Transylvania.[22] Becker and colleagues argue that the shared formal rules of local communities and the "well-respected administration increased citizens' trust in local public services" (2015: 40). The Austro-Hungarian Empire provided various public goods in exchange for the taxes collected, such as bridges,[23] road infrastructure, and stable administrative practices.

In the early thirteenth century, we find in the Austro-Hungarian territories "truth courts" (*loca credibilia*) run by both the judiciary and the (Catholic) Church, signifying that formal bureaucratic institutions had an earlier history in this region. By contrast, Wallachia and Moldavia relied at this time much more heavily on feudal rule.

By comparison to the formalism and uncertainty of the fiscal contract with the Ottomans, under the Hungarian annexation, citizens' expectations were more clearly constructed. Responsibilities were no longer placed solely on the ruler, the delegated figures of authority having a clearer mandate. However, as late as the nineteenth century, enforcement and monitoring mechanisms were not very effective: tax collection would involve troops who would occupy "entire villages, search the houses of delinquent taxpayers, and proceed to remove anything of value" (Janos 1989: 340).

Much like elsewhere in Central Europe at that time, Transylvanian citizens were called upon to contribute in order to support ongoing military campaigns. In the fifteenth century, various taxes were proposed with the specific purpose of financing offensives against the Ottomans or standing armies (Bonney 1999: 266). The legitimacy of such taxes would have been higher than those collected in the Romanian Principalities, as the taxpayers would also be direct beneficiaries (i.e. from a security provision). Their usage was nevertheless very limited.

Given the same population, with the same level of development, over certain periods there was a much better correlation between the extractive and redistributive functions of the fiscal system. Transylvanian taxpayers also had the advantage of their proximity to Western markets, thus creating more flourishing urban centers with a sharp increase of urbanization in the seventeenth century. The development of existing urban centers, alongside supporting administrative services, had been pursued actively in previous centuries by the policies promoted during the Hungarian annexation of the fourteenth and fifteenth centuries (under, for example, King Mathias Corvinus). After the decline of the Hungarian Kingdom, much of the administrative system was overshadowed by Ottoman law. The still predominantly agrarian population subsequently suffered the same fate as that in the Romanian Principalities, becoming trapped by exploitative land-owning elites (Janos 1989: 335).

Duties owed and resources

The Romanian territories found themselves under single rule for a brief period in 1600, under Michael the Brave.[24] Under his rule, the issue of finances became very important and informed the actions that led to unification. At a time when debt had reached a record level, Michael the Brave's decision to rebel against the Ottoman Empire "while risky, . . . was nevertheless reasonable from an economic point of view" (Murgescu 1996: 251). Michael duly leveraged his military position of fighting against the Ottomans to ensure financial support from Western powers. Historical records contain evidence of this in his correspondence (in Latin) with such Hungarian intermediaries of Emperor Rudolf II as Nicholas Puffy and Bartholomeus Pezzen (Murgescu 2012: 46).

There was a marked increase in fiscal burdens in the sixteenth century (see Table 10.2): "relatively limited in Transylvania, considerable in Moldavia, and extreme in Wallachia . . . the comparison to other [European] states shows unequivocally the exceptional nature of this increase before 1594" (Murgescu 2010: 39). This benefited the people of Transylvania as much as it did its rulers, because the system here was much more effective in extracting its due share. Also, rulers in Transylvania never had a sense of autonomy—being previously annexed by the Kingdom of Hungary—as the rulers of the Principalities constantly strived for.

If we account only for per capita monetary duties, we would find Wallachia on a level with the Venetian state. Nevertheless, we can see that a heavier fiscal burden was felt in Wallachia if we look at in-kind taxation: 134 kilos of wheat per capita. Bearing a similarly large agricultural capacity, Transylvania was only taxed 40 kilos of wheat per capita (Table 10.3). Overall, Transylvanian duties, both monetary and in-kind, were in line with those within the Ottoman Empire.

In comparison to the other Romanian territories, Transylvania benefited in several unique ways. Firstly, the province possessed significant resources of precious metals, and *aspri* silver coins were produced in large quantities here throughout the sixteenth century. Secondly, it benefited from an increasingly advantageous exchange rate over the years. Transylvania predominantly used coins of Hungarian circulation (e.g. florins), as opposed to the Ottoman dinar that was experiencing faster depreciation. Thirdly, fiscal collections in Transylvania had less to do with diplomatic affairs. Rulers of the Romanian Principalities had the additional burden of the high value of bribe payments (*plocon* or *peșcheș*) to secure their rule and their borders. Transylvania was

Table 10.3. Comparative fiscal duties in the sixteenth century

State	Duties owed in gold coins per capita	Duties owed in kg of wheat per capita
Poland (1580)	0.14	10
Egypt (1596)	0.15	–
England (1600)	0.25	21.5
India (1600)	0.34	86
Transylvania (1590)	**0.4**	**40**
Ottoman Empire (1581–3)	**0.5**	**60**
Moldavia (1590)	**1**	**67**
Venice (1600)	2	50
Wallachia (1590)	**2**	**134**
Low Countries (1650)	4.5	148

Source: Murgescu 1996: 286–8.

much more clearly placed under the protection of Hungary, with which it shared its fate in good and bad times. As such, fiscal collection here was mainly about funding adminstrative and military expenses, similar to the Western bureacratic system.

The introduction of a bureaucratic system of tax collection only occurred in Romania as a whole after the eighteenth century. Even though "the system of collection remained ineffective, the revenues would be collected anyway by individual bureaucrats, who used the power of their office to extort the bribes that would keep them in a style regarded as commensurate with their social status" (Janos 1989: 341).

Essentially, the success of early bureaucratization in Transylvania was that it provided the authorities with a way to monitor tax payments. Much more advanced records of property and life events were not only possible because of the manner in which the administration worked, but also its own institutional survival over time. Ottomans did not intervene in Romanian territories' domestic administrative affairs; this meant that they neither created (in the Romanian Principalities), nor destroyed (in Transylvania) the existing records. This meant that over the centuries ownership of private and public property became traceable.

Concluding Remarks

This chapter has illustrated in the case of Romania the importance of the mechanisms through which fiscal collection is exerted. The extent of their legitimacy and authority is sourced in important elements such as the (un) coupling of collection and redistribution functions, whether the collection of taxes is done for the benefit of domestic or foreign entities and who is responsible for collection.

As this volume sets out to show, political culture and political institutions matter greatly in the taxpaying process. In the case of a functioning, trust-worthy state, the leap of faith means that personal resources would be invested for the common interest; taxpayers at least believe it to be so. Throughout most of Romania's history, the leap of faith merely meant sur-rendering willingly personal resources. Without the administrative capacity to systematically monitor and enforce, let alone redistribute, paying taxes in this case study generally meant taking personal responsibility within your social group.

According to existing theories, fiscal compliance occurs when citizens believe: (1) that they will get something in return, and (2) that they will be punished if they do not comply. The case study of Romania illustrates what happens if these two conditions fail to coincide. Rulers paid because they acted under a contractual logic: they maintained their privileges and rights (i.e. they got something in return) as long as they paid, and they expected to be punished if they did not comply. In contrast, citizens were subjected to a much more discretionary collection mechanism with limited monitoring capacity. They paid their tax when they could not escape it, being pressured by recognizable figures of authority. Importantly, both the enforcement and redistribution functions were done through informal intermediaries, such as local noblemen or Church representatives.

I use this case study to argue that there is more to paying taxes than a simple logic of returns. As Marcelo Bergman points out: "tax evasion has cultural roots in social norms and institutional arrangements" (2009: 2). In the Romanian case study, neither social norms nor institutional arrangements worked in favor of systematically acquiring the taxpayer's consent in the fiscal collection process. There was a process of collection, but without consent. Within the context of the semi-periphery, where little beyond declarative support came from the Ottomans, paying their taxes was not a priority for the impoverished population. In contrast, social norms as well as institutional arrangements did apply some pressure in the fifteenth and early sixteenth centuries to the urban areas of Transylvania, where a nascent bureaucratic system provided benefits of predictability and rule enforcement for tradesmen and guild workers.

One of the key insights of this chapter is the historical role of localism. This is in contrast to the mainstream understanding of the process of state-building as a process of consolidation of formal administrative structures. Looking at the historical experience of Romanians with fiscal authorities, we see a fluency of rules and institutional actors. But, beyond these shifting structures, there is a constancy in the normative power in local communities, or small elite groups. Compliance in Romanian territories is a product of common agreement, much like in more developed states, the difference being that the mechanisms of deliberation and benefit distribution remain hidden as informal channels.

The second departure of this chapter from mainstream Romanian studies literature was to treat all Romanian territories within the same comparative framework. Because of contextual (i.e. foreign influence) and institutional differences (i.e. administrative practices) scholars tend to analyze them separately. Romanian territories present themselves as a sort of natural experiment, with different administrative and fiscal systems during pre-modern times. A variation we can observe is that the predictability of the bureaucratic administrative system in Transylvania does seem to have created a certain civility in citizens' interactions with the state. In contrast, Romanian Principalities have gone through a consolidation of patrimonial practices and opportunistic self-interest maximization. As various studies on fiscal compliance suggest, the extent to which Romanians perceive the collection process to be beneficial to them makes a difference. For a state to be able to create this perception, it must be able to respond to the wants and needs of the tax-paying population.

There are several avenues through which the present analysis can be strengthened or expanded. On the one hand, as this volume proves, there is much to be learned from comparative historical analysis. While the Romanian case study bears great similarities with Italy, it differs significantly from Sweden or England. Both single cases and comparative studies that investigate further the long-term effects of the coupling of regulations with practices would be informative. On the other hand, Romania shares many contemporary behavioral patterns with other periphery countries, thus a wider historical comparative analysis on informal mechanisms of distribution and enforcement in developing countries could be revealing.[25]

Notes

1. [*A fost un răstimp în care de mirare este cum n-a ajuns acest popor la stingere totală. Stăteau asupra lui stolurile prădalnice ale birarilor și dăbilarilor.*]
2. Based on the author's interviews with public affairs specialist, Adelina Țânțariu, and on the analysis of fiscal collection data series at www.dpfbl.mdrap.ro/analize_bugete.html.
3. See "Willing to Pay?" dataset, http://willingtopay.eu/; and the World Values Survey datasets, www.worldvaluessurvey.org/WVSContents.jsp.
4. I refer to Bogdan Murgescu's modified measure of urbanization, to include smaller towns (i.e. over 2,000 inhabitants) and not only larger agglomerations (i.e. those of over 5,000 or 10,000 inhabitants) (Van Zanden 2005).

5. While the regulation of their status varied over time, especially in terms of duties owed and the ruler appointment system, they can be characterized as a quasi-colony, as they were a conventional part of the Ottoman Empire.
6. In the aftermath of the Crimean War (involving foreign powers that were heavily influencing the Romanian state at that time—the Russians and the Ottomans), Romanians found an innovative way to unite the territories of Moldavia and Wallachia by electing the same leader, Alexandru Ioan Cuza, at the same time in both Principalities, thus creating from a political perspective the modern state of Romania.
7. *Pravalniceasca Condică* by Alexandru Ipsilanti, 1780, Wallachia; *Legiurea Caragea*, 1818, Wallachia; *Callimachi Code*, 1817, Moldavia.
8. 1831 in Wallachia, and 1832 in Moldavia.
9. *Regulamentul Organic: Partea Politică şi Administrativă* [Organic Statute: Political and Administrative Section], 99. www.digibuc.ro.
10. www.digibuc.ro.
11. *Proclamaţia de la Padeş* by Tudor Vladimirescu, 1821; *Proclamaţia de la Islaz* by the Revolutionary Government, 1848.
12. Tax exemptions were made for those engaged in military service or those who could not afford to pay (e.g. women, children, serfs).
13. Ruling decisions of Constantin Brâncoveanu from Sâmbăta de Sus Monastery.
14. Denominated Phanar Lords—derived from Phanar, which was the name of the area in Istanbul where the Constantinople Patriachate resided, along with a concentration of the Greek population from the capital.
15. *Condica vistieriei Ţării Româneşti din periaoda lui Constantin Brâncoveanu.*
16. Based on Bogdan Murgescu's historical analysis (Murgescu 2012: 119).
17. Numerous contemporary fictional accounts portray this shifting dynamic of power in favor of these foreign rulers.
18. Calculations made by Dragoş Ungureanu from the National Patrimony Institute.
19. *Certa puncta* (1769) reproduced by Augustin Bunea, Episcopii Petru Pavel Aron şi Dionisiu Novacovici, sau istoria românilor transilvăneni de la 1751 până la 1764, Blaj, 1902, pp. 404–12, in Murgescu (2001: 118).
20. *Certa Puncta* (1769) (Rules on the reports between noblemen and peasantry in Transylvania).
21. Ruling decisions of Constantin Brâncoveanu from Sâmbăta de Sus Monastery.
22. Hungarian rule spans 1866 to 1918, but this section also looks at the period when the Austrian Empire exerted authority over Transylvania (including Banat and Bukovina provinces). Transylvania became Romanian territory in 1918, at the Great Unification (*Marea Unire*).
23. A seventeenth-century bridge in Oradea was under the guarantee of the Austrian constructor until recently.
24. He was a wealthy nobleman himself, holding high offices (e.g. Ban of Craiova, a position similar to that of a treasurer), and possessed a vast personal fortune, acquired especially through land purchases (Murgescu 2012: 45; see also P. P. Panaitescu 2002).
25. I am grateful for the key insights provided by Cornel Ban, Dan Brett, Bogdan Murgescu, Marina Nistotskaya, Viorel Panaite, Andreas Stamate, and Vladimir

Topan. I am also indebted to the various experts interviewed for this chapter from the National Agency for Fiscal Administration (ANAF), the Romanian Orthodox Church (BOR), and the National Bank of Romania (BNR). This chapter benefited from the generous advice and close guidance of Sven Steinmo. All limitations and faults belong to the author.

References

Ban, C. (2014), *Dependență și dezvoltare: economia politică a capitalismului românesc.* Cluj-Napoca: Editura Tact.

Ban, C. (2016), *Ruling Ideas: How Global Neoliberalism Goes Local.* New York: Oxford University Press.

Barbu, D. (2000), "O arheologie constituțională românească." *Studii și documente.* University of Bucharest Publishing House, isbn: 9735754819.

Barkey, K. (2008), *Empire of Difference: The Ottomans in Comparative Perspective.* New York: Cambridge University Press.

Becker, S. O., K. Boeckh, C. Hainz, and L. Woessmann (2015), "The Empire is Dead, Long Live the Empire! Long-Run Persistence of Trust and Corruption in the Bureaucracy." *The Economic Journal* 126(590): 40–74.

Bergman, M. (2009), *Tax Evasion and the Rule of Law in Latin America: The Political Culture of Cheating and Compliance in Argentina and Chile.* University Park, PA: Penn State Press.

Bonney, R. (ed.) (1999), *The Rise of the Fiscal State in Europe c.1200–1815.* New York: Clarendon Press.

Darling, L. T. (1996), *Revenue-Raising and Legitimacy: Tax Collection and Finance Administration in the Ottoman Empire, 1560–1660* (Vol. 6). Leiden: Brill.

Dimitrov, V., K. H. Goetz, and H. Wollmann (2006), *Governing after Communism: Institutions and Policymaking.* Lanham, MD: Rowman & Littlefield.

Dobrogeanu-Gherea, C. (1910), *Neoiobăgia: studiu economico-sociologic al problemei noastre agrare.* Ed. Librăriei SOCEC & Comp.

Fischer-Galați, S. A. (1959), *Ottoman Imperialism and German Protestantism, 1521–1555.* Cambridge, MA: Harvard University Press.

Gabor, D. (2010), "(De)Financialization and Crisis in Eastern Europe." *Competition & Change* 14(3–4): 248–70.

Ghica, I. (2014 [1880]), *Scrisori către Vasile Alecsandri.* Bucharest: Humanitas.

Helmke, G. and S. Levitsky (2004), "Informal Institutions and Comparative Politics: A Research Agenda." *Perspectives on Politics* 2(4): 725–40.

Janos, A. C. (1989), "The Politics of Backwardness in Continental Europe, 1780–1945." *World Politics* 41(3): 325–58.

Karaman, K. K. and Ş. Pamuk (2010), "Ottoman State Finances in European Perspective, 1500–1914." *The Journal of Economic History* 70(3): 593–629.

Kitschelt, H., Z. Mansfeldova, R. Markowski, and G. Tóka (1999), *Post-Communist Party Systems: Competition, Representation, and Inter-party Cooperation.* New York: Cambridge University Press.

Levi, M. (1988), *Of Rule and Revenue*. Berkeley, CA: University of California Press.

Light, D. and D. Phinnemore (2001), *Post-Communist Romania: Coming to Terms with Transition*. New York: Palgrave Macmillan.

Linz, J. J. and A. Stepan (1996), *Problems of Democratic Transition and Consolidation: Southern Europe, South America, and Post-communist Europe*. Baltimore, MD: Johns Hopkins University Press.

Lupan, H. N. (1937), *Studiu asupra impozitelor si taxelor agricole in Romania in comparatie cu alte tari*. Bucharest: Monitorul Oficial Imprimeria Nationala.

Madgearu, V. N. (2014), *Curs de economie politică* (reprinted edition). Bucharest: Humanitas.

Migdal, J. S. (2001), *State in Society: Studying how States and Societies Transform and Constitute one Another*. Cambridge: Cambridge University Press.

Mungiu-Pippidi, A. (2002), *Politica după comunism*. Bucharest: Editura Humanitas.

Murgescu, B. (1996), *Circulația monetară în Țările Române în secolul al XVI-lea*. Bucharest: Editura Enciclopedică.

Murgescu, B. (ed.) (2001), *Istoria României în texte*. Bucharest: Corint Press.

Murgescu, B. (2010), *Romania si Europa: Acumularea decalajelor economice (1500–2010)*. Iași: Editura Polirom.

Murgescu, B. (2012), *Țările Române între Imperiul Otoman și Europa Creștină*. Iași: Editura Polirom.

Panaite, V. (2013), *Război, Pace și Comerț în Islam: Țările Române și Dreptul Otoman al popoarelor*. Iași: Editura Polirom.

Panaitescu, D. (2014), "The Ottoman Empire and the Preservation of Wallachia's Fiscal Potential (1730–1774)." *Revista Economica* 66(6): 59–76.

Panaitescu, P. P. (2002), *Mihai Viteazul*. Bucharest: Corint Press.

Pippidi, A. (2010), "The Development of an Administrative Class in South-East Europe." In W. P. Van Meurs and A. Mungiu-Pippidi (eds.), *Ottomans into Europeans*. London: Hurst, 111–34.

Pop, L. (2006), *Democratising Capitalism? The Political Economy of Post-Communist Transformations in Romania, 1989–2001*. Manchester: Manchester University Press.

Rădulescu-Motru, C. (2012 [1937]), *Psihologia Poporului Român*. Bucharest: Paideia Press.

Skocpol, T. (1979), *States and Social Revolutions: A Comparative Analysis of France, Russia and China*. Cambridge: Cambridge University Press.

Stan, L. (ed.) (2009), *Transitional Justice in Eastern Europe and the Former Soviet Union: Reckoning with the Communist Past*. Abingdon: Routledge.

Stan, L. and L. Turcescu (2011), *Church, State, and Democracy in Expanding Europe*. New York: Oxford University Press.

Stan, L. and D. Vancea (eds.) (2015), *Post-Communist Romania at Twenty-Five: Linking Past, Present, and Future*. London: Lexington Books.

Tilly, C. (1992), *Coercion, Capital, and European States, AD 990–1992*. London: Wiley-Blackwell.

Ureche, G. (2011), *The Chronicles of the Land of Moldavia, 16th Century*. Bucharest: Litera. Available (in Romanian) at https://books.google.co.uk/books?id=ePFgCwAAQBAJ&printsec=frontcover&source=gbs_ge_summary_r&cad=0#v=onepage&q&f=false.

Van Meurs, W. P. and A. Mungiu-Pippidi (eds.) (2010), *Ottomans into Europeans*. London: Hurst.

Van Zanden, J. L. (2005), "Early Modern Economic Growth." In M. Prak (ed.), *Early Modern Capitalism: Economic and Social Change in Europe, 1400–1800*. London: Routledge, 69–87.

Volintiru, C. (2012), *Institutional Distortions, Clientelism and Corruption: Evidence from Romania*. Bucharest Academy of Economic Studies, Research Center in International Business and Economics (RCIBE), Working Paper No. 1.

Zachariadou, E. (2006), *The Great Church in Captivity 1453–1586*. In M. Angold (ed.), *Cambridge History of Christianity* (Vol. 5). Cambridge: Cambridge University Press, 169–86.

11

Willing to Pay? The Politics of Engendering Faith in the Post-Communist Romanian Tax System

Arpad Todor

Despite the fact that Romania has constantly had one of the worst performing tax systems, with the highest levels of tax evasion among EU countries, a recent experimental study on tax compliance found that Romanian subjects are significantly less likely to cheat than Italian and UK subjects in similar experiments.[1] This high tax morale[2] is furthermore backed by opinion poll data showing that Romanians tend to believe tax avoidance is not excusable. To explain the puzzling gap between the willingness to pay and the constant underperformance of the tax system, I investigate the process of the post-Communist creation of a new extensive and comprehensive tax system and its failure to motivate its subjects to pay their taxes. As the most recent democracy, with the newest tax system, least influenced by path dependencies, the Romanian case allows us to investigate easily the explanatory power of various competing theories of tax compliance looking at the weight of competing causal factors within the same condensed time frame. This case study furthermore allows us to gain an insight into how to improve tax compliance in developing countries in the contemporary world.

I argue that the structure of incentives created both for those paying mainly personal income taxes (PIT) and for firms paying corporate income taxes (CIT) makes it rational to avoid paying them. The high instability and low quality of the legal framework in combination with the absence of political debate on fiscal issues; the high level of taxation combined with widespread tax evasion, high tolerance for state budget debt and generous tax breaks for large firms; and low spending on infrastructure and other public services, have signaled constantly that the tax system is not governed by any significant mechanisms generating reciprocity and laying down the base for a fair fiscal contract. Furthermore, dismal social expenditure (except in pensions, an area with a broken connection between contribution and benefits) creates the impression that average citizens do not receive much from the state in exchange for paying their taxes. Overall, given the constant failure to create an adequate legitimacy for the tax system, the capacity to directly tax citizens and companies has slowly decreased in recent years, in parallel with an increasing reliance on indirect taxes.

To substantiate my argument I analyze historical evolutions and examine the current trends. First, I elaborate the puzzle motivating this investigation and briefly present the main theoretical approaches on tax compliance that inform my inquiry. Second, I discuss several features of the Communist tax systems and the influence of those features on the initial choices and subsequent developments of the new tax system. Third, I analyze the most important characteristics of the post-Communist Romanian tax system that shaped its capacity to generate tax revenues. Fourth, I evaluate some characteristics of the structure of state expenditure, focusing on the absence of significant welfare policies and the consequences for inequality. To conclude, I discuss the implications of my analysis on the volume's aim to untangle the mechanism through which states have developed comprehensive tax systems and motivated their citizens to comply with their tax obligations.

The Puzzle

By all metrics, Romania has experienced significant changes in the last quarter of a century since the fall of the Communist regime, transitioning to a market economy and achieving measurable improvements in many areas of institutional quality, and quality of the political process. All these evolutions allowed it to join the European Union in 2007 and experience high rates of economic growth after the first decade of transition. Yet Romania is a constant laggard in the area of taxation compared to other post-Communist countries that joined the EU. Today, Romania still has the lowest tax revenue as a percentage of GDP in the EU,[3] the highest levels of tax evasion, and one of the worst performing tax collection systems (PricewaterhouseCoopers 2014).

Nevertheless, a recent experimental study on the willingness of subjects to comply with their tax obligations under various incentive structures found that, on average, Romanian subjects were highly cooperative and less likely to cheat than participants in Italy and the UK. The results from the nine Romanian experimental rounds[4] showed a compliance rate ranging from 70 percent to 82 percent, rates that are significantly above the Italian average, and especially above the results from the three locations in the UK (Oxford, London, and Exeter). Although the lowest compliance rate (70 percent) was obtained in round six of the nine, where a 50 percent income tax was applied, this was still 20 percent above the Italian (51 percent) and the British (48 percent) rates. This gap is all the more intriguing since, unlike Italy and the UK, which have steep progressive tax systems, Romania has had a flat personal income tax since 2004 of 16 percent; thus, the 50 percent tax rate should have appeared extremely high for Romanian participants.

The relevance of the subjects' high compliance rate for the entire Romanian population is strongly backed by other experimental studies and opinion poll data. For example, in a study of full-time students from four countries (Romania, Austria, Russia, and Hungary),[5] participants from Romania and Russia tended to identify low-trust scenarios as being more representative of the situation in their countries (Kogler et al. 2013: 172). When faced with a similar incentive structure, the students did not differ that much in their responses; however, differences were apparent when they were confronted with a scenario similar to that from their own country (Kogler et al. 2013: 176). Opinion polls tend to tell the same story. For example, in the 2005 Rural Eurobarometer (Fundația pentru o Societate Deschisă 2005), 83.2 percent of respondents considered that paying taxes is very important. Also, the October 2007 Barometer of Public Opinion (Fundația pentru o Societate Deschisă 2007), a country-level representative sample, revealed that 70 percent of the respondents believed that not paying their taxes, assuming that they could avoid them, is never justified, while only 10 percent considered that it is justified always or most of the time.[6] Furthermore, a 2008 opinion poll (Fundația pentru o Societate Deschisă 2008) showed that 80 percent of respondents believed that it is unacceptable for corporations not to declare revenue, while only 3 percent considered this partly or completely acceptable.[7]

These findings contrast with the observation that the Romanian tax system has the poorest performance among EU countries in terms of the tax gap and difficulty of paying taxes. In other words, although Romanians do not trust their country's institutions, living in a society with high levels of corruption and an inefficient tax system, they do believe that taxes should be paid and are willing to pay when presented with an ideal tax system.

The literature on the relationship between tax compliance, institutional quality, and trust can be divided into three main groups, based on their core mechanisms of generating compliance: state capacity, deterrence, and cultural–behavioral-based approaches. In her influential account, following Schumpeterian tradition, Levi (1989: 1) argues that "[the] history of state revenue production is the history of the evolution of the state." Her theory of the tax state is built around the notion of "quasi-voluntary compliance" (1989: 52–3), compliance dependent on the population's perception of the number of non-cooperators. Centered on the state, but focusing on the relationship between taxation policies in the light of political structures that have shaped various political conflicts, Steinmo has developed an approach to understanding the differences between diverse tax systems. While multiple checks and balances in the US led to a fragmented tax system, the Swedish corporatist model led to a unitary, stable, and efficient tax system. British politics, on the other hand, dominated by strong parties, has led to an unstable tax system (Steinmo 1996). Steinmo argues that tax compliance can be seen as a "fiscal exchange" that manifests a positive correlation between the chance of winning from the common pot and citizens' willingness to pay. In a similar analysis, focused on the post-Communist space, Easter (2002) has compared Russia and Poland in order to explain how various political constraints led to the structuring of the tax system. While in Russia the tax extraction system was the result of elite bargaining over taxing corporate profits, in Poland the extraction strategy is centered on taxing household incomes.

Parallel to the state-centered literature, starting with Allingham and Sadmo's theory of tax compliance based on taxpayers as *utility maximizers*, various authors have analyzed deterrence mechanisms as a function of the chances of being detected, the size of fines, and the potential gains from tax avoidance. Most theoretical models based on deterrence imply that increasing fines and control intensity would lead to lower tax evasion and add elements such as the amount of information available to tax authorities, the formulation of penalties and responsibilities, audit probability, and non-compliance penalties (Luttmer and Singhal 2014). Building on this literature, a new generation of models focuses on the subjective nature of each individual's assessment of the probability of being detected. While these theoretical models can be useful to understand some features of citizen–tax authority interaction, their explanatory power is rather low given that most tax systems in the world are not based on deterrence, and do not offer much guidance for tax authorities in their efforts to improve compliance (Luttmer and Singhal 2014).

The third strand of literature has developed around the concept of tax morale as an implicit psychological contract between the state and its citizens, where loyalty is very important while rewards and punishment can crowd out intrinsic motivations (Frey 1997; Frey and Feld 2002). For example, Kirchler (1999) discusses tax compliance as a social exchange between the state and citizens, while Porcano (1988) and Alm, McClelland, and Schulze (1992) emphasize that tax compliance could be improved if government accentuated tax compliance as a fiscal exchange. A different type of approach to tax compliance is developed by Bergman (2009), who argues that the level of tax compliance is a function of the "compliance equilibria" reached in different counties, equilibria that are highly dependent on deeply rooted social norms. Instead, other studies have employed games centered on the public good to analyze what kind of variables influence tax evasion levels (Feld and Tyran 2002; Frey and Feld 2002; Scholz and Lubell 1988).

Focusing specifically on the Romanian case, Bădescu (2007), Rothstein (2004; 2005), and Uslaner and Bădescu (2004) advance different explanations for the link between generalized trust, people's incentive to pay taxes and the quality of governance. Rothstein (2004) writes that even in a low-trust society like Romania, the establishment of universal and impartial institutions that implement public policies aimed at reducing economic inequalities generates social capital of the type necessary to support economic development. Instead, Uslaner and Bădescu (2004: 35) argue that "When corruption is rampant, as in Romania, people become inured to it. They don't think worse of their fellow citizens, who must get by in any way they can in a system that seems rigged toward those at the top. People are disturbed by corruption in government, but they may feel powerless to do much about it." Thus, Uslaner and Bădescu stress that the causal link moves from economic equality to social trust. Also, while generalized trust does not lead to higher levels of personal tax compliance, it influences people's propensity to accept higher levels of PIT (Bădescu 2007: 319). Bădescu argues that trust, perception of state capacity, and tax compliance are linked through three causal mechanisms: (1) if there is a generalized perception that most people avoid paying taxes, it is rational to try the same strategy; (2) perceiving that the mechanism for spending taxes is inefficient and rigged by corruption stimulates noncompliance; (3) those who believe that poverty is caused by a lack of work and individual merit would be more prone to avoiding paying taxes (Bădescu 2007: 308).

All in all, the explanatory models advanced by different theoretical accounts of compliance focus on the same core variables, but give them different weights and put different emphases on the causal links among them. To understand what kind of theoretical model can offer more insight into the causes that lead to the puzzling data that motivates this inquiry, in the following sections I will investigate how the state, and the tax system in particular, relates to citizens. The historical narrative starts with the Communist period, when most developments that influenced the post-Communist period occurred.

Path Dependencies

Starting with August 23, 1944, when Romania switched sides in World War II and turned against Nazi Germany, the USSR's influence on Romania quickly increased and led to the installation of the Petru Groza cabinet in March 1945 and the fraudulent 1946 elections, culminating in the forced abdication of the last monarch and the proclamation of the Popular Republic in December 1947. Under close supervision from Soviet advisers whose authority was enhanced by the presence of Soviet troops (Pop 2006), the economy was transformed into a socialist one, with the elimination of practically all private property and the collectivization of agriculture and tax extraction. The new approach to increasing tax compliance was detailed in Law no. 344 from December 1947, which introduced harsh penalties against tax evasion but also the option of paying previously avoided tax in order to escape prison sentences. For the first time, tax evasion was regarded as equivalent to state sabotage and was sanctioned by harsh punishments.

While various forms of small private economic activities survived, during the Communist period most economic actors were state-owned enterprises (SOEs) and the exact level of taxation of their profit was established through negotiations between the Ministry of Finance and the SOEs. Also, workers were mainly taxed through hidden payroll deductions, directly retained by the SOEs; thus employees were not even aware they were being taxed. As the Communist regime started to transform the economy and eliminate private economic actors, a new set of regulations was elaborated with Decree no. 202/1953 regarding the modification of the Penal Code. This law introduced a chapter on offences against the economic system, which defined tax evasion as sabotage. While this regulation was eliminated from the 1969 Penal Code, Law no. 18/1968 regarding the control of goods owned by natural persons who had obtained them illegally introduced the state's right to evaluate people's wealth and to compare it with their existing means of income (Virjan 2012: 7). According to this law, any unsubstantiated wealth was taxed at a rate of 80 percent.[8] Given the substantial size of the shadow economy, especially in the agricultural sector, the discretionary ability of tax authorities to apply arbitrary formulas to evaluate income and expenditure, and the limited means available to appeal decisions in the courts, this law was occasionally used as a discretionary tool of repression. While no official data exists on how widespread the application of this regulation was, the law created such a climate of insecurity that the 1991 Constitution included a special formulation in Art. 44(8): "Legally acquired assets shall not be confiscated. Legality of acquisition shall be presumed."[9] Basically, this constitutional provision limited the possibility of enacting laws that would require the obligation to prove the source of someone's wealth, a limitation that was confirmed by a 1996 decision of the Constitutional Court that declared unconstitutional the still unabolished 1968 law.

Another development, peculiar to Romania's final decade under Communist rule, is represented by the self-imposed austerity measures begun in 1982, following the 1973 oil crisis since which the balance of payments had deteriorated and foreign debt increased (Pop 2006: 16). According to Ban (2012),

Romania embarked upon a harsh austerity program that led to a collapse in living standards and the explosion of an informal economy. Following the 1982 debt crisis, the combination of Stalinist and nationalist views on development policies lead the Ceaușescu regime to embark on a course of rapidly paying off all foreign debt and prioritizing industrialization. These policies led to a significant decrease in consumption, extensive food and other goods shortages, and led to an exhaustion of the regime's sources of legitimacy. Furthermore, to justify the decrease in the availability of goods (Ben-Ner and Montias 1991), the Communist regime imposed a *program of rational nutrition* that set a strict basic food quota for each person. Combined with a chronic undersupply of official groceries and severe limitations on imported food, all the conditions for the development of a parallel system of food production and distribution developed. Thus, a large part of the population was using that alternative system, a factor that implicitly meant that they participated in tax evasion activities and were liable to harsh punishments, a situation that significantly affected their institutional trust in the decades to come. Within this context, the percentage of goods acquired through the shadow economy has significantly increased and the process that indirectly affected Romanians' propensity to pay taxes during the Communist regime has developed as a coping mechanism for the inefficiency and scarcities of official production and poor distribution of goods, especially food.

The Communist legacy was responsible for equally deleterious outcomes in the area of business taxation. Despite their limited development, non-state-run enterprises have been subject to detailed tax regulation since 1968, when Decree no. 65 introduced a steep taxation system with rates from 10 percent to 45 percent (Rotaru 2009). Subsequently, Romania increased the progressivity of its taxation policy in this sector, introducing tax rates of up to 77 percent, a change that generated only insignificant revenues as the state's interest in controlling these businesses was limited. Also, given the high integration of production streams (Pasti 2006: 358) the socialist system had separated the organization of production from cash flow as trade among firms took place through planning allocations and not profit- or efficiency-based mechanisms (Pop 2006: 18). All in all, these legacies would prove to have long-lasting effects during the transition period from communism to a free market economy.

The Unfinished Post-Communist Fiscal Contract

Given the significant differences between the logic of a tax system designed for a centralized as opposed to a market-based economy, the post-Communist authorities faced significant dilemmas regarding the transition toward a new tax system. Also, the initial choices were made under conditions of economic downturn and rapidly decreasing state revenues, as well as limited access to capital markets (Ban and Tamames 2015). Given that the price system had been bureaucratically determined, the process of price liberalization inflicted significant economic pain, with a hugely inefficient and energy-intensive industry (Pop 2006: 16) in need of significant restructuring. As hard budgetary constraints started to affect big SOEs, they started to proactively avoid paying taxes. By the end of 1991, the state abandoned its coordinating functions in the economy (Pasti 2006: 356) and the effects of price liberalization and firms' restructuring led to protests and a period of high mobilization by the unions (Pop 2006: 22). The initial reforms adopted under pressure from the IMF led to a deleterious recession, contraction of credit, increasing inter-company arrears, and the collapse of purchasing power (Ban and Tamames 2015: 77).

Furthermore, the absence of an indirect taxation system and a widespread lack of trust in most state institutions (with the exception of the army) made it difficult to rapidly create and implement new fiscal rules and institutions. Thus, in practice the new government had chosen to enact a CIT system that borrowed many of the features of the Communist system for taxing independent activities. The first tax reforms began in early 1991 with the introduction of a CIT based on a sixty-seven-step scale starting at 5 percent (for income between 25,001 RON and 50,000 RON) and rising to 77 percent (for income above 955 million RON), a tax rate among the highest in the world. Meanwhile, foreign investors were given special status and corporations with full foreign ownership paid no taxes for the first two years after they started to earn profit from their investments. Subsequently, the Ministry of Finance could further offer them a 50 percent cut on their CIT. The mixed ownership corporations were granted a permanent 50 percent CIT cut. It is worth mentioning that at that time Romania had basically no Foreign Direct Investments (FDI)[10] and that while these tax facilities did not trigger any relevant FDI influx, they were used as a means of tax evasion and by immigrants from Middle Eastern countries to open various import–export businesses. Also, Law no. 82 from 1991 (*Accounting law*) criminalized the entering of false data in companies' books, an offence punishable with imprisonment from six months to five years. Nevertheless, in practice, the chance that small mistakes would occur was very high, an aspect that generated significant discretionary power for the tax authorities and high incentives for tax evasion. Basically, the widespread norm was that all companies were given small fines and made bribery payments to the tax inspectors.

The initial tax system was so poorly designed that by the end of 1991, with a direct contribution from the World Bank, the progressive taxation of the CIT was scrapped and a system with just two levels was introduced. This changed again in 1995 to a unique 38 percent rate.[11] The first comprehensive regulation concerning tax evasion was enacted through Government Ordinance no. 17 of August 1993, defining the contraventions for breach of financial and fiscal regulation. Subsequently, according to Law 87 from 1994, tax evasion was defined as any avoidance of paying taxes to any of the state budgets or funds by natural or legal Romanian or foreign persons (Virjan 2012: 3). The limited success of the tax system in adapting to new economic conditions is reflected not only in the decrease of tax/GDP revenues from 34 percent to 28 percent by 1995, a percentage that remained constant until 2015, but also a decreased tax effort (Mertens 2003: 548), a situation further aggravated by various tax exemptions and tax breaks that perpetuated *soft budget constraints* until EU accession (Daianu, Kallai, and Lungu 2012: 164). Two important milestones that switched the approach toward a more coherent and predictable tax system came in 2005 with Law no. 241/2005 and Cabinet Decree no. 873 of July 28, 2005. They modified the fiscal regulation with new measures for fighting tax evasion in the areas of alcohol and oil taxation (Daianu, Kallai, and Lungu 2012: 8). The most important institutional consolidation was enacted in 2004 when the National Agency for Fiscal Administration (NAFA) unified the previously fragmented fiscal duties. While the 2014 Report by the Accounting Court shows some noticeable improvement in the NAFA's functioning, a systemic improvement of the tax system is still to be felt. Furthermore, despite the fact that one of the main aims in creating the NAFA was to reduce the widespread corruption among tax authorities, by 2016 four of the five former NAFA general directors had been prosecuted for corruption by the anti-corruption agency.

Even within the context of a region with high tax instability, the Romanian tax system stands out. The initial choices created a locked-in effect that made the Romanian tax system one of the worst in the region, a situation further aggravated by the high level of corruption (Transparency International n.d.). While the Ministry of Finance constantly attempted to clarify the tax code system with the aim of increasing the state's collection capacity, a lack of adequate foresight led to continuous modifications and very low predictability of revenue collection. More than a thousand modifications of the legislation were introduced over a period of twenty-five years, with countless situations where a new modification of the tax code in parliament was further modified by a government Emergency Ordinance just days after it came into force. For example, the 2003 Fiscal Code was modified one hundred times between 2004 and 2013, the number of words tripled to 190,000, and only twenty-five Articles out of the initial 298 remained unchanged (Medrega 2013).

It is no wonder that in 2015 the Romanian tax system still exhibited one of the worst performances: in the Ease of Paying Taxes measure, Romania ranked 134th out of the 170 countries evaluated, the worst in the EU (PricewaterhouseCoopers 2014). Despite the implementation of the flat tax in 2004, its worst ranking was in the number of different taxes to be paid by businesses annually (including the personal taxes on their employees' salaries), totaling ninety-six in all. Only recently did Romania achieve some perceptible progress in the area of compliance cost, according to World Bank data. Despite the still high number of payments (thirty-nine), the total time necessary to prepare, file, and pay taxes has decreased to 200 hours and come closer to the EU average of 166 hours, better than Italy at 269 hours.

As in other countries, the complex and dysfunctional Romanian tax system goes hand in hand with a low enforcement capability. Although taxation levels reach 43.2 percent, above the EU average of 41 percent (Olescu 2015), due primarily to high social security contributions (SSC) and value added tax (VAT) rates, fiscal evasion for 2013 was estimated at 16.2 percent of GDP, 75 percent (12.21 percent of GDP) related to VAT[12] and 15 percent stemming from unpaid social insurance contributions from workers without an employment contract or paid partially outside a legal contract.[13] Overall, Romania has the worst VAT collection capacity, with only 56 percent of the income extracted (compared to 83 percent in Estonia or 71 percent in the Czech Republic), and the lowest social insurance contribution collection capacity, reaching only 72 percent, among the worst in the EU (Consiliul Fiscal 2014). A 2015 Report by the Court of Accounts (Bratu 2016; Curtea de Conturi a Romaniei 2015) reveals a huge imbalance in tax compliance between labor and capital, showing that businesses accounted for 96.5 percent of *arrears*, with the top 2.7 percent of companies responsible for 75.7 percent of the outstanding amount. The report also underlines a limited interest by NAFA in cracking offshore tax evasion: firms identified with a high risk of tax evasion and transfer pricing are multinational corporations, a fact widely reflected in mass-media reports. Furthermore, the report also identifies significant shortcomings in terms of procedural equity, with multiple cases in which entities operating under similar conditions receive different treatment. Thus, unlike the older EU member states, where the distribution of income from direct and indirect taxes is balanced, tax revenues in Romania are skewed toward indirect taxes such as VAT and excise duties. For example, revenues from PIT decreased from 5.3 percent of GDP in 1995 to just 2.7 percent in 2002, and then hovered around 3.3 percent, while revenues from CIT decreased from 5.3 percent of GDP to a low of 2.3 percent in 2005, and then recovered to 3.3 percent of GDP. On the other hand, despite high tax evasion, indirect taxes (VAT and excise duties) increased their share of total tax revenue from 33.7 percent in 1997 to 45.2 percent by 2010 and have remained constant since, above the average of other post-Communist countries (42.3 percent) or the old EU member states (36.2 percent).[14]

All in all, despite significant evolution since the fall of the Communist regime in 1989, Romania still ranks bottom, alongside Bulgaria, in almost all relevant indicators of institutional capacity to collect revenues. With an average tax revenue as a percentage of GDP of only 28 percent between 1995 and 2012, Romania is 11 percent under the EU average (Pana 2016b). By comparison, other post-Communist countries are performing significantly better in this dimension: Hungary's tax revenue as a percentage of GDP is 38.6, Slovenia's 37.6, the Czech Republic's 35.3, and Poland's 31.8.

Unlike in consolidated democracies, despite the continuing malfunction of the tax system, as well as the widespread frustration it causes, tax reforms have rarely been the subject of intense political debate or confrontation (Steinmo 1996), regardless of the political coalition in power. The constant modifications of the tax code legal statute were mostly needed to correct various mistakes, clarify incoherencies, or close widely used loopholes. Also, political parties have made no attempt to detail their proposals for tax reforms in their electoral programs beyond generalities; government pro-grams have contained just general aims, such as reducing tax evasion and increasing revenue targets, and have not detailed how to achieve these goals. It is no wonder that Romania was one of the countries where the neoliberal flat tax reform was put on the political agenda by the Ministry of Finance of the Social Democratic Party and gained the support of the prime minister. However, the party abandoned the reform due to opposition pressure from the Romanian president (who was also the ex-leader of the Social Democratic Party). Subsequently, the flat tax was proposed by the right-wing Truth and Justice Alliance as a major electoral theme and was later implemented through a government Emergency Ordinance, without any debate in parliament. The 2015 adoption of the new tax code offers another example of the lack of political debates around fiscal issues. The new law has been adopted twice in parliament through general political consensus, after the president sent it back with objections regarding the reliability of the revenue streams, given the planned tax cuts (especially the decrease of VAT from 24 percent to 19 percent). Despite the presence of parliamentary scrutiny (see Daunton, Chapter 6 in this volume), unlike Italy, Sweden, the UK or the US, where tax reforms involve significant debates and negotiations with a large number of societal actors (unions, business associations, the Church, think-tanks), Romania continues its his-torical trend of no political debates around taxation and its link with expenditure, especially the welfare state. In the following section I will discuss the link between the fiscal issue and the post-Communist develop-ment of the welfare state.

The Welfare State and Inequality

Although during the first decade of post-Communism transition Romania's economic policies were highly inconsistent, especially with the constant friction between internal actors and interest groups aligned with external institutions (Ban 2013; Pasti 2006), after the start of the EU-accession negotiations the Romanian development model became coherent and remained fairly stable under alternate governing coalitions. The move from uncoordinated capitalism (cocktail capitalism) toward a "dependent market economy" relied on multinational banks, FDI, and proactive policies to promote liberalization and the privatization of public utility companies. The move has also influenced the tax system and the functioning of the welfare system (Ban 2013). While this development model was associated with higher than average rates of economic growth (Ban 2013: 7), it also increased the shift of the tax burden toward labor and consumption and increased inequality. The post-2007 economic crisis further exacerbated this shift, as costs of the economic crisis have been transferred away from capital, a change reflected by the fact that the national net income received by wage earners decreased from 48 percent to just 40 percent by 2013, while the average is 65 percent in the US and 60 percent in France (Georgescu 2015).

A direct effect of its low budgetary revenues is the fact that Romania also has one of the lowest rates of public investment and the worst infrastructure in the EU. Furthermore, the efficiency of those expenditures is rather low given the high levels of corruption, especially in public procurement (Consiliul Fiscal 2014: 16). Even though Romania became a member of the European Union in 2007, its socio-economic development lags behind the EU average in almost all areas with no indication that it is catching up. Like some other post-Communist countries, Romania is facing demographic pressures, especially a declining population, high emigration, and a pensioners-to-employees ratio that is worse than in many developed EU member countries and is forecast to dramatically worsen in future decades (Expert Forum 2012).

Like many other Communist countries, Romania started with a low level of economic inequality. During the transition to post-Communism, the Gini coefficient steadily increased, given both the move to capitalism and the limited effect of transfer policies. According to World Bank data, the Gini coefficient increased from 23.3 in 1989 to 31.8 in 1998, ranging between 29.5 and 30.46 by 2006, and increased above 35 in 2008.[15] An analysis of the impact of flat-tax reform on inequality reveals that, as expected, most of the gains from the PIT flattening went to the top 20 percent of income earners, stimulated consumption only within this group, and led to a perceptible increase in overall income inequality in Romania (Voinea and Mihaescu 2009). Thus, while EU accession led to a decrease in inequality, post-2008 financial crisis economic growth was unequally distributed and led to an increase in the Gini coefficient from 33.4 in 2010 to 34.7 in 2014 (Pana 2016a). It is worth mentioning that the Romanian state's social policies have been totally ineffective in limiting this increasing inequality. On the other hand, the massive emigration of three million people (15 percent of the total population) after EU accession (emigration that significantly increased remittances, especially in rural regions), had a positive effect on revenues in many of Romania's poorest regions. Nevertheless, despite this huge emigration, Romania continues to rank the worst of all EU countries in terms of inequality and risk of poverty.[16]

As Romania has the lowest tax revenue and GDP in the EU, social protection and education expenditure rank last in the EU. Nevertheless, the total cost of pensions is in third place as part of total public expenditure (Pana 2016b). Overall, "data from Eurostat reflects an increase of spending on social protection benefits from 378.7 Euro/inhabitant in 2002 to 916.57 Euro/inhabitant in 2009 but despite the 2.4 times increase, it is still very far from the 7823.13 Euro/inhabitant, the average spending in the EU-15 (the old EU member states)" (Todor 2015: 81). One of the most important reasons or incentives for citizens to trust the state with their money is that they receive in return good public services or support for social cohesion through an adequate redistribution. Despite the fact that social services expenditure as a percentage of total expenditure has reached a high level in Romania, the area that consumes most resources is the pension system, while the amount of resources spent on other categories such as family and child benefits, or sickness and disability benefits is dismal.[17] This situation was partially caused by the rapid increase in unemployment during the harsh economic adjustments of the 1990s, combined with the mass pension programs designed to alleviate unemployment. Also, through the implementation of special pension programs for those who have worked in the military, police, justice, or secret services, the link between social contributions and the level of pensions became highly distorted, significantly decreasing taxpayers' incentive to report real wages. For example, the special pension system offers an average pension that is three times higher than the regular pension and generates ongoing public outrage.

In May 2010, "Romania enacted one of the most aggressive and regressive fiscal retrenchment programs" (Todor 2014: 39), justified by budgetary pressures triggered by the post-2007 economic crisis. Most importantly, Prime Minister Boc's Cabinet committed itself to the goal of cutting social security costs from 2.9 percent of GDP to 2 percent (the EU average is 5 percent), as mentioned in the *Social Assistance Reform Strategy*.[18] Although these plans were never put into practice because of the results of subsequent elections, it is worth stressing that debates on the future of the welfare state or the link between taxation and the welfare state were hardly relevant during the 2012 electoral battle. Blyth argues that the REBLL (the Baltic states, Bulgaria, and Romania) group's approach to austerity during the economic crisis under the supervision of the troika (the International Monetary Fund, the European Central Bank, and the European Commission) is unique, given that it was caused by their growth model based on foreign borrowing, high FDI inflows, and dependence on remittances—a model highly vulnerable to external shocks. The austerity measures contained mostly expenditure cuts and only regressive tax increases such as VAT and labor taxes, which led to a significant increase in the levels of tax evasion (Blyth 2013: 129). Even worse, today Romania has one of the highest percentages of working poor, as Eurostat data indicates (14.2 percent compared with the EU average of 5.5 percent or the new member states average of 7.1 percent), a situation that disproportionately affects young cohorts and is explained by the lack of indexing of most personal deductions within the context of PIT flattening (Pana 2015).

All in all, the limited Romanian welfare state is neither truly functional nor based on very clear and predictable rules. Given the country's low taxation capacity, welfare consumes a high proportion of the state budget and is constantly used as a scapegoat for the significant underinvestment in infrastructure or areas such as education. In addition, because the current population decrease will further shrink the future benefits of regular employees, the system is perceived as highly unfair.

Conclusions

This chapter set out to investigate the process of creation of a new post-Communist Romanian tax system, the main characteristics of the efforts to create its rules and institutions, and how these evolutions affected the relationship of citizens with the tax system. The investigation started from the puzzling observation that Romania appears to exhibit two extremes: on the one hand, it has developed the worst tax system in the EU in terms of the quality of its functionality, the tax gap, and its general instability, and on the other hand Romanians appear to have high tax morale and are willing to pay when faced with ideal tax institutions.

To explain this puzzle, I have reviewed the main theoretical approaches on tax compliance and investigated the historical processes that have led to the current situation of the tax system. This investigation allowed me to explain what constellation of various explanatory variables accounts for the gap between observed and manifested tax compliance. Far from being simple, the observed gap is caused by a complex set of factors, most of them related to low institutional quality. Romania's tax system is neither stable nor efficient, but is burdensome, inefficient, and undermines its own legitimacy as it allows people in powerful and influential positions to easily avoid paying taxes. Romanians do not live, yet, in a well-functioning society and do not, rationally, trust government-run institutions to any degree. Despite the fact that most Romanians do not consider that they receive adequate services and welfare protection for their taxes, they appear to be willing to pay, believe that everyone should pay, and see the fight against corruption as the main aim in trying to improve the current situation. The historical analysis showed that some constants of the structure of incentives created for both those paying mainly PIT and firms paying CIT made it rational to avoid paying taxes. Not only has the legal framework regulating taxation been highly unstable and unpredictable throughout the entire post-Communist period, but these hundreds of smaller or bigger adjustments have not been the subject of significant political debate and negotiation among relevant social actors. The combination of high numbers of taxes, high levels of taxation, significant tax evasion, and corruption, which have led to low spending on infrastructure, public services, and social expenditure, limits the chances of creating an adequate legitimacy for the tax system and the underlying social contract supporting it (see also Volintiru, Chapter 10 in this volume, on the long-term explanations for this situation). All this has led to an increased resistance to direct taxation and increasing reliance on regressive indirect taxes. Nevertheless, it is worth stressing that data reveals that tax avoidance is not widespread in terms of the percentage of the population that participates in paying it. In fact, data reveals that most tax avoidance (CIT and VAT) happens in the corporate sector. Thus, unlike Italy where tax avoidance can be explained along a North–South divide (see D'Attoma, Chapter 5 in this volume) or religious differences (see Hien, Chapter 4 in this volume), these dimensions appear to be irrelevant in Romania. Also, while Volintiru's analysis reveals that the historical legacy significantly differs from successful countries such as Sweden (see Nistotskaya and D'Arcy, Chapter 2 in this volume) or the UK (see Daunton, Chapter 6 in this volume), this chapter shows that almost all relevant causality can be traced to post-Communist Romanian history.

The divergent combination of high tax morale and widespread tax evasion implies that ameliorating tax compliance cannot be undertaken significantly through deterrence mechanisms since strong punishment in less than perfect institutional settings easily transforms into discretionary power that encourages corruption. Both in the Communist and post-Communist period, legal provisions offered tax authorities significant leverage in order to impose harsh punishment on those that evaded taxes. Nevertheless, no data indicates that these mechanisms have been efficient, as the results actually prove the contrary.

This analysis shows that even in the presence of significant tax free-riders, quasi-compliance does not necessarily crowd out compliance if the instruments used to tax different parts of the population differ significantly. Also, the quasi-compliance explanation does not take into consideration the fact that people might crave a change in the quality of institutional operation. These findings also argue against trust-based explanations. By analyzing various opinion polls collected throughout the last two decades, Bădescu (2007) concludes that for the average Romanian, the most important ability of the state is to fight corruption—that is, fight with direct results on limiting the big tax evaders. Another finding reported by Bădescu (2007) using a 2004 survey is that most Romanians favor limited state taxes as a percentage of GDP, especially given the high level of perceived corruption. Bădescu (2007: 312) writes that opinion poll data reveals that many Romanians cannot correctly evaluate the link between the structure of taxation and its impact on inequality. Data consistently shows that Romanians do not have faith in tax authorities in particular and state institutions in general to spend their taxes wisely. Nevertheless, the historical analysis shows that rationally speaking, Romanians do not have many reasons to trust the state in how it fairly collects and spends their taxes, and they are right in their evaluation that those with money are less likely to pay their share of taxes. While Romania is both a low-trust society with comparatively low institutional quality, identifying public policy solutions to exit such social traps (Rothstein 2005) requires an in-depth understanding of causal links among relevant variables, as well as how they can be altered through various government policies. Before anything else, inadequate trust of poorly functioning and corrupt institutions eliminates any relevant triggers and incentives for improvement.

These findings strongly support the conclusion that Romanians might exhibit highly cooperative behavior under ideal institutions, but they experience low tax morale given their perceptions of existing tax institutions and how they operate—these are not contradictory positions. Yes, Romanians are willing to pay if they face transparent and fully functional institutions, but when they recognize a low-trust, low-compliance scenario they defect (Frey and Torgler 2007: 136; Kogler et al. 2013: 176). This brief review of some of the most important historical evolutions shows that based on historical events, rational citizens should manifest a low level of tax compliance given that taxes have been usually used inefficiently. Accordingly, reforms that would increase the fairness of taxation, especially the fight against high-level corruption, directly linked with high-level tax evasion, could generate a virtuous circle that could change the way people relate to institutions, even in the absence of an increased level of interpersonal trust.[19]

Notes

1. Research conducted within the "Willing to Pay? Testing Institutionalist Theory with Experiments" ERC Grant agreement no. 295675, coordinated by Prof. Sven Steinmo. I gratefully acknowledge the assistance of Alexandra Diaconescu, Dinu Guțu, Andrada Nimu, Daniela Panica, Sebastian Țoc, and Andrei Vlăducu in organizing the experiments in Bucharest at the National School for Political Science and Public Administration.
2. Tax morale is defined as the intrinsic motivation to pay taxes in Torgler (2003).
3. Tax revenue as a percentage of GDP decreased from 34 percent in 1992 to 28 percent in 1997 and remained constant until 2015. Daianu, Kallai, and Lungu (2012: 164). Eurostat website (2017) Table: Total tax revenue by country, 1995–2016 (% of GDP). Available at: http://ec.europa.eu/eurostat/statistics-explained/index.php/File: Total_tax_revenue_by_country,_1995-2016_(%25_of_GDP).png.
4. The experiments were organized in nine rounds in Bucharest in May 2014 and involved a total of 135 subjects. Participants were selected randomly from an electronic database created for the purposes of that experiment. While most people in the pool were undergraduate students from the National School for Political Science and Public Administration, around 35 percent were recruited following the dissemination of posters in downtown Bucharest.
5. The study involved 1,319 students: 95 percent in Economics or Business Administration, "from the University of Vienna in Austria, the University of Debrecen in Hungary, the Babes-Bolyai University in Cluj-Napoca, Romania, and the National Research University and the Academy of National Economy in Moscow, Russia. 329 students participated in Austria (57.8% female; mean age 22.0, SD = 3.4), 280 students in Hungary (68.6% female; mean age 21.1, SD = 2.1), 400 students were recruited in Romania (62.5% female; mean age = 21.7, SD = 1.4), and 341 students participated in Russia (52.8% female; mean age = 18.82, SD = 1.9)" (Kogler et al. 2013: 172).
6. On a scale of (1)–(10), where 1 = never justified and 10 = always justified, 53.1% answered that avoiding taxes is never justified (1), 10% answered (2), and 8.4% answered (3); while 3% chose (8), 2.2% chose (9), and 7.6% answered (10) = always justified.
7. On a scale of (1)–(10) where 1 = completely unacceptable and 10 = totally acceptable, 59.2% answered (1), 13.4% answered (2), and 7.4% answered (3); whereas 0.8% chose (8), 2.6% chose (9), and 2.6% chose (10) = totally acceptable.
8. Article 2 provided: "The value of assets whose origin is not substantiated is subject to an 80 percent tax. Substantiating the origin of assets means the obligation of the person to prove the licit character of means used for acquiring or increasing the assets." See https://cristidanilet.wordpress.com/2011/06/23/opinie-despre-prezumtia-liceitatii-dobandirii-averii/.
9. www.cdep.ro/pls/dic/site.page?den=act2_2&par1=2#t2c2s0sba44: "(8) Averea dobândită licit nu poate fi confiscată. Caracterul licit al dobândirii se prezumă."
10. FDI reached $5 per capita in 1992 and $9 per capita in 1993 according to IMF data. Romania ranked last throughout the entire post-Communist period in terms of FDI per capita among the ten new post-Communist EU member states.

11. The next major development came in 2000 when the CIT was cut to 25 percent and the tax on profits from exports decreased to 5 percent (Sfetcu 2013).
12. The low VAT collection capacity is a constant of the entire post-Communist period. Romania ranked bottom in its capacity to collect VAT, and by 2014 the VAT evasion rate reached 44 percent.
13. Estimated at 1.57 million people—27.7 percent of the total active labor force (Consiliul Fiscal 2014: 18).
14. Eurostat (2015): Indirect Taxes as % of Total Taxation—Total.
15. See http://data.worldbank.org/indicator/SI.POV.GINI?locations=RO.
16. Eurostat data indicate that around 22.5 percent of the population is still at risk of poverty after social transfers. See Table 1: "At-risk-of-poverty rate after social transfers, 2011–13" at http://ec.europa.eu/eurostat/statistics-explained/index.php/ Income_distribution_statistics#Database.
17. Although pensions are labeled as social expenditures in Romania, the general perception of the pension is that it is a right earned by paying social contributions during the years when a person is active in the labor market. A 2010 decision by the Romanian Constitutional Court declared pensions a *patrimonial right*, and implicitly excluded them from the sphere of social expenditures (www.ccr.ro/files/prod ucts/D0871_10.pdf).
18. Strategia privind reforma în domeniul asistenței sociale 2011–13 [National Strategy for reform in social services]: www.mmuncii.ro/pub/img/site/files/ 58bd6ffc9844fbc4a8a639672450872b.pdf.
19. I am grateful to Cornel Ban and Bo Rothstein for their insightful comments on the initial draft of this chapter, and to Alexandru Mustață, who helped me with the editing of the text.

References

Alm, James, Gary H. McClelland, and William D. Schulze (1992), "Why Do People Pay Taxes?" *Journal of Public Economics* 48(1): 21–38.
Bădescu, Gabriel (2007), "Trust, Corruption and Tax Evasion in Romania." In Nicolas Hayoz and Simon Hug (eds.), *Tax Evasion, Trust, and State Capacities*. Bern: Peter Lang, 307–26.
Ban, C. (2012), "Sovereign Debt, Austerity, and Regime Change: The Case of Nicolae Ceausescu's Romania." *East European Politics & Societies* 26(4): 743–76.
Ban, Cornel (2013), "From Cocktail to Dependence: Revisiting the Foundations of Dependent Market Economies." Global Economic Governance Initiative. Boston, MA: Boston University, February 12. www.bu.edu/pardeeschool/files/2014/11/ Dependent-market-economy-Working-Paper.pdf.
Ban, Cornel and Jorge Tamames (2015), "Political Economy and the Ghosts of the Past: Revisiting the Spanish and Romanian Transitions to Democracy." *Historein* 15(1): 62–82.
Ben-Ner, Avner and J. Michael Montias (1991), "The Introduction of Markets in a Hyper-centralized Economy: The Case of Romania." *Journal of Economic Perspectives* 5(4): 163–70.
Bergman, Marcelo (2009), *Tax Evasion and the Rule of Law in Latin America: The Political Culture of Cheating and Compliance in Argentina and Chile*. University Park, PA: Pennsylvania State University Press.

Blyth, Mark (2013), *Austerity: The History of a Dangerous Idea*. Oxford and New York: Oxford University Press, 2013.

Bratu, Victor (2016), "Radiografia Curții de Conturi pe ANAF: Procentul încasărilor stă pe loc de 10 ani / ANAF și multinaționalele / Presiune pe contribuabilii mici, ignorarea celor mari / Rambursări de TVA cu încălcarea legii / Decizii ignorate de executare silită / Lipsesc aplicațiile informatice." *CursDeGuvernare*, February 3. http://cursdeguvernare. ro/radiografia-curtii-de-conturi-pe-anaf-procentul-incasarilor-sta-pe-loc-de-10-ani-anaf-si-multinationalele-presiune-pe-contribuabilii-mici-ignorarea-celor-mari-rambursari-de-tva-cu-incalcarea-l.html.

Consiliul Fiscal (2014), *Annual Report 2013*. www.fiscalcouncil.ro/RA2013Engleza. pdf.

Curtea de Conturi a Romaniei (2015), "Sinteza Raportului de Audit Privind Contul General Anual de Execuție a Bugetului de Stat Pe Anul 2014." Bucharest: Curtea de Conturi a Romaniei. www.curteadeconturi.ro/Publicatii/SINTEZA_cont_gen_exec_bug_2014.pdf.

Daianu, Daniel, Ella Kallai, and Laurian Lungu (2012), "Tax Policy under the Curse of Low Revenues: The Case of Romania (Part I)." *Romanian Journal of Economic Forecasting* 15(1): 156–86.

Easter, Gerald M. (2002), "Politics of Revenue Extraction in Post-Communist States: Poland and Russia Compared." *Politics & Society* 30(4): 599–627.

Expert Forum (2012), "Cine Va Mai Plăti Pensiile 'Decrețeilor' in 2030?" Working Paper no. 3, Bucharest 2012. http://expertforum.ro/wp-content/uploads/2012/11/Cartea-alba-a-pensiilor-RO_11nov.pdf.

Eurostat (2015), *Taxation Trends in the European Union*, DG Taxation and Custom Union. Luxembourg: Publications Office of the European Union.

Feld, Lars P. and Jean-Robert Tyran (2002), "Tax Evasion and Voting: An Experimental Analysis." *Kyklos* 55(2): 197–221.

Frey, Bruno S. (1997), *Not Just for the Money: An Economic Theory of Personal Motivation*. Cheltenham, UK and Brookfield, VT: Edward Elgar.

Frey, Bruno S. and Lars P. Feld (2002), "Deterrence and Morale in Taxation: An Empirical Analysis." CESifo Working Paper.

Frey, Bruno S. and Benno Torgler (2007), "Tax Morale and Conditional Cooperation." *Journal of Comparative Economics* 35(1): 136–59.

Fundația pentru o Societate Deschisă (2005), "EuroBarometrul Rural." www. fundatia.ro/sites/default/files/baza%20de%20date%20Eurobarometrul%20Rural% 202005.rar.

Fundația pentru o Societate Deschisă (2007), "Barometrul de Opinie Publică." www. fundatia.ro/sites/default/files/baza%20de%20date%20octombrie%202007.zip.

Fundația pentru o Societate Deschisă (2008), "Atitudini Față de Muncă În România/ Attitudes towards Work." www.fundatia.ro/sites/default/files/baza%20de%20date% 20Atitudini%20fa%C8%9B%C4%83%20de%20munc%C4%83%20%C3%AEn% 20Rom%C3%A2nia%202008.rar.

Georgescu, Florin (2015), "Capitalul În România Anului 2015." Bucharest. http://blog. prospectiv.org/2015/11/capitalul-in-romania-anului-2015-florin.html.

Kirchler, Erich (1999), "Reactance to Taxation: Employers' Attitudes towards Taxes." *Journal of Socio-Economics* 28(2): 131–8.

Kogler, Christoph, Larissa Batrancea, Anca Nichita, Jozsef Pantya, Alexis Belianin, and Erich Kirchler (2013), "Trust and Power as Determinants of Tax Compliance: Testing the Assumptions of the Slippery Slope Framework in Austria, Hungary, Romania and Russia." *Journal of Economic Psychology* 34(C): 169–80.

Levi, Margaret (1989), *Of Rule and Revenue*. Berkeley, CA: University of California Press.

Luttmer, Erzo F. P. and Monica Singhal (2014), "Tax Morale." *Journal of Economic Perspectives* 28(4): 149–68.

Medrega, Claudia (2013), "10 Ani de Cod Fiscal: 100 de Modificări Legislative Și Un Text de Trei Ori Mai Lung | Ziarul Financiar." *Ziarul Financiar.* www.zf.ro//zf-24/10-ani-de-cod-fiscal-100-de-modificari-legislative-si-un-text-de-trei-ori-mai-lung-11718563.

Mertens, Jo Beth (2003), "Measuring Tax Effort In Central and Eastern Europe." *Public Finance & Management* 3(4): 530–63.

Olescu, Emilia (2015), "Tara Noastra Se Afla Pe Ultimul Loc in UE, ca Procent de Colectare a TVA. Interviu Cu Roxana Popel, Head of Tax CMS Romania." *BURSA*, March 9. www.bursa.ro/tara-noastra-se-afla-pe-ultimul-loc-in-ue-ca-procent-de-colectare-a-tva-263425&s=print&sr=articol&id_articol=263425.html.

Pana, Marin (2015), "Țara În Care Munca Nu Aduce Bunăstare: O Analiză Comparativă a României Cu Statele UE." *CursDeGuvernare*, November 23. http://cursdeguvernare.ro/tara-in-care-munca-nu-aduce-bunastare-o-analiza-comparativa-a-romaniei-cu-statele-ue.html.

Pana, Marin (2016a), "Când PIB Crește Odată Cu Sărăcia: Coeficientul Inegalității Sociale În UE âi Colegele de Pluton Ale României." *CursDeGuvernare*, March 14. http://cursdeguvernare.ro/cand-pib-creste-odata-cu-saracia-coeficientul-inegalitatii-sociale-in-ue-si-colegele-de-pluton-ale-romaniei.html.

Pana, Marin (2016b), "Cum Îşi Cheltuieşte România Bugetul: O Comparaţie Cu Practica Europeană." *CursDeGuvernare*, March 23. http://cursdeguvernare.ro/cum-isi-cheltuieste-romania-bugetul-o-comparatie-cu-practica-europeana.html.

Pasti, Vladimir (2006), *Noul Capitalism Românesc.* âtiinţe Politice Opus. Iaşi: Polirom.

Pop, Liliana (2006), *Democratising Capitalism?: The Political Economy of Post-Communist Transformations in Romania, 1989–2001.* Manchester: Manchester University Press.

Porcano, Thomas M. (1988), "Correlates of Tax Evasion." *Journal of Economic Psychology* 9(1): 47–67.

Pricewaterhouse Coopers, World Bank Group (2014), "Paying Taxes 2014. A Comparison of Tax Systems in 189 Economies Worldwide." PwC. http://documents.worldbank.org/curated/en/14333146831382983o/pdf/886380WP0DB20100Box385194B00PUBLIC0.pdf.

Rotaru, Constantin (2009), "SISTEMUL FISCAL DIN ROMÂNIA ANILOR 1945–1989|." *Articole*, October 10. www.constantinrotaru.ro/2009/10/10/sistemul-fiscal-din-romania-anilor-1945-1989/.

Rothstein, Bo (2004), "Social Trust and Honesty in Government: A Causal Mechanisms Approach." In János Kornai, Bo Rothstein, and Susan Rose-Ackerman (eds.), *Creating Social Trust in Post-Socialist Transition*. New York: Palgrave Macmillan, 13–31.

Rothstein, Bo (2005), *Social Traps and the Problem of Trust*. Cambridge: Cambridge University Press.

Scholz, John T. and Marc Lubell (1988), "Trust and Taxpaying: Testing the Heuristic Approach to Collective Action." *American Journal of Political Science* 42(2): 398–417.

Sfetcu, Nicolae (2013), "Reforma Impozitelor Directe În România, 1990–2005." *Set Things*, December 26. www.aluzii.ro/reforma-impozitelor-directe-in-romania-1990-2005/.

Steinmo, Sven (1996), *Taxation and Democracy: Swedish, British, and American Approaches to Financing the Modern State*. New Haven, CT: Yale University Press.

Todor, A. (2014), "Romania's Austerity Policies in the European Context." *Romanian Journal of Society and Politics* 9(1): 25–42.

Todor, A. (2015), "Romania's Social Protection Programs Reforms During the Economic Crisis." *Romanian Journal of Society and Politics* 10(2): 79–93.

Torgler, Benno (2003), "To Evade Taxes or Not to Evade: That Is the Question." *Journal of Socio-Economics* 32(3): 283–302.

Transparency International (n.d.), "Romania Corruption Index." www.transparency.org.ro/index_en.html.

Uslaner, Eric M. and Gabriel Bădescu (2004), "Honesty, Trust and Legal Norms in the Transition to Democracy: Why Bo Rothstein Is Better Able to Explain Sweden Than Romania." In János Kornai, Bo Rothstein, and Susan Rose-Ackerman (eds.), *Creating Social Trust in Post-Socialist Transition*. Basingstoke: Palgrave Macmillan, 31–53.

Vîrjan, Bogdan (2012), *Infracțiunile de Evaziune Fiscală*. Bucharest: C. H. Beck.

Voinea, Liviu and Flaviu Mihaescu (2009), "The Impact of the Flat Tax Reform on Inequality the Case of Romania." *Romanian Journal of Economic Forecasting* 12(4): 19–41.

Part VII
Conclusion

12

Taxation and Consent

Implications for Developing Nations

Marcelo Bergman and Sven H. Steinmo

So What?

We conclude this volume with a simple and blunt question: So what?[1] Perhaps the historical narratives in this book are fun to read and interesting for historians, but do they matter? In other words, do these "stories" have anything to teach us beyond the narratives themselves? This concluding chapter is devoted to answering this question. We argue that the analyses offered here are more than simply interesting stories about different countries and instead offer insights into how and why some countries have been better able to build positive relationships between citizens and their states than others. Though the substantive focus here has been on taxes and tax compliance, we further believe that these lessons have significant implications that go far beyond the study of fiscal policy.

Specifically, these analyses teach us important lessons about both citizens *and* states. Many models of development are built on classical economic theory that assumes an essentially hostile relationship between citizens and their states in which citizens and taxpayers are mostly driven by short-term self-interest and their desire to pay as little as possible. The analyses contained in this book demonstrate that this is not the right way to think about this relationship. It is clear that citizens can be intimidated into paying taxes. In societies that are more successful in collecting taxes, however, citizens and taxpayers willingly take a "leap of faith" and pay their taxes because of some sense of public good, common identity, and/or sense of equity. While it is clearly the case that short-term self-interest plays a role in citizens' willingness to pay, it is equally clear that citizens are also driven by social norms, a desire for fairness, a sense of belonging, and even their social values.

In recent years there has been a powerful narrative suggesting that markets are better than states and that a key problem in the modern world is that states have become too strong. In our view this is wrong. The analyses contained in this book suggest that the opposite may even be true. We see in several of the previous chapters that strong states can in fact elicit higher levels of *voluntary* compliance. Schneider, Buehn, and Montenegro (2010) estimate that the average of economic activity hidden from tax authorities in the developing world (where the weakest states are found) is 35.7 percent of GDP, while in OECD countries where most strong states are located, the hidden economy is 18.7 percent. It may seem counter-intuitive, but it apparently takes a strong state to deliver the kinds of goods and services that citizens are willing to pay for. Intimidating citizens into paying taxes can be done, but this is the behavior of a weak state. Moreover, heavy reliance on intimidation is an extraordinarily inefficient way of collecting revenue and is likely to generate very high levels of defection and evasion.

Citizens are more willing to take the "leap of faith" and comply with state authorities when the state is sufficiently capable of delivering goods and services that are worth paying for and sufficiently able to reinforce social norms of compliance. We will discuss the relationship between state capacity and social norms below, but the main point here is that a positive compliance equilibrium can be built only where states have high levels of information about their society and have coherent legal rules that are applied to the whole of society fairly.

The analyses in the preceding chapters have clearly shown that it is precisely those states that are strong that have managed to develop a two-way street with taxpayers and thereby move beyond the predator–victim relationship. The lessons from the five cases examined in this book allow us to disentangle the variables that have been shown to work and present a sequence model or phased paths that may lead to better compliance. It is this type of state strength that allows a culture of compliance to co-evolve with state capacity.[2]

This concluding chapter summarizes several aspects of tax compliance developed throughout this project, highlighting what has worked in tax compliance and what the lessons are for countries worldwide. Rather than recapitulating the narratives themselves, we look to use learned lessons to guide future debates as well as make scholars and practitioners from different latitudes aware of several topics that are not generally developed in the research. Thus, in the last section we offer our conclusions as to what we believe needs to be taken into consideration when countries want to reduce tax evasion and enhance compliance. We stress that in addition to smart taxes, adequate tax rates, and strong institutional capacities, governments should be thinking how to elicit the "leap of faith" from the population. Only then will tax compliance be sustainable.

The chapter is divided into four major sections. The first highlights the importance of effective states and the emergence of stable institutions in compliance behavior. In the second section we draw from the historical narratives explored in this book and examine the foundation stones for building fiscal legitimacy. In other words, what kinds of general policy have successful states followed in contrast to those that have been much less successful in generating high levels of consent? The third section identifies the "lessons learned" from our studies and the routes taken to improve compliance behavior. Finally, we conclude with a series of policy implications drawn from our comparative narratives, other studies on taxation, as well as from our behavioral experiment research. Our aim here is to offer insights into the kinds of policy that seem to have worked in the more successful cases we have examined and not to make predictions about what exact policies any specific country should follow.

Strong States and Successful Societies

Margaret Levi's classic, *On Rule and Revenue*, characterizes tax compliance as a relationship between predators and subjects. In this view, governments extract as much as they can get away with by providing services and/or through extortion. States will provide only as much as they have to in order to get the revenues they need and taxpayers will pay only as much as they have to in order to avoid punishment. This "fiscal exchange" can vary from country to country, to be sure, but the basic calculation is always the same. The state's goal is to maximize revenue and the taxpayer's goal is to pay as little as possible. In this view, the differences in tax systems around the world and the explanation for different rates of tax compliance are essentially a product of the different bargains that have been struck between adversaries.[3]

In this book we tell a different story. In our view, in the more *successful societies* people's willingness to comply with tax authorities transcends the ability of rulers to extract resources from their citizens and has much to do with other variables such as culture, trust, fairness, and social cohesiveness. Formal institutions are important, but they are only part of the story.

Promoting positive social norms

As we have seen in the "Willing to Pay?" experiments, there are a number of motivations that affect individuals' compliance decisions, just as there are a wide range of individuals in every country (see Andrighetto et al. 2016;

D'Attoma, Volintiru, and Steinmo 2017; Zhang et al. 2016; as well as the forthcoming volume *Willing to Pay?*). To be sure, even in countries such as Sweden some people still cheat the taxman (and maybe even steal from their neighbors), while in countries such as Romania or Italy many people abide by tax laws even when they know there are many others who do not. In all societies there are those who will act according to what they think is "right" (or fair, or just, or equitable, or even altruistic) even when a cost–benefit analysis should lead them in the opposite direction. Finally, a large share of people in any society will try to adjust their behavior to what they believe is expected within that society—the social norms (Bicchieri 2006; Conte and Andrighetto 2013; Elster 1989; Tetlock 2000; Traxler 2010).

This is where institutions become important. Institutions (both formal and informal) are rule systems. High compliance societies have more efficient and coherent institutions that signal and monitor desired behaviors or choices in clear and transparent ways. Low compliance societies have unstable and less efficacious institutions that neither give clear signals nor effectively monitor the behavior of their members. In a society in which violating social rules or laws is rarely punished, people will begin to defect. The more people who defect, the more others will mold their behavior in the same way and eventually defection itself may become the norm (Andrighetto et al. 2013). When a critical mass of defectors is built, it becomes extremely difficult to reverse this equilibrium (Bergman 2009).

This overlooked aspect of taxation has important implications for the enforcement capacities of states. A key reason that Italy cannot replicate the tax administration of Sweden today is because of the large number of self-employed individuals. The self-employed are harder to monitor and more likely to cheat on their taxes everywhere (Gerxhani and Scham 2006; Pisani 2014). Large numbers of small companies and self-employed individuals (who mostly work within a cash economy) make it exceptionally difficult to monitor effectively these millions of taxpayers. Consequentially, nearly everyone in Italy knows someone who under-reports their real income. For example, it is commonplace in Italy for medical doctors and dentists to offer their patients' two prices: one price if you pay in cash and a higher one if you need a receipt. Eventually this behavior becomes "normal."

Similar stories are found throughout Latin American countries, where personal income tax is largely evaded (Barreix, Benítez, and Pecho 2017; Ondetti 2015) as well as in Africa (Kedir 2014). On the other hand, Sweden can achieve high rates of compliance in part because for most people taxes are automatically reported and paid by employers. But compliance is also high in Sweden because Swedes themselves monitor for the state. Not only are all citizens' tax reports available online, but also it is virtually unthinkable that a medical doctor, for example, would offer a patient different prices according to whether they would like a receipt or not. In fact, Sweden is increasingly becoming a cashless economy. As a consequence, tax authorities need only identify a few tax evaders to maintain a positive equilibrium. Where monitoring is extensive and administration is consistent, norms are easily reinforced. Conversely, where many taxpayers can effectively hide income from the authorities and few are caught, evasion has become a socially acceptable norm—at least among large segments of society.

In sum, compliance co-evolves with efficient administration, effective institutions, and a society in which most people believe that everyone is paying their fair share. Even self-employed people can be encouraged to higher levels of compliance, but this requires states to firmly develop the necessary institutional foundations. Brute deterrence will ultimately get mediocre results. Strong states can generate high revenues at lower cost because their citizens are willing to cooperate and even monitor each other. This kind of relationship is not easy to develop, of course. As we have repeated often in this volume, "Getting to Sweden" is hard. But the key point here is that this relationship must be built upon socially cooperative foundations, not on threats and intimidation.

Building a sense of identity and/or purpose

Humans have a profound and natural motivation to belong (Axelrod 1986; Baumeister 2011; Elster 1989). In this book we have seen multiple cases where state actions have created a sense of belonging and/or helped facilitate a sense that the state and society have a common purpose. Where this happens, citizens are more willing to pay taxes.

Studies in tax compliance have very rarely explored the effect of social cohesion in taxation. Still, the apparent correlation between cohesive societies and levels of tax compliance should not be surprising. In the laboratory we have found that compliance is higher as the group gets smaller. In general one can say that smaller groups increase the level of interpersonal trust and thus the levels of contribution to the common good are higher. More broadly, it seems clear that societies capable of constructing a widely shared national narrative are more able to demand sacrifices from their citizens. Most obviously, in periods of war, national disasters, or external threats, people's willingness to pay taxes increases.

Cohesiveness is of course a social construction. Cohesiveness is *not* the same thing as homogeneity. The United States, after all, has been since its inception a highly diverse country, with immigrants from all around the world, which enforced slavery until the middle of the nineteenth century. Still, as we saw in Carolyn C. Jones's analysis (Chapter 9 in this volume), this country managed to manufacture a sense of identity and common purpose in the mid-twentieth century.

There are no a priori salient natural traits that make one country more cohesive than another. Social cohesiveness can stem from, for example, isolation, from sharing common goals, from shared beliefs and/or religion, from shared social mores, or from external threats. Smaller groups have a natural tendency to be more cohesive but it is not a prerequisite.[4]

In Latin America, the two countries with the highest compliance rates are Uruguay and Chile, which are among the most cohesive countries in the region, while Mexico and Brazil (despite having strong tax administrations) exhibit relatively high levels of non-compliance (CEPAL 2016). Central American countries with deep social divisions such as El Salvador and Guatemala collect very little tax revenue while Costa Rica and to some extent Panama have only moderate levels of tax evasion. Here too we see that Latin American countries where people feel they truly belong to a national narrative and common purpose enjoy better rates of tax compliance.

Political considerations also play a role in cohesiveness. Lieberman (2003) has shown that South Africa's elite racial coordination in the first half of the twentieth century allowed it to command great tax sacrifices from its members, whereas in Brazil elite regional fragmentation inhibited the emergence of an upper-class sense of purpose and common identity. As a result, whites in South Africa were able to raise significant tax revenues and compliance, while Brazil lagged significantly behind in that respect.

Building Fiscal Legitimacy

The famous Allegory of the Good and Bad Government painted by Lorenzetti located in the city councillors' room of Siena's fourteenth-century City Hall has been seen as a masterpiece of what constitutes good governance. One of the few texts included with the paintings clearly says that a governor can collect taxes and tributes because he has promoted justice and fairness.[5] In this painting we see that even as far back as Middle Ages Italy, it was understood that it was the obligation of the state to promote the common good (*ben commune*) through fairness and justice.

In this section of our chapter we will explicitly explore how and why some cases turn toward what we will call "virtuous circles" while others appear stuck in "vicious cycles". First, successful states produce tangible goods. Second, they distribute those goods and raise revenues fairly. Fairness, as we shall see, can be a rather complex concept in which both procedural justice and equity matter. Third, in order for the state to be perceived as fair it must be able to monitor its citizens and enforce its laws. Under these conditions, and perhaps only these conditions, society itself may promote norms of cooperation and cohesion.

Good government, then, can produce a positive feedback loop that may allow the strong state to speak softly even while they may still carry a big stick.

Lennart Wittberg of the Swedish Tax Authority captures the dynamic in this way:

> There are also indirect effects of trust that may have a larger meaning. Most taxpayers are willing to do right if others do. A belief that the tax administration has the ability to ensure that others pay the right tax is therefore of great importance for their own will to do the right thing. Another indirect effect is that trust contributes to perceived justice, which in turn affects behavior.
>
> (Wittberg 2010, authors' translation)

We have seen several routes through which this process could happen, including increasing taxes on workers in Sweden in the 1930s and 1940s; lowering taxes in the seventeenth and eighteenth centuries in the UK; and even propagandizing citizens as the country mobilized for war in the 1940s in the US. In each of these successful cases, governments made a case which either connected taxpayers and taxpaying to collective benefits and/or used tax and compliance as a focal point for social solidarity.

The case histories in this volume have also given us several examples in which the state was far less successful in building consent—or perhaps did not even really try. As Clara Volintiru and Arpad Todor each demonstrated in their chapters (10 and 11, respectively) on Romanian history, the Romanian state never built a sense that the citizens belonged together or that the state was an agent of society. Instead the state was seen as a foreign institution at first dominated literally by foreign powers and then later dominated by alien and hostile dictators. Though a variety of different tax collection mechanisms were tried none of these proved effective at convincing Romanians that they and their states had common identities or interests. Todor's work demonstrates that even the move toward a very low, flat-rate tax in the twentieth century could not break this cycle, not because a foreign power still ruled over Romania, but because the state itself was considered a hostile and predatory force.

Italy offers an analogous, if not quite as extreme, example. Here the state was dominated by foreign rulers in the seventeenth and eighteenth centuries. But in this case it appears that it was internal fragmentation that weakened Italy's ability to come together and develop a sense of common purpose. First, as Hien shows (Chapter 4), the Catholic Church did much to undermine the legitimacy of the modern Italian state. But as John D'Attoma also shows (Chapter 5), the continued conflicts between North and South have done nothing but exacerbate these problems. Still today the state and its administrative apparatus are burdened by rules, laws, and legal protections that prevent the administration—and specifically its tax collectors—from building the coherent administrative tools like those we have seen in Britain, Sweden, and the United States.

Alexander Gershenkron's famous essay, *Economic Backwardness in Historical Perspective* (1962), argues that countries that entered the modern era relatively late can be advantaged by the fact that in late development capital and labor resources can be concentrated in ways that make it possible for them to leapfrog past the early developers (Germany and Japan are the primary examples). The logic here is that late developers could import the institutions, economic structures, and technologies developed outside their country and refine them to suit their local circumstances in sometimes very efficient ways. Consequently, they quickly start up and enter global markets while maintaining relatively low wages and thereby gain competitive advantage and even overtake more established political economies (Gershenkron 1962).

The narratives found in this book and elsewhere lead one to suspect that the advantages of importing administrative technologies are not always so obvious. The Romanian case provides perhaps the best example of this. In their desperate desire to attain revenue efficiency and greater levels of effectiveness after the fall of Communism, Romanian governments introduced one of the most "advanced" and modern tax systems in the world. The idea of a "flat tax" system was at the cutting edge of economic thinking of the day. As we saw in several countries examined here, by the mid-1980s the highly progressive and highly complex tax systems that had developed over the previous fifty years throughout Western democracies have been brought into question. Even the Swedes had moved away from the very high marginal tax rates toward a more "efficient" tax system. A number of Eastern European countries including the Romanians took this idea one step further and introduced a flat (16 percent) tax, the logic being that if it were so low everyone would be willing to pay. As we learned in Todor's chapter, things did not work out exactly as planned. Why? The answer seems to be that simply introducing new technologies requires an administrative and social foundation in which those technologies (whether tax policy or something else) could and would be administered fairly and efficiently. In other words, imposing a flat tax without first having developed efficient monitoring systems for controlling the misbehavior of political and administrative elites did nothing to build the legitimacy of the system as a whole.

The most important lesson here is that leapfrogging usually fails because it does not establish the social and administrative foundations for building consent. Institutions need to perform effectively for the equilibrium to emerge and be sustained. Many countries in the developing world are able to raise tax revenues, yet they are still unable to foster voluntary compliance, and therefore they fall short of generating sustainable, cost-effective systems. The early state-building project in Central America, for example, rejected tax progressivity and fairness (Schneider 2012). The interests of economic privileged groups were instead protected and this led to the belief that the system was unfair. The result has clearly been to produce weak taxation regimes despite the fact that these countries emulated similar tax structures promoted by international organizations. The post-Communist regimes in Ukraine, Russia, and to some extent Poland, were able to exert coercion and improve tax administrative capacities during the transition to market economies, but so far they have fallen short of building the kind of institutions that enhance trust and equity (Berenson 2017). In all these cases, the virtuous circles of compliance, trust in governments, and valuable public goods has not yet been established. Clever tax policies and large bureaucracies do not replace solid social institutions.

Countries that have long histories of adverse relationships between citizens and their governors face difficulties in raising taxes. This is obvious. What has received less attention is that building a "culture prone to compliance" can take generations. Quick fixes rarely work. Of course, Guatemala cannot be Sweden, but what Guatemala's officers can do is learn from Sweden's sixteenth-century experience: building the foundations of a monitoring system through the co-opting of strong groups (in Sweden's case the Lutheran Church) in order to foster mechanisms of compliance. Guatemala does not need to wait a hundred years to enhance compliance; it can be done in a much shorter time span. Yet it still may be a matter of decades or generations before a new culture of compliance fully emerges.

Lessons Learned

The historical narratives contained in this volume describe how "ecologies of compliance" (or non-compliance) were construed and evolved over time. In all of the 180+ countries in the world today only a tiny handful have achieved anything like the kind of willing compliance we see in Scandinavia in the twenty-first century. Indeed, one might say that even Italy (one of the less successful countries in this study) is significantly better at generating tax revenue than many other countries across the developing world. This section examines what states can do to bolster the foundations for successful compliance: building consent.

Monitoring

Several chapters in this book have demonstrated that consent is built on effective monitoring and measuring mechanisms being in place before a heavy tax burden is imposed. In Sweden, for example, because the cadastral system was established very early and effectively, the state and the local community developed the capacity to monitor both those who paid taxes and those who did not. As a consequence, the state developed the ability to enforce rules broadly and relatively effectively. In the Italian and Romanian cases, in contrast, the state failed to develop institutions that could monitor its citizens and/or taxpayers effectively. Consequently, many taxpayers defected. This is not because Italians or Romanians are more dishonest than Swedes (Andrighetto et al. 2016). Rather, it is because Italian and Romanian institutions differentiated between groups and regions in such a way that nearly everyone felt that the system was unfair. The result has been a norm of non-compliance.

In countries where tax evasion is prevalent, even good tax laws cannot mitigate the adverse effect of the wide predisposition of citizens to cheat. Citizens can effectively cooperate together to evade the state. In these cases the vicious cycle of non-compliance and ineffective tax authority is hard to break.

What is perhaps most remarkable about the Swedish case is that the state relied on local parishes and church officers to collect the necessary information. Rather than rely on a strongly hierarchical public administration, the king devolved recording and reporting duties to local parishes, which had direct knowledge of local taxpayers, and allowed them to run tax collection.[6] In other words, tax capacities were developed in conjunction with non-state actors in order to first guarantee the ability to monitor taxpayers and promote fair application since inception.

Other countries took different routes but kept a similar logic: They built capacity to gather information first and then applied the law in such a way that government was perceived as fair. As Daunton shows, England also developed the ability to monitor taxpayers at the parish level with the specific aim of building consent. Similarly, the American state was in a somewhat unique position because as the nation expanded across the continent the government developed sophisticated administrative and technical expertise to monitor and measure the nation. Later in the twentieth century it developed strong administrative capacities in the Internal Revenue Service, which then propagandized citizens with a key unifying message (taxes to fight Axis).[7]

In many societies people are afraid of the state. Consequentially, the state's ability to monitor its citizens or even their financial records is legally limited. In several cases this could be for good historical reasons. Still, if the state does not have the capacity to effectively monitor its citizens it cannot deliver the goods and services, or tax citizens in ways that people feel are fair. There can be no doubt that the enormous amount of information the British, Swedish, and American tax authorities have about their citizens puts them light years ahead of their Italian and Romanian counterparts. This may feel intrusive to those whom the tax authorities audit, but the fact that the state can do these things means that other citizens can be relatively confident that laws are being abided by and those that should pay, do pay.

Enforcement

Under the classical tax compliance paradigm that evolved from Allingham and Sandmo (1972), enforcement is simply about deterrence. According to this view, self-interested individuals want to maximize rents and therefore they will cheat on taxes unless the perceived probabilities of detection and/or punishment are high.

In our view, this misses the key point about compliance: We generally pay taxes in private, for benefits that are public (Downs 1957). Tax compliance is both a private and a public act because we are social animals who are strongly motivated by social norms. In short, we are more willing to pay if we believe that everyone (or nearly everyone) is paying as well. This is why enforcement is so important. Taxpayers want to know that others are also contributing to the collective, and most citizens will abide by the rules to the extent that they believe that such an environment is maintained. In other words, the main function of solid enforcement is *not* to intimidate the taxpayer into paying taxes, but is instead to help convince citizens that everyone pays and thereby build high tax morale (Wittberg 2010; 2012). Enforcement thus serves first and foremost a social purpose: the creation of "ecologies" of compliance that help people believe that cheats will be caught and punished. Taxpayers need to see that cheats are detected and punished, and that the tax administration is efficient and applies the laws and regulations fairly. Only under these conditions will a culture of compliance prosper.

Once again, individuals are not purely rational estimators of gains and losses. Instead, people anchor expectations on what a social norm dictates. Therefore, when many people cheat (Italy, Romania), that will be the expected behavior. Poor enforcement reproduces these perceptions, and the vicious cycles are hard to break. When a norm emerges (a new tax or a new rule) the state must make sure that most people adhere to it and they will aggressively enforce the norm. Then, when most people already comply, moderate enforcement will maintain the equilibrium. Successful states exert strong enforcement at the outset of a new law and then apply selective and moderate enforcement to guarantee sustained cooperation.

Equity/fairness

Human beings show strong preferences for equity and fairness in the laboratory and in the real world alike (Bowles and Polanía-Reyes 2012; Fehr 2006;

Kastlunger et al. 2011; Nicolaides 2014). Simply put, states that promote equity and fairness have higher compliance rates. Fairness, to be sure, has multiple meanings or interpretations. First, fairness in taxation means that individuals will be more likely to comply if they believe they will be treated equally with others to whom they could reasonably be compared (this is called horizontal equity). Second, the vast majority of taxpayers everywhere believe that the rich should pay higher taxes than the poor—taxes should be built on the ability to pay (this is called vertical equity). Finally, the state should apply its rules equally to all citizens (this is called procedural justice) (Kumlin 2002; Rothstein 2000; 2011).

It may seem obvious, but it is important to note that rulers cannot foster compliance environments where corruption is rampant. No one wants to be a sucker (Levi 1988) and if citizens view elites as tax evaders, there is little reason for them to willingly comply. As Ukraine President Petro Poroshenko noted in his first State of the Nation address in June 2015: "The image of the state is formed in citizens' eyes by the tax inspector, the customs man, the cop. While they're on the take, people won't believe the sincerity of our anti-corruption intentions" (cited in Berenson 2017). We concur and argue that without a strong and independent prosecution office and zero tolerance against corruption, a tax compliance environment will be hard to establish. Chile and Singapore are good examples, demonstrating how low levels of corruption correlate with low levels of tax evasion. Conversely, the Philippines, Indonesia, and Mexico have both high corruption and significant tax evasion.

Citizens' perceptions of fairness matter precisely because tax compliance is not a simple tit-for-tat game. Instead of being a direct exchange, as in the market, where I only pay for the things I can own, touch, or see, citizens often pay for things that they personally do not want and cannot use. When individuals believe that governments are producing goods that are fairly distributed, this perception can produce more willingness to pay regardless of whether they personally receive the benefits. For example, people are willing to pay for pensions as long as mature adults receive adequate benefits, and most people are willing to pay for children's education even if they have no children of their own.[8] In short, the social perception that taxes are converted into shared social equity can transcend the short-term self-interest paradigm. As social creatures, people also care for the common well-being.[9]

In order to foster a fair system, taxes should target a large taxpayer base, be general, and be widely applied. Unfortunately, too many governments in need of resources look for quick revenues usually raised among those who cannot escape enforcement (bank deposits, certain transactions, imports and exports controlled by customs, gasoline taxes, and so on). In our view, this is a sure recipe for failure down the road. People who pay taxes should not feel they are victims or just the unlucky ones. Fairness is gained when those who pay believe that the tax authorities go the extra mile to tax those who cheat.

In summary, states can enhance compliance if they build their tax systems fairly. Fairness in taxation has several dimensions: It implies: (1) that tax rates are proportionate to the level of income or the ability to pay (progressivity); (2) that people are treated equally; and (3) that rights are granted to the individuals (including courts and institutions) that protect these rights (procedural fairness).

Recommendations for Policies

We conclude with an even narrower and more specific set of recommendations that are drawn from the lessons learned in this book as well as the five-year "Willing to Pay?" investigation funded by the European Research Council. Perhaps unsurprisingly, our recommendations overlap with many ideas and policies that have been promoted by several international organizations including the IMF, World Bank, and OECD. Our emphasis, however, is less on revenue collection from a technical perspective and instead focuses on measures intended to build stronger relationships between taxpayers and tax authorities. We do not suggest that all these policy ideas could be implemented at any one time, but rather that they are goals that we believe would contribute to building better relationships between citizens and their states. Ironically, perhaps, they also imply that measures should be taken that are specifically designed to be—or are dependent upon—stronger states.

The following is essentially a list of several policy guidelines derived from the lessons of this project. By no means do we cover the full range of tax policies that should be considered, nor do we suggest that all of these measures can or should be implemented at once. These are guidelines governments may benefit from, and that have been somewhat overlooked in the literature. We instead list them and make very brief remarks, as they are clearly tied to the central theme of those books.

- *Strong information systems.* This should be top priority. States should develop tools to monitor the incomes and transactions of individuals and corporations both within and outside their national borders. Therefore, tax administration should have access to other information systems such as welfare programs, credit cards, and financial transactions, and invest heavily in capabilities to identify them with taxpayers. Of course they should be used very restrictively to protect individual rights.

- *Build third party payment/information systems.* Successful tax policies combine taxpaying and tax information requirements. Large taxpayers, employers, corporations, banks, and so on are agents that can provide useful information to the state. Successful cases have shown that compliance increases dramatically when these steps are successfully implemented.

- *Permanently develop monitoring capacities to signal to taxpayers that the tax agency knows a great deal about income and financial transactions.* Tax administrators in large non-compliance societies should privilege wide monitoring over audit policies. Effective monitoring has wide coverage of taxpayers, while tax audits reach very few taxpayers and are usually ineffective in reducing the number of tax evaders. Italy probably audits more taxpayers, but Sweden and Britain have higher compliance rates.

- *Invest heavily to improve cadastral records.* Property taxes are very progressive but they are widely evaded in the developing world. Therefore, an important element in producing legitimacy and fairness is to have a strong property tax. States need to coordinate politically with local governments, which usually levy such taxes; not an easy task.

- *Ensure simplicity.* Complexity breeds evasion. Only levy taxes that can be enforced. Many taxpayers, given the chance to cheat, will do so, even in Sweden. Two variables make the difference in compliance between countries: (1) withholding and monitoring mechanisms; and (2) the individual's willingness to take high risks and cheat. Firstly, policies should promote taxes that are: "compliance friendly"—that is, easy to report, those withheld at source or through a third party, such as VAT; income taxes based on multiple information requirements readily available to the tax administration agency; and property taxes based on accurate land and property registers.

- *Make everyone pay something.* This is a critical point, particularly in the developing world where a significant share of citizens is exempt from personal direct taxes. However, to guarantee fairness and inclusion, and to make demands for state effectiveness, all people should contribute. When everybody pays, people feel included. This means that *even the poor should pay something.* This might be controversial, but as derived from other principles, membership to a community should cost something. Of course, progressivity should be strictly maintained.

- *Start with the rich (they should pay dividends) and monitor your borders.* This is critical, since the middle class through fudging and evasion, and the rich through legal exemption, avoid paying a significant share of their income. All taxation success stories began by taxing the rich and slowly expanding toward the middle class. Countries should not be afraid of capital flight, because the costs of not taxing the rich in the long run are higher. Developing countries might benefit from cooperation with OECD countries and international organizations in closing tax havens and promoting cooperation with countries for releasing financial information. Large sums of tax-evaded funds from the rich are hidden in banks and assets in OECD countries, as well as in tax havens.

- *Punish severely and consistently.* Send to prison dozens or even hundreds of tax evaders per year. Do not settle disputes with reduced fines, because they incentivize tax evaders. This does not mean that the state only relies on "the stick" to enhance compliance. The main purpose is to signal to compliers that cheats are severely punished, promoting fairness in taxation.

- *Be uncompromising with corruption.* Corruption is perhaps one of the most corrosive factors in compliance behavior. It unravels trust, fairness, and equality. Authorities should send a message that corruption will not be tolerated, despite the fact that initially many agents and taxpayers will be willing to take bribes. Corruption probably will not be completely eliminated, but citizens will know that governments are not complacent.

- *Take as many steps as possible to reduce the cash economy.* Informal economies augment individual incentives to cheat. Temporary reliefs gained through tolerating informal markets tend to undermine development and also tax compliance. Countries with low compliance equilibria tend to produce dual economies or at least large informal markets that have perverse effects and, due to the social cost, are hard to reverse.

- *Fiscal balance matters, but people will comply if they feel they receive valuable goods in exchange.* This is critical for the developing world. The story of Britain, Sweden, and the USA has shown that taxes need to be shown promoting the public good. Paying off national debts might prevent financial crisis but citizens do not perceive this as beneficial. Taxes should produce clear and tangible public goods, either in infrastructure, education, and/or healthcare services, or to fight wars or expel a threat to the country's security.

- *Raise taxes in good times.* Taxes enacted in prosperous times can produce public goods that enhance wide compliance, nurturing a virtuous circle. Conversely, taxes promoted under crisis might be necessary but most likely they will be quick fixes and not long-term solutions. If governments are forced to raise taxes to alleviate a specific need, they should reduce them once the goal has been attained. Britain in the eighteenth and early nineteenth centuries raised taxes during wars, but returned to previous levels afterwards.

- *VAT should not be the only or most important tax although it should be promoted or kept.* VAT has been the workhorse of tax systems in the developing world because it effectively creates incentives for compliance. Tax authorities should take steps to include the informal economy (through withholdings, reporting, and low rates) into the VAT base.

Conclusion

No one should take these policy ideas and suggestions as absolute maxims that must be applied in any and every case. Indeed, as the historical chapters in this volume demonstrate quite clearly, there are many routes to a modern, efficient, and successful tax system. Surely, the Swedish example continues to be a model that could be emulated, but no one should be so naïve as to believe that the Swedish story could be repeated or copied in full. Still, the central points that can be drawn from the Swedish (as well as the British and American cases) in contrast to the Italian and Romanian examples are that consent is contingent on four basic factors which may seem obvious, but are worth repeating here: (1) the state must develop the capacity to monitor its citizens and lands in order to administer taxes in ways that citizens can consider to be fair; (2) citizens are far more "willing to pay" when they see that they get something in return for the taxes they pay, and that other citizens pay their share; (3) tax revenues finance public programs and institutions that contribute to greater social justice and equality, but a punitive tax system which pretends to tax the rich, but then allows them to evade, generates little revenue but much skepticism toward the state; (4) the more successful regimes have been able to raise taxes while creating a common sense of identity or purpose.

Governments across the world today are under great pressure to finance public programs, improve infrastructure, and satisfy citizens' expectations. Too often though, taxes are used as sticks to herd the taxpayers into compliance and/or discriminate between different groups in society. When they do so, the state is more likely to be seen as a predator than as an agent. In this case, few taxpayers will be willing to take the Leap of Faith.

Notes

1. A note from Sven Steinmo: As I was coming toward the end of this large project on tax compliance in (mostly) developed nations I grew increasingly interested in thinking about the implications of this research for the developing world. Surely, the routes followed (some obviously more successfully than others) should have some implications for countries which have not yet been able to build sustainable and efficient tax systems? I had recently read the marvelous book, *Tax Evasion and the Rule of Law in Latin America*, by Marcelo Bergman (2009) and had been deeply impressed with this book generally and its obvious links to many of the arguments we have been developing in our European Research Council-funded project. To this end I invited Professor Bergman to collaborate with me on the concluding chapter of this book. My idea here was to see if it would be possible to move from the study of

several historical cases to explicitly examining their implications for quite different countries who very often are struggling now with issues confronted by the more advanced countries decades and perhaps even centuries ago. Especially given the fact that this book will be available "Open Access" to anyone in the world with an Internet connection, we take the somewhat unusual step of moving from history to policy. Of course, it will be up to the reader to decide whether this was a wise move or not.

2. Marc Berenson offers a fascinating comparison of tax policies and compliance in which he makes almost exactly this point. He introduces his book with the following: "Effective governance occurs when the state and society interact with each other in a dualistic process through trust" (Berenson 2017: 2). We strongly recommend this book to those interested in a similar analysis to that found here, but particularly to those interested in the implications for the post-Communist world.

3. Levi indeed recognizes the importance of what she calls quasi-voluntary compliance that is contingent to both the exchange equity (she fully develops this dimension) and horizontal fairness (making sure that others pay). However, she does not really extend the implications of this last dimension, probably because hers is a top-down theory, while we promote an endogenous equilibrium, a co-evolving approach.

4. A comparison between Rwanda and Burundi provides a fascinating example. Both countries have been torn apart due to ethnic conflict and violence. Yet, Rwanda today is noted for having one of the most effective and efficient tax administrations and highest level of tax compliance in the developing world. Burundi, in contrast, continues to suffer from an inability to provide coherent administration and governance. A consequence is very low tax compliance (Bank 2010; Tumwebaze 2013).

5. The text within the lower border of the image reads: "This holy virtue [Justice], where she rules, induces to unity the many souls [of citizens], and they, gathered together for such a purpose, make the Common Good their Lord; and he, in order to govern his state, chooses never to turn his eyes from the resplendent faces of the Virtues who sit around him. Therefore to him in triumph are offered taxes, tributes, and lordship of towns; therefore, without war, every civic result duly follows—useful, necessary, and pleasurable."

6. Several countries around the world today are experimenting with various versions of "tax farming" in which non-state actors (usually for-profit businesses) are tasked with collecting revenues for the state (Stella 1993). The experiments are ongoing and the results are mixed. In addition, the wide range of withholding systems in income tax and VAT are centered on this basic principle: Let employers or large firms collect the lion's share of the revenues, and have the tax administration concentrate on controlling these large agencies and firms (Bird 1989: 232–6).

7. Tax capacities therefore are closely linked to the information systems that governments develop. As Jones's paper shows for the USA, a key element for successful compliance rates has been the W-2 form that employers file for each employee, enabling the IRS to gather information.

8. In Latin America a deep sense of injustice and inequality has hindered the ability of governments to make progressive tax reforms and elicit fair tax regimes (Mahon, Bergman, and Arnson 2015). Elites are hesitant to support redistributive systems

even when they have mustered strong political capacity (Ondetti 2015). In general, whether there are low legal tax burdens, such as in Mexico and Chile, or mass evasion and corruption, such as in Brazil, taxpayers remain skeptical and defiant about the ability of Latin American states to enhance fairness through fiscal policies, and therefore compliance remains low in most countries.

9. Anthony Down's (1960) classic essay, "Why Government's Budget is too Small in a Democracy," presents the dilemma that citizens are less aware of the benefits they receive from taxation (paved roads, clean air, public safety) than they are on the direct costs of taxation. Consequentially, he argues, citizens overvalue the taxes they pay considering the benefits they wish for. We take this point seriously, but taken too far it ignores the point that many citizens *are* willing to pay for services and goods that they do not directly benefit from *if they believe these goods and services are distributed fairly*.

References

Allingham, M. and A. Sandmo, (1972), "Income Tax Evasion: A Theoretical Analysis." *Journal of Public Economics* 1: 323–38.

Andrighetto, G., J. Brandts, R. Conte, J. Sabater-Mir, H. Solaz, and D. Villatoro (2013), "Punish and Voice; Punishment Enhances Cooperation when Combined with Norm-signalling." *PLOS ONE* 8(6), e64941.

Andrighetto, G., N. Zhang, S. Ottone, F. Ponzano, J. D'Attoma, and S. Steinmo (2016), "Are Some Countries More Honest than Others? Evidence from a Tax Compliance Experiment in Sweden and Italy." *Frontiers in Psychology*. http://dx.doi.org/10.3389/fpsyg.2016.00472.

Axelrod, R. M. (1986), "An Evolutionary Approach to Norms." *The American Political Science Review* 80(4): 1095–111.

Bank, A. D. (2010), *Domestic Resource Mobilization for Poverty Reduction in East Africa: Burundi Case Study*. Regional Department East A. www.afdb.org/fileadmin/uploads/afdb/Documents/Project-and-Operations/Burundi%20case%20study%20final.pdf.

Barreix, A., J. C. Benítez, and M. Pecho (2017), *Revisiting Personal Income Tax in Latin America: Evolution and Impact*. OECD Development Centre Working Paper No. 338.

Baumeister, R. F. (2011), "Need-to-belong Theory." In P. A. M. Van Lange, A. W. Kruglanski, and E. T. Higgins (eds.), *Handbook of Theories of Social Psychology: Volume Two*. London: Sage.

Berenson, M. (2017), *Trust and Taxes: From Coercion to Compliance in Poland, Russia and Ukraine*. Cambridge: Cambridge University Press.

Bergman, M. (2009), *Tax Evasion and the Rule of Law in Latin America*. University Park, PA: University of Pennsylvania Press.

Bicchieri, C. (2006), *The Grammar of Society: The Nature and Dynamics of Social Norms*. New York: Cambridge University Press.

Bird, R. M. (1989), "The Administrative Dimensions of Tax Reform in Developing Countries." In M. Gillis (ed.), *Tax Reform in Developing Countries*. Durham, NC and London: Duke University Press, 315–46.

Bowles, S. and S. Polanía-Reyes (2012), "Economic Incentives and Social Preferences: Substitutes or Complements?" *Journal of Economic Literature* 50(2): 368–425.

CEPAL (2016), *Estudio Económico de América Latina y el Caribe 2016: La Agenda 2030 para el Desarrollo Sostenible y los desafíos del financiamiento para el desarrollo*. Estudios Económicos de América Latina y el Caribe. Santiago de Chile: CEPAL.

Conte, R. and G. Andrighetto (2013), *Minding Norms: Mechanisms and Dynamics of Social Order in Agent Societies*. Oxford: Oxford University Press.

D'Attoma, J., S. Volintiru, and S. Steinmo (2017), "Willing to Share? Tax Compliance and Gender in Europe and America." *Research & Politics* 4(2). http://dx.doi.org/ 10.1177/2053168017707151http://dx.doi.org/10.1177/2053168017707151

Downs, A. (1957), *An Economic Theory of Democracy*. New York: Harper & Row.

Downs, A. (1960), "Why Government's Budget is too Small in a Democracy." *World Politics* 12: 541–63.

Elster, J. (1989), *The Cement of Society: A Study of Social Order*. Cambridge and New York: Cambridge University Press.

Fehr, E. (2006), "Inequality Aversion, Efficiency and Maximum Preferences in Simple Distribution Experiments: Comment." *American Economic Review* 96(5): 1912–17.

Gershenkron, A. (1962), *Economic Backwardness in Historical Perspective*. Cambridge, MA: Harvard University Press.

Gerxhani, K. and A. Scham (2006), "Tax Evasion and Income Source." *Journal of Economic Psychology* 27(3): 402–22.

Kastlunger, B., S. Muehlbacher, E. Kirchler, and L. Mittone (2011), "What Goes Around Comes Around? Experimental Evidence of the Effect of Rewards on Tax Compliance." *Public Finance Review* 39(1): 150–67.

Kedir, A. (2014), "Tax Evasion and Capital Flight in Africa." In S. Ajayi and L. Ndikumana (eds.), *Capital Flight from Africa: Causes, Effects, and Policy Issues*. Oxford: Oxford University Press, 323–45.

Kumlin, S. (2002), *The Personal and the Political: How Personal Welfare State Experiences Affect Political Trust and Ideology*. Gothenburg: University of Gothenburg.

Levi, M. (1988), *Of Rule and Revenue*. Berkeley, CA: University of California Press.

Lieberman, E. (2003), *Race and Regionalism in the Politics of Taxation in Brazil and South Africa*. New York: Cambridge University Press.

Mahon, J., M. Bergman, and C. Arnson (2015), *Progressive Tax Reform and Equality in Latin America*. Woodrow Wilson Center Report for the Americas. Washington DC.

Nicolaides, P. (2014), *Tax Compliance Social Norms and Institutional Quality: An Evolutionary Theory of Public Good Provision*. European Commission Working Paper No. 46.

Ondetti, G. (2015), "Once Bitten, Twice Shy: Path Dependence and the Magnitude of Tax Burden in Latin America." Paper presented at the Politics of Taxation in Latin America Conference, Cornell University, Ithaca, NY.

Pisani, S. (2014), *An Approach to Assess how the Activity of the Italian Revenue Agency Affects Compliance*. Rome: Italian Revenue Agency.

Rothstein, B. (2000), "Trust, Social Dilemmas, and Collective Memories." *Journal of Theoretical Politics* 12(4): 477–501.

Rothstein, B. (2011), *The Quality of Government: Corruption, Social Trust, and Inequality in International Perspective*. Chicago, IL: University of Chicago Press.

Schneider, A. (2012), *State-Building and Tax Regimes in Central America*. New York: Cambridge University Press.

Schneider, F. G., A. Buehn, and C. Montenegro (2010), "New Estimates for the Shadow Economies all over the World." *International Economic Journal* 24(4): 443–61.

Stella, P. (1993), "Tax Farming: A Radical Solution for Developing Country Tax Problems?" *IMF Staff Papers* 40(1): 217–25.

Tetlock, P. E. (2000), "Cognitive Biases and Organizational Correctives: Do Both Disease and Cure Depend on the Politics of the Beholder?" *Administrative Science Quarterly* 45(2): 293–326.

Traxler, C. (2010), "Social Norms and Conditional Cooperative Taxpayers." *European Journal of Political Economy* 26(1): 89–103.

Tumwebaze, P. (2013), "Rwanda Tops Region in Tax Compliance." *Rwanda New Times*, September 23.

Wittberg, L. (2010), *Bemötande och förtroende* [*Encouragement and Trust*]. Stockholm: Swedish Tax Agency.

Wittberg, L. (2012), "Using Communication to Influence Taxpayer Culture." Paper presented at the IOTA Workshop, Prague.

Zhang, N., G. Andrighetto, S. Ottone, F. Ponzano, and S. Steinmo (2016), "Willing to Pay? Tax Compliance in Britain and Italy: An Experimental Analysis." *PLOS ONE* 11(2). https://doi.org/10.1371/journal.pone.0150277.

Name Index

Note: Tables and figures are indicated by an italic *t* and *f*, respectively, following the page number.

Åberg, A. 45
Adams, C. 182
Agell, J. 66, 68
Ahlqvist, B. 68
Ahlstrom, S. E. 214
Alexander, D. C. 190
Allingham, M. 25, 153, 183
Alm, J. 25, 120–1, 253
Almond, G. A. 106
Ambrosetti, C. 118
Andersson, J. G. 67
Andrews, J. A. 182, 191
Andrighetto, G. 6, 275, 276, 282
Archer, W. R. Jr. 191
Armey, D. 191–2
Axelrod, R. M. 277
Axelsson, P. 40

Bădescu, G. 254, 265
Baigent, E. 37, 40, 47
Ballerini, A. 95
Balogh, B. 190
Bame-Aldred, C. W. 83, 84
Ban, C. 227, 255–6, 257, 261
Banfield, E. 15, 81, 85, 106
Barbu, D. 233
Barenson, M. 4
Barkey, K. 230
Barr, J. 189
Barreix, A. 276
Barron, J. D. 181
Baumeister, R. F. 277
Beck, W. 120–1
Becker, L. A. 43
Becker, S. O. 241
Beckett, J. V. 136
Bell, S. 166
Benedict XV, Pope 114
Benítez, J. C. 276
Ben-Ner, A. 256
Bennet, J. 214
Bensel R. F. 184
Berenson, M. 276, 281, 284, 289 n.2
Berggren, H. 59

Bergman, M. 6, 8, 26, 108, 122, 244, 253, 288–9 n.1
Bergström, V. 60, 66
Berlin, I. 189, 208–9
Berlusconi, S. vi, 15, 106, 120, 122
Berman, S. 48
Bevir, M. 162
Bhatti, J. 106
Biagini, E. F. 142
Bianchi, L. 112*f*
Bicchieri, C. 276
Bigoni, M. 106
Binney, J. E. D. 133
Björklund Larsen, L. 74
Blair, T. 164
Blum, J. 204, 207
Blum, W. 215
Blyth, M. 67, 69, 163
Bollati, G. 84
Bonney, R. 230, 231, 241
Boorstin, D. 213–14
Bordignon, M. 43, 45
Boréus, K. 68, 69, 73
Bowles, S. 283
Brâncoveanu, C. 234, 237–8, 239, 240
Bratu, V. 259
Braun, R. 9
Bregnsbo, M. 42
Bresciani, A. 92
Brewer, J. 132, 133, 134, 136, 137
Broers, M. 89–90
Brown, G. 163
Brown, R. H. 184
Brownlee, W. E. 185, 188, 199, 218
Buehn, A. 274
Buisseret, D. 37
Burg, D. F. 44
Burrow, J. W. 146

Calvin, J. 88
Cameron, D. 59, 161
Cannari, L. 83, 84
Cantor, E. 208
Cantril, H. 204

Caradja, I. V. 239
Carlsson, I. 70
Carr, J. 161, 173
Carruthers, B. G. 44
Carter, J. 190, 192
Carter, N. 111
Cartocci, R. 106
Ceaușescu, N. 24
Ceccarini, L. 98
Cercel, P. 239
Charles XI 48
Chiarini, B. 83
Chiri, S. 83
Chote, R. 163
Clark, M. 96, 111, 116, 118, 119, 120
Clift, B. 162
Coffman, D. M. 137
Colbert, J. B. 4
Conte, R. 276
Cooper, J. A. 187
Cosciani, C. 118
Coughlin, C. 201
Crane, J. 214
Croce, B. 85
Cummings, R. 25, 108

Dahlberg, S. 73
Daianu, D. 258
D'Alessio, G. 83, 84
D'Arcy, M. 35, 43, 45
Darling, L. T. 230, 234
D'Attoma, J. 6, 83, 276
Daunton, M. 50, 143, 144, 145, 146, 147,
    148, 150, 157, 158, 162
D'Azeglio, M. 84
De Gasperi, A. 117
de Tocqueville, A. 22
Diamanti, I. 86, 98
Dickie, J. 92
Dimitrov, V. 227
Dobrogeanu-Gherea, C. 233
Dovring, F. 34, 36
Downing, B. 43
Downs, A. 283
Doyle, W. 133
Du Rietz, G. 48, 67
Duggan, C. 95, 96
Dulles, A. F. 214
Dunleavy, P. 170

Easter, G. M. 253
Edling, M. 184
Edlund, J. 108
Egger R. Jr. 192
Einhorn, R. 184
Eisenhower, D. 213, 214, 215
Ekman, G. 61, 71

Ellis, E. 185
Elster, J. 276, 277
Elvander, N. 63
Englund, P. 66, 68
Engqvist, L. 68
Enste, D. H. 87t
Erik XIV of Sweden 47
Erlander, T. 64, 65
Erlingsson, G. Ó. 61–2
Ertman, T. 35, 36, 43
Evans, P. 9

Fehr, E. 283
Feld, L. P. 108, 253, 254
Feldt, K.-O. 67, 68, 69, 70
Ferrera, M. 95, 116
Fielding, S. 157
Fifield, J. W. Jr. 215
Finlayson, A. 170
Finn, M. 141, 142
Fiorio, C. V. 83
Fischer-Galati, S. A. 230
Flaherty, J. 184
Flora, P. 50
Flynn, J. J. 190
Ford, G. 190
Forssberg, A. M. 42, 43, 44
Frey, B. S. 25, 108, 253, 254, 265
Friedman, M. 188, 189
Fukuyama, F. 106

Gabor, D. 227
Galbiati, R. 83
Galli, G. 97
Gambles, A. 139
Garelli, F. 98
Garibaldi, G. 92
Gelissen, J. 57, 58
Gentile, G. 96
Georgescu, F. 261
Gershenkron, A. 280
Gerxhani, K. 276
Ghica, I. 233, 239
Gille, H. 39, 41
Gilmour, D. 117
Gini, C. 111
Ginsborg, P. 87, 99–100 n.5
Gioberti, V. 84
Giolitti, G. 101, 113–14
Gladstone, W. 18, 141–2, 143, 144–5, 145–6, 150
Glanner, T. H. 183
Glete, J. 35, 36, 37, 40, 41, 43, 44, 45, 46, 47, 48
Goetz, K. H. 227
Goodwyn, L. 185
Gorski, P. S. 88
Grab, A. 81, 89, 90, 91, 92
Gramsci, A. 85

Grasso, M. 164–5
Gregory XVI, Pope 92
Griffiths, T. 133, 140
Grindle, M. S. 26
Gustav Vasa 36, 41, 44, 46–7, 62
Guzzini, S. 98

Hafer, J. J. 181
Hall, R. 191, 192
Hall, S. 167
Hallenberg, M. 36, 42, 44, 46, 47–8
Hamilton, A. 184, 185
Harling, P. 140
Hart, A. 108
Hartmann, S. M. 212
Hay, C. 162
Hayek, F. 214
Heaps, W. A. 182
Hedborg, A. 66
Heidenheimer, A. J. 50
Helmke, G. 230
Henrekson, M. 60, 62–3
Herberg, W. 213
Hickenlooper, B. B. 212
Higgs, E. 40
Hilderbrand, M. E. 26
Hilton, B. 140
Hindmoor, A. 166
Hines, N. W. 212
Hirschman, A. O. 156
Hoffman, P. T. 45
Hollinger, D. A. 218
Holm, J. 36, 42, 44, 47
Hood, C. 170
Hoover, H. 186
Hope-Jones, A. 147
Hopkins, C. H. 214
Hoppit, J. 133, 137
Humbert II of Savoy 117
Hunt, P. 131, 133, 140
Huntington, S. P. 9, 14, 108
Huret, R. D. 182, 184, 190, 191, 192

Ihalainen, P. 42
Ingalls Wilder, L. 216
Innes, J. 135

Jacobsson, K. 74
Janos, A. C. 232, 241, 242, 243
Jansson, J. 63
Jefferson, T. 22
Johansson, Å. 61, 71
Johansson, A. L. 66
Johansson, D. 36, 42, 44, 47, 48, 67
Johansson, J. 69
Johansson, O. 72
John III of Sweden 47

Johnson, D. C. 191
Johnson, L. B. 215
Jones, C. C. 205, 209, 211, 212, 214, 215
Jones, T. 84–5

Kahl, G. 192
Kain, R. J. P. 37, 40, 47
Kallai, E. 258
Kalven, H. Jr. 215
Kane, J. 37, 44
Karaman, K. K. 230, 231
Karl XI of Sweden 45
Karnad, J. 183
Kastlunger, B. S. 284
Katz, R. S. 98
Kay, J. 20
Kaye, D. 209
Kedir, A. 276
Keeble, J. 160
Kelikian, A. 94
Kellems, V. 216
Keller, M. 185
Kertzer, D. I. 93, 94
Kessler-Harris, A. 203
Khruschev, N. 213
Kidder, J. L. 171
King, M. 20
Kirchler, E. 253
Kiseleff, P. 233
Kiser, E. 37, 44, 58
Kitschelt, H. 227
Kogler, C. 252, 265
Kohn, R. H. 184
Kornhauser, M. 182, 186, 192, 199, 200
Kruse, K. 189, 215
Kumlin, S. 284

La Follette, R. Sr. 185
Langford, P. 133
Leff, M. 188
Leonardi, R. 15, 106
Levi, M. 9, 11, 26, 35, 43, 57, 58, 108, 231, 252, 275, 284
Levin, J. 203
Levitas, R. 163
Levitsky, S. 230
Lewin, L. 66
Lewis, A. 84
Lewis, J. 183
Lext, G. 42
Liberatore, M. 95
Lieberman, E. 278
Light, D. 227
Liliequist, J. 46
Lindberg, I. 61, 68
Lindert, P. H. 9
Lindgren, A. 66

Lindkvist, T. 36, 37, 44, 46
Lindström, S. 67
Linz, J. J. 227
Lister, R. 163
Logan, O. 92, 93, 96, 97
Long, H. 202
Longstreth, F. 6
Lorenzetti, A. 278
Löwnertz, S. 60
Lubell, M. 108, 254
Lundstedt, S. B. 43, 45
Lungu, L. 258
Lupan, H. N. 232
Luttmer, E. F. P. 253
Lynch, K. A. 39

Macdonald, J. 134
MacDonald, R. 164
Mack Smith, D. 96, 111
Mackie, G. 107
Madgearu, V. N. 232
Magnusson, L. 66
Mahoney, J. 7
Mair, P. 98
Major, J. 164–5
Malmer, H. 62
Mammarella, G. 97
Mandler, P. 140
Manestra, S. 83, 112, 113, 115, 118, 120,
   121, 124–5
Marigliani, M. 83
Marino, M. 83
Marshall, J. 182
Martin, I. W. 9, 166, 171
Martini, C. M. 87
Marty, M. E. 213
Marzano, E. 83
Mathias, P. 132, 134
Mathias Corvinus 241
Matthew, H. C. G. 142, 143
Maugham, J. 161
May, E. T. 213, 214
Mazzini, G. 84, 92
McCarthy, J. 215
McClelland, G. H. 253
McGerr, M. 185
McKee, M. 120–1
McKibbin, R. 143
Medrega, C. 258
Mehrota, A. 9, 166, 185, 186, 196, 199
Mellon, A. W. 186, 211
Melloni, A. 98
Mertens, J. B. 258
Michael the Brave 242
Michelmore, M. C. 193
Middleton, R. 131, 150
Migdal, J. S. 14, 231

Mihaescu, F. 261
Montenegro, C. 274
Monti, M. 81, 122–3
Montias, J. M. 256
Moore, B. Jr. 43
Morgan, J. P. 200, 201
Morgenthau, H. 204, 205, 208–9, 211
Munck, T. 43
Mungiu-Pippidi, A. 227, 234
Murgescu, B. 229, 231, 235, 236, 239, 242
Murphy, R. 162
Mussolini, B. 96, 97, 110, 115–66
Myrdal, G. 22, 66
Myrdal, J. 46, 47

Nanetti, R. Y. 15, 106
Napoleon 81, 89–90, 92, 139
Neal, L. 49
Neild, R. 145
Neveux, H. 43, 46
Neville, P. 116
Nicolaides, P. 284
Nicotri, P. 86–7
Niebuhr, R. 215
Nilsson, J.-J. 41
Nistotskaya, M. 35
Nitti, F. 114
Nixon, R. 213
Nordin, J. 42, 43
Nordin, S. 67
Norquist, G. 191
North, D. C. 26, 59

Obama, B. 193
O'Brien, P. K. 131, 132, 134, 136, 137, 140
Odegard, P. H. 206
Oden, B. 39, 40, 41
Ogborn, M. 46
O'Gorman, F. 139
Olescu, E. 259
Olson, M. 35
Ondetti, G. 276
Österberg, E. 43, 44, 46
Ostrom, E. 35

Paler, L. 108
Palme, O. 66
Pamuk, Ş. 230, 231
Pana, M. 260, 262
Panaite, V. 230, 234, 236, 237
Panaitescu, D. 236
Pasti, V. 256, 257, 261
Patriarca, S. 81, 84, 107
Paul, R. E. 201, 204, 209
Pecho, M. 276
Peel, R. 18, 140–1, 141–2, 143, 147, 150
Peralta Prieto, J. 61, 70, 71

Pew, J. H. 214, 215
Pezzen, B. 242
Phinnemore, D. 227
Pierson, P. 8
Pilatini, C. 84
Pippidi, A. 237, 240
Pisani, S. 83, 276
Pius IX, Pope 93–4, 96
Pocock, J. G. A. 139
Polanía-Reyes, S. 283
Pollard, J. 94, 117
Pommerehne, W. 108
Pop, L. 117, 255, 256, 257
Pope, T. 158
Porcano, T. M. 253
Poroshenko, P. 284
Postel, C. 185
Poulsen, B. 34
Prasad, M. 9, 166
Prest, J. 135
Preti, L. 120
Prina, G. 81, 90–1
Puffy, N. 242
Putnam, R. D. 15, 81, 85, 106, 108

Quadagno, J. 203

Rabushka, A. 191, 192
Rădulescu-Motru, C. 232
Rand, A. 216
Rao, G. 184
Raponi, D. 92–3
Reagan, R. 182, 191, 216, 219 n.9
Reale, A. 84
Reinhart, C. M. 131
Reitan, E. A. 133
Retsö, D. 34, 46
Reuter, H.-R. 88
Riall, L. 83, 85
Richards, D. 167–8
Richardson, H. C. 184
Riches, D. 40, 45
Risen, C. 215
Roantree, B. 158
Roberts, M. 36, 41, 42, 43, 47
Rocco, A. 96
Rodriguez, E. 48
Roeder, L. 181
Rogoff, K. S. 131
Romani, R. 93, 94, 95
Roosevelt, F. D. 186, 189, 201, 202, 203, 217
Roosma, F. 57, 58
Roper, D. 186
Rosenman, S. 201
Ross, M. L. 108–9
Rotaru, C. 256
Rothstein, B. 27 n.1, 35, 254, 265, 284

Rudolf II, Emperor 242
Ruml, B. 188, 189, 210

Sabatini, F. 106
Sabetti, F. 108
Sacks, A. 108
Sadoveanu, M. 225
Sahlgren, M. 73
Sandmo, A. 25, 253, 283
Santoro, A. 83, 97, 106, 120
Saville, J. 167
Scham, A. 276
Schneider, A. 281
Schneider, F. 83, 87t, 108, 284
Schoeneman, G. 217
Scholz, J. T. 57, 58, 108, 254
Schön, L. 49, 60
Schulze, W. D. 253
Schumpeter, J. 4
Scott, J. C. 37, 40
Seligman, E. R. A. 198, 205
Selmi, M. 97
Seltzer, L. H. 199, 200, 204
Selznick, D. O. 209
Sestito, P. 83
Shays, D. 182
Shildrick, T. 164
Shoup, C. S. 189
Singhal, M. 253
Skocpol, T. 9, 192, 231
Sköld, P. 37, 39, 41, 42
Slaughter, T. P. 184
Smith, K. 108
Smith, M. 167–8
Smith, R. 135
Söderberg, J. 34, 46
Södersten, J. 60, 66, 68
Solmi, A. 96
Sparrow, J. T. 209
Specter, A. 191
Spicer, M. W. 43, 45
Stalans, L. 108
Stan, L. 227, 234
Stanley, L. 163
Stasavage, D. 137
Stebbings, C. 147
Stedman Jones, G. 141
Steinmo, S. H. 6, 7, 9, 13, 20, 33, 60, 63, 67, 69, 85, 145, 162, 190, 253, 260
Stenkula, M. D. 48, 49, 60, 62–3, 67
Stepan, A. 227
Stevenson, A. 213
Sträng, G. 67, 69, 70
Stridh, A. 72
Stuck, S. 189
Surrey, S. S. 204, 213
Svallfors, S. 73

Taft, C. P. 214
Tamames, J. 257
Taparelli d'Azeglio, L. 94–5
Tarrow, S. G. 108, 113
Taylor, M. 144
Teorell, J. 35, 107*t*, 109*t*
Tetlock, P. E. 276
Thálen, L. 67
Thärnström, B. 71
Thatcher, M. 20, 155, 157, 164–5
Thelen, D. 185
Thelen, K. A. 6, 7
Therner, B. 67
Thompson, H. 162, 163
Tilly, C. 9, 22, 35, 36, 40, 43, 45, 48, 231
Timmons, J. F. 58
Todor, A. 262
Tomlinson, J. 162
Torgler, B. 25, 84, 87, 108, 162, 166, 265
Torrance, J. 133
Townsend, F. 202
Trägårdh, L. 59
Traxler, C. 276
Trump, D. 15, 20
Tullio-Altan, C. 85
Turcescu, L. 234
Turcitul, M. 239
Ture Jönsson 47
Turley, C. 160
Tursun Beg 237
Tyler, T. 108
Tyran, J.-R. 254

Unger, I. 184
Ureche, G. 237, 240
Uslaner, E. M. 254

Van Meurs, W. P. 234
van Oorschot, W. 57, 58
Vancea, D. 227
Vanoni, E. 117, 118, 124
Velde, F. R. 137
Verba, S. 106
Virjan, B. 258
Voinea, L. 261
Volintiru, C. 227
Volintiru, S. 276

Walston, J. 116
Ward, W. R. 136
Watson, M. 162, 163, 164
Weber, M. 87
Weiner, M. 14
Weir, D. R. 137
Wigforss, E. 68
Wiggins, A. L. M. 216–17
William III of
   England 131
Williams, D. K. 216
Williamson, V. 192
Willigan, D. J. 39
Wilson, M. R. 184, 189
Wincott, D. 157
Wisselgren, M. J. 39, 40, 41
Wittberg, L. 72, 279, 283
Wollmann, H. 227

Zachariadou, E. 234
Zanella, G. 83
Zelenak, L. 186, 189, 190
Zelizer, J. 188, 190
Zhang, N. 6, 19, 83, 276
Zizza, R. 83

Subject Index

Note: Tables and figures are indicated by an italic *t* and *f*, respectively, following the page number.

American Civil War 22, 183, 199
American Federation of Labour 185
American War of Independence 133
Austria, national defaults on debt 131
Austro-Hungarian rule in Transylvania 226, 241–3

Boer War 149
Brazil 278
Brexit 19, 20
Britain *see* United Kingdom/Britain
Byzantine Empire 234

cadastral surveys and surveying 286
France 47
Italy 38, 113
Romania 38
Sweden (*geometriska jordeböcker*) 37–8, 38*f*, 39*f*
UK 38, 47
Calabrian Mafia (*ndrangheta*), Italy 120
Calvinism 87, 88
Catholic Church
early modern period, Sweden 36, 41
in England and Wales 134
Italian state, conflict with (nineteenth century) 13–14, 82, 85–7, 89–95, 98, 109–10, 228, 234, 279
Italian state, North/South division in relations with 15, 111, 113–14, 123
and Italian state from Mussolini to Democrazia Cristiana 96–8
Ireland 139, 140
Catholicism
and just taxation, Italy 94–5
mainstreaming in Italian politics 114
and tax 'fudging'/evasion 14, 82, 85, 87, 88, 98
Center Party, Sweden 67
Central America, state-building project 278, 281
Chile 278, 284
Christian Democratic Party, Italy 15, 97–8, 117
Church of England 82, 134–5, 214
Civiltà Cattolica, La (Jesuit periodical) 92, 93, 94, 95

Cold War 213–14
Communist Party (Partito Communista Italiano), Italy 117
"compliance equilibria" 8–9, 274, 287
and social norms 253–4
UK 9, 131
Conservative (Tory) Party, UK
1815–51 139–40, 141, 143
1979–90 20, 155, 164–5
2010/2015 155, 156, 157, 163
Corn Laws, Britain 139–40, 141
corruption
Italy 86–7, 98, 110, 117, 120, 122
policy recommendations 287
Romania 24–5, 252, 254, 258, 261, 265
state 284
Costa Rica 278

Democratic Party, USA 216
Dissenters, Britain 134
Domesday Book 40

East India Company 133
El Salvador 278
enforcement 26, 283, 287
UK 160
equity/fairness 3–5, 9, 12, 13, 18–19, 21, 22, 28, 57–9, 69–70, 72–3, 94–5, 218–19, 230–5
horizontal 284, 285
and procedural justice 27, 283–5
of tax collection 57–8, 72
vertical 284, 285
European Union (EU), Romanian accession 251, 258, 261

fascism, Italy 83, 96–7, 110, 115–16, 123
fiscal capacity, and the evolution of modern states 4, 9–10
fiscal contract and legitimacy, as foundation for compliance 43, 57
for mass income tax, USA 205–7, 207–9
Reformed Lutheran Church of Sweden and 10, 11, 34, 41–3, 82, 89
and state building 278–81
France 136
late expansion of cadastral mapping 47

France (*cont.*)
  national defaults on debt 131
  tax "farming" 132, 133, 134
French Revolution 89, 92, 95

Germany, national defaults on debt 131
global financial crisis (GFC, 2008) 157, 163, 173, 261
Google 161
Great Dacke Rising (1542–3), Sweden 44
Great Depression 186, 201
Great Exhibition (1851), London 141
Greece
  Etairea anti-Ottoman revolutionary society 233
  national defaults on debt 131
  tax evasion 81, 83
  tax evasion, and religiosity 87, 87*t*
Guatemala 278, 281

Her Majesty's Revenue and Customs (HMRC), UK 156
  "Compliance Perceptions Survey" 160
  "ghosts"/"moonlighter" distinction 159
  "Liechtenstein Disclosure Facility" 162
  powers of enforcement 160
  "sweetheart deals" 161–2
"HSBC files", UK 161–2
Hungarian Kingdom 241, 242

Indonesia 284
Internal Revenue Service (IRS), USA 21, 23, 181, 190–1
Italian–Ethiopian War 115
Italian People's Party (Partito Popolare Italiano) 114
Italy 13–17, 22, 79–127, 279–80
  1972 to the present 119–22
  amoral familialism 81–2, 85, 98, 106–8, 123
  Anti-Risorgimento 92–4, 95
  budgetary allocations (1811) 91*t*
  Calabrian Mafia (*ndrangheta*) 120
  Catholic Church/State conflict, nineteenth century 13–14, 82, 85–7, 89–95, 98, 109–10, 228, 234, 279
  Catholic Church/state relations, improvement, WWI 114
  Catholic Church/state relations, North/South division 15, 111, 113–14, 123
  Catholic Church/state relations from Mussolini to Democrazia Cristiana 96–8
  Catholic mainstreaming in Italian politics 114
  Catholicism and tax 'fudging'/evasion 14, 82, 85, 87, 88, 98
  Christian Democratic Party 15, 97–8, 117
  "civic virtue", North/South divide 15, 106

clientelism 98, 108, 110, 115, 117, 119, 123
Communist Party (Partito Communista Italiano) 117
Constitution (1947) 117, 123
corruption 86–7, 98, 110, 117, 120, 122
dazio consume (indirect consumption taxes) 90
"economic miracle" 118–19
explaining tax compliance, historical perspective 106–24
fascist period 83, 96–7, 110, 115–16, 123
faulty 'Italian character' 84–5, 107
first republic 16, 83, 117–19
Fund for the South 117, 118
government accountability 15
government performance 106, 107*t*
high-trust/high-efficiency/high-compliance environment in the North 111, 114, 115
Italian People's Party (Partito Popolare Italiano) 114
just Catholic taxation 94–5
Lateran Treaties 96, 97
Liberal Democrats (Parti Liberale Democratico) 114
Liberal Party 89, 92, 95, 100–1 n.10, 114
low-efficiency/low-trust/low-compliance environment (North and South) 108–10, 113, 116, 117–18, 119, 120, 122, 123–4
low-efficiency/low-trust/ low-compliance environment in the South 111, 112, 114, 115, 116
manette agli evasori (handcuffs for evaders) 120
milling tax 91
Napoleonic occupation 82, 89–91, 100 n.9
Napoleonic "War on Religion" 89–90
national cadasters 38, 113
national defaults on debt 131
Neapolitan *camorra* 120
Non Expidite doctrine 94
North to South fiscal transfers 98
North/South divisions 15–16, 106–8, 107*f*, 109–10, 111–15, 112*f*, 116, 117, 118, 123, 279
"*otto per mille*" law 86, 100 n.7
papal infallibility doctrine 94
parastati 116
political strife (early twentieth century) 113–15
quality of government by region 109*t*
Quanta Cura encyclical 93–4
Radical Party (Parti Radicale) 114
regional governments introduced 119–20
religiosity and tax evasion 87, 87*t*
Republic vs. dynasty vote (1946) 117
rise of socialism 123
Risorgimento 92–3, 111–15, 123

'Second Republic' 117, 122
small-business and self-employed sector 16, 110, 121–2, 123–4, 276
Socialist Party (Partito Socialista Italiano) 114, 117
Studi di Settore (Sector Studies) 16, 121–2, 123–4
Tangentopoli corruption scandals (early 1990s) 86–7
tassa personale (income tax) 90
tax amnesties 16, 120–1, 123
tax collection reforms, Napoleonic 90–1
tax evasion v–vi, vii, 13–17, 81–98, 106–10, 117–18, 120, 121, 122–3
tax evasion, and Church-state conflict 85–7, 87t
tax evasion, Mussolini's view 97, 115, 123
tax evasion, North/South divide 15, 98, 106–8, 107f, 124 n.1, 264
tax evasion rates 83, 85, 97–8, 106, 121
tax evasion rates by region (1998–2002) 107f
tax morale in laboratory conditions viii, 6, 14, 82, 85, 98
tax reforms (1972) 110, 120
tax reforms (1990s) 110, 121–2
tax reforms (*Legge Vanoni*, 1951) 118
tax reforms, fascist period 115–16
tax reforms, Napoleonic 90–1
trade union movement strength (1976) 119
transformismo 114, 115
unification 13, 24, 82, 93, 98, 108, 109–10, 111, 113
vicious circle 8, 122
welfare state expansion, fascist period 116

Kingdom of Italy 81, 89, 90
Kingdom of Naples 89

Labour Party, UK 143, 149, 150 *see also* New Labour Party, UK
Lateran Treaties 96, 97
Liberal Democrats (Partito Liberale Democratico), Italy 114
Liberal Parties
Italy 89, 92, 95, 100–1 n.10, 114
Sweden 15, 63, 65, 66, 67
UK 148, 149
London interbank offered rate (LIBOR) scandal (2017) 167
Lutheranism 87
Luxembourg leaks scandal (2014) 161

Mexico 278, 284
Moldavia 225, 229, 231, 234, 235, 236–40, 242
Church census records 232
formal and informal systems of payment 239–40

governor appointments 237
Legal Codes 233
loans and debts 237–8
monasteries in newly established territories 235t
and the Ottoman Empire 226, 236–40
periphery status and contractual legitimacy 236
tax collectors and duties owed 237–9
unification with Moldavia as Romanian Principality 233, 235
see also Romania

Napoleonic/French Revolutionary Wars 18, 131, 132, 138
National Agency for Fiscal Administration (NAFA), Romania 258, 259
National Association of Manufacturers, USA 215
National Council of Churches (NCC), USA 214–16, 218
neoliberalism 13
Sweden 13, 68–9
Neapolitan *camorra*, Italy 120
New Democracy Party, Sweden 72
New Labour Party, UK 20, 155, 157, 162–3, 163–4, 165
New Spirit, The (Disney, 1942) 207–8

Orthodox Christianity, and tax evasion 87, 87t, 88
Orthodox Church, Romania
and Ottoman Empire 234
redistribution system 226, 228, 229, 234–5
and the state 24
taxation system 234
Ottoman Empire and Romania 226, 231
fiscal system 230
and "protected lands" status 232
Wallachia and Moldavia 236–40

Panama 278
Panama Papers scandal (2015) 161
Papal States 89, 92, 93
Philippines 284
Piedmont 93
Statuto Albertina 92
Poe v. Seaborn (1930), USA 211–12
Poland 281
tax system compared with Russia 253
policy recommendations 285–7
cadastral record investment 286
cash economy reductions 287
for corruption 287
fiscal balance 287
information systems 285
make everyone pay something 286

policy recommendations (*cont.*)
  monitoring capacities to signal to taxpayers knowledge of income and financial transactions 286
  punish severely and consistently 287
  raising taxes in good times 287
  the rich, and monitoring borders 286–7
  simplicity 286
  third party payment/information systems 285–6
  VAT 287
political culture, co-evolution with political institutions 7–9
Pollock v. Farmers' Loan and Trust Co. (1894), USA 185, 199
Pomperispossa in Monismanien (Lindgren) 66
Poor Law (1601), England 135, 148, 149
  amendment Act (1834) 135
Protestant Federal Council of Churches, USA 214
Protestantism
  and support for Risorgimento 92–3
  and tax morale 87–8

"quasi-voluntary compliance" 11, 12, 26, 34, 43, 57, 134, 252–3, 265, 289

Radical Party (Parti Radicale), Italy 114
Reformed Lutheran Church of Sweden catechetical records (*hursförshörslängder*) 38–9, 41
  role in state monitoring and legitimation 10, 11, 34, 41–3, 82, 85, 89, 134, 135, 228, 231
religion and tax morale 87–9, 87*t*
Republican Party, USA 216
Roman Catholic Church *see* Catholic Church
Romania 23–5, 223–70, 279
  austerity measures (1982) 255–6
  austerity measures (current) 263
  Austro-Hungarian administration 226, 231
  balance of power between administrative and ecclesiastical authorities 228
  Brâncoveanu reforms 237–8, 239
  bribe payments (*peşcheş* or *plocon*) 239, 242
  bribery 257
  business taxation 256
  Cabinet Decree 873 (2005) 258
  Ceauşescu regime 24, 256
  Church (Orthodox/Catholic) system of redistribution 226, 228, 229, 234–5
  cisluire land tax 232
  Communist period 24, 254–6, 263
  "compliance equilibria" approaches 8, 253–4
  corporate income tax (CIT) rates 257–8, 264
  corruption 24–5, 252, 254, 258, 261, 265
  cultural divisions 24

debt crisis (1982) 256
Decree 202 (1953)
Decree 65 (1968) 256
deterrence mechanisms 253
Ease of Paying Taxes ranking 258–9
emigration and remittances 262
EU accession (2007) 251, 258, 261
excise duties 259
Fiscal Code (2003–13) 258
fiscal duties in the sixteenth century 242, 243*t*
"fiscal exchange" theory 25, 253
Foreign Direct Investment (FDI) 257, 266 n.10
foreign investors' tax breaks 257
Government Ordinance 17 (1993) 258
haraci/tribut taxes 234, 239
hidden payroll deductions 255
high tax morale and low compliance rates 250, 251–3, 263–5
historical analysis, reasons for 227–9
historical role of localism 244
Hungarian rule 230, 246 n.22
imbalance of tax compliance between labor and capital 259
incentive structure for personal taxes (PIT) and corporate taxes (CIT) 250
income inequality 261–2
indirect taxes 251, 257, 264
informal institutions and social norms 230–1, 244
joint labor (*clacă*) taxes 240
judeţe 232–3
Law 344 (1947) 255
Law 18 (1968) 255
Law 82 (1991) 257
Law 87 (1994) 258
Law 241 (2005) 258
Legal Codes 233
legitimacy and expectations on redistribution 230–5
as low-trust society 265
military campaigns against the Ottomans 241
military support payments 239
monasteries in newly established territories 235, 235*t*
monitoring failures 282
National Agency for Fiscal Administration (NAFA) 258, 259
national cadasters 38
national net income post global financial crisis 261–2
nationalist movements 233–4
noblemen/boyars (*boieri*) 232, 239–40
offshore tax evasion 259
Organic Statute 233

Orthodox Church and the Ottoman
Empire 234
Orthodox Church and the state 24
Orthodox Church taxation system 234
Ottoman Empire 116, 231, 234
Ottoman Empire and "protected lands"
status 232
Ottoman fiscal system 230
patrimonial system 226, 228, 237
peasant landowner class 235
Penal Code (1969) 255
pension system 262
Petra Groza cabinet 254–5
Phanar Lords 238–9, 246 n.14
personal income tax (PIT) 264
personal income tax (PIT), flat rate reform
(2004) 252, 259, 260, 261, 263, 280
personal income tax (PIT) revenues
(1995–2002) 259
post-Communist fiscal contract 256–60
post-Communist tax system 250–65
price liberalization 257
produce (dijma) taxes 240
and quasi-voluntary compliance
theory 252–3, 265
as quasi-colonial peripheral state 226, 228–9,
233–4, 243–5
rational nutrition program 256
redistribution of public goods 228–9
religiosity and tax evasion 87, 87t
Russian protectorate Statute 233
shadow economy 255, 256
Social Assistance Reform Strategy 262
social contract with the people 226–7, 243–5
social security contributions (SSC) and
collection 259
social services expenditure 25, 262
state-owned enterprises (SOEs) 255, 257
symphonia 234
tax collection in folklore 225
tax collection system 226, 251
tax collection without consent 225–45
tax evasion 23, 24, 225, 244, 250, 251, 257,
258, 259, 263, 264, 265
tax evasion Communist period 255, 256
tax farming 240
tax morale in laboratory conditions viii, 23,
25, 225, 251–2
tax reforms and political debate 260, 264
tax revenue as percentage of GDP 251,
259, 260
taxation structure, link with impact on
inequality 265
taxes, intermediaries and bureaucratic
genesis 231–4, 236, 240
theoretical accounts of compliance 252–4
trade liberalization 240

unemployment levels 262
unification 225, 242
urbanization levels across the regions 229
utility maximizers theory 253
value added tax (VAT) and
collection 259–60, 263, 267 n.12
vicious circle 8, 228
welfare state and inequality 261–3
willingness to pay and underperformance
gap 250, 252, 263–5
see also Moldavia; Transylvania; Wallachia
Russia 281
tax system compared with Poland 253

Second Vatican Council (1962–1965) 98
Singapore 284
Småland rebellion (1542–3), Sweden 47
small-business and self-employed sector,
Italy 16, 110, 121–2, 123–4, 276
small to medium size enterprises (SMEs),
UK 160–1
social cohesion and taxation 277–8
Social Democratic Party, Sweden 11–13, 14,
56–7, 59–74
Socialist Party (Parti Socialista Italiano),
Italy 114, 117
South Africa 278
Spain, national defaults on debt 131
Spirit of' 43, The (Disney, 1943) 209
state capacity 4, 26–7, 59, 60–2, 67–9, 70–2
state as predator 25–7
state/s 3, 278–9
administrative and monitoring systems 27,
277, 281–3
building a sense of identity and/or
purpose 277–8
building fiscal legitimacy 278–81
horizontal equity 284, 285
intimidation and coercive behaviours
274, 277
leapfrogging failures 280–1
procedural justice and fairness 27, 283–5
promoting positive social norms 7–8, 275–7
quality of government, western Europe 107t
redistribution 58–9, 72–3, 226, 228–9,
230–5, 241–2
strong states and successful societies 275–8
tax compliance as private/public act 283
vertical equity 284, 285
see also policy recommendations;
welfare state
Sudan 3
Sweden 4, 7, 10–13, 22, 31–78, 124, 253, 279
bevillning tax 49
Center Party 67
center-right government (1976–81) 67
center-right government (2006–14) 73–4

Sweden (*cont.*)
  Church role in state monitoring and
    legitimation 10, 11, 34, 41–3, 82, 85, 89,
    134, 135, 228, 231
  "citograf system" 61
  continuity of tax state 35, 40, 51
  contrasted with other European
    countries 35, 36–7, 38, 40, 44, 47, 48,
    49–50
  corporate taxes 60–1
  corporate tax reduction (1980s) 68, 69
  corporatism 56, 60, 61
  Dags att deklarera ("It is Time to Do Your
    Taxes") booklet 71
  defending a challenged tax system (1970s
    and 1980s) 65–72, 73
  direct taxation, transition to modern form
    of 49–50
  direct taxes, pre-modern 49
  direct taxes, increase in household share 60
  early modern period 35–48
  early modern period, importance 35, 36
  electronic data-processing system
    (EDP) 70–1
  enlightenment and propaganda 63–4
  "Feldt's Lads" 69
  geometriska jordeböcker (cadastral maps) 37–8,
    38f, 39f
  Great Dacke Rising (1542–3) 44
  grundskatter ('basic tax') 49
  horizontal fiscal contract (between
    subjects) 11, 34, 43, 45
  income tax increases, postwar 60
  income tax individualization, postwar 65
  income tax reduction (1980s) 68, 69
  indelningsverket (military allotment
    system) 11, 34, 44–5, 46, 48, 49
  individual tax assessments, early modern
    period 36
  jordeböcker (land registers) 36
  labour market arrangement 60–1
  Landsorganisationen (LO) 63, 65–6
  late industrial development and tax
    structure 11, 34, 48–50
  logic of fairness and new understanding of
    taxes 69–70
  mantalspenning (poll tax) 49
  marginal tax rates 66, 67–8
  neoliberalism 13, 68–9
  origins of high compliance 33–51
  "outsiders" (*utanförskapet*) concept 73–4
  paying taxes and constructing the welfare
    state (1945–70) 59–65
  "People's Home" (*Folkhemmet*) notion 60
  perceptions of fairness and tax
    compliance 8, 12, 13, 57–9, 72–3
  personnummer 40, 50, 61

popularity of tax agencies 118
population statistics, early modern
  period 38–9, 41
progressive taxation 49, 60, 65–6, 69
progressivity reduced (1980s) 68
"quasi-voluntary compliance" 11, 12, 34, 43,
  57, 134
Reformed Church parish catechetical records
  (*hursförshörslängder*) 38–9
religiosity and tax evasion 87, 87t
Riksskattenämnden tax collection
  authority 62
role of social democracy in creating tax-
  compliant citizens 56–74
royal bailiffs 36, 41
self-monitoring 276–7
"*Skattefria Andersson*" (Tax Evader Andersson)
  election film 64
Småland rebellion (1542–3) 47
Social Democratic Party 11–13, 14, 56–7,
  59–74
social structure, early modern period 10–11,
  34, 46–8, 134
standing army, early modern period 40, 45
state monitoring capacity, early modern
  period 10, 11, 18, 34, 35–40, 134
state monitoring capacity, updated 50, 51,
  282–3
Sudan compared 3
Tabellverket population statistics 39–40, 41
tax collection, state capacity (1945–70) 60–2
tax collection, state capacity questioned
  (1970s and 1980s) 67–9, 73
tax collection, technical progress and
  improved state capacity 70–2
tax collection losses (post-1980s) 33
tax evasion 62, 64, 66, 67
tax farming 46, 47–8
tax gap vi–vii, 33
tax planning 66, 67, 68
tax reforms (1972) 73
tax reforms (1980s) 67–71
tax return complexity (1950s) 61
tax return simplification (1971) 71
tax return simplification (1987) 72
tax revenue as percentage of GDP
  (1965–2013) 33
taxeringsnämnd (TN) tax return control
  committee 61–2
taxes and solidarity 74
tithe registers (*boskapslängder*) 42, 42f, 51 n.2
trade unions and labor movement 56, 60,
  63, 65–6, 69
trust in public institutions 72, 109
Vasa ship 45–6
vertical fiscal contract (between State and
  subject) 10, 34, 36, 43–6, 47–8, 50

virtuous circle 8, 12, 35, 36, 43, 50–1
wage earners' funds 65–6
welfare state 13, 50, 51, 56, 59–65, 67, 68, 73, 74
withholding tax system 61
Swedish Employers' Confederation (Svenska arbetgivareföeningen, SAF) 69
Swedish Tax Agency 72

tax collection
  and equity/fairness 57–8, 72
  Italy 90–1
  Moldavia 237–9
  Romania, without consent 225–45
  Sweden 33, 60–2, 67–9, 70–2, 73
  Transylvania 241–2
  UK 134–5
  USA 181–93
  Wallachia 237–9
tax compliance
  behaviour 5, 25–7
  "equilibria" 8–9, 131, 253, 274, 287
  mechanisms 58t
  see also equity/fairness
tax evasion 6, 25
  Greece 81, 83, 87, 87t
  Italy v–vi, vii, 13–17, 81–98, 87t, 106, 107f, 115, 117–18, 120, 121, 122–3, 124 n.1, 264
  Romania 23, 24, 225, 244, 250, 251, 255, 256, 257, 258, 259, 263, 264, 265
  Sweden 62, 64, 66, 67
  UK 85, 136, 160–1, 173–4
  USA 21, 83, 187, 192, 201–2, 216–17
taxation
  balance between a strong state and a successful society 4
  and consent, implication for developing nations 273–88
  as collective action problem (CAP) 35, 45
  and "security" 64
  untaxed economic activity developing world/OECD as percentage of GDP 274
  see also policy recommendations
Tea Party, USA 192
Trade Union Confederation (Landsorganisationen/LO), Sweden 63
trade unions
  Italy, movement strength (1976) 119
  Sweden 56, 60, 63, 65–6, 69
  UK 143, 150
Transylvania 225, 229, 230, 231, 244, 245
  Austro-Hungarian rule 226, 241–3
  bureaucratic monitoring 232
  collection and redistribution 241–2
  duties owed and resources 242–3
  early development of administrative capacity 241–3

monasteries in newly established territories 235t
urbanization 241
see also Romania

Ukraine 281
"ultimatum game" 8
United Kingdom (UK)/Britain 17–21, 36–7, 40, 44, 129–77, 253, 279, 282
  absence of national defaults 137–8
  Anti-Corn Law League 140
  assessed taxes on wealth 136, 138, 146
  Board of Inland Revenue 147–8
  bond-holders (1750–1800) 138
  bonds, dividends and tax 147
  cadastral surveying, England 38, 47
  capital gains tax 158
  Catholics in Ireland 139, 140
  CEOs in the public sector, and burgeoning management 166
  Chartists 140, 141
  Church of England 134–5, 139
  Church-state symbiosis 82
  Code for Fiscal Stability 162
  Commission for Examining the Public Accounts (1780) 133
  compliance equilibrium 9, 131
  Conservative governments (1815–51) 139–40, 141, 143
  Conservative governments (2010/2015), and austerity 155, 156, 157, 163
  constitutional radicalism 142
  Corn Laws 139–40, 141
  council tax 158
  Cromwell's government 136
  customs and excise duties 132, 133, 136–7, 140–1, 149–50
  earned/unearned income differentiation 149
  fairness and transparency 18–19
  French revolutionary/Napoleonic wars expenditure 132, 138
  "ghosts" and "moonlighters" 159–60
  Gladstone's budget (1853) 141, 142
  government expenditure as percentage of GDP (1815–1890) 139, 141, 150
  historicizing contemporary tax morale 155–75
  hypothecation rejection 144, 145
  income tax 50, 136, 138, 139, 140, 141, 142, 143, 146–7, 148–9, 150
  Jobseeker's Allowance 165
  land taxes 135–6, 138, 146
  Liberal government and tax reform (1906–14) 148, 149
  LIBOR (London interbank offered rate) scandal (2017) 167

United Kingdom (UK)/Britain (*cont.*)
local government spending (late 19 th century) 148–9
local tax commissioners 134, 135, 138
losing consent (1815–50) 139–41
MPs' expenses scandal 167, 173, 175 n.1
national debt repayments 131, 138, 139, 140, 145, 150
National Health Service (NHS) 157, 166
Naval Defence Fund 145
New Labour (Blair) government (1997–2007) 20, 155, 157, 162–3, 163–4, 165
New Public Management and marketization of public services 166, 170–1
offshore tax evasion 161–2
parish role in civil government 18, 135
parliamentary accountability and surveillance of tax and spending 133–4, 141, 143–6
parliamentary annual votes and close scrutiny of accounts 144–5
parliamentary scrutiny committees (1782–92) 133–4, 137
pay as you earn (PAYE) system 157
"people's budget" (1909) 149
"phone hacking scandal" (2011) 168
political rhetoric of elites (1820–40) 141–3, 150
postwar tax state (1945) 157–62
poverty and welfare attitudes 164–5, 165*f*
public trust and tax policies 166–7, 167*f*
public-private partnerships (PPPs) 166
(re)creating consent (1850–1914) 141–50
religiosity and tax evasion 87, 87*t*
sanctity of credit 137–8
self-assessment of taxes 157–8
shadow (hidden) economy 156, 159–60
small- to medium-sized enterprises (SMEs) tax evasion attitudes 160–1
smuggling 136
state borrowing and interest rates 137–8
state-taxpayer relationship 132–8, 141, 142–3, 146–50
support for Risorgimento 92–3
"sustainable investment rule"/"golden rule" 163
state profligacy and "illogical banalities", focus group examples 168–72
tax avoidance schemes 161
tax collection 134–5, 146–50
tax evasion 85, 136, 160–1, 173–4
tax gap (2005–13) 33
tax morale in decline (1983–2011) 157, 158*f*
tax morale in laboratory situation viii, 6, 19, 85, 156

taxation, war and good government (1688–1914) 131–51
Thatcher government (1979–1990) 20, 155, 164–5
Thatcherism shaping public opinions and social values 164–5
trade unions 143, 150
value-added tax (VAT) 158
virement ban 144, 145
welfare state 20, 150, 157, 165
YouGov poll (2010) on knowledge of the welfare budget 165
United States of America (USA) 7, 21–3, 179–222, 253, 277, 279
1776–1900 tax collection, citizens and compliance 181–93
1776–1913 invisible tax, invisible collection 183–5
1913–1941 finding common ground 185–7
1970–2010 chain reaction, eroding consent 189–92
American Federation of Labour 185
American Institute of Certified Public Accountants 192
Americans for Tax Reform organization 191
anti-tax politics 21, 191, 193
Armey plan 191–2
Battle Stations for All pamphlet (1943) 208
Board of Tax Appeals (1924) 186
Bureau of Internal Revenue 183
civic religion 213–16
Civil Rights Act (1964) 215–16
Civil War 22, 183, 199
Cold War ideology 213–14
Committee on Ways and Means 191
"common ground model" 21, 183, 189
community/common-law marital property systems 211–12
Current Tax Payment Act (1943) 210
"daylight savings" approach to government finance 210
death and inheritance taxes 187, 192
definition and measurement of income and wealth 183
Democratic Party 216
Dr Francis Townsend's Plan 202
excise tax returns on corporate income made public 199
fairness in taxation, perceptions 9, 21, 22, 218–19
Federal Land Survey 38
flat income tax rate proposal 191–2
Huey Long's Share Our Wealth plan 201, 202
income tax 187–9, 199, 202–3, 204–5, 209–11, 217
Internal Revenue Service (IRS) 21, 23, 181–2, 190–1

John Fries rebellion 184
legibility for citizens 199–201
legitimacy for mass income tax 205–7, 207–9
National Association of Manufacturers 215
National Council of Churches
 (NCC) 214–16, 218
New Deal programs 207, 208, 217
patronage system 184
"pick-up" scheme (1920s) 187, 192
"pink slips" 187, 200
Pledge of Allegiance (1954) 214
postwar period 211–17
progressive tax system attacked 189–92
progressive taxation, rise of 185–7
prohibition against Church-state
 cooperation 22
Protestant Federal Council of Churches 214
racial minorities and social security 203
Reagan administration 192
"relief, not rights" classification 203
"Report on Postwar Taxation" 211
Republican Party 216
Revenue Act (1924) 200
Revenue Act (1934) 187, 200
Revenue Act (1937) 201–2
Revenue Act (1940) 204
Revenue Act (1942) 187–8, 189, 204
Revolutionary period and tax collection 184
Risorgimento, support for 92–3
Roosevelt administration 187, 188–9, 201,
 202, 204, 205, 217
Ruml Plan 210
scientific taxation 185, 186
Sixteenth Amendment 186, 187
social legitimacy of the state 183
social security and welfare 22, 202–3,
 215, 217
Spiritual Mobilization 214, 215
stock market crash (1929) 200
tariffs/excise tax regimes and land
 sales 183–4, 185, 198–9
tax codes, Section 509(a) 191
tax collection process 182–3
tax compliance, mid-twentieth
 century 198–219
tax evasion 21, 83, 187, 192, 216–17
tax evasion (1930s) 201–2
tax gap vii
tax haven states 187
tax justice movements (1970s) 190
tax loopholes and exemptions
 (1960s) 189–90
"Taxes to Beat the Axis" slogan 23
Tea Party 192
Truman administration 213, 216
Victory Tax (1942) 204
war bonds saving 205–7

"Whiskey Rebellion" (1791–1794) 184
"Window tax" 184
women workers 212–13
World War II war bonds and income
 tax 204–11, 217
Zoot Suit Riots (1943) 209
United States v. Dickey (1925) 200
Uruguay 278

Vatican 13–14, 82, 89, 92, 96
 reform (1960s) 98
Vatican City 93

Wall Street crash (1929) 200
Wallachia 225, 229, 231, 234, 235,
 236–40, 242
 Church census records 232
 duties and loans (1694–1703) 238t
 formal and informal systems of
  payment 239–40
 governor appointments 237
 Legal Codes 233
 loans and debts 237–8
 monasteries in newly established
  territories 235t
 Ottoman Empire 226, 236–40
 periphery status and contractual
  legitimacy 236
 "Registry of Wallachia's Treasury" 237
 tax collectors and duties owed 237–9
 unification with Moldavia as Romanian
  Principalities 233, 235
 see also Romania
welfare state
 Italy, North/South divide 116
 Sweden 13, 50, 51, 56, 59–65, 68, 73, 74, 78
 UK 20, 150, 157, 165
 USA, and social security 22, 202–3, 215, 217
"Whiskey Rebellion" USA (1791–1794) 184
"Willing to Pay?" project vii–viii, 5–7, 27 n.2
 British subjects viii, 6, 19, 85, 156
 Italian subjects viii, 6, 14, 82, 85, 98
 Romanian subjects viii, 23, 25, 225, 251–2
World Bank 257, 285
World War I
 and Italy 110
 and the UK 149–50
 and the USA 22–3, 186, 201
World War II
 and Italy 97, 110, 115, 117, 123
 and Romania 254
 and tax changes, UK 157
 and tax increases, Sweden 62
 and the USA 22–3, 192, 193, 204–11, 217–18

YouGov poll (2010) on knowledge of the
 welfare budget 165